Private Governance

Private Governance
Creating Order in Economic and Social Life

Edward Peter Stringham

OXFORD
UNIVERSITY PRESS

OXFORD
UNIVERSITY PRESS

Oxford University Press is a department of the University of Oxford.
It furthers the University's objective of excellence in research, scholarship,
and education by publishing worldwide.

Oxford   New York
Auckland   Cape Town   Dar es Salaam   Hong Kong   Karachi
Kuala Lumpur   Madrid   Melbourne   Mexico City   Nairobi
New Delhi   Shanghai   Taipei   Toronto

With offices in
Argentina   Austria   Brazil   Chile   Czech Republic   France   Greece
Guatemala   Hungary   Italy   Japan   Poland   Portugal   Singapore
South Korea   Switzerland   Thailand   Turkey   Ukraine   Vietnam

Oxford is a registered trade mark of Oxford University Press
in the UK and certain other countries.

Published in the United States of America by
Oxford University Press
198 Madison Avenue, New York, NY 10016

Cataloging-in-Publication Data is on file with the Library of Congress.

9780199365166

1 3 5 7 9 8 6 4 2

Printed in the United States of America on acid-free paper

To legal centralists of all parties.

CONTENTS

Foreword by Peter Boettke   *ix*

PART ONE: Why Private Governance?
1. Introduction   *3*
2. Beyond the Deus ex Machina Theory of Law   *9*
3. Rules from Voluntary Associations as an Alternative to Coercive Ones: Governance as a Club Good   *21*

PART TWO: Privately Governed Markets in History and Modern Times
4. Markets without Enforcement: Reciprocity and Reputation Mechanisms in the World's First Stock Market   *39*
5. The Evolution of Rules in Exclusive Clubs: From Coffeehouses to the London Stock Exchange   *61*
6. Markets Creating Transparency: Competing Listing and Disclosure Requirements from the Big Board in New York to the Alternative Investment Market in London   *79*
7. How Technologically Advanced Markets Can Work Even When Fraud Is "Legal": Ex Ante Risk Management by PayPal and Other Intermediaries   *100*
8. Bundling Private Governance with Bricks and Mortar: Private Policing in California, North Carolina, and Beyond   *113*
9. The Most Personal Form of Private Governance: Individual Self-Governance   *134*
10. When Third-Party Review Is "Necessary": Adjudication by Contract   *148*
11. Does Private Governance Work in the Most Complex Markets? Successful Risk Management on Wall Street Even in the Wake of the 2008 Economic Downturn   *165*

PART THREE: Lessons of Private Governance
12. The Relationship between Public and Private Governance: Does the State Help or Crowd Out Good Governance?   *193*

13. Applying Hayek's Insights about Discovery and Spontaneous Order
    to Governance   206
14. The Unseen Beauty that Underpins Markets   226

Acknowledgments   237
References   239
Index   269

FOREWORD

Edward Peter Stringham's *Private Governance: Creating Order in Economic and Social Life* is wonderfully written and chock full of compelling case studies of precisely how individuals and communities achieve governance without turning to government. Stringham provides examples that cross time and cultures, from the origins of financial markets to the complicated transactions that define our modern global economy.

Traditional political economists believe that without a strong state authority, private actors will prey upon those weaker than themselves. In so doing, traditional political economists commit errors of both overpessimism and overoptimism. The standard analysis is overly pessimistic about the ability of individuals and communities to find rules that enable them to live better together and to realize the social gains from cooperation rather than devolve into social conflict without the establishment of a coercive state authority. But the standard analysis is also overly optimistic about the state's ability to establish binding constraints on itself so that societies are not just trading off the threat of private predation for public predation.

History is filled with examples of aggressive and oppressive public predation, so this intellectual error of overoptimism is one of the most costly ever committed. The committing of that error was made possible, though, because of the first error, overpessimism, which hides from view, as Stringham puts it, "the unseen beauty that underpins markets." It is in correcting that error that Stringham's major contribution resides.

Building on the insights of James Buchanan and his "Economic Theory of Clubs," Stringham demonstrates in ways beyond the theoretical imagination of even Buchanan how far one can stretch the basic argument for private governance. But theoretical imagining, let alone normative pontificating, is not what Stringham is content to do. Instead, he demonstrates in one example after another that individuals are able to come together, devise rules, and agree to mechanisms of enforcement in ways that transform situations of potential conflict into opportunities of mutually beneficial and reinforcing cooperation.

His narrative introduces the reader to something that is absolutely beautiful: the amazing capacity of diverse individuals to realize peaceful cooperation and productive specialization without the explicit threat of violence by a geographic monopoly on coercion. Readers will see this beautiful cooperation in Amsterdam and London as the institutions of modern finance are born, as well as in advanced technology such as PayPal and in the rise of private arbitration. Along the way, Stringham also shows how a state monopoly on governance distorts cooperative tendencies and introduces social cleavages and conflicts where otherwise they would not appear. In short, public government can crowd out effective private governance.

Along these lines, Stringham's application of his theory of private governance to the financial crisis of 2008 is a most welcomed perspective on the idea that Wall Street requires government control and a helping hand to function properly. Stringham argues that private governance mechanisms were already in place and working before the crisis, but government regulations and bailouts distorted those mechanisms and prevented them from functioning as they would have in the absence of the state's coercive interference.

Throughout this book, Stringham successfully marries the best ideas from property rights economics, law and economics, public choice economics, and Austrian economics to form his own private-governance perspective. He constantly tests this perspective through examinations of how individuals and groups find myriad ways to police both themselves and other participants for the activity under examination.

Stringham tells an inspiring story, but not a utopian one. It does not require any change in human nature. He treats individuals as they are—sometimes sinners, sometimes saints, sometimes smart, other times not so smart—documenting the ways they muddle through and figure out that cooperating is better than not cooperating to realize the gains from trade and innovation.

Edward Peter Stringham has written an inspiring book about the unseen beauty of the cooperative abilities of mankind. All social thinkers should take notice of how diverse individuals have developed a variety of private institutional arrangements that enable them to live better together and to realize the great gains from peaceful cooperation and productive specialization. This "marvel of the market" is indeed a thing of beauty.

Peter Boettke
University Professor of Economics and Philosophy
George Mason University

Private Governance

PART ONE

Why Private Governance?

CHAPTER 1

༄

Introduction

It's the year 1762, and you are a London stockbroker in the narrow Exchange Alley between Cornhill and Lombard Streets. You haven't been doing too well recently, but share prices for this one long purchase you made have been going up. Everything is looking perfect. But at settlement time you notice your trading counterpart in an expensive-looking new coat, and he tells you he's not going to deliver your shares. He says, "What are you going to do? Sue me? Did you forget that courts refuse to enforce these contracts?" In eighteenth-century London a defaulting broker *could* have been common, but such a predicament was *not* in fact common. Without the ability to rely on external courts, brokers transformed coffeehouses into private clubs that created and enforced rules. Each club aimed to admit only reputable brokers, and those who broke the rules would be kicked out and labeled a "lame duck." The private club known as Jonathan's Coffeehouse eventually became the London Stock Exchange, which adopted as its motto "My word is my bond." The rules did not come from government, but from the private sector, from private governance.

In modern times PayPal and eBay and other payment processors and clearinghouses also create order in markets and facilitate exchange. Private governance describes the various forms of private enforcement, self-governance, self-regulation, or informal mechanisms that private individuals, companies, or clubs (as opposed to government)[1] use to create order, facilitate exchange,

---

1. Here I use the terms *government*, *private*, and *club* according to their dictionary definitions from Merriam-Webster (2013): "Government: the group of people who control and make decisions for a country, state, etc"; "Private: intended for or restricted to the use of a particular person, group, or class"; and "Club: a group of people who meet to participate in an activity." Regulators, police, or courts provided by local, state, or national governments are considered governmental because they make decisions for everyone in a region (regardless of whether people agree), whereas rule makers or enforcers at private colleges or stock exchanges are private and only apply to people who do business in those venues. I discuss the differences more in chapter 3.

and protect property rights. From the world's first stock markets in the seventeenth century, to private policing in the early days of San Francisco, to millions of credit card transactions governed by private rules today, *Private Governance* makes the case that privately produced and enforced rules are more common, effective, and promising than most of us believed. Credit card transactions, electronic commerce, and the world's most sophisticated financial transactions are made possible because of private governance.

The heart of this book is case studies with examples that include the following:

1. My Word Is My Bond. In seventeenth-century Amsterdam and eighteenth-century London, the world's first stock markets were surprisingly complex, with short sales, forward contracts, and options contracts even though none were enforceable in official courts of law. In these markets the forces of reputation acted as an alternative to government enforcement. The most advanced markets the world had ever seen and modern capital markets owe their existence to private governance.

2. The Hidden Law of Online Commerce. Millions of electronic transactions occur every day without a thought. Even though government has difficulty tracking down anonymous fraudsters, transactions are protected by a complex system that manages and prevents fraud before it occurs. The better intermediaries deal with fraud ex ante, the more irrelevant the inefficacy of government law enforcement becomes.

3. Where the Streets Are Policed with Gold. With the California Gold Rush tens of thousands of people moved to San Francisco, but early on government police were entirely absent. Even after they were created, they were considered worse than the private criminals. To deal with the problem of crime, including crime from government, merchants organized a private police force that had a thousand members by 1900 and still patrols San Francisco today. Bundling protection with real estate enables merchants to have a more responsive police force than government.

4. *Compromis* Is Not a Compromise. Alternative dispute resolution (and the *compromis* document agreeing to arbitrate) allows parties wanting third-party adjudication to have cases adjudicated in the manner they want. They get to select the rules, the procedures, and who adjudicates a dispute. Private parties are willing to pay money to hire private judges who are experts and adjudicate disputes as the disputants prefer.

5. Derivatives as Anything but Derivative. Derivative markets are among the most sophisticated and largest markets in the world, with the value of notional contracts outstanding exceeding world GDP multiple times over. Collateralized debt obligations, credit default swaps, and other complex products create new bundles of property rights that are not the creation of government. Although they are wildly misunderstood, and often vilified

for causing crises, these financial instruments work remarkably well at mitigating risk and expanding the scope of markets.

Private Governance describes some of the major mechanisms that private parties use to produce social order and highlights how modern markets would not be possible without them. Analytical narratives weave together history and economics to show readers how private governance works. The hypotheses are: that potential problems such as fraud are pervasive, but so are private solutions; that private governance is a far more common source of order than most people realize, but few people notice it; and that private parties have incentives to devise various mechanisms for eliminating unwanted behavior, and among them the efficacy of nonviolent mechanisms is particularly underappreciated. This book explores some of the different mechanisms, including sorting, reputation, assurance, bonding, and various forms of ex ante risk management, that underpin markets.

The approach of private governance stands in contrast to what Gallanter (1981) and Williamson (1983) labeled legal centralism, the idea that order in the world depends on and is attributable to government law. Legal centralism is widely held among lawyers, lawmakers, and even free-market thinkers who believe that "the protection and enforcement of contracts through courts and civil law is the most crucial need of a peaceful society; without such protection, no civilization could be developed or maintained" (Rand, 1966, p. 299).

Yet, whether one likes or not, often government law enforcement is absent, too costly to use, or unknowledgeable about or uninterested in protecting property rights or contracts. Because government regulators, police, and courts are, to put it in the nicest way possible, "imperfect," private parties have potentially important unmet needs. Such parties can either live with problems or attempt to solve them. What do they do? People can rely on government, or they can devise private solutions. Williamson (1996, p. 121) writes that most researchers ignore "the variety of ways by which individual parties to exchange 'contract out of or away from' the governance structures of the state by devising private orderings." Williamson (2005, p. 16) concludes his Ely Lecture to the American Economic Association by saying, "I submit that our understandings of economic organization and public policy pertinent thereto have been needlessly impoverished by failures to pay heed to the lessons of governance. The economics of governance is an unfinished project whose time has come."

Williamson calls on researchers to study all areas of governance, and this book focuses on, you guessed it, private governance. One of the premises of this book is that just as one should not assume the effectiveness of governmental legal solutions, one should not assume the effectiveness of private legal solutions. Although not legal centralists in the traditional sense, many radical libertarians are legal centralists of a sort who simply substitute private enforcers for government enforcers of law. If a potential problem comes up, the libertarian legal centralist is prone to say, "That would be illegal in my ideal world." Yet even the best private police or courts might not be able to solve a problem in a cost-effective way, so private parties may have to live with certain trade-offs or seek alternative solutions. Instead of relying on legalistic mechanisms to facilitate trade and protect property rights, private parties have created countless private mechanisms to underpin exchange and make markets work.

Although I believe normative discussions of what qualifies as a legitimate market system are necessary and useful, as Kant pointed out, ought statements imply can statements, so one also needs to have economic discussions about how matters can or cannot work.[2] The examples in this book are not hypothetical solutions but rather real-world solutions from private governance. Focusing on actual rather than hypothetical examples eliminates the need to speculate about whether certain problems could be solved. For example, one need not debate whether complex financial transactions can take place without external enforcement (something that Olson [1996] asserts is impossible), if one can observe them taking place for centuries. The examples discussed in this book are tremendously important for creating modern markets, but countless other examples of private governance exist. After some theoretical discussions from the 1970s about private order, economists including Bruce Benson, Robert Ellickson, Avner Greif, Terry Anderson, and P.J. Hill were pioneers in documenting examples, and I now believe the research potential for this topic is nearly limitless.

An implicit assumption in many normative debates is that private solutions cannot be relied upon for complex problems. Can private governance facilitate cooperation in sophisticated transactions, in large groups, in heterogeneous populations, under conditions of anonymity, or across long distances? Or will problems such as free riding and prisoners' dilemmas lead to market failure? All of these are empirical questions whose answers are usually assumed rather than investigated.

Yet mechanisms of private governance are far more ubiquitous and far more powerful than commonly assumed. Mechanisms of private governance work in small and large groups, among friends and strangers, in ancient and modern societies, and for simple and extremely complex transactions. They

---

2. This book focuses on economics rather than philosophy, but readers interested in philosophical discussions of a privately governed society can read Barnett (1998); Chartier (2013); Casey (2012); Huemer (2013); Long and Machan (2008), Narveson (2008), Rasmussen and Den Uyl (2010); Sanders and Narveson (1996); Skoble (2008) and Watner, Smith, and McElroy (1983). My normative ideals are represented in those works. Economic books about this subject include Anderson and Hill (2004); Benson (1990, 1998); De Jasay (1997); and Friedman ([1973] 1989), and books making rights-based and economic arguments include Hoppe (1989) and Rothbard (1973, 1977, [1982] 1998). For an overview of this literature, see Stringham (2005a, 2007), Powell and Stringham (2009), and Boettke (2005, 2012).

often exist alongside, and in many cases in spite of, government legal efforts, and most of the time they are totally missed. The more that private governance solves problems behind the scenes, the more people overlook it and misattribute order to the state. Milton Friedman, for example, recognizes that private rule enforcement could work, but considers it rare: "I look over history, and outside of perhaps Iceland, where else can you find any historical examples of that kind of a system developing?" (Doherty and Friedman, 1995).[3] After reading this book, I hope Friedman would answer instead that private order is all around us. Private governance is everywhere and responsible for creating order not just in basic markets but also in the world's most sophisticated markets, including futures and advanced derivatives markets. If the success of private governance were limited to the examples in this book, the track record should be rated superb. Yet they are a fraction of what has worked and will work in the future. I hope this research inspires others to document some of the countless mechanisms that have made markets as robust as they are.

Research in private governance not only gives a better understanding of how markets work, but also has many normative implications. Where legal centralists assume that government is the source of order and look to additional rules and regulations to deal with potential problems, the necessity and effectiveness of their solutions are usually unconsidered. According to Spinoza (1670, c. 20), "He who tries to determine everything by law, will foment crime rather than lessen it." In this perspective order comes about privately, and attempting to legislate outcomes can have the opposite effect. Government is often dysfunctional and crowds out private sources of order, or it is simply absent or too costly to use. With so many government officials ignorant of or even outright hostile to markets, how much should one attribute the existence of markets to them? Providers of private governance recognize government is not the solution, so they take the initiative and devise private ones.

Friedrich Hayek used the word *marvel* to describe the price system and its role in coordinating disparate individuals. The mechanisms of private governance are just as marvelous and are responsible for creating order in markets. As Thomas Paine ([1791] 1906, p. 84) writes:

> Great part of that order which reigns among mankind is not the effect of government. It has its origin in the principles of society and the natural constitution of man. It existed prior to government, and would exist if the formality

3. Friedman was asked about societies with fully private enforcement, so I may be misrepresenting his position. Nevertheless, even in societies with government, private governance plays a crucial rule. As Galanter (1981, pp. 19–20) states, "Societies contain a multitude of partially self-regulating spheres or sectors, organized along special, transactional or ethnic-familial lines ranging from primary groups in which relations are direct, immediate and diffuse to settings (e.g., business networks) in which relations are indirect, mediated and specialized."

of government was abolished. The mutual dependence and reciprocal interest which man has upon man, and all the parts of civilised community upon each other, create that great chain of connection which holds it together.

The invisible hand analogy in economics sheds light on underappreciated processes of coordinating behavior, and the study of private governance sheds light on the underappreciated mechanisms that create order. Markets, from soup to nuts, are where they are because of private governance. Yet the more seamless private governance is, the fewer people notice it or appreciate its beauty. Private governance is so often missed, but it makes markets possible.

CHAPTER 2

༺༒༻

Beyond the Deus ex Machina
Theory of Law

2.1. INTRODUCTION

In Euripides's (408 B.C.) play *Orestes*,[1] the stage is set by describing Orestes's grandfather Atreus, who killed Thyestes's children and feasted on them, and Orestes's father, Agamemnon, who is later murdered. Soon after, Orestes kills his mother and becomes sick from a cruel wasting disease, his mother's blood goading him into frenzied fits. Orestes's sister Electra spends half her life weeping and wailing about her being a maid unwed, unblest with babes, and dragging out a joyless existence as if forever. Orestes's uncle, Menelaus, arrives to look for his wife Helen, whom he suspects has been murdered by Orestes, but Helen's body is nowhere to be found. Menelaus finds Orestes and his friend Pylades with a sword at the throat of Menelaus's daughter, Hermione, and they threaten to kill her and burn the family palace. "Ah me! what can I do?" Menelaus declares. With 95 percent of the play complete (the final 2.5 pages remain in the Coleridge translation), matters are looking pretty grim. But right before the very end Apollo appears from above with Helen, whom he has rescued from death. Apollo announces that Helen is granted immortality in the mansions of Zeus and will be honored with drink-offerings as a goddess forever. Apollo tells Orestes that Orestes will return to Athens and go on trial before the gods, but win his case, marry Hermione, and become ruler of Argos. Apollo takes the blame for forcing Orestes to murder his mother and says he will bring about reconciliation. Apollo says that Menelaus will become ruler of Sparta, and Menelaus wishes Helen well in heaven's happy courts and gives

---

1. I create this paragraph abridgement almost entirely using exact phrases from the translation by Coleridge (1893).

his blessing to Orestes to marry his daughter. Apollo declares, "Repair each one to the place appointed by me; reconcile all strife." The end.

It might be nice if the world's problems were solved that way, but commentators from Aristotle to Nietzsche argue such writing is questionable.[2] The deus ex machina (god from the machine) plot device is named for Greek plays that used gods played by actors suspended on cranes to suddenly solve characters' problems. One sees this in all sorts of movies where problems are solved last minute by an outside entity. In the end of the not-so-acclaimed movie *Jurassic Park 3* the characters are saved by the U.S. Navy, and in the end of the even less acclaimed movie *Matrix 3*, Keanu Reeves is saved by a mysterious supercomputer named . . . Deus Ex Machina.

Not only is the deus ex machina popular in poorly written fiction, it is also popular in bad social science. In many social science and policy debates theorists think of potential problems and assume government can solve them (Demsetz, 1969). Although they do not view government law enforcement (regulators, police, and courts, which I will refer to as "the law") as a literal deus ex machina, most theorists view the law as exogenous corrective device. Whether the issue is security property rights or facilitating exchange, the idea is that government can and will fix problems.

Ellickson (1991, p. 138) uses "the phrase legal centralism to describe the belief that governments are the chief sources of rules and enforcement efforts." Legal centralism takes various forms, but all forms assume that markets would not be able to fully function without government rules and regulations.[3] In addition to assumptions about the ability of markets to function without government, legal centralism includes assumptions about the efficacy of government. For Williamson (1983, p. 520), "Most studies of exchange assume that efficacious rules of law regarding contract disputes are in place and that these are applied by courts in an informed, sophisticated, and low-cost way. . . . The 'legal centralism' tradition reflects this orientation."

The strongest forms of legal centralism consider legal rules or regulation costless (notice, for example, that the Securities and Exchange Commission almost never mentions the costs of its policies), while weaker forms of legal centralism recognize some costs of legal rules or regulations but still consider them absolutely necessary. For Ellickson (1991, p. 138), "The quintessential legal centralist was Thomas Hobbes, who thought that in a society without a

2. Abel (1954) argues that Euripides's use of the deus ex machina plot device is not a fault but an excellence that intends to get the audience to think about the secular versus the divine. Abel may be right to defend Euripides specifically, but I doubt whether he would defend the use of the deus ex machina plot device in movies starring Keanu Reeves.

3. Legal centralism is found among various normative frameworks, among advocates of rights, utilitarianism, wealth maximization, and much else, regardless of one's support for markets or other political perspectives.

sovereign, all would be chaos," but he argues that such thinking strongly influences law and economics scholarship today: "The seminal works in law and economics hew to the Hobbesian tradition of legal centralism." My professors James Buchanan and Gordon Tullock are often skeptical of government in general, yet they ultimately follow Hobbes and believe that government enforcement is essential for markets. As Buchanan (1975, p. 163) writes, "The protective state has as its essential and only role . . . one of enforcing rights to property, to exchanges of property, and of policing the simple and complex exchange processes among contracting free men."

Classical liberals typically advocate two main functions for the government legal system: protecting property rights and enforcing contracts to deal with force and fraud. One could support one function but not the other (e.g., calling on government to protect property rights but relying on private mechanisms for facilitating exchange), but most believe government must do both. As Richard Epstein (1999, p. 285) comments, "Under its classical liberal formulation, the great social contract sacrifices liberty, but only to the extent that it is necessary to gain security against force and fraud. Perhaps we might go further, but surely we go this far." Epstein suggests that one would be a "naïve visionary" to "believe that markets could operate of their own volition without any kind of support from the state." Likewise, Rajan and Zingales (2004, p. 293) write, "Markets cannot flourish without the very visible hand of government, which is needed to set up and maintain the infrastructure that enables participants to trade freely and with confidence." Such a sentiment is also found in Mises ([1927] 2002, p. 39): "The state is an absolute necessity, since the most important tasks are incumbent upon it: the protection not only of private property, but also of peace, for in the absence of the latter the full benefits of private property cannot be reaped." And the sentiment is found in Kirzner (1985, p. 680), who writes, "Preservation of this fundamental framework of individual rights calls for government that protects these rights against potential enemies."

The strongest forms of legal centralism consider property rights and exchange impossible without government enforcement, while weaker forms of legal centralism recognize property rights and exchange as possible without government enforcement, but believe they would be extremely limited. To authors such as North (1990), Landa (1994), Olson (1996), Frye (2000), and Soto (2000) advanced markets and sophisticated exchange crucially depend on government making them legal centralist in some ultimate sense. Soto (1989), for example, describes how most Peruvians live on private property that is not recognized in any government registry, but ultimately Soto (2000) believes that advanced markets would require government to codify these property rights. Similarly North (1990) and Olson (1996) recognize that exchange often occurs in absence of government enforcement (one need not use law to trade among families, friends, or close-knit groups), but ultimately they argue that sophisticated markets such as those in capital markets would be impossible without government enforcement. A common prediction is that cooperation breaks down as groups become larger or more heterogeneous, or trade takes place through time (Landa, 1994, p. 60; Frye, 2000, p. 34). Although Frye (2000) recognizes that private governance is important, he believes that private governance must be ultimately be subordinate to and backed up by law and that advanced markets cannot work without law.

2.2. WHEN THE ASSUMPTIONS OF LEGAL CENTRALISM DO NOT HOLD

Legal centralism is a clean theory that lets people declare, "Here is how I would like the legal system to shape the world," and is thus understandably popular. It does, however, rest on many theoretical and empirical assumptions, and if some of those assumptions do not hold, the theory may not be useful for understanding or shaping the world. Whether one likes it or not, "market augmenting" (Olson, 2000, p. xi) legal agents might not exist, be inaccessible, have diverging interests, or know too little to help out. Instead of assuming that government has the ability and interest to solve problems, we must look to see if certain conditions are met. Whenever a potential problem exists, one should ask the following questions:

> Do regulators, police, and courts have the ability to solve the problem in a low-cost way?
> Do regulators, police, and courts have the knowledge to solve the problem?
> Do regulators, police, and courts have the incentive to solve the problem?

Where the legal centralist assumes that the answers to these questions will be yes, the researcher of private governance considers the possibility that regulators, police, and courts may be lacking in important ways. Knowledge and incentive problems exist (Barnett, 1998; Benson, 1990; Boettke, 2005, 2012; Hoppe, 1989; Pennington, 2011; Rothbard, 1973, 1977; Stigler, 1975; Stringham and Zywicki, 2011a). Whether one hopes for government to eliminate fraud, deal with principal-agent problems, protect property rights, or enhance markets in any other way, simply assuming government will solve the problem is a nonstarter. If the answer to one or more of the above questions is no, then unmet needs exist, and then we should ask:

> When unmet needs exist, will the private sector have the ability, knowledge, and incentive to solve them?

In many cases there is no solution, and people just have to live with the problem. In many cases, however, private parties will notice problems and look for solutions through private governance. The chapters in this book describe cases in which market participants clearly could not rely on regulators, police, and courts to solve their problems. This explains why parties need to turn to private governance. Thinking about institutional, Austrian, and public choice economic insights in the area of governance gives reasons to question the legal centralist approach.

2.2.1. Do Regulators, Police, and Courts Have the Ability to Solve the Problem in a Low-Cost Way?

"What? This $25 long-distance phone card is bogus?" The thoughts "I've been had" and "This cannot be happening to me" raced through my mind. I contacted various law enforcement agencies and lawyers to initiate a lawsuit. For weeks I sat by the phone, but for some reason nobody returned my call. I have been living with this missing $25 and devastation for the past two decades. . . . Actually I did lose $25, but I never ended up making any of those calls. How much good would it have done? I could have assumed that relying on courts would have been relatively low cost. But assuming something so does not make it so. Because the cost of initiating a lawsuit, including the cost of my time, far exceeded what I reasonably could expect to get back, I preferred treating the $25 as a sunk cost over spending time and money through avenues with little prospective gain. At the time I had no private solution either, but the fact that legal solutions are costly or often nonexistent should be the starting point of our analysis, as that reality shapes how individuals and businesses choose.

A $25 phone card is trivial, but it's actually the just tip of an iceberg. Each day trillions of small transactions take place, and although theoretically it is possible to take a party to court each time another party does not follow through with its part of the bargain, at a minimum doing so would be very costly. What percentage of transactions in your typical day do you think could be easily enforced in courts of law? Where would you even begin? Even the most litigious person must weigh the expected benefits of initiating a lawsuit (what you could be awarded times the estimated probability of winning the lawsuit) with the cost of hiring a lawyer and going to trial, the hassle of dealing with the courts, the value of your time, the inconvenience of having assets held up in the legal system, the negative repercussions of being seen as a litigious person, and so on. Whenever the cost of enforcement exceeds the value of what is at stake or what one can reasonably expect to gain through law, then private parties must simply live with the problem or seek private solutions.[4]

---

4. I am not arguing that the many litigious parties and million lawyers in the United States do not exist. Their mere existence, however, does not prove that they are augmenting markets. Instead, many simply are using the state according to Bastiat's ([1848] 1995) description, in which "The state is that great fiction by which everyone tries to live at the expense of everyone else."

How significant are the costs of formulating, implementing, complying with, and enforcing rules (Hertog, 1999, p. 225)? How significant are the costs of hiring lawyers, going to trial, having facts verified and interpreted, and after the trial, getting the party in the wrong to rectify the situation (Barzel, 2002; Bernstein, 1992; Hart and Moore, 1999; Klein and Leffler, 1981; Telser, 1980; Tirole, 1999)? The costs of using courts are often significant, and whenever they outweigh what is at stake in a lawsuit, most people will not bother with the law. Galanter (1981, p. 3) describes how "courts resolve only a small fraction of all disputes that are brought to their attention. These are only a small fraction of the disputes that might conceivably be brought to court and an even smaller fraction of the whole university of disputes," and transactions with disputes are but a fraction of the total number of transactions.

Shadow-of-the-state theories of order suggest that even if most transactions are not litigated, the prospect of litigation, punitive damages, or high fines makes the expected costs of bad behavior too high. Yet the greater the "transaction costs" of using various aspects of the law, the greater the likelihood that the legal system deviates from textbook ideals (Williamson, 1996, p. 142). That helps explain why even with high fines, government cannot stamp out drugs in society, or even prisons, and that helps explain why many petty fraudsters continue to exist even though fraud has been illegal since time immemorial.

The cost of using the legal system can be significant not just for small dealings but for large dealings as well. Businesses that have millions of dollars at stake in transactions or require fulfillment to move forward with business do not want to have assets tied up in government courts. When I worked on a trading desk in the late 1990s, we needed to make sure each poorly executed trade was rectified by the end of each day, not the end of the year. Our trading desk worked out dozens of potential problems daily, and not once did we or our counterparts initiate a lawsuit.

The cost of using the legal system can be significant not just for straightforward transactions but even more so for complex ones. In simple models two parties agree to exchange two assets, and government simply needs to verify whether each party delivered (Buchanan, 1975, p. 104). Sophisticated transactions, however, often involve complex bundles of goods that are not easily verifiable by third parties (Lancaster, 1966; Hart and Moore, 1999; Dore and Rosser, 2007). For example, a court can observe parts of a bundle, such as whether custom software was installed on customers' machines, but be less able to evaluate the other more subjective and more important elements of the product. When goods have a thousand attributes (Microsoft Windows and Macintosh operating systems each have tens of millions of lines of code that interact with each other), government may be able to reasonably evaluate only a handful of them. How significant are the costs of writing contracts describing multifaceted and heterogeneous goods, stipulating the myriad of possible contingencies (if that's even possible), remedies when specific performance is not met, or relying on the legal system to fill in these details (Barzel, 2002, p. 37; Lind and Nyström, 2007)? When was the last time you sued Microsoft or Apple when your computer crashed?

The cost of using the legal system may be significant only in a few areas, or it may be extremely widespread. One of the biggest markets is the labor market (according to some estimates, labor accounts for roughly 75 percent of national income [Gomme and Rupert, 2004]), yet Vandenberghe (2000, p. 541) describes it as being full of implicit contracts that are "too vague to be legally enforceable." Have you ever worked with someone who shows up to work and follows all the rules but is not effective at actually producing value? Does law enforcement help businesses make unproductive employees more productive, or does it make it difficult for companies to fire them? If regulators, police, and courts do not have the ability to solve a problem in a low-cost way, then unmet needs will exist.

2.2.2. Do Regulators, Police, and Courts Have the Knowledge to Solve the Problem?

In fall 2011, thousands of protesters converged in downtown Manhattan through the Occupy Wall Street movement, demanding that government rein in and increase regulations on the financial sector. One list of demands at the website OccupyWallStreet.org (2011) called for everything from "outlawing credit rating agencies" to "immediate across the board debt forgiveness for all. Debt forgiveness of sovereign debt, commercial loans, home mortgages, home equity loans, credit card debt, student loans and personal loans now!" Despite the economic nature of most of their demands, a *New York Magazine* survey (Klein, 2011) of Occupy Wall Street protesters found that in response to the question "Who is the chairman of the Federal Reserve?" 42 percent answered "Don't know" (only 38 percent could answer correctly), in response to "What is the 'S.E.C.'?" 68 percent answered "Don't know," and in response to "What is the Dodd-Frank Act?" 84 percent answered "Don't know."[5] For a movement that focuses on economic issues, protesters' knowledge of economics (not to mention their knowledge about the importance of bathing at least once per month) does not appear to be that strong. Without irony, Harvard law professor and now U.S. senator Elizabeth Warren states, "I created much of the intellectual foundation for what they do," and "I support what they do" (Johnson, 2011). Meanwhile, on the productive and better-dressed

---

5. For readers who did not live in the United States at the time of this survey, the correct answers were Ben Bernanke, the Securities and Exchange Commission, and a major set of financial regulations signed into law in 2010.

part of Wall Street, trillions of dollars of shares exchange hands. The masters of the universe on Wall Street could sit around and hope that the state will be a "market-augmenting government" that will "expand the dominion of markets by providing rules that facilitate voluntary and reliable trade" (Azfar and Caldwell, 2003, p. 3) and hope for "effective judicial enforcement of complicated contracts" (Glaeser, Johnson, and Shleifer, 2001, p. 854). Or they can recognize that government officials often lack an understanding of the markets they are allegedly bolstering. While private parties are figuring out how to make incredibly complex financial deals possible, government officials are debating banning short sales or imposing price controls on interchange fees (Zywicki, 2011).

Ludwig von Mises and Friedrich Hayek argue that government is not omniscient and that without markets in consumer and producer goods, central planners cannot calculate whether the value of what they are producing is worth more than its costs (Hayek, 1945; Mises, [1920] 1990; Salerno 1990).[6] Hayek describes the market as a discovery process in which different people get to test out different ideas and see what best fulfills customer desires. Profits and losses provide constant feedback about whether firms are serving their customers, but such feedback is absent with government. Although Hayek used terms such as *discovery* to describe the process of common-law judges figuring out the best legal rules, he did not entertain the idea that all rules and regulations be subject to the market test (Stringham and Zywicki, 2011). But what if he did? How will a monopolist government best identify problems, and how will it know where to devote scarce resources? How will government measure the costs of additional rules and regulations, and how will it measure the potential burden they impose on subsequent parties? What is the likelihood that the government designs and enforces rules in an optimal way, and what is the feedback mechanism when it does not solve problems or makes problems worse? Just as the central planner assumes that without property rights, prices, profits, and markets the government can engage in rational economic calculation, the legal centralist assumes that government, a monopolist legal and regulatory system, can effectively weigh the effects of each rule to prevent problems in markets. If regulators, police, and courts lack the knowledge of what rules or enforcement procedures are augmenting markets and what are harming them, then unmet needs will exist.

---

6. For example, a road might be valuable, but without knowing the opportunity cost of the inputs (stone, cementing agents, labor, and land) or the value of the road to consumers, government can only guess whether the road is worth more than what otherwise could be produced. With markets, producers can see the prices all of their inputs and outputs, which enable them to calculate whether it makes sense to produce any given product or to produce it in a different way. Without markets, such feedback is absent (Mises, [1920] 1990).

2.2.3. Do Regulators, Police, and Courts Have the Incentive to Solve the Problem?

San Francisco has a lot of gentle people with flowers in their hair, but it also has a fair share of down-and-out drug addicts. I remember walking down the aisle in the Safeway grocery store across from the San Francisco Giants' ballpark, AT&T Park, and observing a man lying flat in the middle of the aisle, staring up into the air.

Several employees came over, thinking he had fallen. "Are you okay?" one asked.

"Yes, I am completely fine."

"May we help you get up?"

"No, there is no problem whatsoever. What is the problem?" he asked, bothered that they were asking questions of a normal person simply minding his business. In his drug-influenced alternate universe there was no problem with him lying there for hours, but to a high-volume grocery store each minute of his presence meant lost sales in the short run and fewer customers in the long run. To Safeway, matters like this are a potentially big problem.

When something is a big problem to a merchant such as Safeway, especially to a merchant that pays so much in taxes, one could assume that government police will set their priorities accordingly. But the San Francisco Police Department has other priorities. Even a well-meaning government police force has to prioritize its time, and no matter how important the issue is to Safeway, the police can lack incentives to cater to Safeway's needs. In San Francisco, the police classify a merchant call about removing an unwanted guest as a low-priority event and usually will not send anyone at all.

James Buchanan and Gordon Tullock asked economists to consider the possibility that government agents consider their well-being when making decisions. Buchanan never applied public choice to law (instead Buchanan [1975] describes government enforcement mechanistically, like an alarm clock acting), but what if he did? A weak version of the public choice hypothesis is that law enforcement officials care about the public but also consider their own well-being when making choices. They might like protecting property rights or facilitating economic exchange on other people's behalf but not be very motivated, in the same way that many government teachers work, but not as hard as they could. A stronger version of the public choice hypothesis is that law enforcement officials care about their personal well-being and not that of their subjects. Police objectives can include relatively benign failings such as keeping patrolling to a minimum, consuming leisure, or pursuing overtime, or more malevolent failings such as using the law to extract resources or exert power. Legal centralists' wishes notwithstanding, law enforcement officials may not have maximizing utils in society or maximizing Kaldor-Hicks efficiency in their objective function.

Surveys indicate that elected officials are seen as "influenced by special interests, looking out for themselves" (Pew Research Center, 2010, p. 50), and only one in five Americans says "they can trust the government in Washington almost always or most of the time"(Pew Research Center, 2010, p. 13). Are law enforcers, regulators, judges, or police different, or should we consider the possibility that law enforcers care about advancing their career, income, power, or leisure? Should we assume that officials sprout angel's wings when they step behind a regulator's desk or put on a policeman's uniform or a judge's robe? The many cases of police brutality and prosecutorial misconduct (Roberts and Stratton, 2008; Balko, 2013) suggest that the hypothesis of self-interest is at least often true. When government is not sufficiently motivated to solve people's problems, then unmet needs will exist.

2.2.4. If Unmet Needs Exist, Will Providers of Private Governance Attempt to Meet Them?

If regulators, police, and courts are deficient in any of the above ways, then potentially important unmet needs can exist. Here the private sector will either have to live with a problem or attempt to solve it. Why wouldn't they? Of course, providers of private governance are not dei ex machina. Imperfect knowledge, conflicting interests, transaction costs, and other collective action problems will always prevent the economy from reaching nirvana. In some cases, especially with problems on government-owned land that lacks a residual claimant, there are no private solutions, or private solutions that are not worth implementing. (A residual claimant is typically an owner of an enterprise who profits when things go well, and earns losses when things do not. Government property is typically not owned and no one makes profits or suffers losses based on its good or bad management.) For example, it does not make sense to hire an armed guard to watch over a $100 bicycle. Certain problems might persist simply because providers of private governance have yet to figure out solutions.

In many cases, however, private parties can profit by ameliorating problems, and the more important the solution, the larger the potential profit opportunity (Klein, 2002). Putting governance into the hands of private parties encourages them to look for creative solutions, just as entrepreneurs look for ways to better serve consumers. Demsetz (1967, p. 352) maintains that issues (such as establishing the property rights in beaver) are more likely to be addressed as the value at stake increases. Is the same true for unmet needs of governance? The question is more than just academic. Before conducting business everyone must evaluate whether one can rely on regulators, police, or courts to protect one's property or facilitate exchange. Setting up in areas with lots of criminals, such as Washington, DC, and simply assuming that regulators, police, and courts care about one's problems may not be the best business model. Because regulators, police, and courts are so often incapable of or uninterested in solving problems, private parties must rely on mechanisms of private governance. PayPal founder Peter Thiel once told me that one can observe suboptimalities in the world and complain about them or consider the tremendous good one can create by eliminating them. PayPal noticed an existing set of problems and found ways to solve them. The company helped facilitate nonrepeat transactions between complete strangers around the world and enriched many people as a result.

Providers of private governance will never solve all problems, in the same way that entrepreneurs will never invent every possible product. But just as profit lures entrepreneurs to find ways to better serve customers, profits lure providers of private governance to find better ways of protecting property rights and facilitating exchange.

2.3. SUMMARY AND THOUGHTS

Legal centralist tendencies seem engrained in many people. I recall the Friday in July 2000 when my professor and I had just landed in Prague, a city that was rapidly liberalizing but still had many remnants of communism. On our way for food and drink, my professor was attempting to take money out of a perfectly modern bank machine. The machine required the user to retrieve the card before the machine dispensed the cash, but when he did not retrieve his card in time, the machine thought he forgot it and sucked it in. He stated, aghast, "What do I do? The bank will not be open until Monday." His free-market credentials notwithstanding, my professor's reaction was nothing less than "Let me seek help from these nearby police officers." After some protestations, I realized the futility of convincing him that GE Capital may not give the Czech police keys to their bank machines. The Czech police, predictably, were unable to retrieve his card. Why didn't GE Capital give the Czech police access to their vaults? Why did they even spend private resources on security when they could rely on around-the-clock protection from government? To ask these questions is to answer them. No deus ex machina solution was available, so my professor had to wait until Monday; GE Capital judged the best outcome to be holding potentially lost cards for safekeeping rather than allowing former communist policemen to open its bank machines.

Despite its popularity, legal centralism may not be helpful for attempting to understand and shape the world. Market participants have to be aware of imperfect government solutions, not just with bank cards but with all areas of economic life. Depending on the severity of its deficiencies, government may be anything from an inept protector of property rights and facilitator of economic exchange, to their primary disruptor. Throughout history governments have had a tremendous track record of undermining property rights and interfering with markets, but even if one assumes that government is ultimately beneficent, one must recognize that government does not meet all needs, and that explains why people turn to private governance.

Rather than assuming that government will fix one's problems, people know they must take many steps if they want their problems addressed. The examples in this book describe not hypothetical deus ex machina solutions but actual solutions of private governance. If you are a broker in seventeenth-century Amsterdam, should you assume that government officials understand your advanced financial transactions and will work to make them possible? If you are a broker in eighteenth-century London, should you assume that officials want to make your market as orderly as possible? If you are a merchant in nineteenth-century San Francisco, should you assume that government police will make sure your shop is safe? If you are an online processing company at the beginning of the twenty-first century, should you assume that government will protect you from anonymous fraudsters? If you are a multinational firm with millions of dollars at stake in a transaction, should you assume that courts around the world will adjudicate your case in a fast and fair manner? The legal centralist perspective might be correct. Government agents may have the knowledge, incentive, and ability to solve the public's problems in a low-cost way. Or they may not. The demand for private governance exists because government is not a deus ex machina.

CHAPTER 3

ளை

Rules from Voluntary Associations
as an Alternative to Coercive Ones

Governance as a Club Good

3.1. INTRODUCTION

Francis introduced himself to his platoon mates in the 1981 movie *Stripes*:

> The name's Francis Soyer, but everybody calls me Psycho. Any of you guys call me
> Francis, and I'll kill you. Also, I don't like no one touching my stuff. So just keep
> your meat-hooks off. If I catch any of you guys in my stuff, I'll kill you. And I don't
> like nobody touching me. Any of you [derogatory noun]s touch me, and I'll kill you.

Psycho certainly found *one* way to set the ground rules between him and his
platoon. When nobody touched him or his stuff, he could have attributed that
favorable outcome to his threats. But with a few exceptions, most people recognize that cooperation can occur for many reasons. Where the government
seeks to influence behavior with the threat of the use of force, the private
sector has many other options for motivating behavior, and most of them do
not involve the threat of the use of force. Regardless of what one thinks about
coercion from a normative point of view, a large body of literature in psychology indicates that people are most often better motivated using noncoercive
means (Sidman, 1989; Frumkin, 2010).[1]

---

1. For a brief introduction to this literature, see Myers (2004, pp. 318–32). For example, managers could motivate employees by threatening lashes or deportation to Si-
beria, but instead managers almost always use rewards for good performance. Despite
the harsh penalties in the Soviet Union, its system of motivation was never as effective
as the system of noncoercive incentives found in most private sector firms (Boetttke,
1993, p. 143; Maltzev, 1996, p. 108; Rothbard, 1990, p. 157).

Williamson (2005) describes some of the many ways in which private parties take steps to encourage good and discourage bad behavior. For example, two people contemplating a deal will think about the risks of opportunistic behavior but will also think about ways to minimize such risks. To a legal centralist, any cooperation must be attributable to the state, but in actuality, cooperation can be attributable to steps taken by the individual parties, membership clubs, corporations, and other voluntary associations. Williamson (2005, p. 14) explains that private parties take steps to minimize opportunism because "even in states that make best efforts to provide protection for property rights and contract enforcement, the state's access to information and the state's protection and enforcement mechanisms are inherently limited." Effective economic governance includes mechanisms such as credible commitments, reputation mechanisms, vertical integration, private protection of property rights, and profit-motivated contract enforcement (Williamson, 2005, pp. 14–15). The demand for order exists and is most often met by providers of private governance.

Moving beyond the "government provision"/"no provision" dichotomy reveals that many private organizations already create and enforce rules. The amount of private governance in current society is far greater than people commonly recognize and governance can be analyzed as a club good that can be provided in a multitude of ways. Merriam-Webster defines a club as "an association of persons for some common object usually jointly supported" or "an association of persons participating in a plan by which they agree to make regular payments or purchases in order to secure some advantage." How people with common goals meet their needs together is an often unexplored question. Clubs allow members to opt into preferred governance structures, and they create incentives for cooperation within. The simple ability to screen or exclude unwanted members gives clubs a powerful tool to discourage bad behavior without relying on the use of force. Competing clubs must constantly prevent or alleviate potential problems in ways that their members prefer. Private governance harnesses the benefits of competition, experimentation, and constant feedback that are seen in markets but not in government.

3.2. RULES THROUGH VOLUNTARY ASSOCIATIONS: CONSIDERING GOVERNANCE AS A CLUB GOOD

"No playing golf in tennis shorts! You cannot be here like that," Danny declared to one fellow whose inseam was not long enough. On another occasion Danny instructed a woman in a sleeveless collared shirt: "You will have to change your shirt, or else you will have to leave the course." Although Danny was in some ways strict, he was not a member of the tyrannical fashion police imposing restrictions on an unwilling public. Instead Danny was the starter and caddy master at the Country Club in my hometown of Brookline, Massachusetts, and he was simply enforcing the "restrictions" or club rules that members had chosen. As the oldest country club in the United States, the Country Club is a particularly traditional club whose members want to be surrounded with the positive externalities (spillover benefits to nonpayers) associated with turquoise golf slacks. The customer is in charge.

I begin by mentioning the Country Club not to suggest that everyone must shop at Brooks Brothers or J. Press but because it is an obvious example of how clubs create rules at the behest of their members. Other, less formal or less exclusive clubs include the Elks Lodge, a commune, a co-op, a workingmen's club, a camping club, a church, a bowling club, or any other sports club. Club rules range from country-club formality to Burning Man informality—a festival that caters to hippies, hipsters, and other poorly dressed people.

Nozick (1974, pp. 297–334) describes an ideal world in which people can opt into communities with different characteristics. Clubs enable this. According to the legal centralist, "Government must set the rules of the road" (Forty Fourth President of the United States, 2009, p. 689). But clearly many rules apply at smaller levels and need not be society-wide. Rules can range from a dress code at the country club to actual rules of a specific road or set of roads. The country club not only selects the rules for its golf course but also decides the speed limit for its roads, who can travel on them, and when. The same is true of other sources of private governance such as shopping malls, apartment complexes, and stock exchanges.

In his economic theory of clubs, Buchanan (1965) makes the case that economists should not assume that goods are either pure public goods that need to be shared by everyone in society or pure private goods that can be consumed only by one person. Instead, Buchanan suggests that all goods can be analyzed as club goods for which the optimal size of the club depends on each good. In this framework the optimal size of a club to consume an ice cream cone is usually one person, and the optimal size of a club to use a lighthouse (in theory but not in actuality [Coase, 1974]) might be infinite, because a lighthouse is a pure "public good."[2] However, most goods fit somewhere in between. A club of a thousand people shares a golf course, and a club of a hundred people shares a swimming pool in an apartment complex. The members of a country club or an apartment complex share not only their golf course or swimming pool but also the rules of the course or pool. Most apartment complexes have rules about when residents can use the pool and what time of the night one's voice has to be lowered. These rules are not set by government but are set by a type of private club.

2. Of course, even the optimal number of consumers for a lighthouse is much less than infinity because thousands rather than billions of people usually use lighthouses. Furthermore, despite claims to the contrary, lighthouses have historically been provided privately and paid for by users of a port (Coase, 1974; Block and Barnett, 2009).

Clubs can be geographically based and have a comprehensive set of rules for many aspects of life (as in a boarding school or a kibbutz), or clubs can be made for solving problems at very small margins within one's life, such as a chess club. Whether they realize it or not, most people choose to be members of many various clubs created to solve problems in different areas. Vincent Ostrom (2007) and Elinor Ostrom (2005, p. 283) discuss how governance can come from many sources with overlapping units (polycentrism), and their framework easily can be applied to clubs. For example, at any given time an individual can be a member of a geographically based residential club with rules of conduct between members (what is often subsumed under tort law and criminal law) as well as a business club such as a stock exchange with rules about trading (what is often subsumed by contract law). Membership in a private club can be formal or informal, long term or short term. In any given day a person might frequent a gated community, an apartment complex, an office complex, a corporation, a shopper's club, a country club, and a nightclub. To the extent that rules or forms of security are beneficial, these clubs create and enforce rules within their realms.

It is not too conjectural to claim that most of the world either currently *is* or (for areas currently publicly controlled) easily could *become* a private club. Geographically based clubs can be as small as a store or as large as Disney's Celebration, Florida (10,000 residents) or Las Vegas's City Center (which, with more than 5,000 hotel rooms, is bigger than many towns in the United States). Nongeographically based financial clubs such as MasterCard and Visa encompass billions of people.

In current society, government-managed property lacks private owners that have incentives and the ability to maintain or police the road. It's therefore unsurprising to observe the market "failing" to provide security there. But in shopping malls or other areas with private roads, private security is provided by the mall owner, paid for by tenant members, and free for guests. The rules of private security are most often "Do what you want so long as you are not bothering others."

Californians can easily observe the difference between public and private roads by comparing the number of panhandlers on Santa Monica's governmentally owned and managed Third Street Promenade with Silicon Valley's privately owned and managed Santana Row. Both have many shopping and dining options and attract large numbers of visitors (40,000 daily visitors for Third Street Promenade and 30,000 for Santana Row [DTSM, 2007; Federal Realty, 2011]), but the Santana Row owners can exclude panhandlers from the property's sidewalks at the behest of customers.

Many economists concerned with Kaldor-Hicks efficiency (wealth maximization as measured in dollar terms) argue that rules are needed to deal with externalities (spillover benefits or spillover burdens not captured or paid for by the decision-maker) because private parties lack incentives to internalize costs they impose on others (Musgrave, 2009). Those concerned with rights (Stringham and White, 2004) could reframe the problem as saying that rules are necessary wherever rights violations—including property rights violations—are likely to occur. But most interactions take place between parties at a small enough scale that such "externalities" can either be internalized or have the potential rights violations be dealt with within a club. Even though they have many members, golf clubs, colleges, and stock exchanges have a strong incentive to solve the problem of potential "externalities" within their realms (Foldvary, 1994).

Most advocates of government recognize that laws need not be enforced by global government and instead believe that laws can be enforced at more local levels (Tiebout, 1956; Meese, 1997). It is not that much of a stretch that the vast majority of potential conflicts can be dealt with easily at the level of clubs, which can vary their size on the basis of the extent and optimal way of dealing with "externalities." Most disputes take place among people who have relationships with each other and interact within a specific geographic area, and a club can easily handle such disputes. One could model clubs trading off the ease of solving problems within small groups (the fewer the members, the more likely the common interests) versus the amount of potential externalities between different groups (the greater the number of distinct clubs, the greater the need for interclub interaction). Musgrave (1999, p. 41) maintains that small groups can privatize the "external bads and goods" but believes "that solution, however, is not feasible where larger numbers are involved." Individual clubs, just as with sovereign nations, might not have the individual ability to deal easily with global externalities, international disputes, or disputes between clubs. For those types of disputes, cross-club dispute mitigation and resolution mechanisms may be needed. But even if certain global "externalities" or other sovereignty issues exist, it does not therefore follow that global government is necessary or optimal (Cuzan, 1979; Leeson, 2007d). A rational approach does not think of potential problems and then assume that government can solve them (Demsetz, 1969). The question of externalities should include what the relevant alternatives are. Government as a coercive monopoly has many inherent problems of its own. Governance through clubs has practical and moral advantages over governance imposed by city, state, national, or global government.

This discussion of club size is not to merely suggest that government should be more localized or provided at a smaller scale. One of the most fundamental differences between public governments and private clubs is that private *clubs are voluntary associations* that people join contractually and are free to quit. According to J. A. Ryan (1907, p. 1):

> A voluntary association means any group of individuals freely united for the pursuit of a common end. It differs, therefore, from a necessary association

in as much as its members are not under legal compulsion to become associated. The principal instances of a necessary association are a conscript military body and civil society, or the State; the concept of voluntary association covers organizations as diverse as a manufacturing corporation and a religious sodality.

In contrast to a voluntary association, the state "arrogates to [itself] a compulsory monopoly of police or judicial protection" (Rothbard, 1977, p. 2), which makes people subjects whether they like it or not.[3] The essence of markets is voluntary choice, whereas the essence of the state is imposing its choices on everyone.[4] At different points in history, governments have denied people the right to form voluntary associations in areas such as enterprise or religion.[5] But I consider a world with voluntary associations rather than coercive ones as a normative ideal (in Read's [1964] words, "Anything that's peaceful"),[6] and believe that Tocqueville ([1835] 2010, p. 895) is correct to state that "voluntary associations must be formed, or civilization is in danger." In a world comprised of voluntary associations, all are free to choose their religion, their job, their colleagues, and their friends. Voluntary associations can meet many objectives for creating a civil society (Beito, Gordon, and Tabarrok, 2002; Boettke and Rathbone, 2002; Boettke and Coyne, 2008), one of them being the creation of rules through private governance.

3. Some public choice and public finance economists, including Musgrave (1999, p. 41) and Mueller (2003, p.1 87), argue that states are just like big clubs or that clubs are just like small states. It seems, however, that adopting such language would make it all but impossible to distinguish between government and private provision of religion, industry, schools, or anything else. Instead, I opt to use the dictionary definitions of clubs as voluntary and agreed-upon associations rather than as small governments. For a discussion, see DiLorenzo and Block (2000), Block and DiLorenzo (2001), and Stringham (2006).

4. In this book I focus on governance from voluntary associations rather than coercive ones, which includes government and private criminal organizations. Here the New York Stock Exchange is classified as a private and voluntary organization, the Securities and Exchange Commission as a governmental and not voluntary organization (publicly traded companies and the typical citizen do not have the ability to ignore the Securities and Exchange Commission's rules), and a gang of muggers as a private but coercive organization. Unfortunately, sometimes private groups transform from voluntary to coercive associations, just as O. J. Simpson transformed from a football player to a criminal, but when evaluating them, the distinction between voluntary and coercive is still important. For example, many Mafiosi teeter between legitimate enterprise and extortion, and some other private individuals also cross that line. For analyses of governance in private criminal organizations see Gambetta (1993), Leeson (2007b, 2009), and Skarbek (2014).

5. In England in 1720, the Bubble Act "made it a crime, punishable by death and confiscation of goods, to form voluntary associations and to issue transferable shares" (Dodd, 1894, p. 159).

6. For more see Kukathas (2007) and Rasmussen and Den Uyl (2010).

3.3. PRIVATE GOVERNANCE FOR WHOSE BENEFIT?

What rules should voluntary associations create, and for whom? In *Reason of Rules*, Brennan and Buchanan (1985) advocate applying economic analysis to analyze the costs and benefits of any given rule. Without unanimous political agreement or a hypothetical veil of ignorance behind which people make disinterested constitutional choices, one can debate how practical such a proposal is for evaluating rules that apply to all of society (DiLorenzo and Block, 2000; Block and DiLorenzo, 2001). But Buchanan's framework can be much more easily applied to club rules to which all club members agree.

Those who will be subject to a possible rule (or bundle of rules) can evaluate the expected benefits and costs of any given rule. For example, a person considering joining a country club with a particular fashion rule weighs how much it will likely benefit him (the benefits of being around well-dressed people) against its potential level of inconvenience (the individual cost of having to be well dressed). A country club considering adoption of such a rule will thus estimate how it would affect its members' satisfaction with their product.

This framework is applicable to any rule, including those regarding torts or fraud. A college considering adoption of a rule about noise levels in dormitories compares how much students value quiet with the potential inconvenience of having to be quiet. Similarly, a stock exchange considering adoption of an additional disclosure rule for its members must weigh how much it likely enhances the market versus its cost.

When considering private governance, many people believe that those setting the rules will inevitably stack the deck in their favor. Authors such as Grigg (2010, p. 282) write that "regulatory programs should follow the principle of 'not having the fox guarding the chicken coop.'" This analogy implies that a stock exchange will create rules that help brokers at the expense of investors, an apartment complex will create rules at the expense of tenants, or a firm will create rules at the expense of its employees. The implication is that government, as a disinterested third party, is better suited to create rules than members of a given industry.

The idea that firms' interests are never aligned with those of their business partners should be rejected outright (for whom, after all, are the producers producing?), but it should be recognized that at any given instant trading partners' interests can diverge. Parties can agree to a contract that would be mutually beneficial if everything went according to the original plan, yet after initiating the contract one party might feel the desire to engage in postcontractual opportunism (Klein, Crawford, and Allen, 1978). Leeson (2007a) has criticized some of my work (Stringham, 2006) by saying that even if a proprietary community makes a set of promises, it will have an incentive to disregard its promises in the postcontractual period.

This problem can be characterized as a type of prisoners' dilemma (Hardin, 1997). (In the prisoners' dilemma two partners in crime are apprehended and independently interrogated by police, and although each would be better off if they both kept their mouths shut, they have an incentive to rat on their colleague to lessen their personal cost.) Prisoners' dilemmas can arise in many situations, including among contracting businesses when each is deciding whether to follow its promises or renege. Although both prefer the contract over no contract, each one may choose to not deliver on its half of the bargain. A cunning buyer wants to receive goods without paying, and a cunning seller wants to receive money without delivering. When both parties think this way, no transactions will take place. This is known as the suboptimal Nash equilibrium.

Men are not angels, and the potential for noncooperative outcomes is always real. But the commonly invoked solution of altering payoffs through government enforcement is not the only option (even assuming it even is a practicable option). This is due to the fact that the more the parties can gain by cooperating, the greater the incentive is for them to solve the problem (Klein, 2002). In the prisoners' dilemma story, the two prisoners have no ability to communicate or coordinate their strategies in advance. But private interactions are not held in captivity, nor are they acted upon without any communication. If parties can step outside the prisoners' dilemma, they often can eliminate many of the problems that arise only in one-shot, anonymous situations (Tullock, 1985, 1999). Both parties have an incentive to minimize their potential losses and maximize their potential gain, and if they can coordinate to do so, they both gain.[7] This is not to imply that at any instant private governance (or any other system) has the ability to eliminate all problems, but consumers and providers of private governance do have incentives to find ways of minimizing the problems associated with opportunism. The more effective the solutions, the more they will be demanded by consumers. The same is true about the overall reliability and consumer focus of private governance.

Consider the incentives of a provider of private governance or any other service. The more that clients think they will be cheated after a relationship begins, the less willing they will be to enter that relationship (the demand decreases as the value of the service decreases). On the flip side, the more likely it is that sellers think they will be cheated by a client, the less willing they will be to provide the service (the supply contracts as the cost of providing the service increases). Introducing risks that shift the demand and supply curves inward hurts sellers and buyers alike. Akerlof (1970) describes this in his famous discussion of the lemon problem with used cars (in which if buyers think cars might be lemons, prices become low, and the result is that only sellers of lemons

---

7. For example, in laboratory experiments in which parties can communicate and discuss strategies, the amount of cooperation is extremely high (Levy et al., 2011).

are in the market). Such issues do pose potential problems, but sellers have an incentive to eliminate them by providing assurances to buyers (Klein, 2002; DiLorenzo, 2011). In the car market, for example, sellers rely on various mechanisms such as repeat business, reputation, money back guarantees, third-party verification, third-party warranties, and leases in which the lessor, as the owner of the car, bears the long-run risk of any problem. Sellers have an incentive to assure buyers that they will get their money's worth. When I was shopping for a used car after graduate school, I encountered a couple of stereotypical used car salesmen (I asked, "That car has a twenty-fifth anniversary Mustang emblem on it. What does that signify?" and was told, "That is very special. They come out with one of those once every twenty-five years"!). But rather than take a risk by dealing with less reputable dealers, I chose to pay a price premium (because I had a higher demand) to buy a used car from a trustworthy dealer.

Similarly, providers of private governance have an incentive to provide assurances that they will treat their clients well; otherwise, the demand for their product will not be as high as it could be. A stock exchange that fails to provide assurances or attempts to stack the deck in favor of its members at the expense of investors will attract fewer investors in its market in the long run. Any stockbrokers attempting to create rules that come at the expense of clients do so at their own peril. Likewise, an apartment building that has built-in risks for tenants will have decreased demand for its product in the long run. For the same reason that producers constantly develop ways to provide better products at lower costs, providers of private governance will seek to provide assurance to their clients. For example, not only must a developer of a condominium complex offer a physical unit that customers demand, but in the construction phase he must offer a contract with contingency clauses that the buyers can trust. He must also put in place the framework of the condominium association that will govern the property in the future. Without those, the demand for the product will be less. The incentives are quite similar for rental properties. Exceptions can occur, and in those cases one might want additional assurances (which also can be private), but most of the time the producer has to be only pro consumer.

Even if future customers are not present when private governance mechanisms are put in place, private governance providers must heed future customer demands. Thus, rather than being similar to a fox guarding a chicken coop, private governance is like a farmer guarding the chicken coop on behalf of egg buyers. Successful rules are crafted for the benefit of all constituents rather than at the expense of some. As in other product markets, ultimately the producer must work to please his clients (Mises, [1949] 1998, p. 358), making the relationship what Frederic Bastiat ([1850] 1996) would call a harmony of interests rather than a conflict of interests. Like all market relationships, people will want to opt into a system of private governance only if the expected benefits are positive.

3.4. VOLUNTARY ASSOCIATIONS VERSUS INVOLUNTARY ASSOCIATIONS

One of the main advantages of private governance is that voluntary associations must serve members, and people who want different governance mechanisms are free to join other associations of their choice. The structure, management, and ownership of clubs can take various forms, including clubs that are jointly owned and run by members as well as those owned by shareholders, run by management, and catering to client members. Sometimes clubs with almost no membership requirements or complete open access can work, but Elinor Ostrom discusses how limited access is often necessary. Ostrom (1990, p. 91) writes, "Without defining the boundaries" and without "closing it to 'outsiders,' local appropriators face the risk that any benefits they produce by their efforts will be reaped by others who have not contributed to these efforts." For example, a fishery to which nonowners have unlimited access is prone to a tragedy of the commons, but when a fishery can exclude unentitled parties, the ownership club can cultivate more fish and determine optimal harvesting.

The terms "closing it to 'outsiders'" and "exclusion" have negative connotations to many, but a voluntary association would not be voluntary if everyone were forced together against their will. Political philosopher Kukathas (2007, p. 4) writes, "The fundamental principle for describing a free society is the principle of freedom of association. A first corollary of this principle is the freedom of disassociation." A voluntary association requires the right to exclude nonmembers in much the same way that private property implies the right to exclude unwanted guests. Markets for apartments function only because apartment buildings can exclude nonrenters, the hotel market functions only because hotels can exclude nonpayers, and the restaurant market functions only because restaurants can exclude noncustomers. When government laws prevent owners from excluding nonpaying guests, the result is for many sellers or landlords to simply take their product off the market. The 1990 movie *Pacific Heights* is fictional but reality-influenced account of what happens when two San Francisco landlords cannot evict their diabolical tenant. The character played by Michael Keaton is a bad guy intentionally destroying his landlords' home, but he has the police and courts on his side. Unfortunately, antilandlord laws like this exist in San Francisco and elsewhere, and they help explain why many multifamily properties sit unrented (and those with existing tenants are worth much less than those without tenants [James, 2013]).

Even though exclusion is an important part of a social system based on voluntary relations, the system would be much more inclusive overall. As long as government does not exclude at a society-wide level, exclusion is nothing more than people deciding with whom they want to interact. With government rules, the potential immigrant wishing to get a job or take up residence anywhere in the United States must get permission from the state; otherwise, he is completely shut out of one-third of North America. In a continent governed by disparate clubs, the foreigner needs to get permission from only one club, not the whole of society. Economists have discussed how for-profit businesses are more likely to care about whether someone is a paying customer than irrelevant demographic characteristics (Roback, 1986). When government owns the land, such as public roads, it decides for everyone who will enter them. But privately governed geographic areas, in contrast, make that choice at the club or property level. Even though at any given time one might not be allowed to enter 100 percent of country clubs, office complexes, residential complexes, or nightclubs, the market still offers a tremendous amount of choice, with each club catering to its members. I really don't mind being excluded from the 130 million U.S. homes that I do not own because I know that millions of hotels, landlords, and potential sellers of homes exist. Most shopping centers, restaurants, and hotels accept any paying guest and are often much more open to visitors than publicly governed lands.

The ability of a club to establish membership rules and to exclude nonmembers has multiple benefits, including cooperation among members. Russell Hardin (1997) argues that cooperation without government is possible, but only when the number of people interacting is sufficiently small, because in large group settings the ability to track others makes the incentive to cheat too high.[8] But if people have difficulty cooperating when many are present, clubs enable people to sort into smaller groups in which one can know (or club managers can know) the other members. I see people at my sailing club on a regular basis, and when I'm getting on a boat with someone, I need not worry that he will act like a pirate (Leeson, 2009). Similarly, a member of the Elks Lodge need not worry that the club member at the other end of the bar is going to turn from Jekyll to Hyde.

When advantageous, clubs can be set up among people who have similar characteristics and similar views on what is acceptable behavior. Authors such as Frye (2000, p. 93) argue that government is more necessary the greater the heterogeneity of a population, but assuming that heterogeneity on certain margins causes problems, then clubs could organize among relatively homogeneous groups. Membership requirements and a screening process enable people to sort into clubs in which members are more likely to want to follow a common set of rules. Once people have passed the screening process, they need to worry less about interacting with others with conflicting interests, differing discount rates, or different interpretations of

---

8. Hardin (1997, p. 30) writes, "Two-person prisoners' dilemma is resolvable with cooperation when iterated, but n-prisoners' dilemma for large n not resolvable. . . . Somewhere between a small pastoral society and the more advanced society, the anarchist's model can no longer work because we cannot be engaged in reciprocal, iterated interaction with more than a small percentage of our fellows."

what is acceptable behavior. For example, the diamond merchants described by Bernstein (1992) have been in the business for ages and are less likely to have a basic dispute about what constitutes acceptable business practices. The ethnically homogenous middlemen described by Landa (1981, 1994) have kinship and other ties that help them to cooperate. At the end of the day, these diamond merchants and ethnically homogenous middlemen sell to people of all sorts of backgrounds, so talking about organizing within clubs does not imply an insular society. The club simply allows people to organize on margins that encourage cooperation.

Membership requirements also provide incentives for people to behave once accepted into a club. When continued membership is contingent on adherence to the rules, people have incentives to act cooperatively. Removal of future membership privileges can be a major loss that changes the payoffs of what otherwise might be prisoners' dilemmas. The student kicked out of college, the broker kicked out of the stock exchange, or the credit card holder who has his credit card suspended loses the benefits of all future interaction. Someone who spent $4 million for his seat on the New York Stock Exchange (Hulbert, 2005) will think twice about stealing other members' wallets. With membership requirements and the ability to exclude the unreliable, one is less likely to face potential rule breakers in the first place, and once in the club the prospect of potential expulsion also creates incentives against misbehavior.

Notice that membership requirements enable the enforcement of rules with minimal or often no use of force. When the New York Stock Exchange has the ability to suspend a member's $4 million seat or an apartment building has the ability to change the locks and cash a renter's $1,000 security deposit, it need not fret about any transgression less than $4 million or $1,000, respectively. I am not making the case that clubs, property owners, or individuals should not be able to use defensive force to protect themselves against invaders or to walk rule breakers off their property, but in a very high percentage of cases in which people assume that the use of force is necessary, more effective and less coercive alternatives exist. The simple ability to exclude gives clubs a powerful tool to influence behavior, and it eliminates the need to resort to the threat of physical punishment at every turn. Simply permitting a property owner to exclude nonguests, a company to escort an ex-employee off the premises, a college to expel a student, a stock exchange to suspend a member's membership, or a credit card issuer to suspend a cardholder's account may be the extent of the force needed. Some, such as Samuels (1974), would suggest that escorting someone to the door or ceasing to offer employment is an inherently coercive act, but even if one holds that view, escorting someone to the door or not doing business with him in the future seems fundamentally less coercive than incarceration or corporal punishment.[9] A credit card that

---

9. For a critique of Samuels (1974), see Beaulier (2005).

says, "Please repay your loans if you would like us to continue extending you credit," or a college that says, "Please follow the rules if you want to keep the privilege of being a student," seems incomparable to, "If you do this, then we will put you in jail." If mechanisms of private governance such as exclusion can eliminate the need for physical punishment or incarceration in some (or even all) circumstances, then they should be viewed as quite liberal.

3.5. EMBRACING A MARKETPLACE OF PRIVATE GOVERNANCE

When people are free to join voluntary associations, they can select the types of governance that they prefer. This freedom of choice allows what could be described as a liberal archipelago (Kukathas, 2007) of governance structures. A system of private governance stands in contrast with public government, which imposes rules and regulations on people whether they like it or not. In the area of religion, in which rules were (and often still are) a public matter, everyone must follow regardless of their beliefs. In regular product markets, in which choices of production and distribution were (and often still are) a public matter, everyone gets what government provides regardless of their preferences. I, like many others (Rothbard and Liggio, 1975; Gunderson, 1989; Shorto, 2004; DiLorenzo, 2005; McCloskey, 2006; Kukathas, 2007) believe that historical movements toward more religious and economic liberty have been good. As religion and regular product markets become more private matters, everyone is free to choose what he thinks is best. And as governance becomes more of a private matter, rules and regulations come about through the free choices of individuals.

Over the past few centuries, economists have discussed many of the benefits of markets over various forms of government compulsion and control. Adam Smith ([1776] 1976) showed how markets create incentives for people to work for each other and to conduct business in an honest and reliable way. Carl Menger ([1871] 2007) showed how supply and demand can coordinate without central direction or control. Ludwig von Mises ([1920] 1990) showed how market prices and profits and losses enable producers to evaluate whether something is worth producing; producers make money only by transforming inputs worth less into goods that consumers value more. Friedrich Hayek (1948) showed how the price system helps millions of people coordinate their activities in an ever-changing world. He described how markets can be viewed as a discovery process that helps people see what others want. In contrast, government, as a compulsory monopoly, has an entirely different set of knowledge and incentives.

Although Smith, Menger, and Hayek did not apply their logic about the beneficence of markets to the realm of governance, they could have (Rothbard, 1973; Friedman, 1973; Benson, 1990; Stringham and Zywicki, 2011a;

Boettke, 2005, 2012). Just as Menger ([1871] 2007) applied economic analysis to something as crucial to markets as money, one can apply economic analysis to governance. Governance can be analyzed as a product just like other products that can be supplied and purchased voluntarily.[10] Consider the producers in the markets for country clubs, colleges, stock exchanges, credit card networks, or any sort of private governance. All these producers have an incentive to cater to their clients or members, whether these are long or short term. Producers have incentives to innovate, to keep costs down, and to experiment to see what members want. In shareholder-owned clubs, owners that innovate to better serve members earn profits, and member-owned clubs that innovate bestow benefits directly to their members, so in both cases the incentive is to serve members.

Because clients are in the driver's seat, providers of private governance must constantly evaluate how a mechanism benefits and costs their clients. Consider a stock exchange deciding whether to adopt a new rule that will likely decrease losses from fraud by 1 percent per year. Where the noneconomist would say, "Adopt the rule,"[11] the exchange must evaluate the marginal benefits and costs of the rule from the perspective of member firms, brokers, and their ultimate clients, the investors. If investors ultimately bear the cost and benefits of rules and the total costs of drafting, enforcing, and complying with the rule (Hertog, 1999) exceed the savings, the rule does not make sense. The decision is similar to that of an apartment building choosing not to hire a potentially useful armed guard who is extremely costly. The potential benefits and costs of new mechanisms for encouraging cooperation are not always clear, but private governance enables small-scale rather than society-wide

10. Klein (2002) makes this point about an important mechanism of private governance, the demand and supply of assurance. Certain economists, such as Kirzner, are reluctant to apply economic analysis to factors that affect or determine the framework within which economic exchange takes place. Kirzner writes (2000, p. 67), "We wish to emphasize the insight that, for its very emergence and existence, the market must rely on the presence of extramarket institutions, without which the idea of a market must be a mere dream." He wants to take the framework as external, but from a positive perspective, much of the framework for a market economy is at a minimum influenced or determined by private governance. Not only have the rules of golf clubs emerged privately, but so have the rules of stock markets (see chapters 2 and 3), and as Mises is quoted, "A stock market is crucial to the existence of capitalism and private property. For it means that there is a functioning market in the exchange of private titles to the means of production. There can be no genuine private ownership of capital without a stock market: there can be no true socialism if such a market is allowed to exist" (Rothbard, 1995, p. 426). If the rules of something as crucial as the stock market can be generated without government, then assuming that markets are only made possible because of government is a "mere dream."

11. For example, Albert (2002) argues that if the rate of fraud in a private venue is greater than zero, then government must step in, yet she fails to discuss the expected costs of government enforcement or how government even has the capacity to reduce the amount of fraud, let alone reduce it to zero.

social experiments for evaluating new mechanisms (Caplan and Stringham, 2008). What mechanism is optimal? Private governance is not a governmental one-size-fits-all "solution," and it allows private governance providers to craft solutions that cater to the needs at hand (Hasnas, 1995). Those who develop new solutions reap the immediate benefits of those choices, and in the long run this encourages others to mimic those good mechanisms and abandon bad ones.

Private governance is much more than a selection of rules enforced by the private equivalent of government courts and police. Private governance involves many potential mechanisms for preventing or minimizing the costs associated with disputes. Consider the possible options for ensuring that parties follow through with their contracts. To the legal centralist, this is the realm of contract enforcement in which government (or private courts if one is a libertarian legal centralist) relies on enforcement of formal rules through the threat of ex post punishment. But parties already use many different mechanisms of private governance instead of government enforcement. These mechanisms can be formal, informal, long term, or short term. They can deal with problems ex post or help avoid problems ex ante. They can involve third-party enforcement or create incentives for self-enforcing contracts (Klein and Leffler, 1981; Telser, 1987). They can rely on the discipline of repeat dealings or on trust (Smith, [1766] 1976; Macaulay, 1963). Parties can give deposits to an escrow agent that can disburse funds (Friedman, 2008, p. 104) or hire a bonding or insurance agent that assumes the risk if any party does not follow through with his bargain. Parties can post irrecoverable assets (Williamson, 1996), or they can use reputation bonds, the value of which is forfeited in case of default as a way of committing to cooperation (Greif, 1989; Klein, 1997; Stringham, 2003). They can become a member of a club with strict membership requirements for upstanding merchants only (Stringham, 2002), or they could even require membership in a close-knit clan or religious community (Landa, 1981; Bernstein, 1992; Johnsen, 1986; Leeson, 2007c; Powell, Ford, and Nowrasteh, 2008). Trading partners can be members of trading networks (Greif, 2006; Clay, 1997a, 1997b, Neal and Quinn, 2001; Quinn 1997) or credit card associations (Zywicki, 2000; Stringham, 1999) that act as a proxy for or guarantee of trust. They can have a system of informal or elaborate norms to encourage cooperation (Posner, 2002).

I agree with Ellickson (1991) and Williamson (1996) that most people put far too much emphasis on legal rules as the source of order, but even if one assumes that certain problems require legal rules, one need not assume that a compulsory monopoly must provide them. Historically, many legal systems have not involved a government monopoly (Benson, 1988, 1989, 1990, 1994a, 1998; Stringham and Curott, 2010; Stringham and Zywicki, 2011b) and are much more concerned with the parties in the dispute than with advancing the interests of the state (Benson, 1994a; Barnett, 1985, 1986). Literatures such as those on legal pluralism (Galanter and Lubin, 1992) and restorative justice (Jenkins 2006) show that law can be provided in many ways and that many of those ways are much more sensible and humane than those of government.

Often enforcement mechanisms are not even necessary. The more accurately that risk can be assessed and priced into a contract, the less external enforcement is needed. Lenders, for example, are usually quite good at estimating the likelihood of default, and they price that default risk into the interest rate of a loan (Merten, 1974). The high interest rates on pay day loans, credit card loans, and junk bonds help make possible transactions where recovery of assets is difficult (Staten and Johnson, 1995). Much of what legal centralists consider legal problems might better be thought of as risk management problems.

3.6. SUMMARY AND THOUGHTS

Individuals rely on private governance in many aspects of their lives. And much of (or even all of) the order that exists may be attributable to private governance rather than the state. Clubs, as voluntary associations, allow people to interact in manageable numbers with others who have similar goals or levels of reliability, and they create incentives for good behavior once in. These private mechanisms create incentives for cooperation without relying exclusively on the threat of physical punishment that many economists say is needed in large or heterogeneous populations. Clubs enable people to opt into the set of governance structures that they prefer rather than forcing the same set of rules on everyone in society. Private governance allows for variation, experimentation, and solutions that vary according to the challenges at hand. From a positive perspective, governance can be analyzed as a club good in which private provision of rules is already prevalent. From a normative perspective, private governance could be more prevalent and could substitute for government in areas that most people think must be the domain of a compulsory monopoly.

In his framework for utopia, Nozick (1974, p. 329) outlines an ideal world in which individual communities set whatever rules they want and the only role for the overarching state is to oversee the system. I think that the assumption that the state creates the framework for markets is an unrealistic view of the state,[12] but one can believe that while still allowing for a very large percentage of governance to be private. Private governance is already quite pervasive, and it easily could be expanded to more areas.

---

12. I agree with Benson (1994a) and Holcombe (2004) that the state and its law enforcement apparatus were created not to provide public goods or enhance markets but instead as a means of extracting revenue for those in control of the state.

PART TWO

Privately Governed Markets in History and Modern Times

CHAPTER 4

୶

Markets without Enforcement

Reciprocity and Reputation Mechanisms in the World's First Stock Market

4.1. INTRODUCTION

It's the year 1614 in Amsterdam, and you are one of the pioneers in the new market trading shares in the United East India Company (the Vereenigde Oostindische Compagnie). The company is making shiploads of profits trading in India, and it just financed Henry Hudson's voyage to North America. The world has never seen anything quite like it. Twelve years ago, more than a thousand people invested in what was originally going to be limited set of voyages to the East Indies, after which the assets would be liquidated and proceeds distributed (Barbour, [1950] 1976, p. 79; Dehing and 't Hart, 1997, p. 54). But after the ships returned with such high profits, the managers decided to send them out again and to make the Dutch East India Company an ongoing venture (Neal, 1990a, p. 195). After twelve years, the dividends for the initial investment were 100 percent, a handsome return, but many investors wanted to cash out and sell their shares. Without central direction, a secondary market for shares emerged in which brokers applied trading techniques, such as forward contracts and short sales, that they had learned in commodity markets. What rules would govern the trading of these shares, and who would enforce the rules? What would happen if someone intentionally or unintentionally defaulted? Nobody had ever been in this situation.

Economists such as North (1990, p. 57) argue that "complex contracting . . . in a world of impersonal exchange must be accompanied by some kind of third-party enforcement." But in seventeenth-century Amsterdam, government officials were not supportive of the stock market, as they viewed trading as a type of gambling that could be used to manipulate prices (Garber, 2000, pp. 30–34; Neal, 1997, p. 63). In February 1610 the government passed the first of many edicts against forward contracts and short sales. Despite these prohibitions, a sophisticated stock market, including an advanced stock options market, flourished.

Situations like this arise frequently. Most theorists, including a large percentage of anarchist libertarians (e.g., Tannehill and Tannehill, 1970), are wedded to the idea that exchange must be enforced with rules against fraud or widespread cheating and conflict will occur. But as a practical matter, many areas lack formal rules. From relatively simple markets such as eBay to complex markets such as that for (the often unfairly maligned) credit default swaps, private sector innovators are usually years ahead of government officials. In a world where government officials think they can prevent stock market declines by outlawing short sales (whether the prohibition comes in 1610 or 2010—after four hundred years government officials are just as oblivious to how markets work), the private sector cannot rely on government to advance markets. The idea that government is in the background to assist and advance markets is a heroic assumption made by most economists, including those who are otherwise skeptical about government (Mises, [1949] 1998; Buchanan, 1975; Friedman, 1962; Hayek, 1973).

Even in areas in which government theoretically is available to enforce rules, the rules are often unusable, easily avoided, or too costly. For example, it's not practical to sue a restaurant if a meal does not live up to expectations. Likewise, it's not practical to take every business partner to court if he does not meet your expectations (Macaulay, 1963). Even the most litigious person must weigh the expected benefits of initiating a lawsuit (what he could be awarded times his estimated probability of winning the lawsuit) against the cost of hiring a lawyer and going to trial, the hassle of dealing with the courts, the value of his time, the inconvenience of having assets held up in the legal system, the negative repercussions of being seen as a litigious person, and so on. The costs of using courts are often significant, and whenever they outweigh what is at stake in a lawsuit, most people will not bother with the law. For these transactions, trading partners are in what might be considered a de facto state of lawless anarchy.

When reliance on formal rules is not an option or is too costly, people will rely on informal mechanisms of eliciting cooperation instead. One of the most straightforward yet most important mechanisms is what Gordon Tullock, inspired by Adam Smith ([1766] 1982, p. 538), calls the discipline of continuous dealings. According to Smith, with repeated interactions people have an incentive to follow through with their contracts or else others will not want to deal with them. In Axelrod's (1984) computer tournaments, for example, the most effective strategy was a simple tit-for-tat strategy in which people act cooperatively except with others who cheated them. In general, treating others how they treat you or adopting norms of reciprocity can eliminate cheating (Ridley, 1997). The literature on self-enforcing contracts describes many other ways that parties can structure relationships to ensure that each party has an incentive to cooperate (Telser, 1987; Klein and Leffler, 1981).

Still, many theorists question how far these results can be extended. Although authors such as North (1990, p. 56) recognize that cooperation without external enforcement is possible, they theorize that it can occur only in very limited settings. Hardin (1997, p. 30), for example, argues that an important limit is the number of people involved: "While the two-person prisoners' dilemma is resolvable with cooperation when iterated, the n-persons prisoners' dilemma for large n is not resolvable and requires the law and its regular application." Others such as Tullock (1972, p. 69) argue that the discipline of continuous dealings breaks down with complicated transactions: "Transactions in which large payments will be made in the future would be impossible if we depended solely on the discipline of continuous dealings." Likewise, Landa (1994, p. 60) writes, "The 'discipline of continuous dealings' cannot be relied on to protect contracts if credit transactions are important." Olson (1996, p. 22) writes that although some trades can be self-enforcing and work without government, this is not true for transactions "in the capital market . . . that *require* impartial third-party enforcement" (1996, p. 22).

But rather than using game theory to debate whether cooperation is or is not possible in relatively large advanced markets without enforcement, a more fruitful approach is to study actual markets to see how they work. In the history of the world's first stock markets, parties extended the discipline of continuous dealings through reputation mechanisms among large numbers and with complicated contracts. With a bilateral reputation mechanism, when one party cheats, the other party boycotts him in the future. But with a multilateral reputation mechanism, when one party cheats, all other parties boycott him in the future. The governance is private and completely informal. Even if two parties have never interacted before and have no intention of interacting again, both will think twice about damaging their valuable reputation for a short-run gain (Greif, 1993). This informal mechanism of governance serves as a substitute for external enforcement. After showing the details of how this mechanism worked in the world's first stock market, I suggest that similar reputation mechanisms are prevalent in the modern world among sellers on eBay, restaurants, stores, and for that matter almost all businesses.

4.2. THE EMERGENCE OF THE WORLD'S FIRST STOCK MARKET

The history of the world's first stock market (as well as that of other early financial markets) is totally at odds with the predictions of academics who have a government-centric view of markets and believe that markets emerge only after government creates the framework. In Douglass North's (1995, p. 9) words, "The search for efficient economic organization leads us to political organization, since it is the polity that defines and enforces the rules of the game," and North-influenced scholar McNally (2007, p. 183) writes, "A free economy thus requires a strong state." Yet the society that became what de Vries and van der Woude (1997) characterize as the world's "first modern economy" had nothing close to a strong state (t' Hart, Jonker, and Zanden, 1997, p. 3). The Netherlands had been under the control of Spain until the Dutch Revolt began in 1568 over issues that included economic and religious liberty; the revolt ended in 1648 when the Netherlands was recognized as independent. The institutional structure was highly fragmented and decentralized, and that helped Amsterdam become Europe's center of commerce and most advanced market.

One can see evidence of how advanced the market was in the Dutch golden age by looking at buildings in Amsterdam built at that time or observing the art by Rembrandt, Vermeer, and scores of other painters who were able to focus on painting ordinary life rather than on royalty or subjects that pleased governments. Visit the Rijksmuseum in Amsterdam to see the 1606 painting by Pieter Isaacsz titled *Allegory of Amsterdam as Centre of World Trade* (figure 4.1). A 1639 poem from East India Company director Joost van den Vondel features the lines, "Wherever profit leads us, to every sea and shore / For love of gain, the wide world's harbours we explore" (Fisher, 1997, p. 78). By the middle of the seventeenth century, the Dutch had 16,000 ships and "at least half of Europe's total seagoing tonnage" (Crouzet, 2001, p. 71).

The two largest publicly traded companies were the East India Company, founded in 1602, and the West India Company, founded in 1621, which were the biggest joint stock ventures to date (Dehing and 't Hart, 1997, p. 54).[1] They allowed numerous investors (see table 4.1) to reap the benefits of foreign trade without risking their entire fortunes.[2] Over the course of 120 years,

---

1. Companies with transferable shares date back to classical Rome, but these were usually not enduring endeavors and no considerable secondary market existed (Neal, 1997, p. 61). The first modern joint stock company was the Muscovy Company, which was chartered in England in 1553 (Kindleberger, 1984, p. 196).

2. Kellenbenz (1957, p. 134) explains the creation of East India Company shares: "Trade and speculation in shares first appeared there when in 1602 the six local 'chambers' for East Indian trade were united into a general Dutch East India Company. According to the official pronouncement, every inhabitant of the United Provinces had an opportunity to participate in the Company. At the beginning the rights deriving from the initial payments were called 'paerten,' 'partieen,' or 'partijen,' the word being taken over from the practice of 'participation' in the shipping business. It was not until 1606 that the word 'actie' (i.e., share) seems to have come into use. The possibility of trading these 'participations' was assured by the fact that each owner of shares could, by payment of a fee, transfer holdings, in whole or in part, to another person."

Figure 4.1
Allegory of Amsterdam as Centre of World Trade, Pieter Isaacsz, 1606

Table 4.1. INITIAL INVESTORS IN THE AMSTERDAM CHAMBER
OF THE EAST INDIA COMPANY IN 1602

	All investors		Chief investors	
	Number	Guilders invested	Number	Guilders invested
North Netherlanders	785	2,023,715	40	635,100
South Netherlanders	302	1,418,700	38	871,160
Germans	38	137,900	3	60,000
English	3	6,900	0	0
Portuguese Jews	2	4,800	0	0

Source: Data are from Israel, 1995, p. 346.

dividends on the original capital of the East India Company averaged 22.5 percent annually, making it an attractive investment (Neal, 1990b, p. 17).[3] By 1688 the East India Company had more than twenty thousand employees and more than three hundred ships traveling between the East Indies and Europe (Israel, [1989] 1991, p. 258; 1995, p. 942).[4] Figures 4.2 and 4.3 show one of their factories and one of their merchants in front of company ships. The West

3. Dehing and 't Hart (1997, p. 41) estimate that price inflation in the century was negligible, and according to de la Vega (1688, p. 164), ordinary loans received interest of 2.5–3.0 percent. For more on interest rates and banking in seventeenth-century Netherlands, see French (2006), Neal (2000), Dickson ([1967] 1993, p. 474), and Dehing and 't Hart (1997, p. 53).
4. The trade included spices, tea, coffee, silk, and cotton (Israel, 1989, pp. 336–38).

Figure 4.2
V.O.C. Factory in Hoegly, Hendrik van Schuylenburgh, 1665

Figure 4.3
A Senior Merchant of the V.O.C., Jacob Mathieusen, in Batavia, Aelbert Cuyp, 1660

India Company was never as successful as the East India Company, and its market value reflected this (see figures 4.4 and 4.5).[5]

Modern New Yorkers can thank the East India Company for financing the voyage of Henry Hudson during which he charted the Hudson River (New York's North River) and the West India Company for creating their trading

5. In 1672 West India shares were almost worthless, and the company had to be re-structured (de la Vega, 1688, p. 174; Israel, 1989, p. 294). The Netherlands had other companies, but none was as long lasting or large as the East and West India companies, which constituted most of the stock market (Israel, 1989, pp. 109–12; Dehing and 't Hart, 1997, p. 54; de la Vega, 1688, p. 173).

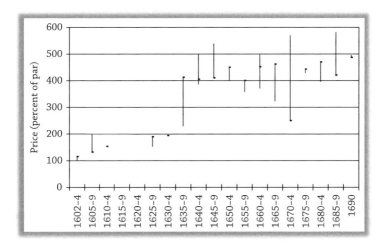

Figure 4.4
Share Prices of the East India Company in Amsterdam, 1602–1690
Source: Data are from Garber (2000, p. 77); Israel ([1989] 1991, pp. 86, 186); Israel (1995, p. 848); Kellenbenz ([1957] 1996, p. 134).

post and eventual settlement, New Amsterdam, just a decade and a half later. Russell Shorto (2004) makes the case that New York City's as well as America's religious and economic freedom are largely inherited from the Dutch and that New York is the financial and cultural center of the world because of this legacy.

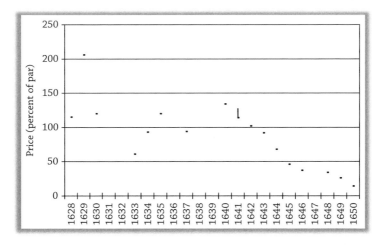

Figure 4.5
Share Prices of the West India Company in Amsterdam, 1628–1650
Source: Data are from Israel ([1989] 1991, p. 163).

In the early years shareholders of the East India Company wishing to sell or buy a share had go to the company and pay a fee to have the shares transferred to someone else's name (see figure 4.6). The company allowed people to do this only at limited times (De Vries and Van Der Woude, 1997, p. 151), and delays often occurred (Neal, 1997, p. 62). Because such a process was tedious, brokers at one corner of the Amsterdam Bourse (see figures 4.7, 4.8, and 4.9) began to specialize in trading stocks. With stocks that could be traded back and forth, it did not make sense to go to the company and transfer ownership of the share after each trade. Traders created, *rescontre,* settlement dates every three months (Neal, 1997, p. 62), thus making the contracts basic forward contracts. Come settlement date, either shares were transferred or traders could pay the difference between the transaction price and the current price (Dickson, [1967] 1993, p. 491).

The introduction of forward contracts had many advantages, but also created the possibility that come settlement date the other party would be unintentionally insolvent or willfully fraudulent. In cases such as this, the legal centralist looks to government to enforce contracts. But what seems to be an unwavering empirical regularity throughout history is that government officials do not have the best understanding of economics and finance or of the purpose of short sales and forward contracts more specifically. In 1608 shares in the East India Company fell from 200 to 130 (prices were quoted

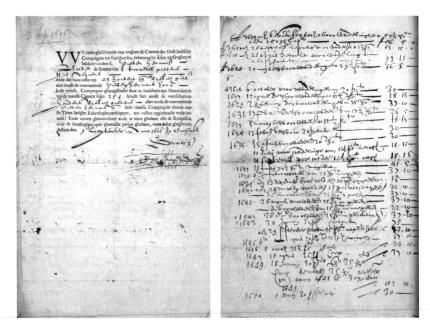

Figure 4.6
V.O.C. Share, 1606

Figure 4.7
Beurs van Hendrik de Keyser, Claes Janszoon Visscher, 1611

Figure 4.8
De Beurs van Amsterdam, Boëtius Adamsz, Bolswert, Michael Colyn, and Pieter Cornelisz Hooft, 1609

as a percentage of the initial public offering price), and officials believed that outlawing short selling would prevent further price drops (Kellenbenz, [1957] 1996, p. 134). They passed ordinances against short sales, prohibiting selling *in blanco* (selling something one does not own) as well as *windhandel* (trading in wind). The new ordinances required that only owners of shares could make sales and that sellers had to actually transfer their shares within

Figure 4.9
Beurs van Amsterdam, Claes Janszoon Visscher (II), P. C. Hooft, 1612

a month (Wilson, 1941, p. 14; Kellenbenz, [1957] 1996, pp. 134–35). In the following decades official prohibitions continued; additional ordinances were passed in 1621, 1623, 1624, 1630, 1636, and 1677 (Dehing and 't Hart, 1997, p. 55; Garber, 1994, p. 78; De Vries and Van Der Woude, 1997, p. 151) that outlawed all but the simplest transactions. Visit the Amsterdams Historisch Museum and you can see a set of plates (see figure 4.10) depicting stock traders as playing with money and phrases that translate to "away with dandy speculators," "squeeze the speculators tight," "down with the speculators," and "away with actions and speculators." An engraving (figure 4.11) from the time depicts "wind traders" of the market. However, even though government outlawed many types of contracts, officials did not actively punish those who made them.[6]

To the legal centralist, if government does not enforce contracts in a stock market, then they will not take place. But the Amsterdam traders were cleverer than blackboard theorists such as Ferguson (2001) or Glaeser and Shleifer (2003), who assert that financial markets emerged because of government. We can see how markets actually worked by analyzing some firsthand accounts, the best of which was published in 1688 by stockbroker Josef Penso de la Vega.

---

6. Schama (1987, p. 348) writes, "Confined within its handsome Flemish-mannerist colonnaded court, the Bourse was more or less left to its own regulation. Rules were not so much devised by the city for the exchange, as barriers set between it and the rest of the town's commerce."

Figure 4.10
Anti-speculator Plates from Eighteenth-Century Netherlands

Figure 4.11
Wanhopige handelaren [desperate traders] *in de beurs van Amsterdam*

Written in his native Spanish in the form of a dialogue, *Confusion de Confusiones* is a sort of seventeenth-century FAQ, most likely for people looking to get into the stock market.[7] In the book de la Vega describes numerous transactions including short sales, forward contracts, option contracts, and other transactions that occurred even though they were unenforceable in courts of law.

4.2.1. Short Sales without External Enforcement

First, let us consider short sales. As a quick review, when someone thinks a share is undervalued, he buys, which helps the undervalued share rise toward its true underlying value (how much it would be worth if the firm's future profitability could be known). When someone thinks a share is overvalued, he sells, which helps an overvalued share fall to its true underlying value. It's easy for the bull without shares to act on his judgment, as he simply buys, but a bear without shares has nothing to actually sell, and in simple spot markets the voice of a whole group of people would remain unheard. Enter short selling, in which a buyer and seller make a contract today and agree to exchange shares at a certain price at a future date. Sometime between now and the settlement date, the short seller in this forward contract needs to procure shares that he will deliver. If the short seller forecast correctly, share prices fall, and he buys on the cheap to deliver at the originally agreed-upon price. But if the short seller forecast incorrectly, he must purchase shares for more than he thought and deliver them at the originally agreed-upon price. Such contracts add liquidity to the market and help all people exercise their judgment to move share prices to the perceived true market value. The risk to both parties, however, is that the party forecasting incorrectly will renege on his half of the bargain come settlement date. A short seller faces unlimited downside risk as the shares he must procure for delivery rise, and those who do not make arrangements to have shares to deliver (a naked short seller does not borrow shares from his broker at the time of the initial contract) can easily find himself in a position in which he simply cannot or does not want to deliver.

When such contracts are unenforceable, various outcomes could occur. Although a legal centralist would assert that such contracts would be impossible, let's see what actually happened in seventeenth-century Amsterdam. De la

---

7. De la Vega, a Sephardi of Portuguese origin, was born around 1650, grew up mostly in Amsterdam, and wrote mainly in Spanish but also in Hebrew and Portuguese (Amzalak, 1944, p. 33; Boer and Israel, 1991, pp. 443, 451; Penslar, 1997, pp. 33–34). In *Confusion de Confusiones*, one character, the shareholder, "is usually the vehicle for the pronouncement of the author's judgments" (Kellenbenz, 1957, p. 133). Kellenbenz (1957, p. 136) writes, "If one is able to look through or around the literary peculiarities of the volume, he will find in it a reasonably realistic description of the whole stock market."

Vega begins by referring to the ordinances that prohibited short sales: "Frederick Henry, too, a shining star in the house of Orange-Nassau, promulgated (with wise motives) an ordinance for these provinces, according to which he who sold shares for future delivery without putting them on a time account should be exposed to a danger (because he sold something he does not own) that the buyer will not take the pieces at the time fixed upon" ([1688] 1996, p. 152).[8] But even though these contracts were unenforceable, people engaged in short sales nevertheless. De la Vega (p. 153) recognizes that people would be tempted not to deliver when the price took an unfavorable turn: "There are many persons who refer to the decree [which proclaims the unenforceability of short sales] only when compelled to do so, I mean only if unforeseen losses occur to them in their operations." When a deal was looking unprofitable, someone could legally "appeal to Frederick" (de la Vega, p. 153) and declare that their bargain was not valid. But if enough people did this, no one would agree to deal with short sellers. This was not common, as de la Vega (p. 153) noted: "When a loss occurs, the losers are expected to pay at least what they have available at the moment, and it might be expected that, when the wound is fresh, there would be no new injury. . . . Other people gradually fulfill their obligations after having sold their last valuables and thus meet with punctuality the reverses of misfortune." Despite the ability of short sellers to call upon the law to get out of their predicaments, doing so was not prevalent; short sellers instead attempted to deliver what they owed. I discuss the reasons why below.

4.2.2. **Forward Contracts without External Enforcement**

Beyond short sales, other transactions with unclear legal status took place. Forward contracts were negotiated with settlement dates many months in advance. De la Vega describes them:

> The third kind of transaction takes place *at later dates* still. Here the shares must be delivered and be paid for on the twentieth and twenty-fifth of the month which is specified in the contract, unless one makes use of the mysterious prolongations of which I disapprove because they damage the credit and endanger the reputation [of the party who asks for the prolongation]. For these time bargains the brokers use printed *contract forms* with the customary stipulations and conditions of the business. On these forms spaces are left only for the names, dates, and prices. When two copies have been filled out and signed, the

---

8. The first laws prohibiting short sales were passed before the time of Stadholder Frederick Henry, the chief executive of the Netherlands from 1625 to 1647, but the traders referred to the ordinances of Frederick Henry because many were passed when he was in office.

contracts are exchanged by the two parties; [later,] and after the establishment of the profit or loss in the business by the rescounters [settlement], they are re-exchanged by the signatories. (pp. 181–82)

Forward contracts also required traders' counterparts to be available and to deliver what they owed when the time came.

Again, the legal centralist would assume that the law was the reason why traders followed through with contracts, but from *Confusion de Confusiones* one can see that time bargains were prohibited. De la Vega writes:

> As to the unactionable feature of any speculative transaction to be settled by the payment of the differences, you are right in remarking that with *cash trans-actions* the regulation lacks pertinence. It is, however, valid in the case of *time bargains* unless the seller has the shares transferred to the time account of the purchaser within a fortnight. Then the buyer is obliged to take up the shares, or declare himself insolvent.
>
> Though the opinion prevails generally that this regulation does not apply in the case of the seller but only in that of the buyer, this is an error introduced by bad practice. The lawyers assert that the seller as well as the buyer is allowed to raise the objection [envisaged by Frederick Henry's edict].
>
> The public also presumes that, if the seller of stocks buys them back (from someone who had purchased them earlier), the law does not apply. That is un-doubtedly an error also. (For instance), the edict does not apply when I buy shares at [540], sell [at 520], and declare before witnesses that the stock so sold will serve to settle the account of shares previously purchased. By this action I have declared myself debtor for the difference of 20 per cent [of the face value] which I have lost. Therefore I am not permitted to appeal to the regulation, since I have already assumed the debt; I must pay the difference or become insolvent. But if I have bought a share at [540] from one and without subsequent declaration I sell him another share at [520], [the seller in neither case really owning the stock,] I need neither declare myself bankrupt in order to free myself [from the obligation] nor disappear in order to shake loose [I can merely appeal to the edict]. (pp. 182–83).

Shares needed to be transferred within two weeks of the initial transaction; otherwise, a contract would violate the law. But, like good economic heroes (Block, [1976] 1991), the traders simply ignored the law and engaged in these mutually beneficial trades.

4.2.3. Options without External Enforcement

Although many people believe that options were invented around the time that the Chicago Board Options Exchange opened in 1973, this is actually a few centuries off. The options market flourished in seventeenth-century Amsterdam, and again it was not because of the law. De la Vega (p. 182) describes the contracts: "For the *option business* there exists another sort of *contract form*, from which it is evident when and where the premium was paid and of what kind are the signatories obligations." Here too options contracts had an uncertain legal standing. De la Vega writes:

> As to whether the regulation is applicable to *option contracts*, the opinions of experts diverge widely. I have not found any decision that might serve as a precedent, though there are many cases at law from which one [should be able to] draw a correct picture. All legal experts hold that the regulation is applicable to both the seller and the buyer [of the contract]. In practice, however, the judges have often decided differently, always freeing the buyer from the liability while often holding the seller [to the contract]. . . . With regard to the put premium, however, there are also great differences of opinion, for, while the scholars assume that no [legally valid] claims can be made because of the regulation, there are contrary decisions by the courts, so that law and legal opinion, the regulation and the reasons for the decisions are contradictory. The theory remains uncertain, and one cannot tell which way the adjudication tends. (p. 183)

It is unclear whether everyone or just some people were legally allowed to default on their options contracts. Either way, with whole classes of contracts unenforceable, the options market cannot be attributable to government enforcing the rules of the game.

4.2.4. Hypothecation without External Enforcement

Seventeenth-century traders were quite creative, and they allowed shareholders to borrow money using shares as collateral. After buying of shares there were three choices: sale of shares, transference of the shares into one's own name at the bank, or hypothecation, in which one could borrow money at up to 80 percent of the shares' value. This, in de la Vega's (p. 152) words, "is done even by the wealthiest traders without harm to their credit." De la Vega (p. 182) describes the contract: "The *forms for hypothecating* are different also. Stamped paper is used for them, upon which regulations concerning the *dividends* and other details are set down, so that there can be no doubt and no disagreement regarding the arrangements." Even though parties engaging in this trade signed clear contracts, in this area too it was unclear what was legal. De la Vega writes:

> The same uncertainty of adjudication exists with respect to the hypothecation of stocks. While it is generally assumed that, if the shares fall below the value used as the basis of the loan, the mortgagee is obliged to pay in the difference or

declare himself insolvent, a few very speculative minds have argued (uncertain doubtless because of the paucity of facts to sustain their position) that if the shares have not been transferred to the time account which I as money lender maintain, within a fortnight after the start of hypothecation arrangement, and if the shares remain in the account [of the borrower] until the date of payment [of the loan], I can raise objections [under the regulation] in order to garner a profit as well as to save myself from a possible loss. (p. 184)

When the collateral fell below the value of the loan, market practices required the borrower to sell his shares and repay the loan. But according to some, the borrower was not legally obliged to repay if he had not transferred the shares into the moneylender's account. But such a practice could not have been common; otherwise, no such transactions would have taken place.

4.2.5. **Other Derivatives without External enforcement**

As the century went on, share prices for the East India Company soared. With laborers earning approximately 0.9 guilders daily ('t Hart, 1997, p. 33) and share prices at 15,000 guilders, one's entire lifetime earnings would have been required to purchase a single share. The company considered neither a stock split nor a stock dividend. Nevertheless, traders began to offer derivatives of standard shares to allow those with less wealth to participate. In addition to offering payment of difference contracts in which traders did not actually exchange the shares but instead paid the difference between contract price and market price at settlement date, they also offered contracts on much smaller scales. This is described by de la Vega:

> Some clerks have discovered that the speculation in ordinary shares (which are called *large* or *paid-up shares*) was too hazardous for their slight resources. They began, therefore, a less daring game in which they dealt in small shares. For while with whole shares one could win or lose 30 gulden of Bank money for every point that the price rose or fell, with the small shares one risked only a ducaton [three gulden] for each point. The new speculation, called trading in *ducaton shares*, began in 1683. (p. 185)

Ducaton shares, named for a coin in the Netherlands, were equivalent to one-tenth of a large share, and people could trade in even smaller units as well (de la Vega, p. 188). De la Vega gave an analogy for the process of creating this new security:

> When a mirror is broken, each piece of crystal remains a mirror, the only difference being that the small mirrors reflect one's countenance in miniature and

the large ones in larger size. . . . Stocks shares are similar to mirrors . . . persons broke this mirror [the large "East" shares] and cut the crystal into pieces by agreeing to regard each 500 pounds of the large shares as 5,000 small ones. (p. 187)

Trading in these shares was more affordable and allowed more people to access the market (Dehing and 't Hart, 1997, p. 55). De la Vega (p. 186) declared, "This branch of trade has been increasing during the last five years to such an extent (and mainly with a certain group which is as boisterous as it is quick-witted) that it is engaged in by both sexes, old men, women, and children." It was so popular that de la Vega (p. 188) writes: "Even children who hardly know the world and at best own a little pocket money agree that each point by which the large shares rise or fall will mean a certain amount of their pocket money for their small shares. . . . If one were to lead a stranger through the streets of Amsterdam and ask him where he was, he would answer, 'Among speculators,' for there is no corner [in the city] where one does not talk shares."

The trade of ducaton shares was an unofficial business, but people participating in the trade worked out a somewhat elaborate system of monthly or semimonthly settlements. Parties paid a cashier to keep records and inform them on settlement date what they were due or owed. The following passage gives details:

On the first day of each month when the clock of the Exchange shows one-thirty p.m., the cashier is told the price of the shares by two impartial stock-exchange men and, in accordance with these statements, he specifies the value of the small shares. This comedy is called "raising the stick," because formerly a stick was raised by the cashier, until this custom was given up because of the noise that was made each time. (pp. 185–86)

Where the legal centralist presumes that the third party necessary to settle a contract must be government, here the speculators hired a private third party. Government did not ultimately enforce ducaton contracts. By the time the government courts addressed ducaton trading, it was only to declare it illegal. De la Vega (p. 208) reports, "In the ducaton speculation the damage was still more disturbing. (Speculation [in ducaton shares] was declared by court to be a game or a bet, and thus the transactions in them were denied the character of true business.) Therefore it was not even necessary to appeal to Frederick Henry's decree to refuse payment." In the examples given above, official regulations outlawed whole markets instead of assisting them. For such extralegal markets to function, some other mechanisms must have existed to ensure that traders followed their contracts.

4.3. THE MECHANISMS THAT MADE THE FIRST STOCK MARKET WORK

The first stock market had complex trades through time among people with often diverging interests, making it a prime candidate for prisoners' dilemma problems. Yet the brokers took various steps to enable quite sophisticated financial contracts. At the most basic level, many prisoners' dilemmas can be avoided when people can communicate, choose their trading partners, and deal with each other on a regular basis (Tullock, 1985, 1999). In his *Lectures on Jurisprudence*, Adam Smith describes how in England forward contracts were unenforceable (see chapter 4) but that continuous dealings and reputation create incentives for people to deliver what they owe. Smith describes markets and the stock market specifically:

> Of all the nations in Europe, the Dutch, the most commercial, are the most faithful to their word. . . . This is not at all to be imputed to national character, as some pretend. . . . It is far more reduceable to self interest, that general principle which regulates the actions of every man, and which leads men to act in a certain manner from views of advantage, and is as deeply implanted in an Englishman as a Dutchman. A dealer is afraid of losing his character, and is scrupulous in observing every engagement. When a person makes 20 contracts in a day, he cannot gain so much by endeavouring to impose on his neighbours, as the very appearance of a cheat would make him lose. ([1766] 1982, p. 538)

Even for contracts that take place through time, both parties in a transaction often realize that they will be better off following through with their bargain and continuing the relationship than reneging on their bargain and potentially ending a relationship. In light of this history, let us revisit Landa's (1994, p. 60) assertion that "the 'discipline of continuous dealings' cannot be relied upon to protect contracts if credit transactions are important." Not only is this assertion at odds with the history of financial markets, but it contains an important linguistic problem as well. The word *credit* comes from the Latin *credere*, which actually means to "believe or trust," implying that people must assess someone's trustworthiness before making a transaction. Credit does not imply that transactions require third-party enforcement.

Business partners can establish trustworthiness in many ways. One is if two parties build a long-term relationship with each other. In these cases each party will realize that current customers are also potential future customers and so will think twice about cheating. Let us also revisit Hardin's (1997) and North's (1990, p. 58) assertion that cooperation breaks down when the number of traders becomes too large. Here too the Amsterdam Bourse was a prime candidate for prisoners' dilemma problems, as the number of brokers one could encounter around the Bourse (including money and commodity brokers) was more than one thousand by century's end (Dehing and 't Hart, 1997, p. 53; Bloom, 1937, p. 183), and pretty much anyone else could show up to make trades (de la Vega, 1688, p. 185). The many traders on the Bourse did not have close familial or religious ties (Stringham, 2003, p. 335), but they extended the discipline of continuous dealings through a multilateral reputation mechanism (Greif, 1989, 1993; Clay, 1997a, p. 511). With their multilateral reputation mechanism the cost of cheating became the souring of a relationship not only with the victim but with everyone else who found out. When parties can share information about the reliability of others, cheating has repercussions (Milgrom, North, and Weingast, 1990). Even if two parties have no prior experience and no expected future interactions, the reputation mechanism not only allows them to see if the other is likely to cooperate but also creates incentives for them to do so.

Many passages from *Confusion de Confusiones* illustrate the importance of reputation mechanisms. De la Vega (p. 172) writes, "The Exchange business is comparable to a game. Some of the players behave like princes and combine strength with tenderness and amiability with intelligence, but there are some participants who lose their reputation and others who lack devotion to their business even before play begins." Few people want to deal with an untrustworthy broker. De la Vega (p. 201) writes, "Since the status, the insignificant capital, the low reputation, and the limited trustworthiness of such people are well known, they do not dare attempt to carry on any considerable business."

Although brokers with bad reputations were precluded from most dealings, the stock market was not a closed club.[9] Despite the fact that anyone could enter the Bourse, traders had to build their reputations before they could make substantial trades. For example, in one dialogue in de la Vega's book, a novice believes his limited capital would preclude him and that "there would be nobody to give me credit," but he is told that he can start with options until he "gains in reputation for his generosity as well as his foresight" (pp. 150–51).

At the Bourse each broker had to work for business. Capitalists and merchants could trade themselves, so they would choose a broker and pay his fee (de la Vega, p. 179) only if they saw value in the arrangement. This creates incentives for brokers to act judiciously, which is confirmed by de la Vega (p. 176), who writes, "So great is the loyalty of some brokers to their principals, whom they usually call their masters, and so great is their industry, their activity, their zeal, and their vigilance that the customers get their money's worth." The brokers needed to act in a virtuous manner if they wanted patronage.

---

9. The brokers also came from various backgrounds. De la Vega (p. 185) remarked, "There exists an infinite number of these free brokers. This occupation is [in many cases] the only recourse for impoverished [businessmen], and the best place of refuge for many ruined careers." Although many brokers lived opulently, "Nevertheless there are numerous people in the business simply for the reason of providing decently for their families" (p. 190).

Williamson (1983) discusses how one can commit to not acting opportunistically by posting an irrecoverable bond (a hostage in Williamson's terminology) that will be forfeited if cheating occurs. The irrecoverable bond can take many forms; it can be an actual bond held by a third party, or it can be one's reputation, which will be forfeited or destroyed if one cheats. Putting one's reputation on the line with each transaction is like posting a bond for each trade (Bernstein, 1996). When the value of the bond exceeds what could be had from cheating, the "need" to rely on third-party enforcement or threat of punishment is eliminated.

For this reason, traders had an interest in keeping promises and abiding by their word. The following passage from *Confusion de Confusiones* illustrates this well:

> [To be sure, there is widespread honesty and expedition on the Exchange. For example,] the business in stocks and the bustle of the sales which are made when unforeseen news arrives is wonderful to behold. Nobody changes the decisions which he makes in his momentary passion, and his words are held sacred even in the case of a price difference of 50 per cent; and, although tremendous business is done by the merchants without the mediation of brokers who could serve as witnesses, no confusion occurs and no quarrels take place. . . . Such honesty, co-operation, and accuracy are admirable and surprising. (p. 172)

Deals struck on the spur of the moment did not have enforceable contracts, yet they did not break down.[10] In such an anarchic market, continuous review and adjudication of contracts in the courts was not feasible, yet in the absence of legal oversight, bargains were kept. Because of the discipline of continuous dealings, "such honesty, cooperation, and accuracy" is unsurprising.

In the first century of equity trading, the degree of financial innovation was considerable even though most financial instruments were outlawed by the state. The market was neither a simple spot market nor a small market in which everyone had familial or religious ties. It involved large transactions through time and fluctuations that could have tempted parties to default. Despite the many potential complications, brokers abided by their contracts not because of legal compulsion but because of private mechanisms.

---

10. In addition to the examples of people upholding their contracts, de la Vega stated that when people made legitimate errors, the other parties would not hold them liable. De la Vega (p. 171) writes, "It is an inviolable practice on the Exchange (which once was a mere usance) that that the party making a mistake is not obliged to suffer for it, if a transaction, not done at the price of the day, contains an error of 10 percent [of the par value]."

4.4. SUMMARY AND THOUGHTS

Because government did not create and enforce the rules of the first stock market, one cannot observe cooperation and wrongly attribute the cooperation to the threat of law, as is common in the "shadow of the state" arguments (Sachs, 2006). Even though modern markets theoretically have the state in the background, how much does one rely on government and much rely on informal mechanisms of private governance similar to those in seventeenth-century Amsterdam? Take a minute to think about the percentage of interaction and dealings in your life that could be reasonably adjudicated by third parties. It would be extremely costly if to bring each of these interactions to court, not to mention what that would do to one's business and personal relationships over the long run.[11] Most people find it more cost effective to rely on reputation mechanisms rather than on courts (even private ones).

Parties can choose to interact in small, close-knit groups (Landa, 1981, 1994), to interact among those who follow a common set of norms (Posner, 1996), or to extend reputation mechanisms that facilitate trade between relative strangers. Diners can go to a restaurant that they know is good, a restaurant that their friends say is good, or a restaurant that reviewers say is good. Publications such as the Michelin Guide and Zagat's as well as online review systems such as Citysearch and Yelp help parties share information about the reliability of restaurants. The auction website eBay uses a multilateral reputation mechanism very similar to that of the Amsterdam Bourse. Because users transmit information about the reliability of others, even people who have no experience with a party have pretty good information about whether the other party will deliver what they promise. Exceptions occur, but the expected costs associated with the rare noncontractual performance are much less than what it would cost to utilize the legal system on a regular basis.[12]

Sellers thinking about cheating risk damaging their reputation not only with their specific customers but also with all others. Ceteris paribus, reputation mechanisms will be more prevalent or more comprehensive in markets in which the risk of cheating or what is at stake is higher. When buying a $3 umbrella from a street vendor in Manhattan, I do not worry about whether the vendor has an established history or whether his wares are top quality. But when selecting an investment company, I look to ones that are unlikely

---

11. Of course, many litigious people exist, but a high percentage of them use the legal system opportunistically rather than to settle legitimate disputes. For a discussion of how the law is used to redistribute resources rather than to enhance markets, see Lopez (2010).

12. On one hand, Albert (2002) chides eBay for having a rate of fraud that is above zero and proposes its control by government regulations regardless of cost. I, on the other hand, willingly embrace the small risks of doing business on eBay compared with what would be the stifling costs were government to attempt to enforce dealings there.

to risk tarnishing their valuable (and reliable-sounding) names, such as Fidelity or Prudential. Reputation becomes extremely valuable in these markets (Klein, 1997).

In most markets, parties need to build reputations if they want others to deal with them. A bank, for example, does not give a million-dollar mortgage to someone without an established credit history, but it will extend a small line of credit and then gradually increase it based on its estimate of the borrower's reliability. A borrower who defaults may gain in the short run, but lenders use a multilateral reputation mechanism to share information that then influences the defaulter's credit rating. An ideal loan has the risk of default properly priced into the interest rate, and although some borrowers default, most do not. Those who never establish a good credit history will not obtain considerable loans, and everyone else who wants access to lending markets will need to pay back what they owe.

The establishment of reputation often comes gradually over time, but access to markets can be hastened. Investments in advertising to build a brand name are equivalent to posting an irrecoverable bond (Klein and Leffler, 1981) that will be forfeited if the advertiser does not live up to expectations. Coca-Cola is not likely to switch its formula to trick its customers into buying an inferior product that they do not want. Parties can also hire third-party certification agencies to help convey information about their reliability (Klein, 1997, 2002). Underwriters Laboratories and THX Limited, for example, put their stamp of approval on electrical appliances and stereo equipment, respectively, so that consumers can rely on the reputation of those firms rather than investigate each individual producer. Alternatively, parties can contract with a bonding agency that vouches for someone and assumes any risk if that party does not deliver on his promises. Consumers need not know whether a plumber has enough money in the bank to pay if he accidentally floods a condo, as long as the plumber is bonded by a reputable company that has those funds. Businesspeople often look to their acquaintances to vouch for potential hires, contractors, or clients (Granovetter, 1995) before getting into a relationship that involves considerable risk. Everyone has experience with this.

As long as information about the reliability of prospective trading partners can be shared, many of the incentives for cheating are eliminated. Notice that these reciprocity and reputation mechanisms do not rely on actual or threatened use of force. They also, whether public or private, do not rely on formal rules. Therefore, they can work across political boundaries or in any area where external enforcement is difficult. These mechanisms are at work in the vast majority of exchange and, for that matter, human interaction.

CHAPTER 5

༺༻

The Evolution of Rules
in Exclusive Clubs

From Coffeehouses to the London
Stock Exchange

Go into the Exchange in London, that place more venerable than many a court, and you
will see representatives of all the nations assembled there for the profit of mankind.
There the Jew, the Mahometan, and the Christian deal with one another as if they were
of the same religion, and reserve the name of infidel for those who go bankrupt.
—Voltaire ([1733] 1961, p. 26)

5.1. INTRODUCTION

By the end of the seventeenth century and beginning of the eighteenth century, officials in London often lacked the ability to enforce basic laws (they
were an "ungovernable people"), and a gin craze took off as well (Defoe, 1727;
Brewer, 1983). Maybe the stimulus for development was the freedom, or
maybe it was the booze (Peters and Stringham, 2006), but London ended up
with the most developed stock market in the world. As in Amsterdam, government officials in London were never supportive of these new markets and
made various transactions illegal. Officials banned stockbrokers from the
Royal Exchange, but the brokers ended up developing an advanced market in
coffeehouses (Mortimer, 1801, p. xvi).[1] As the market grew in size, it started

1. The market consisted of stockbrokers and stockjobbers or what we now call stockbrokers, market makers, and other types of agency traders, but for simplicity of exposi-
tion, I will usually refer to everyone who traded in stocks as stockbrokers.

attracting many good but also many unreliable brokers, and this posed a dilemma because keeping track of who was reliable became more difficult. Markets without formal rules often work quite well (reputation, reciprocity, and other informal mechanisms work wonders), but sometimes formal rules are "necessary" (or to use more economic terminology, they enhance trade at the margin). Although Kirzner asserts that one of the institutional prerequisites of markets is "enforceability of contract" and without it "the market cannot operate" and that therefore "those institutions cannot be created by the market itself" (Kirzner, 2000, p. 83),[2] my research about the history of stock markets shows that the rules of the stock market emerged *from* the market.

The rules of the stock market came from brokers themselves as they transformed coffeehouses into private clubs to create and enforce rules. Government officials were neither particularly knowledgeable about modern economics and finance nor particularly interested in the well-being of stockbrokers. The stockbrokers, however, both understood and cared about the problems they faced, so rather than sitting around and waiting for nonexistent government solutions, they took the initiative and altered what economists call the microstructure of the market (O'Hara, 1995; Carlos and Neal, 2006; Neal and Davis, 2005, 2006). Brokers experimented with ways to notify each other about defaulters, fines, entrance fees, subscription fees, and membership requirements. Their ultimate enforcement mechanism ended up being exclusion of anyone who did not meet certain requirements or follow the rules.[3] Brokers experimented with various rules and finally documented them in 1812 in what they described as a "collection of laws . . . for the government of the members" (Committee for General Purposes of the Stock-Exchange, 1812, p. 9).

The transformation of coffeehouse to exchange was not unique to the London Stock Exchange. Other institutions founded in or by coffeehouses include Lloyd's of London (Lloyd's Coffeehouse), the Baltic Exchange (Virginia and Baltick Coffee House), the Philadelphia Stock Exchange (Merchants Coffee House); Shawmut Bank (Old Exchange Coffee House), the Dublin Stock Exchange, Sotheby's, and Christy's. The coffee shops were not like Starbucks and sold booze. According to humor magazine Punch (1882, p. 84), "Most Coffee-Shops sell other things than Coffee" and "Most Coffee-Shops do not sell Coffee at all." Garraway's was popular for stockbrokers and was later described as "a sandwich and drinking room, for sherry, pale ale, and punch. Tea

2. Kirzner (2000, p. 85) mentions the potential importance of "shared ethical perspectives" (presumably independent of government), but he talks about the need "most likely, for governmental, extra-market enforcement."

3. For excellent histories of the London Stock Exchange, see Wincott (1946), Morgan and Thomas ([1962] 1969), Jenkins (1973), and Michie (2001). Neal and David (2005, 2006) also provide excellent analyses of the rules of the London Stock Exchange.

and coffee are still served" (Timbs, 1866, p. 9). Out of these informal environs, brokers ended up creating a system of formal rules.

Transforming coffeehouses into an exclusive club eliminated what could have been a tragedy of the commons situation in which cheating undermined the market. The exclusive club both reduced the admission of unreliable people and created incentives for cooperation of members. Exclusive membership served as a forfeitable bond and made unenforceability in courts of law irrelevant. The history of the London Stock Exchange shows that "the rules of the game" for the most sophisticated markets evolved endogenously *from the market* rather than from government.

5.2. GOVERNMENT OR ENDOGENOUS EVOLUTION OF RULES

It would be nice to start this book with a satisfyingly round sentence: "on the ——th day of —— in the year of our Lord ——, the Stock Exchange, London, came into being." Alas for those with tidy minds, the Stock Exchange is a typically British institution. No-one can say with any certainty exactly when it started. Like Topsy, it almost seems it never was born, but just "grow'd." (Wincott, 1946, p. 1)

England's first major joint stock company was the "Mystery and Company of Merchant Adventurers for the discovery of regions, dominions, islands, and places unknown," founded in 1551 (and later known as the Muscovy Company, chartered in 1555).[4] Other major English companies included the Levant Company, the English East India Company, and the Virginia Company, chartered in 1581, 1600, and 1606, respectively.[5]

At first, ownership of stocks was not widespread, and transactions most often consisted of one owner divesting his shares to someone on a restricted list of eligible buyers (Jenkins, 1973). Over time, however, brokers in other

---

4. Business ventures with multiple shareholders became popular with *commenda* contracts in medieval Italy (Greif, 2006, p. 286), and Malmendier (2009) provides evidence that shareholder companies date back to ancient Rome.

5. Many of these companies were given certain monopoly privileges by government, but the importance of these privileges in the emergence of a market for secondary shares should not be overestimated. First, some companies were given monopoly privileges years after they were founded. Second, their privileges were in relationship to other English firms but often did not affect foreign competition. For example, the Muscovy Company had a "monopoly" of trade with Russia, but it was a relatively small player in the region compared to merchants in the Hanseatic League, which had trading routes with Russia for centuries. Likewise, in the seventeenth century the English East India Company faced competition from the Dutch East India Company, the Danish East India Company, the French East India Company, the Portuguese East India Company, and the Swedish East India Company. If we go by the dictionary definition of monopoly as "exclusive supply," then no monopoly existed. These companies' monopolies were similar to the monopolies of taxi cabs in New York, a market that is certainly not free but still has a fair amount of competition.

commodities began specializing in stocks (Kindleberger, 1984, p. 196).[6] The earliest document I found that describes stockjobbers in England was a letter from 1691 (Wary, 1691), and by 1692 the weekly periodical *Collection for Improvement of Husbandry and Trade* was publishing stock prices for eight companies (Houghton, [1692] 1727; Neal, 1987, p. 99). By the end of the seventeenth century, at least 150 joint stock companies existed (Jenkins, 1973).[7] Early stockbrokers traded at the Royal Exchange, which housed other merchants such as grocers, druggists, and clothiers (Wincott, 1946, p. 7). Government, however, looked down on this market and in 1696 passed an act titled To Restrain the Number and the Practice of Brokers and Stockjobbers.

Without being able to trade in the Royal Exchange, stockbrokers congregated by 'Change Alley around Cornhill and Lombard streets (Reed, 1975, p. 5; see figure 5.1).[8] Especially after London prohibited them from congregating on the street in 1700, their main trading venues became Jonathan's and Garraway's coffeehouses (see figures 5.2, 5.3, 5.4, and 5.5). One broker put out the following advertisement in 1695 in *Collection for Improvement of Husbandry and Trade*: "John Castaing at Jonathan's Coffee House on Exchange, buys and sells all Blank an Benefit Tickets; and all other Stocks and Shares" (reprinted in Mirowski, 1981, p. 564). Another successful stockbroker was described by his peers as "the leader and oracle of Jonathan's Coffee House" (Morgan and Thomas, [1962] 1969, p. 46).

Government officials always looked down on this trade, as Sir Robert Walpole made clear in 1716: "Every one is aware how the administration in this country has been distressed by stock-jobbers" (Francis, 1850, p. 23). In addition to passing rules restricting stockbrokers, the government all but outlawed the formation of new joint stock companies in 1720 with the passing of the

---

6. Jenkins (1973, pp. 19–20) writes, "They were by no means necessarily stockbrokers. They could deal in anything they liked—stockes, gold, haberdashy, fish, bread, carpentry, spectacles, even bows and arrows."

7. In 1694 the Bank of England (a private bank that was given certain monopoly privileges) was founded and started issuing debt so it could lend to the Crown. The term "stock" originally referred to shares in companies, but it also sometimes encompassed government bonds. Mortimer (1762, p. 9), writes that referring to government-related securities as stocks "is highly improper, as they are absolutely public debts, and not stocks." Further muddying the linguistic waters was the fact that some used the term "public funds" to encompass both government bonds and shares in publicly traded private companies (European Magazine and London Review, 1811, p. 35). So the term "stock market" could refer market for equities and the market for equities and bonds.

Ferguson (2001) asserts that the stock market was really mostly a government bond market and that equities only emerged after the government created central banks and markets for government debt. Besides glossing over the equity market in Amsterdam, his account misses the fact that transferable shares in England were present for more than a century before the founding of the Bank of England in 1694, and the stockbrokerage profession dates back at least to 1691.

8. Lombard Street itself was named after the banking houses founded in various cities throughout Europe by merchants of Lombardy (Atwood, 1917, p. 152).

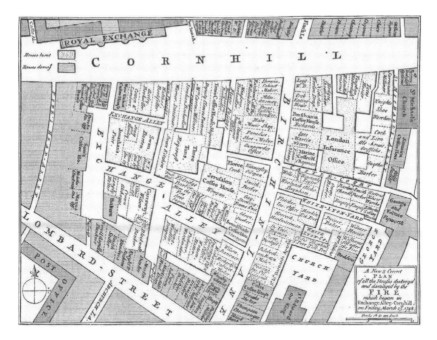

Figure 5.1
Map of Exchange Alley circa 1748

Figure 5.2
Garraway's Coffee House from an Old Sketch

Figure 5.3
Jonathan's from an Old Sketch
Source: Walter Thornbury (1887, p. 472).

Bubble Act.[9] A 1734 bill, "To prevent the infamous Practice of Stock-jobbing," also banned options, futures, and margin trading, and government animosity toward stock traders persisted for well over a century (Harris, 2000, p. 225). Government thought various forms of contracts, including those that were settled with payment of differences rather than actual transfer of shares, were illegitimate. Adam Smith's 1766 *Lectures on Jurisprudence* describes the rationale:

> This practice of buying stocks by time is prohibited by government, and accordingly, tho' they should not deliver up the stocks they have engaged for, the law gives no redress. There is no natural reason why 1000£ in the stocks should not be delivered or the delivery of it enforced, as well as 1000£ worth of goods. But after the South Sea scheme this was thought upon as an expedient to prevent such practice. (Smith, [1766] 1982, p. 538)

9. The Bubble Act was passed in the midst of a government scheme to convert government debts into shares of the South Sea Company. Shortly thereafter the price of South Sea Company stock plummeted, and, of course, government blamed the market for this bubble.

Figure 5.4
Jonathan's Coffee House, H. O. Neal, 1763

Government made various types of contracts illegal, but Smith writes that the law "proved ineffectual." Smith writes:

> In the same manner all laws against gaming never hinder it, and tho' there is no redress for a sum above 5£, yet all the great sums that are lost are punctually paid. Persons who game must keep their credit, else no body will deal with them. It is quite the same for stockjobbing. They who do not keep their credit will be turned out, and in the language of Change Alley be called lame duck. (Smith, [1766] 1982, p. 538)

Contracts were all but unenforceable, but stockbrokers engaged in them anyway. Yet could they deal with the problem of lame ducks? This was the "name given in 'Change Alley to those who refuse to fulfil their engagements. There are some at almost every rescounter [settlement]" (Mortimer, 1762, p. 57).

In the tragedy-of-the-commons story, when an area (such as a fishery or a pasture or in this case a stock market) has certain benefits, newcomers will not consider how their actions decrease the well-being of everyone else in that space. This was definitely a potential problem in the stock market. Although cheaters could make out like bandits, the more widespread cheating became, the more the market would shrivel. Even if interlopers know their actions

Figure 5.5
Waddling Out, from an Old Sketch

will harm the market, they have little incentive to do otherwise. Houghton ([1692] 1727, p. 5) warned, "Without a doubt, if those trades were better known, 'twould be a great advantage to the kingdom; only I must caution beginners to be very wary, for there are many cunning artists among them." With time bargains that had settlement months in the future, one's counterpart might intentionally disappear or unintentionally become bankrupt in the interim. Mortimer (1801, pp. 53–54) states that "problems arise if the person making the trade does not have the ability (cash) to settle, for in many cases a broker and his customer had no money." Various authors described the growing problem of lame ducks that would default and "waddle out of the coffee house" (see figure 5.5).

Where the legal centralist assumes such problems must be dealt with by courts of law, brokers did not have the ability to rely on courts, so instead they figured out various ways to exclude defaulters. Mortimer (1801, pp. 53–54) writes, "The punishment for nonpayment is banishment from Jonathan's but they can still act as brokers at the offices." Expulsion from Jonathan's meant a significant loss of business for a broker (Jenkins, 1973), and this was the first step toward formalized mechanisms for excluding defaulters.

Before the rules were formalized, certain lame ducks would come back into the coffeehouses, and keeping track of all of them was difficult. As a solution, brokers decided to write the names of defaulters on a blackboard as a warning to others not to deal with them. This was a form of noncoercive enforcement against defaulters.

Eventually some brokers decided that they needed to ramp up the exclusion of the unreliable and that coffeehouses open to the public left much to be desired. The plan to eliminate the disarray can be analyzed as closing or privatizing the commons. That enabled reliable brokers to avoid having to deal with, in the words of one historian, "riff-raff" (Jenkins, 1973). In 1761 Thomas Mortimer writes, "The gentlemen at this very period of time . . . have taken it into their heads that some of the fraternity are not so good as themselves . . . and have entered into an association to exclude them from J——'s coffee-house" (reprinted in Smith, 1929, p. 215). In 1762 150 brokers formed a club and contracted with Jonathan's Coffeehouse to use it exclusively.

Each member paid eight pounds per year to rent out the coffeehouse (Morgan and Thomas, [1962] 1969). By transforming Jonathan's into a private club, the members were able to exclude nonmembers and expel those who were unruly. Historians refer to the founders of the club as the "more substantial" (Morgan and Thomas, [1962] 1969, p. 68) and the "better sort" (Jenkins, 1973, p. 45) of brokers. If only reputable brokers were allowed in the club, the potential for bad dealings would be lessened. Any potential interloper who had no concern for paying his debts or for the viability of the market as a whole simply would not be let in. Screening people at the door and excluding those likely to be unreliable was an important step. Furthermore, the ability to kick out someone who did not end up being reliable meant that everyone in the club had to be on good behavior if he wanted to stay in the club.

Creating this exclusive club, or privatizing the commons, was not without controversy. A 1772 letter in *Town and Country Magazine* writes critically that "the brokers at Jonathan's admit none but their own fraternity into their coffee-house, which to prevent strangers intruding amongst them" ("Antilounger," 1772, p. 525). One excluded broker ended up going to government and suing to break up this newly formed club. Government intervened and declared that Jonathan's Coffeehouse did not have the right to exclude outsiders.

In 1773, as an alternative strategy, brokers organized and purchased a building for their own use. This new building was known as New Jonathan's and was open to anyone as long as he paid the daily admission fee, which covered expenses such as rent (Wincott, 1946). In 1773 the *Gentlemen's Magazine* reported, "New Jonathan's came to the resolution that instead of its being called New Jonathan's, it should be called The Stock Exchange, which is to be wrote over the door" (reprinted in Jenkins, 1973, p. 45). Mortimer's (1801, p. 150) description is telling: "Brokers assemble at a very large coffeehouse, called the Stock-Exchange." This coffeehouse / stock exchange had no formal membership and was run by two committees, one representing the coffee-house owners and another representing the customers.

In the early years, this new iteration of the club had not yet formalized membership rules and was basically open to anyone who paid the daily fee. The fee might have been enough to keep out some vagrants, but after a few years it became evident that more formal requirements were warranted. An early nineteenth-century source reports that between "600 and 800 draw their splendid livelihood from this traffic" (Smollett, 1814, p. 209). Enough untrustworthy brokers were still present to cause problems for both investors and brokers (Wincott, 1946). Brokers wanted to have an even more exclusive club, and in 1801 they decided to require that entrants be subscribed members (Morgan and Thomas, [1962] 1969). They posted the following:

> The Proprietors of the Stock Exchange, at the solicitation of a very considerable number of the Gentlemen frequenting it, and with the unanimous concurrence of the Committee appointed for General Purposes, who were requested to assist them in forming such regulations as may be deemed necessary, have resolved unanimously, that after 27 February next this House shall finally be shut as a Stock Exchange, and opened as a Subscription Room on Tuesday 3 March at ten guineas per Annum ending 1 March in each succeeding year. All person desirous of becoming subscribers are requested to signify the same in writing to E. Whit-ford, Secretary to the joint committees on or before 31 inst. In order to their being balloted for by the said committees. (Michie, 2001, p. 35)

Members had to be reviewed and a paid-up member to enter the Stock Subscription Room. Figure 5.6 reproduces print from about 1800 of the market at that time. Organizers stated in 1801 that it "being desirous that the Stock Subscription Room should acquire and preserve the most respectable character and considering that for such purpose it is indisputably necessary to prevent the practice of every disorderly action," they would levy fines on rule breakers, "to be paid to the Secretary of the Committee for general Purposes and by them applied to charitable uses" (Morgan and Thomas, [1962] 1969, p. 69).

The ability to levy fines meant that a member had to be in good standing to retain membership. Where most modern economists focus on government adjusting punishments or fines to discourage bad behavior, here it is done by private parties.

The new Stock Subscription Room faced some challenges. Many brokers did not want the changes to occur and were generally uncooperative. One member

Figure 5.6
On Change from an Old Print, about 1800
Source: Walter Thornbury (1878, p. 487).

was fined but refused to pay, contending that he should not have to go along with the new rules (Morgan and Thomas, [1962] 1969). The future economist David Ricardo was a member at the time, but he eventually resigned (Jenkins, 1973, p. 51). In the following months the Stock Subscription Room disintegrated, and those desiring a more exclusive club had no choice but to go off and start a new exchange.

With much preparation and an offer to old exchange brokers to become members, a group of brokers raised funds by issuing 400 shares at £50 each, of which each person could purchase up to four shares, and constructed a new building over the next year (Morgan and Thomas, [1962] 1969; Reed, 1975). As a new venture the Stock Exchange at Capel Court would have its rules unanimously agreed upon by members. Once again, some of the brokers that did not become members were unhappy. In 1810 some petitioned the government to undermine the Stock Exchange by forcing this private club to open to the public. The proposed bill stated:

> That there is at this time no open Public Market for the sale and purchase of the Public Stocks, Funds, Government and other securities; and that the place wherein the chief part of this business hath been hitherto and is now transacted, is a private room from which the public is excluded; and it would be of great convenience and advantage to His Majesty's subjects if a public open market were established in a suitable situation for the purchase and sale of the said Stocks, Funds and Securities. (Great Britain House of Commons, 1810, p. 60)

A member declared that the 1810 petition was written "under the specious pretext of creating an open Stock Market within the City of London," but that it truly intended "to shelter convicted defaulters and afford new facilities to the criminal designs of notorious and unprincipled gamblers." In this case government did not interfere, and let the club operate as a private club. Government essentially let the club treat the property as private property rather than an open-access commons. With its establishment the Stock Exchange would be "open to honourable men and closed shut for ever to notorious cheats" (Morgan and Thomas, [1962] 1969, p. 72). The Stock Exchange was now able to enact and enforce rules internal to its members; anyone who was not a member was not permitted to do business on the premises (Johnstone, 1814).

In 1878 government finally had good things to say about the Stock Exchange rules, noting that they "had been salutary to the interests of the public" and that the Exchange acted "uprightly, honestly, and with a desire to do justice" (London Stock Exchange Commission, 1878, p. 5). It concluded by saying that the Exchange's rules were "capable of affording relief and exercising restraint far more prompt and often satisfactory than any within the read of the courts of law."

5.3. RULES FOR THE "SAFETY AND PROTECTION OF THE PROPERTY AND INTERESTS OF THE MEMBERS OF THE STOCK-EXCHANGE"

Fraud harms victims and diminishes future trade. London stockbrokers saw this problem and recognized that they could benefit by mitigating it. They experimented with various rules and documented many in their first rule-book in 1812 (figure 5.7). A subcommittee of the Committee for General Purposes of the Stock-Exchange stated that the resolutions were "an attempt (the first indeed that has ever yet been made in this House) to reduce into a regular method the rules and regulations, by which so very important a class of society is to be governed" (Committee for General Purposes of the

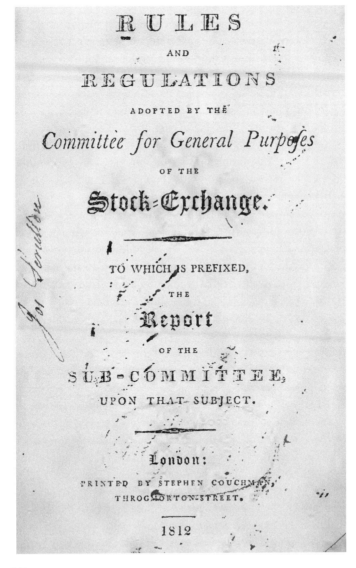

RULES

AND

REGULATIONS

ADOPTED BY THE

Committee for General Purposes

OF THE

Stock-Exchange.

TO WHICH IS PREFIXED,

THE

Report

OF THE

SUB-COMMITTEE,

UPON THAT SUBJECT.

London:

PRINTED BY STEPHEN COUCHMAN,
THROGMORTON-STREET.

1812

Figure 5.7
"Rules and Regulations Adopted by the Committee for General Purposes of the Stock-Exchange," Committee for General Purposes of the Stock-Exchange, 1812

Stock-Exchange, 1812, p. 10). Although the subcommittee said some disputes could be settled within the Exchange using "the known Laws of the Land," it added that "many others (which, from their nature and extent, preclude the possibility of forming any general laws on the subject, so as to meet every contingency) may also be adjusted by the known custom and practice of the market" (p. 10). Government was not the chicken that laid the egg of stock markets. Instead, both the market and rules governing the stock market evolved *privately*.

Although I think rules such as "Thou shalt not steal" are just and should be followed, exactly how brokers should deal with problems such as nonperformance on forward contracts are open questions. What should the repercussions be? Should the exchange undertake retribution, restitution, or simple expulsion? Should an unintentional defaulter be treated the same as an intentional defaulter? If fines exist, should they be flat or graduated, and who should determine them? What should the exchange do when a defaulter had no funds to pay? If the exchange relies on expulsion, should expelled members ever be let back in, and if so, under what circumstances? Should there be any rules about brokers acting in a rowdy manner or about spreading false rumors? These are all tough questions that could long be debated in legislative chambers, regulatory hearings, courts of law, and academic journals, but instead the private governance at the London Stock Exchange left the judgment of the optimal rules to the market. Brokers who reported to their customers, "I didn't think about our counterparty default risk, and I don't actually have the shares that you paid for," would be at a severe disadvantage with respect to those who traded in a venue that minimized such problems. Thus, the Stock Exchange had an incentive to search for rules that would make its market more orderly and more attractive.

The Exchange's 1812 resolutions passed for "the safety and protection of the property and interests of the members of the Stock-Exchange" (p. 6) included rules in the following categories:

Admissions	(14 resolutions)
Bargains	(10 resolutions)
Clerks	(8 resolutions)
Committee	(18 resolutions)
Failures	(12 resolutions)
Partnerships	(1 resolution)
Puts and calls	(1 resolution)
Passing of tickets	(3 resolutions)
Quotation of prices	(5 resolutions)
Settling days	(3 resolutions)

This rulebook is noticeably more readable and less legalistic than anything put out by the Securities and Exchange Commission or the Financial Services Authority. The resolutions' writers stated they wanted to make the resolutions "as clear and comprehensive as possible" (Committee for General Purposes of the Stock-Exchange, 1812, p. 6). The need to attract business made the Exchange act in a judicious manner (Boot, Greenbaum, and Thakor, 1993).

The Exchange's main rule-enforcing body was the Committee for General Purposes, which had thirty members, a chairman, and a deputy chairman, who were elected by the members each year. The committee dealt with the "management, regulation, and direction" of the Stock Exchange. The secretary of the committee kept records of applications and reported "the name of every defaulter that may have been declared in the Stock-Exchange, and insert the same into the minute book" (Committee for General Purposes of the Stock-Exchange, 1812, p. 33). The committee had "the right to expel any . . . members of the Committee who may have been guilty of dishonourable or disgraceful conduct; or who may be otherwise highly objectionable," provided a subcommittee to vote on the matter was created and two-thirds agreed.

The committee also dealt with membership applications, which had to be renewed each year. All new applicants had to be recommended by two members who "have knowledge of the party and his circumstances" (p. 17) and could explain them to the admission committee. Anyone who objected to a new member could express his concern to the committee for consideration. People whose membership was not accepted could reapply after thirty days, but if rejected again they would have to wait until the next year. At any point in time, "Every defaulter ceases to be a member" and "Every subscriber, who shall become bankrupt ceases to be a member" (pp. 18–19). Loss of membership was not necessarily permanent if a defaulter rectified certain wrongs. Certain actions, however, could lead to permanent expulsion: "Every member, who may be guilty of dishonourable or disgraceful conduct, or who may violate any of the fundamental laws of the Stock-Exchange, shall be liable to expulsion." The process of permanent expulsion involved a hearing before a committee at which at least three-fourths of the voting members decided for expulsion.

Members could also request the admission of clerks, who were then the responsibility of those members. A list of approved clerks and their employers "shall be put up and remain in a conspicuous part of the House." To obtain permission, the member had to "send the name of such a clerk to the Committee for General Purposes for their approbation; without whose consent no such clerk shall be admitted" (p. 23). Clerks were not permitted to trade on their own account and were expelled if they did. Clerks were generally forbidden to engage in time bargains unless approved by the Committee for General

Purposes and were posted on the eligible list. Given that time bargains involve considerably more risk, one can understand such a rule.

The Exchange had rules about settlement (p. 20) and what could go wrong in the event of a dispute. The Exchange stated that "all disputes between individuals (not affecting the general interests of the Stock-Exchange) shall be referred to arbitration," and that "the Committee [for General Purposes] will not interfere in such disputes, unless that resource may have proved ineffectual, or unless arbitrators cannot be found ready and willing to determine the case." Here brokers appear to have two levels of adjudication within the Exchange.

The Exchange also had rules about consequences for defaulters. All creditors whose counterparty defaulted were required to report the default to the Committee for General Purposes. Any creditor who violated the rule had his name "affixed in a conscious part of the Stock-Exchange" (pp. 34–35). Other rules outlined the equivalent of bankruptcy proceedings. If someone in default was scheduled to be paid money from another set of trades, the proceeds were split proportionally among the creditors of the defaulter. This prevented a strategic defaulter from reneging on some contracts but collecting on others. A defaulter lost his membership but could reapply if he furnished "his books of accounts and a statement of the sums owing to him and owed by him in the Stock Exchange" and met a few other conditions. A defaulter applying for readmission "shall have his name fixed in a conspicuous part of the Stock-Exchange, at least eight days previous to the application being considered during this Committee." If any members reported "that the conduct of such defaulter has been dishonourable, or marked with any circumstances of impropriety," readmission was denied and the name of the person written on "the *Black Board* in the Stock-Exchange" (pp. 36–37).

The committee stated that "order and decorum" were "so essentially necessary to be observed in all places in this business" (p. 46) and that it needed to inhibit "rude and trifling practices" that would be "injurious to the best interests of the House." The Exchange had fairly strict rules, but none of them seem draconian. As long as defaulters repaid their debts (indicating they had not acted with bad intentions when they defaulted), they could be readmitted. The rules were adopted to inhibit bad behavior and encourage good behavior.

5.4. SUMMARY AND THOUGHTS

The London Stock Exchange emerged when brokers transformed coffee-houses into exclusive clubs to create and enforce rules. With government enforcement lacking, brokers attracted more business by providing assurances against fraud. They did not need to rely on the threat of physical punishment when instead they could include the reliable and exclude the unreliable. Even though the market was growing and had a thousand members by the mid-nineteenth century and two thousand members by 1878 (London Stock Exchange Commission, 1878, p. 5), its ability to enforce rules solved a potential tragedy-of-the-commons situation associated with fraud. By only admitting people who met conditions of membership, the Stock Exchange eliminated most potential problems to begin with. Incentives against cheating were further strengthened by the Exchange's ability to kick out anyone who defaulted once let in. As membership became more valuable, brokers become less likely to want to lose their membership. The value of membership thus acted as a bond, and the ability to exclude acted as a powerful, and nonviolent, enforcement mechanism.

Rather than all-or-none thinking, such as that "all markets require enforcement of property and contract rights" (Grote and McGeeney, 1997, p. 17), a more economic way of thinking examines how private parties can create new rules on different margins. Just as entrepreneurs continually seek to satisfy consumers' unmet needs, providers of private governance continually seek to solve problems that prevent consumers from getting what they want.[10] Organizing the Exchange as a private club meant that members became residual claimants, so problem-solving became a profit opportunity, and the bigger the potential problem, the bigger the profits from solving it.

Some authors suggest that clubs like the London Stock Exchange are the equivalent of governments or private monopolies that unfairly exclude competitors from the market (Welles, 1975). But the Exchange only had a "monopoly" if one defines the relevant market as "conducting trade within the Exchange." Because nonmembers could trade in private offices, the Royal Exchange, the Bank of England, other regional exchanges, or foreign exchanges (Mortimer, 1801; Kregel, 1995; Morgan and Thomas, [1962] 1969; Michie, 1985; Neal, 1987; Stringham, 2002), the market in London is best analyzed as a contestable market under the constant threat of competition.

In the second half of the eighteenth century different groups experimented with different settings to trade stocks or other securities. For example, in 1765 the Bank of England built a rotunda where trading took place, but this did not prove to be successful. An 1824 book described the trading there as of a "less respectable description" (Michie, 2001, p. 44). Brokers were noisy and were generally considered with disrepute (Jenkins, 1973; Morgan and Thomas, [1962] 1969). The London Stock Exchange succeeded because it offered superior rules.

We can generalize this argument. Today even though government regulations make markets much less competitive than they otherwise would be, the

---

10. For a discussion of what they label institutional entrepreneurship, see Boettke and Coyne (2009) and Leeson and Boettke (2009).

London Stock Exchange, the New York Stock Exchange, NASDAQ, and every other exchange must woo customers by having rules and regulations that add value to the market.[11] The stock exchange as a rule-enforcing club is representative of a much wider phenomenon. In each area of one's life, people face different challenges, and in some areas people desire formal rules. A chess club, a sports league, or any firm can create any rules it wants, the costs and benefits of which are borne by the people inside that organization. The London Stock Exchange shows that the rules of one of the most important and sophisticated markets, the stock market, were generated privately rather than from the state.

---

11. Carlton (1984, p. 259) writes, "It is useful to view exchanges as competing (or potentially competing) with each other. As in other markets, competition is a substitute for regulation. The more competition there is, the more likely it is that exchanges themselves will promulgate rules and regulations that benefit and protect consumers in much the same ways as competition in other markets protects consumers." And Mahoney (1997, p. 1447) writes, "An exchange's attempts to charge a monopoly price for its members' services will harm only the members if the exchange faces sufficient competition from other markets. Other exchanges will capture trading volume by offering lower transaction costs and investors will be no worse off by virtue of a foolish attempt to charge a monopoly price in a competitive market. If stock markets face sufficient competition, then, restrictive rules will survive only to the extent they are efficient." See also Macey and Kanda (1990) and Macey and O'Hara (1999).

CHAPTER 6

⌒⌒

Markets Creating Transparency

*Competing Listing and Disclosure Requirements
from the Big Board in New York to the Alternative
Investment Market in London*

6.1. INTRODUCTION

I knew today was lucky day and that was confirmed by this investment opportunity emailed personally to me:

> Dear Friend,
>
> I am a director in the foreign affairs department of the Nigerian National Petroleum Corporation (NNPC). I wish to use this opportunity to notify you of the existence of a certain amount we wish to transfer overseas for the purpose of investments and importation of goods from your country. In May 2001, a contract of sixty-six million United States dollars ($66,000,000) was awarded to a foreign company by my ministry. The contract was supply, erection and system optimization of supper polyore 200,000-bpsd, system optimization of 280,000-monax axial plants and the computerization of conveyor belt for Kaduna refinery. With only the consent of the head of the contract evaluation department, I over invoiced the contract value by thirty four million United States dollars ($34,000,000).
>
> The contract has been completed long ago and the foreign company fully paid off. But in the office files and paper work, the company is still owed USD34M representing the over invoiced amount. Because this amount is derived from the

award and execution of a foreign contract, there is no way the money can be paid locally. That is why I contacted you so that we can do the project together for our mutual benefit. We have concluded every necessary arrangement to transfer this amount to a foreign account as the final phase payment for the said contract. What we need is your bank account into which we can deposit the money and after we shall come over there to share the money with you.

Kind regards,

Mr. Joseph, Victoria Island, Lagos, Nigeria

Since receiving his first letter, Mr. Joseph and I have become close Internet friends and he assures me I can trust him. I also know that fraud is illegal in the United States and Nigeria, so if anything goes wrong I can simply call the Securities and Exchange Commission in the United States or Nigeria and get my money back. My success is guaranteed.

Almost all economists agree that investment markets are a good thing for firms and investors. The process of financial intermediation channels money from savers or investors to firms who need capital, and that enables savers or investors to share in a firm's success. Fraudulent "enterprises," however, are a different matter, and they can range from totally bogus schemes to quasi-legitimate enterprises that actually make money but whose managers swindle part or all of investors' profits. In a world with imperfect information, recognizing the difference between a manager who tried and failed and one who intentionally took money can be difficult, so most people look to government to create transparency. The Securities and Exchange Commission (2012) states its goal is "to protect investors, maintain fair, orderly, and efficient markets, and facilitate capital formation," and its tools include various listing and disclosure requirements for firms accepting money from investors. Lopez-de-Silanes (2004, p. 6) summarizes the most common view: "Regulation of securities is beneficial because it protects investors by mandating disclosure and . . . foments the growth of markets by increasing the supply of truthful information."

As in other markets, the existence of fraud scares investors, and that fear reduces the amount of mutually beneficial investments (Prentice, 2002). Yet just because potential problems exist, it does not follow that transparency, listing, or disclosure requirements must come from (or were innovations of) the state. In fact, the first transparency, listing, and disclosure requirements all predated the Securities and Exchange Commission in America and the precursor to the Financial Conduct Authority in England. When the Securities Act and the Securities Exchange Act were implemented in 1933 and 1934, they simply mandated many of the requirements that the New York Stock Exchange had already adopted. Firms that wanted to be listed and traded at the New York Stock Exchange had to meet certain requirements that helped show they were legitimate firms.

By providing extra assurances to investors, the New York Stock Exchange, the Big Board, increases the demand for its market. Here the exchange acts as a reputational intermediary, providing the equivalent of a Good House-keeping Seal of Approval on listed firms (Macey, 2013). The New York Stock Exchange does not guarantee the lack of fraud, but its listing and disclosure requirements make fraud more difficult and preclude most fly-by-night firms. When competing to make its venue more attractive, each exchange must evaluate the marginal costs and benefits to firms and investors of additional rules and regulations. Other exchanges have their own requirements, and many are more flexible than the New York Stock Exchange. One of the most flexible markets today is London Stock Exchange's Alternative Investment Market (AIM), which caters to smaller firms. When choosing where to list, firms can opt for the strict rules of the New York Stock Exchange or more flexible rules of AIM, but they must consider what will be most attractive to investors.

If rules such as listing or disclosure requirements are so beneficial, private parties can contract to have them. The goodness or badness of the rules becomes internalized into the price of stocks and the exchange where they are traded. Stock exchanges without good assurances (or, on the flip side, with onerous regulations) will lose potential investors, so this creates incentives for stock exchanges to make rules that enhance markets. Mahoney (1997) refers to this role of the exchange as the regulator, and Romano (1998) outlines how such competition encourages exchanges to create rules that that investors trust.

Let us begin by giving a sketch of the origins the strictest listing requirements at the New York Stock Exchange and then provide a more detailed view of the more flexible listing requirements at London's AIM. I highlight both, not to show that one is categorically better or that these are the two best in the world, but to show that different exchanges can offer different listing and disclosure requirements depending on investors' wants. A market for governance offers choices, whereas government regulations do not.

6.2. THE CADILLAC OF LISTING AND DISCLOSURE REQUIREMENTS: THE NEW YORK STOCK EXCHANGE, THE BIG BOARD

If the Exchange [the New York Stock Exchange] had been nothing more than a meeting-place for buyers and sellers of securities, and the borrowers and lenders of funds based on securities—a huge automatic dial to register vibrating values, and a legalized centre of speculation—it would even then have been worthy of an important place in the national annals. But though created only for these functions, it has come to discharge another and

more striking one. In doing so it has formed that connection with the country's development which may be reckoned the most value feature in its history.

—Stedman and Easton (1905, p. 18)

The New York Stock Exchange helped finance American industry by letting the
public participate. The New York Stock Exchange created an attractive market
by prescreening and having rules of conduct for brokers and later for listed
firms.

Similar to other stock markets, the New York Stock Exchange (so named
since 1863) evolved over time. The earliest available written agreements between brokers date to 1791, when signatories agreed to fourteen rules about
trade, and 1792 when twenty-four brokers signed the Buttonwood Tree
Agreement, in which they agreed to "solemnly promise and pledge ourselves
to each other."[1] An association of merchants created the New York Tontine
Coffee House Company in 1791–1792, and opened the Tontine Tavern and
Coffee House (see figure 6.1) in 1793 "for the purpose of a Merchants Exchange with 203 subscribers at $200 each" (Werner and Smith, 1991, p. 216).
In 1794 one commentator wrote:

> The Tontine Tavern and Coffee House is a handsome, large brick building; you
> ascend six or eight steps under a portico, into a large public room, which is the
> Stock Exchange of New York, where all bargains are made. Here are two books
> kept, as at Lloyd's, of every ship's arrival and clearing out. This house was built
> for the accommodation of the merchants, by Tontine shares of two hundred
> pounds each. It is kept by Mr. Hyde, formerly a woolen draper in London. You
> can lodge and board there at a common table, and you pay ten shillings currency
> a day, whether you dine out or not. (Quoted in Bayles, 1915, pp. 360–61)

They adopted a "Constitution And Nominations of the Subscribers To The
Tontine Coffee-House" as early as 1796, and by 1817 brokers created a more
formal membership club and trading venue, the New York Stock and Exchange
Board (Tontine Coffee House, 1796; Stedman and Easton, 1905, p. 62). The
1817 "Rules to be adopted and observed by the 'New York Stock and Exchange Board'" were quite simple and included "fines for non-attendance at
the calling of the Stocks" rules specified that "any member refusing to comply
with the foregoing rules may have a hearing before the Board, and if he shall
still persist in refusing, two-thirds of the Board may declare him no longer a
member" (Stedman and Easton, 1905, p. 64). Members added different resolutions over the years, and by the 1860s, in addition to blacklisting those who
did not follow through with their contracts, to make sure everyone was proper

---

1 Banner (1998, pp. 250–51) argues against the somewhat popular belief that these
two agreements cartelized markets.

Figure 6.1
Tontine Coffee House [on left], *Merchant Coffee House* [in center], *and Wall Street* [on right facing East], Francis Guy, 1797

(see figure 6.2) they had rules prohibiting "indecorous language" (suspension for a week), fines for "smoking in the Board-room, or in the ante-rooms" ($5), and fines for "standing on tables or chairs" ($1) (Hamon, 1865 pp. 26–29; New York Stock Exchange, 1869, pp. 31–33). By 1865 the initiation fee was $3,000 and by 1868 one's membership seat became a valuable property right that could be sold to potential members (Hamon, 1865, p. 12; New York Stock Exchange, 2013). The Exchange moved to Wall Street and Broad Street in 1865 (see figure 6.3) and the current building in 1903 (see figure 6.4).

In addition to rules of membership, the Exchange established rules about the securities that could be listed. Letting any "enterprise," including likely fraudulent ones, approach investors had the potential to create a tragedy-of-the-commons situation where the fraudulent ventures crowded out the good. To deal with this problem, the Exchange adopted listing and disclosure requirements to make the market more transparent. By 1865 the New York Stock Exchange had two lists of securities, the regular list and the secondary list, and the first list would be called at the "First Board" in the morning session that members had to attend. To be on the first list, companies had to apply: "Applications for placing of Stocks on the regular list, shall be made directly to the Board, with a full statement of capital, number of shares, resources, &c." (New York Stock Exchange, 1865, pp. 16–17).

Figure 6.2
Downtown Lunchroom, Thure de Thulstrup, 1888

Over time the New York Stock Exchange adopted more explicit listing requirements and required companies to maintain a transfer agency and registrar that are approved by the Exchange (New York Stock Exchange, 1914, Article XXXIII, Sec. 1); to obtain permission from the Committee on Stock before issuing initial or subsequent shares (Article XXXIII, Sec. 2, Sec. 5); and to comply with various rules of the New York Stock Exchange Governing Committee, which had the authority to suspend dealings or remove a company's shares from the Exchange (Article XXXIII, Sec. 4). By the 1920s, the New York Stock Exchange (1925) required various reports and disclosures from companies.

Although listing and disclosure requirements involve costs to listing firms, they can bestow certain benefits to investors, and in turn listing firms. One can think of the New York Stock Exchange as solving a sort of collective action problem between individual investors and firms. A listing firm nominally bears the costs of compliance, but it willingly does so because the rules increase the value of its stock. If investors value transparency through listing or disclosure requirements, the New York Stock Exchange can require them. That means individual investors need not visit a company's offices if they know that a stock exchange and auditors have reviewed the company's books (Macey, 2013). A stock exchange helps provide an off-the-shelf package of rules for corporate governance, and the costs and benefits of that package become internalized within the exchange. The rules do not address

Figure 6.3
The New York Stock Exchange 1882

all problems, but they can address as many as market participants deem appropriate.

We now know that those running the New York Stock Exchange made a lot of good choices, and that by World War I, it surpassed the London Stock Exchange as the most important exchange in the world. But at the time, the success of the New York Stock Exchange was not inevitable. Adopting stricter rules had the potential to attract more market participants or to push them away to less strict competitors. The New York Stock Exchange always had to compete for business and throughout the years faced competition from the Open Board of Brokers (merged with the New York Stock Exchange in 1869

Figure 6.4
The Floor of the New York Stock Exchange, Secretly Shot with a Camera Hidden in the Photographer's Sleeve. Pearson Publishing Company, 1907

[Stedman and Easton, 1905, p. 214]), the Curb Market and its more formal outgrowth, the New York Curb Exchange (founded in 1921 and renamed the American Stock Exchange in 1953), the Consolidated Stock Exchange of New York (founded in the 1880s, it included many mining companies), and regional exchanges including the Boston Exchange and Philadelphia Stock Exchange (founded in 1834 and 1754, respectively, the latter in the London Coffee House). Investors also could have focused on "the Coal and Iron Exchange, the Coffee Exchange, the Cotton Exchange, the Maritime Exchange, the Metal Exchange, the New York Insurance Exchange, and the Leaf Tobacco Board of Trade" (Markham, 2002, p. 6) to name a few.

Today the New York Stock Exchange competes with NASDAQ and many other stock exchanges worldwide. Firms wishing to list in North America can select from the choices summarized by Cormick (2010) in table 6.1, and similar to the New York Stock Exchange, which had a First Board for the main stocks and Second Board for other stocks, many stock exchanges offer different tiers (represented under a, b, c, etc., in rows of table 6.1), and if firms are willing, they can opt for the Cadillac of listing standards at the New York Stock Exchange. An advantage of markets, however, is that not everyone is required to buy a Cadillac, and market participants will only pay to comply with New York Stock Exchange's stricter rules if they consider them value added. If firms or investors find an exchange's listing or disclosure requirements too onerous or not appropriate for a certain type of form, they can opt into venues with different rules. A market for private governance requires exchanges to continually search for rules that market participants value.

Table 6.1. SUMMARY OF THE LISTING REQUIREMENTS AT MAJOR NORTH AMERICAN VENUES

Requirements	New York Stock Exchange	NASDAQ Global Market	Toronto Stock Exchange	TSX Venture Exchange	Canadian National Stock Exchange	U.S. Over-the-Counter Bulletin Board
Pretax income last year	$2,000,000 (minimum multitiered formula)	a. $1,000,000 b. N/A c. N/A d. N/A	a. C$300,000 b. C$200,000 c. C$200,000	Tier 1: $5,000,000 in NTA; or $5,000,000 in revenue	N/A	N/A
Two-year average pretax income	$2,000,000 (minimum multitiered formula)	a. $1,000,000 (2 out of 3 years) b. N/A c. N/A d. $75,000,000 (2 out of 3 years)	a. C$500,000	Tier 2: $750,000 in NTA; or $500,000 in revenue or $2,000,000 in arm's-length financing	N/A	N/A
Net tangible assets	N/A	a. N/A b. N/A c. N/A d. $75,000,000 and $75,000,000 total revenue	a. C$7,500,000 b. C$2,000,000 c. C$7,500,000 d. N/A e. N/A	See above	N/A	N/A
Market value publicly held stock	$100,000,000 or $40,000,000 (if IPO)	a. $8,000,000 b. $18,000,000 c. $20,000,000 d. $20,000,000	C$4,000,000 (ind.) C$10,000,000 (tech)	Tier 1: $150,000 Tier 2: $75,000	$50,000	N/A

(continued)

Table 6.1. *(continued)*

Requirements	New York Stock Exchange	NASDAQ Global Market	Toronto Stock Exchange	TSX Venture Exchange	Canadian National Stock Exchange	U.S. Over-the-Counter Bulletin Board
# of shares publicly held	1,100,000	1,100,000	1,000,000	Tier 1: 1,000,000 or 20% of Float Tier 2: 500,000 or 20% of Float	500,000 10% of Float	25,000
# Public board lot holders	a. 400 (U.S.) b. 2,200 (if monthly trading vol. of 100,000 shares recent 6 months) c. 500 (if monthly trading vol. 1,000,000 shares recent 12 months)	400	300	Tier 1: 200 Tier 2: 250	150	40
Trading price of listed securities	No minimum	$4.00	No minimum	No minimum (IPO minimum of $0.15 per share)	No minimum	No minimum
Shareholder equity	No minimum	a. $15,000,000 b.$30,000,000 c. N/A d. N/A	No minimum	No minimum	No minimum	No minimum

Source: Reproduced by permission from Cormick (2010).

6.3. MORE FLEXIBLE LISTING AND DISCLOSURE REQUIREMENTS: THE ALTERNATIVE INVESTMENT MARKET IN LONDON

At the other end of the spectrum from the New York Stock Exchange's formal listing requirements are the flexible listing requirements of the Alternative Investment Market (AIM) in London.[2] Founded by the London Stock Exchange in 1995, AIM sets the basic rules and regulations for the exchange, but then approves nominated advisors, or *Nomads*, to oversee individual firms and decide whether firms can list shares. AIM must comply with certain government rules (e.g., as required by the Financial Services and Markets Acts of 2000, the government reviews the prospectus for each company, and firms associated with the market can still be sued by government), but because AIM is classified as an exchange-regulated market, many European Union directives and the United Kingdom's Combined Code on Corporate Governance do not apply (Mendoza, 2008). These Nomads are basically paid (directly by the firm but indirectly by the investors) to ensure that a firm is legitimate before giving it a stamp of approval to go public. If a firm is not legitimate, this damages the reputation of AIM and the Nomad that endorsed the firm.

Nomads are typically investment banks or other financial services firms with experience in helping other firms go public (Financial Times, 2006). The London Stock Exchange sets the rules and must approve companies as Nomads. Such companies must (1) "have practiced corporate finance for at least the last two years," (2) "have acted on at least three relevant transactions during that two-year period," and (3) "employ at least four 'qualified executives'" (London Stock Exchange, 2012a). Nomads must be members of a "firm of experienced corporate finance professionals approved by the Exchange" (London Stock Exchange, 2010b) which prevents fly-by-night organizations or "anything goes" firms from becoming regulators. As a residual claimant on the success of the market, the Exchange does not want to approve private regulators who will undermine the reliability of AIM. At the same time, the Exchange has an incentive to approve any private regulator who is likely to enhance the value of the market.

6.3.1. The Listing Process at AIM

The exchange is open to small firms but does not let just any firm list. To prevent fraudulent firms from getting in, Nomads are hired basically as private gatekeepers to decide whether companies desiring to list are "appropriate for

---

2. Sections 6.3 and 6.4 of the chapter draw from Stringham and Chen (2012).

the market." The Nomad also monitors companies to ensure that exchange-regulated corporate governance standards are met (London Stock Exchange, 2010b). Beyond that, AIM has "no minimum market capitalization, no trading record requirement, no prescribed level of shares to be in public hands, no prior shareholder approval for most transactions, admission documents not pre-vetted by the Exchange nor by the UKLA [United Kingdom Listing Authority] in most circumstances" (London Stock Exchange, 2010, p. 6).

The initial public offering (IPO) process is quite streamlined, and a typical IPO takes from three to six months (London Stock Exchange, 2010, p. 23). Companies already traded on other approved exchanges are eligible for a fast-track option for joining AIM, which takes five to eight weeks (Withers, 2011). For a typical IPO, the Nomad submits an admission document (see table 6.2), which provides disclosure and other information potentially relevant to investors. The privately produced disclosure requirements include "Operating and Financial Review, Capital Resources, Research and Development, Patents and Licenses, Profit Forecasts or Estimates, and Remuneration and Benefits" (London Stock Exchange, 2010b). The Nomad also prepares a legal due diligence report, a working capital report, historical financial information, pro forma financial information, and a report on financial reporting procedures (Hanson Westhouse, 2012). Each of these documents must be available for potential investors for various periods of time, such as ten to fourteen days, before a firm can be admitted (London Stock Exchange, 2010, p. 25). If there are any changes in a firm's "financial or trading position between the balance sheet date of its latest published financial information and the date of the admission document" that could affect the price of the security, the AIM Rules for Companies require the firm to disclose this information in the admission document (London Stock Exchange, 2010, p. 36). In addition to helping coordinate the initial due diligence process for an IPO, a firm's Nomad also provides ongoing consultation, advice, and review (London Stock Exchange, 2012b).

On the front of the admission document firms are required to print: "AIM securities are not admitted to the official list of the United Kingdom Listing Authority" and "The London Stock Exchange has not itself examined or approved the contents of this document" (London Stock Exchange, 2010b, p. 17). Following the guidelines recommended by a 1992 Cadbury Committee report from the London Stock Exchange and the UK Financial Reporting Council (Seidl, Sanderson, and Roberts, 2012), AIM gives firms a comply-or-explain option for rules. This rule allows companies to comply with any rule given by the market regulators or to explain why they should not follow this rule. If certain rules are inapplicable or inappropriate for a certain firm, this provides a way for the firm to skip them. AIM companies (London Stock Exchange, 2010, p. 67) are encouraged, but not required, to follow the UK Corporate Governance Code.

Table 6.3 summarizes the costs of going public as well as continuing listing costs for a firm selling $50 million in shares on AIM versus NASDAQ. Not only

Table 6.2. CONTENTS OF AN AIM ADMISSION DOCUMENT

The very front	• Cover page, including certain "health warnings" and important information for non-UK investors
	• Summarized key information in relation to the company
	• Index
	• List of directors and advisers
	• List of definitions and glossary of technical terms
	• Timetable
	• Placing statistics
The front end: detailed description of the business and the investment proposition	• History of the business
	• Information about the present-day business, current trading, and investments
	• Key business and market trends and prospects; in the case of an investment company, details of its investment strategy
	• Summarized information about directors and key personnel
	• Intellectual property
	• information about the placing or offer for subscription
	• Use of funds
	• Corporate governance policies
	• Share option arrangements and dividend policy
	• City Code information (if applicable)
Risk factors	• Risk factors relevant to the business
Historical financial information	• Historical financial information relating to the company and its subsidiaries—usually audited accounts for the last three years, or a shorter period of time if the company has been in existence for less than three years. If more than nine months have elapsed since the company's financial year end, interim financial information also must be included, which may or may not be audited.
	• An auditor's or reporting accountant's opinion as to whether the financial information shows a true and fair view for the purposes of the AIM admission document
	• If appropriate, pro forma financial information
Other reports	• Experts' reports; these are necessary for mining and oil and gas companies, and they may be desirable for a company with a specialist business (e.g., technology, life sciences, intellectual property).
Statutory and general information: the back end	• A responsibility statement confirming that each of the directors and proposed directors accepts general information: responsibility, individually and collectively, for the information contained in the document, and that to the best of their knowledge and belief (having taken all reasonable care to ensure that such is the case) the information contained in the admission document is in accordance with the facts and does not omit anything likely to affect the import of such information

(continued)

Table 6.2. (*continued*)

Statutory and general information: the back end	• Details of the incorporation and legal status of the company, its registered office, and its objects
	• Information about share capital, including rights attaching to the shares and authorities to issue
	• Further shares
	• Information about the company's articles of association and constitution documents
	• Directors' interest in the company, directorships of other companies, and involvement in previous personal or company insolvencies
	• The name of any person who, so far as the directors are aware, holds an interest of 3 percent or more in the company's issued share capital and the level of that interest
	• Share option plans
	• Material contracts, including the placing or introduction agreement
	• Related party transactions
	• Terms of engagement of the directors and senior personnel summarized tax position
	• Statement by the company's directors that, in their opinion, having made due and careful enquiry, the working capital available to the company and its group will be sufficient for its present requirements, i.e., for at least 12 months from the date of admission of its securities to AIM
	• Material litigation
	• Any "lock-in" statement required by the AIM Rules or the Nomad
	• Level of dilution resulting from any offer
	• Expenses of the issue
	• Terms and conditions of any offer for the sale of shares
	• Sundry information

Source: London Stock Exchange, 2010, p. 40.

are the initial costs of going public on AIM $1 million less, but firms will save upward of $2 million annually going forward because they avoid regulations such as those associated with the Sarbanes-Oxley Act (SOX). The majority of foreign companies listed on AIM (104 of 157) chose to list on AIM between 2004 and 2005 (Rousseau, 2007, p. 54), which coincides with the period when the onerousness of the Sarbanes-Oxley regulations, passed in 2002, became evident. In the words of one broker, "You guys should erect a statue to SOX outside the LSE" (quoted in Grunfeld, 2006).

Table 6.3. THE COST OF LISTING ON AIM VERSUS NASDAQ

Direct listing costs

AIM IPO		NASDAQ IPO	
Nomad/broker fee	2,000,000	Underwriting fee	3,500,000
Corporate finance fee	500,000	Legal fees	500,000
Company counsel	262,000	Miscellaneous expenses	145,000
Nomad counsel	300,000	Printing fees	75,000
Accounting fees	312,000	Accounting fees	65,000
AIM fee	7,300	NASDAQ listing fee	100,000
Registrar fee	45,000	SEC and NASD registration fees	107,000
Total	$3,426,300	Total	$4,492,000

Indirect ongoing costs

AIM		NASDAQ	
Nomad fee	90,000	SOX compliance	3,500,000
AIM annual fee	7,300	NASDAQ annual fee	17,500
Accountants	50,000		
Total	$147,300	Total	$3,517,500

Source: Reproduced by permission from Mendoza (2008).

As the saying goes, the proof of the pudding is in the eating, and by this account the London Stock Exchange and its AIM have been quite successful. Figure 6.5 presents the total number of IPOs at AIM, NASDAQ, and the New York Stock Exchange. The dollar value of those in the NYSE and NASDAQ far surpasses that of AIM, but the AIM enabled IPOs for more firms.

The market attracts firms not just from the UK but from many countries. As the vice president of one Canadian brokerage firm, Mark Maybank, stated:

Everywhere we go in the U.S. or Canada to meetings with potential clients, investors or venture capital companies, the only thing that people want to talk to us about is AIM. We're coming into deals that five years ago would have been part of a drip-feed onto NASDAQ. Now that's flipped completely. (Quoted in Dey, 2006)

And in the words of another financial commentator, "AIM is flourishing and companies from around the world are coming to London exactly because the dead weight of regulation is so much greater in their own markets" (Financial Times, 2006).

With the economic downturn starting in 2008, all markets, including AIM, saw a decrease in the number of IPOs and downward movement in the market capitalization of listed firms. But as of 2012, the London Stock Exchange

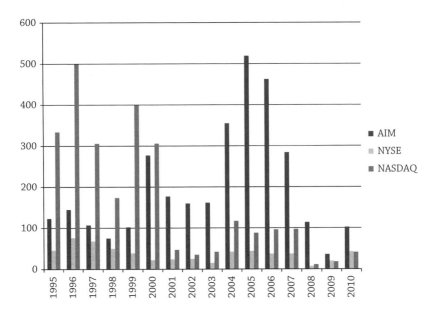

Figure 6.5
IPOs on the London Stock Exchange AIM Market, NASDAQ, and New York Stock Exchange
Source: Data are from AIM Market Statistics, 2012, and Ritter, 2011.

and AIM are experiencing recoveries similar to those of competing markets. Figure 6.6 shows the number of companies on AIM as increasing from 10 companies in 1995 to 1,122 companies in 2012. The number of total firms has decreased from its peak in 2007 (with some of the firms going bankrupt, some being acquired by other firms, some going private, and some moving to other exchanges, such as the London Stock Exchange's main market); as a result, the total market capitalization on AIM is down 27 percent from its peak in 2008 (figure 6.6).

6.3.2. The Process for Dealing with Fraud at AIM and Why Flexible Regulation Does Not Lead to a Race to the Bottom

How well do flexible private regulations work? AIM clearly has attracted many new firms, and as measured by the number of deals and amount of money raised, AIM appears to be a clear success. But what about the longevity of these firms and cases of fraud? There are two potential sources of failure, namely, honest but unintentional firm failure, and deliberate fraud. The result for both is shareholders losing money. Securities fraud occurs when investors are given false information that induces the buying and selling of securities. Oftentimes people debate about whether a firm going into bankruptcy

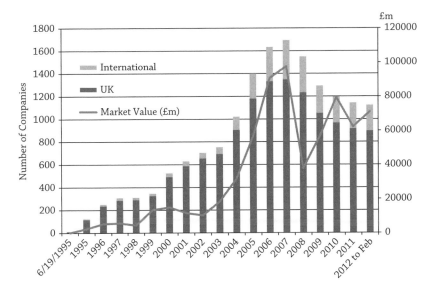

Figure 6.6
Number of Companies and Market Value of Firms Listed on AIM
Source: Data are from AIM Market Statistics, February 2012.

deliberately committed bad choices or just made poor but well-intended business decisions. Without knowing what managers were thinking, sometimes we cannot easily disentangle the two, but the two summed together can be measured by looking at firms' survival rates.

In AIM's case the firms going public get to select the firms that regulate them. Advocates of centralized government regulation argue that allowing competition among regulators can allow firms to shop for regulators that allow them to bend or ignore good rules (Coffee, 1995). London's *Sunday Business* (2007) reports, "Critics claim that AIM, with 1,634 constituents with a combined market value of £90.66bn to the end of 2006 and including 306 non-British firms, is a dustbin for poorly-run businesses." In 2007, former SEC commissioner Roel Campos accused AIM of creating a market like a casino (Treanor, 2007). The number of firms listed on AIM went from a peak of 1,694 in 2007 to 1,091 in 2015 (London Stock Exchange, 2015).

Espenlaub, Khurshed, and Mohamed (2012) conducted a study of the IPO survival rate of firms going public on AIM (the survival rate looks at the percentage of firms that fail various numbers of years after going public) and found it to be very much in line with the survival rate of firms going public on more regulated exchanges. From a comparative point of view, even though firms traded on AIM have had their successes and failures, they do not appear to be significantly different from firms traded elsewhere as a result of fewer government regulations. Khurshed, Paleari, and Vismara (2005) note that

AIM firms utilize IPOs mainly to finance growth and have a high level of equity retention. Critics of AIM companies may highlight the illiquidity of AIM shares relative to larger exchanges. However, average AIM firms have greater liquidity than they would otherwise have on other exchanges (Litvintsev, 2009, p. 26).

Is AIM a good place for firms to raise capital, but also a place where investors are more likely to be swindled? It must be recognized at the outset that no stock market, however regulated, can ever be 100 percent free of listed firms going broke (nor should it be—that is how markets work). The whole point of stock markets is that they allow investors to become partial owners in firms, creating the potential for both higher risks and higher returns. Putting the issue of fraud aside completely, markets for small-cap firms can be especially risky. Nevertheless, although many firms have indeed been delisted from AIM (Matthews, 2010), many were simply purchased (Dawber, 2010), which in no way is an indication of failure. Figure 6.7 plots the performance of the FTSE AIM All-Share Index (an index created by the *Financial Times* and the London Stock Exchange for all equities listed on AIM) versus the Dow Jones Industrial Average. One contains very small firms and the other contains established blue chips, but both have had their ups and downs over the past ten years; the AIM All-Share Index possesses higher variance but not substantially worse or

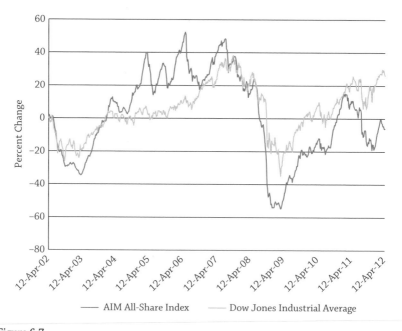

Figure 6.7
Performance of All Firms Listed on AIM Compared with the Dow Jones Industrial Average
Source: Data are from Google Finance Historical Prices, 2012.

better performance overall. Even though many small-cap firms traded on the more privately regulated AIM have faced tough times in recent years, so have firms on more regulated markets. Yet AIM has enabled many smaller firms to raise money and has provided more investment outlets to investors.

Why have failure and fraud not run rampant, as the "race to the bottom" theorists would have predicted? Even though Nomads are hired by the firms that they regulate, both the London Stock Exchange *and* investors must approve these regulators. The London Stock Exchange is the first gatekeeper, as it can expel a Nomad for improperly fulfilling its role. The second gatekeepers are the investors, many of whom are institutional and have repeated experience with the Nomads. If a Nomad establishes a reputation among listing firms for laxity in its regulatory duties (the race to the bottom), that reputation can be easily transmitted to investors. Although investors may find it difficult to fully investigate each of the thousand-plus firms listing shares, they can more easily see if a Nomad is consistently peddling fraudulent firms. As Mendoza (2008, p. 318) states, "Nomads build their reputational capital by servicing clients over prolonged periods of time, and ultimately pledge this highly valuable asset to vouch for the suitability of AIM companies and the accuracy of their disclosures to the market." Nomads include widely recognized firms such as Deloitte and Touche, PricewaterhouseCoopers, JP Morgan, Morgan Stanley, and HSBC Bank. Each of these firms has significant reputational capital that it does not want to risk.[3] Furthermore, to continually improve its regulations, the Exchange has formed the AIM Advisory Group to provide input from Nomads, brokers, advisors, and market participants (London Stock Exchange, 2012a). In this way, AIM can continually receive feedback from its community to encourage and develop its operational efficiency and regulations.

The amount of fraud will never be zero, but AIM has effectively kept its level quite low. In order to completely eliminate fraud, there would have to be no transactions. Since the founding of the Exchange in 1995, AIM has experienced four major instances of alleged fraud. The first involved Langbar International, which in 2005 had its shares suspended from trading and was put under investigation by the Serious Fraud Office for allegedly defrauding investors of £570 million (Mason, 2011). Appropriately, this led to negative repercussions against Langbar International's Nomad, Nabarro Wells. In October of 2007, AIM fined Nabarro Wells £250,000 because it "failed to undertake the necessary level of due diligence to assess the appropriateness of certain companies for admission to AIM" (Kennedy, 2007). Following the incident, Nabarro Wells recorded a loss of £300,000, as compared with the previous year's profit of £183,000, and in April 2008 Ambrian Capital acquired Nabarro Wells for less than £1 million (Evening Standard, 2008).

---

3. For a discussion on the role of reputation, see Shearmur and Klein (1997).

The second largest fine issued by AIM was in 2009 on a Nomad named Blue Oar Securities. In that case, an air conditioning company, Worthington Nicholls, had floated shares at 50p in 2006 and saw them rise to 194p in 2007. But by 2008 financial shortfalls emerged and Worthington Nicholls shares fell to 10p. AIM conducted an investigation and found that Worthington Nicholls had "made announcements to the market which were misleading and/or omitted material information" between 2006 and 2007. AIM publicly censured and fined the Nomad Blue Oar for £225,000. Disgraced, Blue Oar ended up changing its name to Astaire Group and divesting its main division, Astaire Securities, for £2.45 million in 2010 (Bates, 2010. One article in the *Telegraph* concluded, "After all, few things like a good public flogging serve to remind brokerage houses to show a little caution in who they bring to market in the first place—and the importance of never, ever misleading investors" (Taylor, 2009). Another commentator stated, "People will admire them [AIM] for taking a tough line" (quoted in Taylor, 2009), which makes sense because AIM does not want to see the value of its market tarnished.

Although critics could argue these examples of fraud show a failure of the system, it must be recognized that no system, including the extremely regulated markets, has prevented 100 percent of fraud. If anything, the fact that only four known major instances of fraud have occurred among the more than 3,200 firms that have traded in the history of AIM indicates that AIM has been extremely successful in keeping fraud to a minimum. John Pierce, CEO of the Quoted Companies Alliance, notes that for every fraudulent company "there are hundreds of AIM success stories with upstanding management teams working earnestly in the interests of shareholders" (quoted in Taylor, 2009). The ratio is 1 to 800, to be precise. The cases of fraud are quite contained and have not cascaded as the "Regulatory competition leads to a race to the bottom" theorists would have predicted.

6.4. CONCLUSION

When rules listing and disclosure requirement are valuable to investors, providers of private governance have incentives to provide them. Brokers from nineteenth-century New York and twentieth-century London realized they could make their market more attractive by screening firms, creating listing requirements, and requiring disclosure for investors. The requirements were not decided by government, but by the market participants themselves, win or lose, based on the attractiveness of their venue. Those that failed to adopt good rules or that adopted burdensome rules were at a competitive disadvantage, and those that adopted good ones succeeded. Rather than taking part in "a race to the bottom" in which anything goes, the New York Stock Exchange worked to make its market attractive and only put its stamp of approval on firms that warranted trading. One of the main reasons for the success of the New York Stock Exchange and the more recent success of AIM is their effective systems of private regulation. Each offers a different set of private rules and regulations and caters to different market segments.

Where private regulators must always cater to investor wants, government regulators receive no market feedback about the desirability of their rules. I think Stigler (1975, p. 87) is right when he states, "Grave doubts exist whether if account is taken of cost of regulation, the SEC has saved the purchasers of new issues one dollar," but let us assume, contrary to what I believe, that some rules and regulations from the Securities and Exchange Commission, the Sarbanes-Oxley Act, or other government mandates are indeed value enhancing. If they were indeed so value enhancing, then why not let market participants voluntarily adopt them? One exchange could say, "Our companies and member firms are in full compliance with the Securities and Exchange Commission and all other government rules," while another could opt out, just as accredited investors are currently allowed to opt out. If the government rules were so great, then investors would flock to markets regulated by them, and no mandates would be necessary. The fact that mandates are required, however, is prima facie evidence that the rules are not value enhancing and would not pass a market test.

Providers of private governance have done an extraordinarily good job at putting a stamp of approval on legitimate firms and not putting a stamp of approval on bad ones. If investors, the customers of private governance, want to do business in the safest settings, they can do business with firms at New York Stock Exchange, or if investors want to opt out of those rules and trade elsewhere, they can. With private governance, the customer is king, and the servants are providers of private governance. Providers of private governance must remain faithful servants and have entirely different sets of knowledge and incentives than government bureaucrats. The more that providers of private governance make their markets transparent and prevent customers from being defrauded, the more that providers and customers of private governance gain.

CHAPTER 7

⌒⋎⌒

How Technologically Advanced Markets Can Work Even When Fraud Is "Legal"

Ex Ante Risk Management by PayPal and Other Intermediaries

7.1. INTRODUCTION

Private governance underpins high-valued stock transactions, and it underpins everyday consumer transactions as well. In October 1999 a Silicon Valley start-up began enabling electronic payments involving anyone with an email address. No expensive merchant terminal or revealing personal financial information was required. The service that became PayPal had 1,000 users by November, 10,000 by December, 100,000 by February, and 1 million by April (Thiel, 2004). Growth was good, but PayPal had not predicted the degree and sophistication of fraud. Annual revenues for 2001 and 2002 were $14 million and $48 million, respectively (Prashanth, 2004, p. 5), but by early 2001 fraud was costing PayPal more than $10 million *per month* (Levchin, 2008, p. 6). The schemes against PayPal were many. Some fraudsters specialized in stealing and selling passwords, and others specialized in exploiting them. In one common scheme, fraudsters sent themselves small sums from multiple accounts, and at the end of the day they withdrew the money outside of PayPal. By the time PayPal and the users noticed, the fraudster was long gone. What to do?

Electronic commerce is not fundamentally different from more traditional forms of trade, but it poses certain challenges. It vastly expands the size of markets but also exposes people to millions of potential fraudsters around the world. One often has little idea who one is dealing with and whether they are who they say they are. Theorists such as Douglass North argue that exchange without government is possible only in small and simple settings. North (1990, p. 12) states that "realizing the economic potential of the gains from trade in a high technology world of enormous specialization and division of labor characterized by impersonal exchange is extremely rare, because one does not necessarily have repeated dealings, nor know the other party, nor deal with a small number of other people." He writes, "The returns on opportunism, cheating, and shirking rise in complex societies. A coercive third party is essential" (p. 35)

North and others are correct that fraud is potentially profitable and that the traditional discipline of repeated dealings offers little constraint in certain contexts. The only problem with North's theory is that those exact conditions (large groups, technological sophistication, degrees of anonymity, and interaction across political boundaries) also make government enforcement more difficult or impossible. As transactions become anonymous, not only are private parties unaware who is swindling them but so too is government. And even if a government can track down a fraudster, it may have limited ability to recover assets. Suing a fraudster from Nigeria is not easy. To the swindled, government solutions are often too little, too late. Government can have as many rules against fraud as it wants, but as its ability to enforce them decreases, the situation is not much different from fraud being legal.

Rather than observing a problem and doing nothing about it, PayPal realized its fate was on the line and that it had to take action. PayPal developed a sophisticated fraud system that used human and artificial intelligence to help prevent fraud before it occurred. This system constantly monitored account activity and flagged transactions that were likely to be fraudulent.

American Express, MasterCard, Visa, and others associated with the payment card industry also face the conditions described by North. A merchant can fulfill an order only to find out that it was placed on a stolen credit card, or a cardholder might order from a fraudster who has no intention of filling the order, and government's ability to rectify the situation ex post is often close to zero. Rather than setting up a system that depends on government enforcement ex post, intermediaries offer to assume and manage many of the risks of fraud. Financial intermediaries treat risk management like any other economic good, and the better they are at preventing problems ex ante, the less relevant government's inability to deal with problems becomes.

7.2. IT'S NOT SUCH A SIMPLE OR SMALL WORLD AFTER ALL: WHEN LAWS AGAINST FRAUD ARE IRRELEVANT

Fraud hit the new online payment processors hard and led to the downfall of PayPal's competitors eMoneyMail, PayMe, and PayPlace (Jackson, 2004, p. 202). PayPal's founder and CEO, Peter Thiel, started out fairly skeptical of government, so one might expect him to recognize the ineffectiveness of government enforcement initially. But as he relayed to me, "I did not appreciate the whole enforcement of fraud problem until after I was at PayPal. The problem is not solvable in any standard government context."[1] Using traditional methods of ex post enforcement, if one is defrauded, one simply contacts the police, who track down the fraudsters, bring them to court, and order them to repay what they have stolen. Yet doing so is easier said than done. The Internet (and international trade in general) brings people from all over the globe into a single commercial community, but it does not bring everyone under the control of a particular government.

In a more technologically advanced world characterized by impersonal, often anonymous, interaction, problems of government enforcement are often particularly pronounced. At the height of PayPal's initial ascent, U.S. Attorney General Janet Reno (2000) recognized that government enforcement against cybercrime was ineffective. She stated that for government to be able to stop online fraud, it must have the following technological and legal capabilities: (1) "a round-the-clock network of federal, state, and local law enforcement officials with expertise in, and responsibility for, investigating and prosecuting cybercrime"; (2) "computer forensic capabilities, which are so essential in computer crime investigations"; (3) "adequate legal tools to locate, identify, and prosecute cybercriminals, and procedural tools to allow state authorities to more easily gather evidence located outside their jurisdictions"; and (4) "effective partnerships with other nations to encourage them to enact laws that adequately address cybercrime and to provide assistance in cybercrime investigations."[2] If government is deficient in any of these ways, it can lack the ability to effectively enforce laws against fraud.

The overarching spying state has expanded in recent times, but it has not always been so extensive, especially in the early days of Internet commerce. I presented Reno's list to Thiel, and he responded, "Every single one taken by itself seems extremely farfetched. If that's the threshold, it's no wonder it doesn't work." The government officials were hardly experts. He stated, "The level of incompetence we dealt with was amazing." At the time he stated that the FBI did not "even have a working email system." In one case PayPal conducted an internal investigation and determined that a man named

---

1. Personal interview, Palo Alto, October 12, 2004. Unless otherwise noted, quotations from Thiel are from this main interview, although I have had the opportunity to talk with Thiel multiple times.

2. Kubic (2001) of the Federal Bureau of Investigation comes up with a very similar list: "The Internet presents new and significant investigatory challenges for law enforcement at all levels. . . . These challenges include: the need to track down sophisticated users who commit unlawful acts on the internet while hiding their identities; the need for close coordination among law enforcement agencies; and the need for trained and well-equipped personnel to gather evidence, investigate, and prosecute these cases."

Mr. Yagolnitser was defrauding the company of money. After reporting the culprit to the authorities, law enforcement was of little help. Thiel stated:

> The positive place where [government] failed was in providing security. The natural thinking was that when people are defrauding you, you can go to the police. Maybe Mr. Yagolnitser is not going to go to the police, but maybe we can go to the police and report Mr. Yagolnitser. We proceeded to do that. The FBI showed up at his home and concluded he was totally innocent. We'd given them web pages. They were asking us, "What's a banner ad?"

The assumption that technologically advanced markets depend on government seems wildly unrealistic. Another employee of a Silicon Valley security firm told me, "In my view, government is ten years behind what's going on" (personal interview, San Jose, June 30, 2004).

In addition to government being unable to identify who was doing what, they lacked the ability to enforce laws around the globe. Thiel said, "Anything that was outside the U.S. was just hopeless." Thiel also recounted, "There was a jurisdictional dispute between the FBI offices in San Jose and San Francisco over which of them had jurisdiction over Kazakhstan, and which could handle it. So there were some very serious sorts of problems." When interaction takes place across political boundaries, then government often lacks the ability to enforce the rules (President's Working Group on Unlawful Conduct on the Internet, 2000, p. 40).

In theory, each of Reno's four conditions could be met. Governments could be at the forefront of computer technology and have enough resources and ability to track down all cybercriminals. They might be able to identify fraudsters in other countries and work with authorities around the world to prosecute them. But when PayPal was emerging, none of these conditions was close to being met. Since it was passed in 1984, the Computer Fraud and Abuse Act (18 U.S.C. § 1030) has been criticized as "overly vague and too narrow in scope" (Skibell, 2003) and "largely symbolic" (Wible, 2003). Let us consider the limitations of government enforcement from the horse's mouth. Bruce Townsend of the U.S. Secret Service stated, "Law enforcement does not have the financial or technological resources to cope with all these cases" (Swartz, 2004). Government has lacked the ability to track fraudsters down and deal with fraud emanating from around the globe. The President's Working Group (2000) recognizes that "when one country's laws criminalize high-tech and computer-related crime and another country's laws do not, cooperation to solve a crime, as well as the possibility of extraditing the criminal to stand trial, may not be possible." The group adds:

> The solution to the problems stemming from inadequate laws is simple to state, but not as easy to implement: countries need to reach a consensus as to

which computer and technology-related activities should be criminalized, and then commit to taking appropriate domestic actions. Unfortunately, a true international "consensus" concerning the activities that universally should be criminalized is likely to take time to develop. Even after a consensus is reached, individual countries that lack appropriate legislation will each have to pass new laws, an often time-consuming and iterative process.

Former assistant attorney general Michael Chertoff (2001) states, "When we deal with a transborder cybercrime, we need foreign law enforcement counterparts who not only have the necessary technical expertise, but who are accessible and responsive, and who have the necessary legal authority to cooperate with us and assist us in our investigations and prosecutions." "Technical expertise," "accessible," and "responsive" are not words that usually come to mind when thinking of governments around the world.[3] I have documented in more depth the limitations of government enforcement during the time of PayPal's initial ascent (Stringham, 2005b), and many of these conditions that limit the ability of government still exist today.

Thus, conditions that theorists such as North assert make private enforcement "impossible" can also make government enforcement impossible. Thiel stated, "The government approach assumes that you can solve everything after. It might have worked in a small town setting, where everyone knows everyone else, but it clearly does not work in the current world." These problems are pronounced with electronic commerce, but they can be present even with what appear to be the simplest face-to-face transactions. When I lived in San Francisco, my friend's sister decided to buy two laptop computers from a street person who showed her the box with a computer cord coming out of it. She gave him $40, and when she got home she saw that her two laptops were actually two phone books! If a city is big enough, calling the cops and getting an unknown street person arraigned to recover $40 is not that feasible. The lesson was not "Rely on more effective government enforcement mechanisms next time," but instead "Be more careful and practice better due diligence next time."

In settings with high degrees of anonymity, advanced technology, and interaction across political boundaries, private parties must look elsewhere than government. As Thiel stated, "On the positive side, if we had not come up with a technology solution to fraud, we would have simply gone out of business. [Government] might have arrested various low-level people, but we would never have gotten the money back." Most of PayPal's solutions are behind the scenes, so they are often unappreciated by users or social scientists.

At the end of the day, users just need to know they are safe transacting over a network, in much the same way that car owners need not know everything

---

3. When in Prague in 2001, I observed some police officers coming to write a report; they were carrying state-of-the-art mechanical typewriters. Such technology surely enables them to combat cybercrime in a way that Douglass North would imagine.

that went into building the engine. To ensure the customer that their car worked, PayPal assumed many of the risks of fraud.[4] By becoming the residual claimant for fraud reduction efforts, it gained incentives to minimize problems, just as carmakers offering warranties have incentives to make cars more reliable.

PayPal started with many innovations that have now become commonplace. Cofounder Max Levchin helped create the Gausebeck-Levchin test, one of the first commercial implementations of Captcha, in which users are asked to retype distorted text that programs have difficulty recognizing. PayPal also took other measures to verify legitimacy of each account, such as depositing a few cents into customers' checking accounts and asking them to verify those amounts, but with each new safeguard came new types of fraudulent schemes. Consider just one example that Peter Thiel described, a would-be-fraudster taking payments to ship a video game console that was going to be released in two months. The promise "We will send you the XBox videogame console by Christmas" allowed the fraudster to collect the money now and have weeks to plan his getaway. The fraudster had already taken in $800,000 from customers and was in the process of transferring $100,000 to a bank outside PayPal when the company noticed something going wrong. PayPal's interest was different from the intellectual puzzle in a detective novel because the company knew it would be on the hook for money lost. Thiel summarized the issue: "There are two ways of dealing with fraud: Predictive versus backward looking." *Business Week* described PayPal's work as that of a "'pre-crime' detective" (Black, 2002). In the case of the bogus Xbox shipments, PayPal noticed the fraudulent scheme as it was happening and was able to freeze the fraudster's account before much money was lost.

PayPal had expanded its private security team to two dozen employees when the team noticed that they could only effectively monitor a fraction of the transactions. As a solution, Levchin led the development of a fraud-monitoring and prevention system that could spot potentially fraudulent transactions and alert the team to suspicious patterns of behavior (Levchin, 2008, p. 11). Levchin stated, "We mine millions and millions of transactions in real time" (quoted in Schwartz, 2001). PayPal's system looked for patterns, such as many accounts suddenly transferring small sums into one account,

---

4. Although certain laws, such as the Electronic Fund Transfer Act, officially regulate how PayPal deals with victims of fraud, even if the laws did not exist I see little reason why exposing consumers to fraud would have been a profitable business model. Many of the regulations apply only to individuals and not merchants, but PayPal offers fraud protection to all parties. Similarly, the payment card industry has limits on holding individual cardholders liable for fraudulent charges, but even though regulations do not apply to business accounts, merchants are offered many assurances. Merchants also can purchase insurance against chargebacks, indicating that paying others to assume risks is a market phenomenon rather than a product of regulations.

sudden increases in account activity, high-dollar payments, or payments to certain regions of the world (Schwartz, 2001). The company looked at past behavior, but the system was also programmed to learn and to look for new types of fraud over time. If the transactions were likely fraudulent, PayPal would not process them or freeze an account. If the transactions were indeed legitimate, customers could take additional steps to confirm they were making the transaction.

Early on, management recognized that the success of PayPal hinged on how well they assessed and managed risk of fraud. Levchin said:

> I think a good way to describe PayPal is: a security company pretending to be a financial services company. What PayPal does is judge the risk of a transaction and occasional actually take the risk on. You don't really know the money's good; you just sort of assess the riskiness of both parties. (Levchin, 2008, p. 10)

The key was to assess risk and weigh Type I and Type II errors (i.e., assessing a problem as a nonproblem versus assessing a nonproblem as a problem). Losing money because of a fraudulent order is not a good thing, but neither is turning down all orders with a miniscule probability of fraud. PayPal had an incentive to deal with risks in a reasonable way, in contrast to government officials who lack feedback about whether they are being too lax or too zealous.

By reformulating the question, from "How can we rely on government after a problem occurs?" to "What can we do to make sure that problems do not occur?" PayPal eliminated the "need" to rely on government enforcement. To Thiel the reasoning was clear: "There is nothing unique to government about being able to predict things. . . . There is no reason to believe that government is better at predicting than the private sector. . . . In fact government is so bad at it."

PayPal solved an important problem, and it was rewarded. Before PayPal began in late 1999, more than 90 percent of eBay auctions were paid using checks (Schwartz, 2001). Only half a year later, more than 1 million daily auctions on eBay were advertising PayPal as a method of payment. Purchased by eBay for $1.5 billion in 2002, PayPal now has 109.8 million accounts and processes more than $118 billion in transactions per year (Sengupta, 2012). The company's fraud loss rate is an industry-leading 0.5 percent (PayPal, 2012).

PayPal's innovations were matched with innovation from its more traditional competitors. Firms associated with the payment card industry, such as American Express, MasterCard, and Visa, also have taken many steps to reduce the problem of fraud. For example, the payment processor and risk management firm CyberSource was originally a software reseller that realized that "online customers were reluctant to purchase unless their buying experience felt completely secure, simple, and seamless." The company created "one of the first real-time identity verification systems using a unique, automated 'profiling' algorithm" and eventually began marketing to others (CyberSource, 2012b). Purchased by Visa for $2 billion in 2010, CyberSource analyzes the 60 billion annual transactions on the Visa network to reduce the problem of fraud. Predictive analytics, probabilistic risk assessment, and scoring systems help estimate whether a transaction is likely to be bad.

These firms view fraud in a much more economic way than does the theorist who assumes transactions cannot occur without government rules against fraud. CyberSource (2012a, p. 2) characterizes fraud and efforts to deal with it as profit leaks along a risk management pipeline where orders go through automated screening or experience profit leaks with more costly manual review. Profits also leak from lost sales due to rejected orders or paying for chargebacks or not collecting from delinquent customers. The company recognizes that one must weigh the impact of fraud against the cost of enforcement efforts, including "the additional customer experience 'costs' of rejecting valid orders, staffing manual review, administration of fraud claims, as well as challenges with scaling fraud management operations as business grows" (CyberSource, 2012a, p. 2). Among online merchants, 97 percent use validation services such as address verification, and 67 percent use (often more advanced) "proprietary data/customer history tools" such as scoring models that estimate the likelihood that a transaction is valid. An automated scoring model asks questions such as the following ones identified by payment processor FirstData:

> Do the billing and shipping address match?
> Is this an average order amount?
> Did the buyer select rush shipping?
> Is the order for an unusual number of the same item?
> Is the order for a large number of a best selling item?
> Is the order for very high value items?
> Is the shopper using a free web-based email address?
> Is the computing device from which the transaction originates located in a high risk region?
> Is the computing device from which the transaction originates associated with past fraudulent activity (check active database)?
> Does the shopper's phone number have a valid area code?
> Does the shopper's area code match their billing address?
> Additional questions, many of which can be merchant specific. (Ward, 2010, p.10)

The system then accepts, rejects, or flags an order for manual review. Each merchant is able to decide how much risk it is willing to bear when accepting or rejecting transactions and to decide how many fraud prevention tools it wants to utilize. Among merchants using automated screening, "68% of merchants report using at least 3 tools in their automated screening solution and an average of 4.9 tools overall. Larger merchants processing higher order

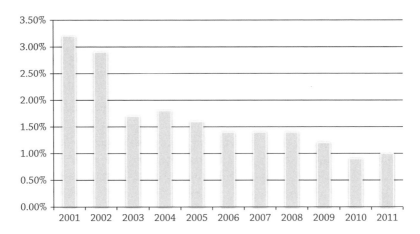

Figure 7.1
Merchant Losses to Online Fraud
Source: Data are from CyberSource (2012a, p. 1).

volumes use an average of 8 tools." The potential for fraud will always remain, but payment processors have been successful at bringing losses from fraud from 3 percent of revenues in 2001 to roughly 1 percent today (figure 7.1). The better the private sector is at eliminating problems, the less "essential" North's essential coercive third party really is.

7.3. THE MARKET FOR FRAUD MANAGEMENT

Law and economics scholars usually think about goods at the margin rather than in all-or-nothing terms, but when it comes to ensuring that parties make legitimate contracts, many abandon their marginalist perspective. Stiglitz writes (2003, p. 74), "The market system requires clearly established property rights and courts to enforce them," and Epstein (1999, p. 285) writes, "The rule of law becomes critical to offer a secure framework for these voluntary transactions to take place." But while scholars influenced by legal centralism suggest that the private sector must wait for government to create a secure framework, the private sector treats the problem quite differently. What legal centralists consider enforcement problems are treated by the private sector as risk management problems.

A loss from fraud is quantifiable, just like any other loss, and firms will take steps to minimize such a loss, just like any other. A firm that can reduce losses for itself captures those benefits, and a firm that can help reduce losses for others can market those benefits to others. PayPal and CyberSource are cases in point. The private sector did not need to look into academic debates about whether fraud management was a public good. Instead these companies saw fraud management as a service that can be priced and sold, thereby filling in a "missing market" in this realm.

The market for fraud management is created by estimating the probability of fraud for various transactions, pricing those risks, taking steps to manage them, and often insuring against those risks. Each of these tasks could be done by separate firms or even by each individual conducting trade over the Internet, but intermediaries such as PayPal bundle many of these services.[5] This eliminates the need for each individual to have to figure out the potential pitfalls and ways to avoid them before making each trade. An individual trader may know little of the probability of fraud for any given transaction, but PayPal has a very good idea.

A crucial step is for payment processors to price the risks of fraud. At the risk of upsetting economists who think human choices cannot be quantified using probabilities because the future is radically uncertain (Lachmann, 1994, p. 120), lenders have done this since time immemorial by charging higher interest rates to parties with higher likelihood of default (Rothbard, 1980).[6] Transacting parties must estimate the likelihood that counterparties will have the ability and intention to follow through on their promises (Duffie and Zhu, 2011) and also what one can expect to recover if a problem occurs. Whereas certain transacting parties, such as mortgage lenders, can theoretically foreclose on the assets purchased with a loan (although in practice this too is difficult), many, such as credit card or unsecured debt lenders, are unable to recover significant assets if the other party fails to follow through on his half of the bargain. Many firms, such as those conducting business over the Internet, have a very limited ability to recover assets from those who defrauded them.

But herein lies the beauty of the market. Even if laws against fraud are ineffective and the possibility of recovering assets from fraudsters is zero, transactions can still take place among even the most risk-averse traders when transacting parties can hire intermediaries to pool and insure risks, thus pricing them into the cost of a transaction.[7] All of this transforms the risk of fraud into a predictable cost of doing business, and it enables parties with various risk profiles to smoothly transact. For example, even if 10 percent of total sales in a particular area go bad, payment processors assuming

5. The traditional payment card industry is less integrated than PayPal, but payment processors often offer many fraud prevention services together. The package of services that a merchant ends up with depends on its willingness to assume risk. For example, some merchants purchase insurance against chargebacks, whereas others do not.

6. Those who believe that human choices cannot be quantified using probabilities should either be unwilling to lend to anyone because "the future is radically uncertain" or be just as willing to lend at the same interest rate for junk bonds and AAA-rated debt (good luck with that strategy).

7. It is quite possible for merchants to hire a third party to pool risks without hiring that same party to assume or insure against those risks.

the cost of fraud will still process them if they can charge transaction fees that are ten percentage points higher.[8] Those transacting in higher-risk areas can use the aptly named high-risk payment processors (some charge merchants upward of 15 percent per transaction), just as more risky borrowers can borrow money by paying higher interest rates. Payment processors constantly collect data on rates of fraud and chargebacks, which are higher with certain product categories such as bankruptcy attorneys, consumer electronics, adult content, gambling, and fortune tellers (alas, fortune tellers cannot always predict the future perfectly). If a merchant gets too many chargebacks, it can be kicked out of its payment processor network, meaning that parties are likely to be pooled with others of similar risk levels. The more accurately risks are pooled and priced into the costs of transactions, the less problematic fraud becomes when recovering assets ex post is not an option.

Although insured risks will not cripple any individual making transactions, higher risk premiums for fraud still discourage trade at the margin. (And the less perfectly risk profiles are pooled, the greater the chance that adverse selection problems encourage more reliable traders to leave the market, further pushing up risk premiums and discouraging trade.) Here payment processors and other financial intermediaries provide their important behind-the-scenes role. Intermediaries make money by facilitating transactions, and any company that can ceteris paribus lower transaction costs, including lower costs of fraud, will gain. This makes the intermediaries beneficiaries of successful fraud management, and the better they are at keeping fraudsters out, the lower the risk premiums they will have to charge. In the constant game of cat and mouse, firms that find better ways of keeping fraudsters at bay are able to provide a better (a lower-cost) service to their customers.

Notice that all of this works even though many potentials for "market failure" exist. First, all of this works even though parties do not have perfect information about the other party or all of the fraudulent schemes that could occur. As long as one hires an intermediary to assume and manage those risks, transacting parties need to trust just that one party. Second, all of this works even in the presence of network effects associated with fraud reduction. The value of a payment system certainly depends on how many others want to use it (PayPal recognized this from day one when it decided to give $10 to each new user and $10 more for referring a friend), but, if anything, network effects help explain why the private sector has managed fraud more effectively. PayPal alone has more users than almost every country has citizens (China, India, and the United States being the only exceptions) and thus

---

8. One of the more problematic aspects of price controls on interchange fees in the Dodd-Frank Act of 2010 is that it will interfere with payment processors' ability to price the cost of fraud into transactions.

has strong incentives to invest in technologies that increase the value of its network. Your local police department or federal government officials do not have those same incentives. On one hand, fraud reduction is often considered a public good, but law enforcement agencies have limited resources, and one should not be surprised if officials around the globe do not consider reducing fraud for merchants or consumers among their top priorities (Reno, 2000). Intermediaries hired to manage fraud, on the other hand, are residual claimants for successful fraud reduction, and they internalize the benefits of their investments.

7.4. SUMMARY AND THOUGHTS

In a high-technology world with relatively anonymous interaction across political boundaries, government's ability to deal with fraud is quite limited. PayPal, and likely most electronic commerce, would not exist had it depended on government to enforce contracts over the Internet. When PayPal realized that it could not rely on government to rectify occurrences of fraud, it found many ways to minimize problems before they occurred.

The risk management services of electronic payment processors are representative of a much wider phenomenon in which firms deal with risks of problems ex ante rather than ex post. Hiring others to conduct proper due diligence (the accounting firm, the underwriter, or the rating agency) helps certify that an entity is the real deal, and hiring others to assume risks reduces firms' exposure when any one thing goes wrong. Having your car stolen and not getting it back is not the worst thing in the world if you purchased insurance, just as having a loan you made defaulted on is not the worst thing in the world if you purchased a credit default swap. Hiring an exchange to facilitate these transactions further reduces risks. In futures markets, transacting parties hire the Chicago Mercantile Exchange or another exchange to assume and manage counterparty default risks. When two parties seemingly make a contract with each other, they are actually each making separate contracts with the futures exchange, so they need not worry about the other party defaulting (Deutsche Borse Group, 2008, p. 16). The futures exchange then works to minimize problems with margin, daily settlement, and other trading requirements. By managing risk in the most sophisticated markets the world has ever seen (Chicago Mercantile Exchange Group processes billions of transactions per year, and the notional value of contracts on all futures exchanges exceeds world GDP [CME Group, 2011]), these intermediaries eliminate the "need" to have billions of contracts enforced in court. Easterbrook and Fischel (1996, p. 283) write that "a rule against fraud is not an essential or even necessarily an important ingredient of securities markets," and the same is true for all markets. Financial intermediaries such as PayPal allow transactions all over the world while keeping problems of fraud to a minimum. Payment processors don't tax half of our income; instead, they provide these crucial services for just a couple of percentage points. Private governance facilitates transactions in lawless parts cyberspace, the Wild West (or more accurately the "Not So Wild, Wild West" [Anderson and Hill, 2004]) of modern commerce.

CHAPTER 8

୶ଚ

Bundling Private Governance with Bricks and Mortar

Private Policing in California, North Carolina, and Beyond

8.1. INTRODUCTION

Attracted by the prospect of gold, thousands of people began descending on San Francisco. The city had only a dozen homes in 1844, but the population expanded to five thousand by 1849 and twenty thousand by 1850. The city also saw tens of thousands more pass through in their search for gold (Barber and Howe, 1865, p. 660). Yet one commentator from 1850 writes:

> There are, however, no police or soldiers to watch specially over the interests of the public. Such a state of things will give rise at the first moment to a sentiment of surprise, almost indignation; nobody could imagine that a government could be so wanting in its essential duties as to not accord direct and official protection to a country ranged under its banner, but many things which the European can scarcely conceive appear natural and simple to the Americans. (Hogg, 1850, p. 344)

Matters were not bad at first, but over time problems of crime started escalating. Criminal groups known as the Hounds or the Regulators ("a gang of ruffians who infested San Francisco in 1849" [Bartlett, [1859] 1877, p. 204]) and the Sydney Ducks ("composed chiefly of Sydney convicts" [Bancroft, 1887, p. 127]) terrorized everyone from Spanish-speaking immigrants (Chilenos; the Regulators threatened to run them out of the city) to American merchants. Soule, Gihon, and Nisbet (1854, p. 227) described the gangs in 1849: "They invaded the stores, taverns, and houses of Americans themselves, and rudely demanded whatever they desired. They could not be refused, for their numbers were so great, while they were well armed, that nobody durst resist them."

San Franciscans had a dilemma but could not rely on a deus ex machina government. Of 1849 San Francisco, Hittel (1898a, p. 725) writes, "There was no police organization or efficient municipal organization of any kind," so "Nothing therefore remained for the citizens but to take the matter into their own hands and provide the necessary remedy in their own way." Rather than noticing a problem and doing nothing about it, San Franciscans decided to create a system of private police. The private police protected individual establishments and sometimes entire neighborhoods without taxation or official sanction. Soule, Gihon, and Nisbet (1854, p. 390) write that by 1851 people "could now lie down to rest at nights without feeling the old constant dread of having their houses robbed or burned before morning." One commentator writes, "In consequence of our unwearied exertions, perfect peace and security exist now in San Francisco" (Gerstäcker, 1853, p. 254).

Long before Samuelson and Nordhaus (2010, p. 377) were theorizing that "history has shown that markets cannot work effectively alone. At a minimum, an efficient market economy needs police to ensure physical security," San Franciscans created a system of private police to ensure their physical security. Private police helped protect individuals when government police were absent or "grossly inefficient and corrupt" (Hittel, 1878, p. 242). In the early 1900s, the private police referred to as Special Police Officers numbered 1,199 (compared to 985 government police officers). And today the network of independent firms now known as the San Francisco Patrol Special Police still provide services such as helping merchants escort unruly patrons or drugged-up vagrants off their property. Unlike security guards in San Francisco, the Patrol Special Police wear badges (see, for example, figures 8.1 and 8.2), are armed, and can protect multiple properties. They were also the good guys in a not so serious movie, *Kuffs*, starring Christian Slater and Milla Jovovich.

Despite the widely held theory that policing is nonexcludable and impossible to charge for (Landsburg, 2010, p. 467; Lipsey and Chrystal, 2007, p. 278), policing is often bundled with real estate, where access *is* excludable and the bundle is priced as a single entity.[1] Whether the "public" good is unarmed security or full-fledged private police, the principles are the same. A shopping center does not charge separately for its security guards—or fountains, sidewalks, and streetlights—and instead prices these collective goods into merchant rents, which are ultimately priced into consumer products. A shopping center does not need to negotiate with each customer for each of these separate amenities and eliminates free riding by indirectly charging all customers

---

1. For a discussion of how tying and bundling arrangements enable the private provision of public goods, see MacCallum (1970), Klein (1987), Foldvary (1994), Deng (2002), and Gordon, Deng, and Richardson (2007).

Figure 8.1
Badge Worn by Patrol Special Police in the Early Twentieth Century
Source: Police Badge Network.

for these collective goods. Similarly, in 1850s San Francisco private police did not need to go into the bar and negotiate with individual patrons for protection against criminals. The problem of free-riding was overcome by bar owners pricing private policing into the cost of drinks.

Interaction in physical space does indeed involve the potential for conflict (or externalities in the neoclassical framework), and although economists like Pigou (1918, p. 194) gave examples of people interacting in physical space causing problems for each other, Knight (1924, p. 586) pointed out that problems persist only if one assumes people are interacting on government-owned property. When physical space is privately owned, the manager has an incentive to make sure the problems are dealt with. One important aspect of management of property is good security, and that can come from everything from white-gloved doormen to fully deputized private police.[2] Customers of retail stores, office parks, hotels, casinos, colleges, and housing complexes all demand a good experience, and if proprietors want shoppers, tenants, guests,

---

2. Unarmed security, armed security, and armed private police provide many of the same services and are somewhat close substitutes (some people use the labels as synonyms). This chapter refers to private police as similar to private security but with many or all police powers, including power of arrest. In modern America, although private police are hired by private parties, they must be authorized by government in much the same way that stockbrokers or other professions require licenses.

Athough unarmed or armed stationary guards often provide all the security required to make an atmosphere safe, in this chapter I focus on private police to highlight that even the most formal police can be private. For excellent overviews of the private security industry, which has twice as many employees as government police and whose revenues have increased in the past ten years, see Benson (1998) and Blackstone and Hakim (2013).

Figure 8.2
Special Police Officer Andrew Briggs, 1922
Source: University of California Jesse Brown Cook Scrapbooks Documenting San Francisco History and Law Enforcement.

gamblers, students, or residents, they must provide the bundle of private and "public" goods that their particular customers want. These businesses win or lose based on the satisfaction of their customers, and therefore they become residual claimants on good policing.

8.2. WHY HIRE PRIVATE POLICE?

San Francisco was in a state of de facto anarchy (using the literal definition of anarchy "absence of government" rather than the alternate definition of anarchy "state of disorder") before the city became incorporated in 1850 and in many ways remained in such a state afterward. Describing 1850 San Francisco, Hittel (1898a, p. 728) writes, "There was no place of office for the first magistrate, or any edifice or building for municipal purposes. There was not a single police officer or watchman; nor a prison for confining a prisoner." Even after government started hiring police in 1850, "The police force was small and inefficient. In case of an arrest the law was powerless" (Bancroft, 1887, p. 137). For Royce (1886, p. 416), "The police force of the city . . . was all this time small, poorly trained, generally neglected, and ill-paid, getting its wages in depreciated city scrip," and for Soule, Gihon, and Nisbet (1854, p. 567) the law was "a matter for ridicule. The police were few in number, and poorly as well as irregularly paid. Some of them were in league with the criminals themselves, and assisted these at all times to elude justice." Thus, even after government was created, clearly their police were not there to serve and protect.

Frye (2000) argues that social cooperation without government breaks down under conditions when a population is heterogeneous or has high discount rates. Both of those conditions were met in San Francisco. Residents came from elsewhere in America, Australia, Chile, China, England, Germany, Mexico, Peru, and the Sandwich Islands (Hawaii). Eighty percent were single males (Soule, Gihon, and Nisbet, 1854, p. 488), and many wanted to get rich quick from gold. Helper (1855, p. 238, p. 37) writes, "Villains from all parts of the world swarmed upon the new soil," and "Words fail us to express the shameful depravity and unexampled turpitude of California society." Bancroft (1887, p. 94) describes gangs "entering various saloons and demanding drink and cigars; if not instantly and cheerfully produced, the rioters would go behind the bar, help themselves and their associates, then smash a few decanters and mirrors." As is common, there was a problem and no government interest or ability to solve it.

Yet bar owners and others did not want to be subject to bands of marauding gangs. Having one's customers beat up or one's property smashed is not exactly a good business model. Bancroft (1887, p. 97) writes, "Fear took hold on the money-makers, and indignation; they swore in their hearts that these things should not be." The January 24, 1850, *Daily Alta California* states, "Our merchants must organize some system of private watchmen." Because the private sector had needs that government clearly did not meet, it decided to create a system of private police.

In 1849 private groups rounded up many of the Hounds and temporarily held them on a boat in the harbor. Arrestees were given trials that followed "all the usual forms of common law procedure in criminal cases," including giving the accused counsel and letting them call witnesses, and "when the evidence failed, the prisoners were acquitted and released" (Hittel, 1898a, p. 726). They found the leader of the Hounds, Sam Roberts, guilty of robbery, assault, and intent to kill, and were pondering sending him and another to prison "in whatever penitentiary the governor of California might direct." In the end they decided against it

(Soule, Gihon, and Nisbet, 1854, p. 560). Most of those found guilty were fined, required to give bonds to "keep the peace for one year," or simply asked to leave the city. Even without incarceration, this brought much of the chaos to an end. These groups were not nearly as liberal as I wish they were, but their punishments were incomparably more liberal than that of the modern legal system, which has more than one million nonviolent offenders behind bars (D'Amico, 2012).

They also were much more liberal than the government police created around that time. In 1851, de Russailh ([1851] 1931, p. 47), a visitor to San Francisco, writes:

> As for the police, I have only one thing to say. The police force is largely made up of ex-bandits, and naturally the members are interested above all in saving their old friends from punishment. Policemen here are quite as much to be feared as the robbers; if they know you have money, they will be the first to knock you on the head. You pay them well to watch over your house, and they set it on fire. In short, I think that all the people concerned with justice or the police are in league with the criminals.

The *Daily Alta California* (1851, p. 1) reports:

> The police established under our charter, and costing the city an immense sum, has been found entirely inadequate. Here as elsewhere, a large portion of their body offer a protection to, rather than a check upon[,] the disorderly and vicious. Men get appointed sometimes as policemen, who are no better than the unhung villains who prowl about our streets at night for theft and robbery.

The politicians were no better. Describing the 1850s, Hittel (1878, p. 243) writes, "In fact, some of the boldest and most dangerous criminals in California were themselves officials." In 1851 and 1856 residents formed vigilance committees and rounded up some of the worst criminals to banish them from the city. One author writing in 1856 referred to most of the members of the 1851 committee as coming "from the elite professional and merchant class of the city," and Royce (1884, p. 461) refers to the 1856 committee as "A Business Man's Revolution." The actions of the 1856 committee also ended up reducing government spending by more than 85 percent (Hittel, 1878, p. 263).[3] That's hope and change I can believe in.

How was all of this financed? Residents privately financed police well over a century before Mancur Olson (1965, p. 95) asserted that "improvements

---

3. Asking criminals to leave the city was a common punishment. In a few cases, such as when a politician named James P. Casey murdered a businessman in 1856, the punishment was much more. Citizens formed an armed vigilance committee, arrested Casey, and had a trial at which "general rules of evidence observed in courts were adopted; the accused heard all the witnesses, cross-examined those against him,

in ... police forces ... cannot be financed without in some sense reducing the economic freedoms of the citizenry, without increasing taxes and thereby reducing the individual's freedom to spend," so they did not realize what they did was actually impossible.[4] A May 19, 1851, article from the *Daily Alta California* (p. 2) describes "two methods by which a police additional to that maintained by the corporation can be supplied"; the first is "to hire persons to watch and guard certain blocks or buildings, the funds necessary being furnished by individuals occupying or owning the particular property to be guarded." One real estate advertisement from the July 26, 1851, *Daily Alta California* (p. 1) indicates the lease will "provide for a day and night watchmen and a fire department attached to the block." The May 19, 1851, article also encourages people to join the volunteer police force and praises it, saying that its members "cost the city nothing—a very important consideration at this time."

Reading through archives from nineteenth-century newspapers and subsequent commentators, one notices certain patterns. From day one, private police protected groups that government police were incapable of, or uninterested in, protecting. For example, government police cared little about policing Chinatown, yet an 1854 article in the *Daily Alta California* (p. 2) reports that the Chinese neighborhood near Sacramento Street "is kept scrupulously clean by the special policeman on that beat, and no portion of the city is more quiet and orderly at night. This, however, has been the work of the Chinese themselves, in putting themselves voluntarily under the supervision of a special policeman, and no praise is due to the city." The government even proposed outlawing private police because too much gambling occurred in Chinatown, but the private police did not seem concerned about prohibiting consensual acts. The government, in contrast, was never friendly to the Chinese and passed various laws against them, including the 1862 "Act to

---

summoned such as he wanted in his favor, had an attorney to assist him, and was permitted to make an argument by himself or his attorney in his own defense" (Hittell, 1878, p. 250). They found Casey guilty, had the verdict reviewed by another private board of delegates, and in the end hanged him. The vigilance committees hanged four people in 1851 and another four in 1856, and although I probably agree with critics of tribunals that utilize capital punishment, in no way does this imply that government would have been any better then or now. In comparison, despite all of the laws that the U.S. government has on the books about due process, in his first four years in office, the Nobel Peace laureate U.S. president ordered drone strikes and killed between 1,534 and 2,681 Pakistanis (New America Foundation, 2012), none of whom were ever accused or tried for any crime. In terms of numbers, these San Francisco vigilantes look like Gandhi compared to the president of the United States.

4. Olson (1965, p. 102, 90) states, "The most notable tradition in nineteenth century economics—the British laissez-faire tradition—largely ignored the theory of public goods," and he also criticizes other economists who "carried the laissez-faire philosophy to an altogether impractical, and perhaps even fantastic, extreme." By developing a theory about how the world must work while ignoring how it actually works, Olson, not the laissez-faire economists, is the one engaging in fantasy.

protect free white labor against competition with Chinese coolie labor, and to discourage the immigration of Chinese into the State of California." Government certainly was not on the side of minorities, as critics of private police such as Benjamin (2009) assume, but here the private sector really did come to the rescue when matters for Chinese residents got bad:

> In 1869 abuse had become so flagrant and the police so indifferent that a Chinese Protective Society was organized among merchants and humanitarians in San Francisco, which employed a staff of special police to patrol the city day and night and to arrest those molesting the Chinese. (Coolidge, 1909, p. 260)

The Chinese were not the only people whom government police were uninterested in or incapable of protecting. In the 1870s the leader of the Workingmen's Party of California (whose direct descendants, no doubt, organized Occupy Wall Street) "predicted that within one year there would be twenty thousand laborers in San Francisco well-armed, well-organized, and well able to take what they wished" and "not only threatened the Chinese with summary treatment, but also inveighed against the capitalists of the state; gave the names of many; revealed in such terms as 'hanging is necessary'" (Hittel, 1898b, p. 600). When mobs threatened violence against businesses hiring Chinese laborers, the businessmen relied on special police officers. Archives of late nineteenth- and early twentieth-century newspapers have numerous examples of special police dealing with rioting workers (see, for example, figure 8.5), and this makes the police unpopular among many historians with a labor union bias. In one notable example, when a mob showed up outside the residence of railroad magnate Leland Stanford, he relied on, not government, but special police. (Dear Rich Stanford University Alumni: Please donate some of your well-deserved wealth to private policing organizations for saving the founder of your university.)

San Francisco had more than one thousand Special Police Officers in different firms at the beginning of the twentieth century, and for perspective that means San Francisco had more private police than 99.5 percent of jurisdictions today have government police (tables 8.1 and 8.2). In recent years their numbers have decreased because of various government restrictions that make it difficult for the Patrol Special Police to hire and do their job, but officers still protect stores, residential complexes, hospitals, restaurants, and bars.

The San Francisco Patrol Special Police Association summarizes the services offered as follows:

Basic Patrol Service
During hours of patrol, officers will make passing calls to check the interior and exterior of your property as well as the surrounding city streets and determine if all is well.

Closing Service
Officers conduct a complete and thorough search of the premises for fire, open windows and unlocked doors. The officer will stand by and assist in making sure all customers and/or employees have left the property and the premises are secure.

Alarm Response
As an additional service to your alarm system, Patrol Special Police Officers will respond to alarm calls usually within a few minutes and provide an on-scene and timely police presence.

Police Calls
During the hours of patrol, Patrol Special Police Officers will respond to your property in the event a police call occurs to assist in the protection of your property and, if necessary, will remain at that location until secured.

Escorts
Patrol Special Police Officers provide escort services for the transport of valuables, deposit of funds or other protective needs.

Other services are available upon inquiry.

Table 8.1. LOCAL GOVERNMENT POLICE DEPARTMENTS AND FULL-TIME EMPLOYEES, BY NUMBER OF SWORN PERSONNEL, 2007

Number of sworn personnel	Departments		Full-time sworn personnel		Full-time civilian personnel	
	Number	Percent	Number	Percent	Number	Percent
All sizes	12,575	100	463,147	100	137,880	100
1,000 or more	48	0.4	153,020	33.0	49,774	36.1
500–999	46	0.4	32,540	7.0	10,915	7.9
250–499	106	0.8	36,963	8.0	12,198	8.8
100–249	424	3.4	61,438	13.3	19,697	14.3
50–99	841	6.7	57,010	12.3	16,638	12.1
25–49	1,573	12.5	53,490	11.5	14,686	10.7
10–24	3,307	26.3	46,344	10.0	10,599	7.7
5–9	3,358	26.7	17,419	3.8	2,933	2.1
2–4	2,219	17.6	4,544	1.0	319	0.2
1	652	5.2	381	0.1	120	0.1

Source: U.S. Department of Justice (2010, p.9)

Table 8.2. LOCAL GOVERNMENT POLICE DEPARTMENTS AND FULL-TIME
EMPLOYEES, BY SIZE OF POPULATION SERVED, 2007

	Departments		Full-time sworn personnel		Full-time civilian personnel	
Population served	Number	Percent	Number	Percent	Number	Percent
All sizes	12,575	100	463,147	100	137,880	100
10,000,000 or more	14	0.1	95,053	20.5	34,304	24.9
500,000–999,999	33	0.3	51,973	11.2	13,726	10.0
250,000–499,999	48	0.4	34,207	7.4	12,086	8.8
100,000–249,999	189	1.5	54,556	11.8	18,591	13.5
50,000–99,999	427	3.4	52,148	11.3	16,153	11.7
25,000–49,999	855	6.8	53,513	11.6	14,278	10.4
10,000–24,999	1,792	14.3	55,507	12.0	15,073	10.9
2,500–9,999	4,111	32.7	48,681	10.5	11,120	8.1
Under 2,500	5,107	40.6	17,510	3.8	2,549	1.8

Source: U.S. Department of Justice (2010, p.9).

Note: The median population served was 3,555.

Despite the theory that "it would obviously not be feasible, if indeed it were possible, to deny the protection provided by . . . police . . . to those who did not voluntarily pay" (Olson, 1965, p. 14), private police have figured out ways to get funding. The most obvious of all is—drum roll please—to provide police services to paying customers! Simply look at the placards indicating that a property has subscribed to a Patrol Special Police firm (figure 8.3). If a property owner wants the luxury of a Patrol Special Police officer checking on the business at night or rushing to the scene in the case of a problem, one has to be a customer. Each Patrol Special Police officer knows whether a particular property owner is a customer and need not worry about getting calls from noncustomers. I am sure some people will think, "It is unfair that paying customers receive service and people without money to spare for the service do not." Do not forget that for issues that government considers unimportant, nobody receives responses.

Whether or not government could theoretically provide lower-cost policing to all residents was irrelevant to nineteenth-century merchants and is irrelevant to subscribers of the Patrol Special Police today. Even though the San Francisco Police Department now has around two thousand officers and a budget of upward of a half billion dollars per year (a staggering $250,000 per officer, which does not include the amount taxpayers spend on pensions or on other hidden costs going directly to police, jails, and the sheriff's department), the mere act of incurring these costs does not mean that citizen needs

Figure 8.3
Placard Indicating Subscription to Patrol Special Police.
Source: Samsast San Francisco Police Badges and Photos.

are automatically met. I sent a survey to 146 customers of the San Francisco Patrol Special Police and asked them, "Why did you not simply rely on the local S.F. Police Department to meet your safety needs?" Customer responses included:

> They scare me—Trust issues.
> They take too long to arrive.
> That's a joke right? I have little confidence in S.F.P.D.

In contrast, when I asked them, "Why did you hire a Patrol Special Police officer?" they offered responses including:

> Faster service, personal touch.
> Protect our clients and customers.
> Officers become familiar with the businesses and potential problems.
> (Surveys collected fall 2009)

People who believe in the deus ex machina theory of government law enforcement assume that private provision cannot meet any needs and government provision will, but in fact the opposite is true.

Over time the San Francisco Patrol Special Police have been subject to regulation. One peculiar and governmentally determined feature of the system is that in each neighborhood only one of the independent firms has a license to operate (figure 8.4) and elements of this setup appear to date to the 1870s (Workmen's Compensation Reporter, 1951, p. 207; Cassel, 2010). According to this system a firm owns a "beat" (the exclusive license to practice in a given area), but it can rent or sell that beat to other firms, in the same way that a taxi

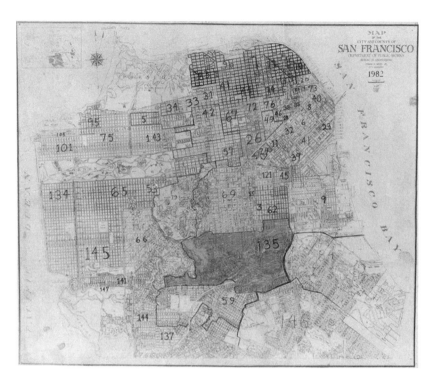

Figure 8.4
Map of Beats for the Patrol Special Police in San Francisco
Source: San Francisco Patrol Special Police Officers Association.

medallion owner can rent or sell the medallion to other taxi drivers. Within each beat, businesses and individuals have the option of being or not being a customer of the firm that owns the beat, or, alternatively, they can hire an unarmed stationary security guard from another company, but they cannot hire a Patrol Special Police firm that does not own that beat. Predictably, certain Patrol Special Police firms, usually those who own and rent the beats, like the beat system, whereas other Patrol Special Police firms that would like to expand their business or those hoping to get into the business do not (personal interviews, San Francisco, 2008). The plot of *Kuffs* involved Christian Slater inheriting the beat from his older brother, so in fiction and real life, these licenses have value. If these individual neighborhoods were private communities, putting policing in the hands of one firm might be a good way of reducing conflict and free-riding in the neighborhood, but when the city owns streets and decides the definition of beats, the best arrangement is unclear.

In 1994 they were stripped of their full police powers, although they still can make citizen's arrests. In the case *Russo & Reyes v. Willis Casey et al.*, 15 F.3d 1089 (9th Cir. 1993), two Patrol Special Police Officers alleged that the San Francisco police chief had conspired to restrict competition. Government police commonly "encourage" businesses to hire off-duty government police officers or companies owned by them or their families instead of Patrol Special Police (Kretkowski, 1995). The case went all the way to the U.S. Supreme Court, but only on a pretrial motion to dismiss; the merits of the case were never debated. In a more recent case (*San Francisco Patrol Special Police Officers Byard et al. v. the City and County of San Francisco and the San Francisco Police Department*), the Patrol Special Police filed a complaint that the San Francisco Police Department was using its regulatory powers to prevent the Patrol Special Police from hiring new employees and using tax-funded resources for profit-seeking enterprises including the lucrative 10(b) overtime contracts. That government police can use law to decide who gets to compete with them is unsurprising.

Beyond San Francisco, other jurisdictions, such as the state of North Carolina, permit quite a bit of private policing. Starting in 1871 Special Policemen were authorized to provide police for railroads as well as utility, construction, and manufacturing companies, and in many areas these private police were the only police one would encounter (Qualkenbush, 2012). Today, according to North Carolina General Statute 74E (the Company Police Act), Special Police Officers have full police powers, including power of arrest, on the property of employers. Currently about seventy-five different private police organizations exist in North Carolina. Some, such as the fifty-officer Allied Barton Company Police Force, are subsidiaries of large firms, such as the fifty-thousand-employee Allied Barton Security Services, which itself provides security to 40 percent of Fortune 500 companies. Nationwide, government police departments average 2.3 law enforcement employees per 1,000 residents (Federal Bureau of Investigation, 2004, table 70); assuming this average is somehow optimal, it would not be a stretch for the fifty deputized officers in the Allied Burton Company Police Force to police a city of twenty-five thousand. In fact, Allied Barton Company Police has more deputized officers than 92 percent of government police departments nationwide (table 5.1).[5]

Another, even larger private police force is that of Duke University, which has 176 full-time employees, including eighty-three nondeputized security officers and sixty-eight deputized private police officers. With a jurisdiction of eight thousand acres (about half the size of Manhattan), fourteen thousand students, thirty-four thousand employees between the university and its medical center, and numerous visitors (Duke University Police Department, 2010, 2012), Duke police deal with a greater population than 95 percent of

---

5. According to Southwick (2005), policing has some economies of scale but also diseconomies of scale that become pronounced after a municipality has twenty thousand residents. Therefore, even if economies of scale exist over certain ranges, they are not large enough to preclude private parties from hiring enough officers to reach that optimum (assuming that the existing police-to-civilian ratios are somehow the optimum).

police departments nationwide (table 5.1). Duke police field thirty thousand calls per year, yet they don't have arrest quotas, tanks, or unmanned drones or walk around in riot gear like government police (Balko, 2006, 2013).

I surveyed some customers of private police in North Carolina,[6] and found responses similar to those of the Patrol Special Police customers in San Francisco. In response to "Why did you not simply rely on the Government Police Department to meet your safety needs?" respondents said that they were "dissatisfied with local agency," that "the County Sheriff's office is over committed," or that they "wanted more personalized service." Economists can develop as many theories as they want about how police are public goods that only government has an incentive to provide (Lipsey and Chrystal, 2007, p. 278), but those theories fly in the face of reality. In contrast to government police, the customers state that the private firm "monitors and polices all of my locations in both plain clothes and uniform," "They assist us in many ways; most importantly—they make the staff feel more secure," and provide "someone to meet my needs" (surveys collected spring 2011). Government is not customer service-oriented elsewhere; the same is true of police. Private parties find it preferable to pay for private service rather than rely on nonexistent government solutions.

8.3. PRIVATE POLICE: TO SERVE AND PROTECT WHOM?

8.3.1. Bundling on the Behalf of Consumers

The idea that the private sector has no incentive or ability to provide police is simply untrue. In fact, the discussion should be shifted from that assumption that "private businesses will not provide a police force" to whether or not police from the private sector can be relied upon. Certain skeptics recognize that private police do indeed exist, but question their desirability. For example, Suffolk Law School's Thurau-Gray suggests that private police "are focusing on the priority of their employer, rather than the priority of public safety and individual rights" (quoted in Goldstein, 2007). Another skeptic, Dan Bay (quoted in Bell, 1997, p. G1) states, "The government entity operates under the public interest, the private entity under the stockholder interest. The potential conflict here is that the stockholder interest will be served before the public interest." In Boston, tenant groups have complained that special police hired by their complex "were overstepping their bounds, arresting young men who lived there for trespassing" (Goldstein, 2007). Worse yet are the private security contractors hired by the U.S. government in its war against Iraq who have been criticized for not caring about the well-being or the rights of the people in Iraq (BBC, 2012).

---

6. I thank my former student Christopher F. Darden for conducting this survey with me.

Are private police or private security inevitably going to, or at least prone to, go against the interest of the public or violate basic rights? Economists interested in private solutions need not endorse every possible type of enforcement as long as the entities doing the enforcing are privately owned.[7] Private individuals are imperfect and can be corrupted or violate rights, just like government police. The potential for fly-by-night, risky, or violence-prone private police made commentators such as Rand (1966) and Nozick (1974) uneasy. The million-dollar question is when or whether the incentives of private parties can be aligned to act in the interest of those who should be protected. At the end of the day, how police act is dependent on the institutional arrangements, their incentives, and whom they are hired to serve.

Consider the incentives in some existing arrangements. One of the most important points is that many often criticized examples of private police should not be considered examples of private policing. In the example from Boston, the "private" police under scrutiny were actually hired by government to police government-owned property (in this case public housing projects). Because these "private" police were hired, directed, and financed by government, in some important ways they were hardly more private than the individual hired to work as a government police officer. Just as government managers rarely work diligently to maximize the value of housing projects to their tenants, the fact that "private" police hired by government do not maximize the value to their tenants or even act in the interest of the tenants is entirely predictable. The conflict that existed in Boston between the tenants and the government landlords is a case in point. Similarly, the "private" security contractors in Iraq ultimately are hired, directed, and financed by the U.S. government, so in these cases one should not be surprised that they act against rather than to protect the Iraqi people. Government decisions to contract out work should not be considered outcomes of the free market (Benson, 1994b; D'Amico, 2009).

Matters are much different, however, when businesses that must cater to customers hire private police on their customers' behalf. The business may do the hiring before the customer enters the picture, but businesses seeking to attract those customers should hire police that cater to the customers. Landlords, shopping centers, colleges, and hotels need to offer the packages most attractive to current and future customers if they want to stay in business. Of course, any given institution or its employee can make poor choices, just

---

7. As Rasmussen and Den Uyl (2009, p. 3) make the case, "'Murder Incorporated' is not regarded in a capitalistic system as a legitimate business firm." At the risk of mischaracterizing my friend Peter Leeson's position, much of his work seems to endorse odd legal arrangements such as having trials by ordeal, battle, or poison (Leeson, 2011, 2012) as long as government does not carry them out. Regardless of the merits of his positive analysis, I doubt many people will find the arguments to be normatively compelling.

as any restaurant worker or restaurant can make poor choices. Because the market provides constant feedback through profits and losses to reward good service and punish bad, businesses will seek to minimize bad behavior among their employees.[8]

Are these assurances enough? For those who assume that some government regulation and oversight are beneficial or necessary, one can still support allowing private policing, provided officers do not violate certain rules.[9] Such a position is much more defensible than the simplistic (and empirically wrong) idea that the private sector cannot police. For those who do not assume that government rules and regulations are enacted to benefit citizens, safety ultimately depends on having the right incentives for private police. In addition to bundling, other market incentives and assurances for consumers exist. One major assurance is police bonding by external companies that can compensate consumers if police do something wrong. Such a policy is like a money-back guarantee or a fidelity bond paid by a third party. In North Carolina private police must be bonded or have liability insurance in the amount of $1 million per incident, and nothing would prevent consumers from requiring this if it were not already necessitated by law. A company that wants to remain bonded or insured will not want to act in a reckless manner. Finally, private agencies such as the International Association of Campus Law Enforcement Administrators (which focuses on universities and has twelve hundred members) and the Commission on Accreditation for Law Enforcement Agencies (which focuses on any police group, whether public or private) share best practices and accredit good agencies or individuals. Academic accreditation already is an important factor for students choosing schools, and accredited police can let potential students know that police at a particular college adhere "to the highest professional standards for campus law enforcement and protective services" (International Association of Campus Law Enforcement Administrators, 2013, p. 1). With these checks in place, police will be less likely to commit wrongs that would risk their ability to remain bonded or accredited.

---

8. Note that none of this analysis assumes that all people working for a restaurant or profit-motivated police company are intrinsically nice. As long as the employer creates an atmosphere that rewards niceness and does not tolerate abuse, then the likelihood of bad behavior will decrease. Visit Internet message boards for police officers, and you can find certain employees of universities complaining about how they have to be nice to their customers, the students. For example, one officer states, "I work for a private university . . . and I can tell you it can be frustrating. The hands off policies, the touchy feely, huggy kissy mentality of some of the powers that be can get old real fast" (Police Forums and Law Enforcement Forums, 2008). However, to help to create an environment that students like is the only reason he was hired to begin with. Although this particular employee might prefer a "get tough on crime" approach, his employer puts the customers' interests above the whims of the officers. Government police lack such constraints.

9. Hasnas (2003) presents this argument even though he believes that government oversight is not beneficial or necessary.

Bundling police with other goods, such as education at a private college, is not very different from bundling software and hardware when the values of each are interdependent. Just as customers are less likely to purchase hardware that lacks good software (Katz and Shapiro, 1994), customers are less likely to want to do business in a proprietary community that lacks good security. Rather than selling computers without an operating system or even basic BIOS software, hardware manufacturers such as Hewlett-Packard have deals with software firms like Microsoft, and more vertically integrated firms such as Apple Computer provide both. Because the availability of one affects the demand for the other, hardware producers such as Blackberry often subsidize software producers (Chen, 2012) and software producers such as Microsoft often subsidize hardware producers (Gralla, 2012). Spillover benefits notwithstanding, it does not follow that software should be put in the hands of government; in fact, this is the last thing one should do, and the same principles apply to policing.

What happens when complementary goods are not bundled and one is provided by government? For a stark contrast, the Duke University police arrested one student, less than one-hundredth of 1 percent of the students enrolled, for a liquor law violation over a two-year period (Duke University Police Department, 2012, p. 26),[10] whereas the government police in the city where I went to college commonly would often arrest eighty students (Melady, 1999), or 3 percent of all students, over a two-*week* period for alcohol-related offenses. Such heavy-handed government tactics can decrease demand for my alma mater, but the Worcester Police Department does not win or lose based on the success of the college or the well-being of students. The idea that government police primarily care about the well-being of public and that private parties do not is an assumption that should be questioned.

8.3.2. Internalizing Externalities by Private Communities

Bundling police with real estate differs from both the idea that police must be provided by a monopolist government and what many consider the only alternative, having multiple itinerant police groups in each area (Friedman, 1989; Frey, 2001). With government police or multiple itinerant police, any one person may be subject to police working for others who may not care about that person's well-being, but with police tied to goods everyone is

---

10. Duke University takes a fairly hands-off approach to alcohol, and when problems occur, resident advisors deal with them administratively (personal interview with Duke resident advisor, North Carolina, October 27, 2012) rather than using the incarceration and prosecution provided by the government legal system. If you think twenty-year-olds should be jailed for drinking, please put this book down and immediately join your local Temperance Society.

purchasing in real space, one need not see police hired by others on a regular basis, if at all. At Duke one typically sees only Duke police, and at Disneyland one typically sees only Disney security. These properties do not have a million competing security firms in exactly the same way that they do not have bathrooms provided by multiple competing porta-potty firms. But neither is a problem.[11] Even though these properties have a monopoly on security within their realms, they must compete for customers' business and offer an attractive deal.

Using security hired by the entity managing the property, as opposed to government or multiple itinerant firms, means that customers of a physical space have opted into a security structure that they prefer. Customers that want to deal with a more hands-off system have that option, and other customers who want lots of security have that option as well. Duke University has fewer rules than Brigham Young University, which has rules about everything from what beverages one can drink to how form-fitting clothing or short skirts can be, and in both cases the customer is in charge. Having customers agree to a common set of rules can both reduce the likelihood of conflict and make clear procedures for dealing with conflict in the event of a dispute. For example, what constitutes a noise violation in an apartment building, and what should the consequences of violations be? One option is for lawmakers to debate the amount of decibels or the type of music deemed offensive; another option is for providers of private governance to offer options to consumers and let the consumer decide.

What happens when parties walk down the street and come into conflict with each other? Does not this create externalities between people who have no prior contractual relationship (Cowen, 1992, p. 254)? Under scenarios in which nobody owns the roads, many problems can arise (Knight, 1924). But when the roads are privately owned, a manager can create a set of rules for all customers and thereby internalize externalities within their realm. Just as two people at a futures exchange might not individually know each other but still have an indirect contractual relationship through the exchange, all students have an indirect relationship with each other and with their university. Students walking down the street at Duke University need not worry about other students who follow a different set of rules because the rules at Duke University are common to all.

Right now government owns a high percentage of, although of course not all, streets, and this poses many dilemmas. But when property is privately owned, the owner can internalize many of the relevant externalities. Many "externalities" are localized (Thorsnes, 2000), so internalizing externalities within

---

11. Machan (2002) also argues that air passengers are fine with agreeing to be under the authority of a single captain for the entire flight rather than having the option of contracting with multiple pilots throughout the flight.

relatively small parcels is quite easy. For example, an individual college dorm or apartment complex can have standards about acceptable levels of noise without putting that decision in the hands of the city, state, or national government. And when the "neighborhood effects" are larger, private communities can be organized large enough to internalize them. For example, the seventy-acre City Center private development in Las Vegas includes large hotels such as the Cosmopolitan, which has three thousand guest rooms and a nightclub that attracts six thousand guests in a night (Friedman, 2012). Its $1.5 million sound system is quite loud, but the property is large enough to have most of its positive and negative "externalities" internalized within the property.

Walt Disney took internalizing externalities to a whole other level (Clark, Miller, and Stringham, 2010). Dismayed by the unsightly motels located next to his eighty-acre Disneyland, he developed Disney World in Orlando as a much larger property with thirty-thousand acres (about twice the size of Manhattan). Thus, all subsequent development could go according to the company's plans. In 1996, the Walt Disney Company opened its privately zoned and developed town, Celebration, Florida, which is now home to ten thousand residents. The town has private rules about everything from the exterior appearance of a home to the color of drapes in windows, and although certain observers call the rules oppressive, they actually cater to customers who like the classic-town feel. The customer has spoken, and median home prices in Celebration are about four times higher than in neighboring towns.

Private communities can be owned by a single entity and subleased (and MacCallum [2002] makes the case that this arrangement has important advantages), or they can be managed by an association of owners who agree to the rules when they move in (Nelson, 2005). Private communities have been growing in recent years, and as many as 60 million Americans live in them (Urbina, 2009). Each has a set of rules of varying strictness, and many are gated or contain full-time security. Surveys indicate that one of the main reasons people live in gated communities is because of security (figure 8.6), and Le Goix (2004) finds that gated communities often have price premiums over otherwise similar nongated communities.[12]

---

12. Although Benjamin (2009) criticizes gated communities in *Searching for Whitopia: An Improbable Journey to the Heart of White America*, Hispanics are actually more likely to live in gated communities than any other group, and "renters, who are more ethnically diverse and less affluent, are nearly 2.5 times as likely as homeowners to live behind gates or walls" (Nasser, 2002). Benjamin also asserts that private police exacerbate bias against the poor and minorities, thereby implying that government police somehow do the opposite. Yet, given that one in three African American males is sent to jail in his lifetime, that American governments incarcerate more African Americans than were enslaved in 1850, and that, for example, in New York City, 96 percent of student arrests (Oh, 2012) and 86 percent of marijuana arrests are of minorities (Hing, 2011), one would have to suffer from some false consciousness toward the state to believe that government police are somehow more on the side of minorities.

Figure 8.5
One of Many Newspaper Headlines about the Special Police in San Francisco
Source: San Francisco Call, 1901.

8.4. SUMMARY AND THOUGHTS

From informal private security to formal, fully deputized private police, the private protection of property rights is common. We need not assume, as Hazlitt ([1946] 1979, p. 69) does, that "necessary" government police "perform productive services as important as those of anyone in the private industry.

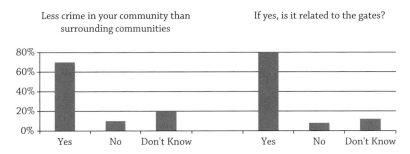

Figure 8.6
Perception of Gates as a Factor in Reducing Crime
Source: Data are from Blakely and Snyder (1998).

They make it possible for private industry to function in an atmosphere of law, order, freedom and peace" when in fact the private sector can and does meet those needs. In San Francisco the Patrol Special Police have been hired by merchants since before San Francisco was a city, and in North Carolina fully deputized private police protect many important assets. Many other examples from history exist (Benson, 1990, 1994a, 1998; Curott and Stringham, 2010; Blackstone and Hakim, 2010, 2013; Pastor, 2003), and the binding constraint seems to be how much government restricts them rather than how much the private sector is willing to produce. Theories that policing cannot be privately financed notwithstanding, markets allow financing of private police through arrangements such as bundling. Police in these arrangements must cater to customers' needs and keep them safe. As Stenning (2000, p. 93) concludes, "It is now almost impossible to identify any function or responsibility of the public police which is not, somewhere and under some circumstances, assumed and performed by private police." Private police are not everywhere, but they do, and are capable of doing, much more than the typical person knows.

CHAPTER 9

⚬∿⚬

The Most Personal Form of Private Governance

Individual Self-Governance

9.1. INTRODUCTION

Police are absolutely necessary.* Except when police are not necessary. In many areas police have a minimal presence, yet peaceful society does not break down. As Rothbard (1973, p. 205) wrote, "Every New Yorker knows, in fact, that he lives and walks the streets, and not only Times Square, virtually in a state of 'anarchy,' dependent solely on the normal peacefulness and goodwill of his fellow citizens." Although not everyone is peaceful toward his fellow citizens, many people are. If everyone were psychopaths, we would all need armed guards (who would also be psychopaths), but luckily we do not live in such a world. The more that individuals police themselves, the less problematic it becomes when police (whether public or private) are not on every corner or in every home. And the more that clubs or voluntary associations can rely on and internalize the benefits of self-governance, the less they need to spend on external enforcement.

Individual self-governance is important for voluntary associations and society as a whole. Consider the recent experience of Georgia, home to some bad people such as Stalin but also home to great wine and some of the nicest people in the world. Over the past century, how much has peace in Georgia depended on Soviet-style police versus the normal peacefulness of the Georgians? The transition after the fall of communism is illustrative. After decades of outright Soviet control, then Soviet-influenced independence, the people of Georgia were ready for a change. In late 2003 their president was former USSR minister of foreign affairs Shevardnadze, but people eventually had enough and took to the streets. The BBC (2005) reports:

> Mr. Shevardnadze told protesters they risked causing a civil war and he deployed hundreds of soldiers on the streets of Tbilisi. At that point, student demonstrators decided to give red roses to the soldiers. Many soldiers laid down their guns. "People were kissing the police and military, it was really spectacular" said Giorgi Kandelaki, a 21-year-old student.

The peaceful "Rose Revolution" led to Shevardnadze's resignation and helped set off a number of liberal economic reforms (so much that today Georgia scores 7.73 on the Economic Freedom of the World Report, compared to 7.81 by the United States [Gwartney, Lawson, and Hall, 2012]).

One of Georgians' most pressing concerns was their police force, whose members served and protected themselves and would routinely stop people, threaten arrest, and extort money (personal interviews, Tbilisi, Georgia, May 16, 2011; Bakuriani, Georgia, August 6–13, 2012, August 10–14, 2013). One diplomat stated, "Everything bad from the post-Soviet days was concentrated in them" (McDonald, 2007). The new president, thirty-five-year-old Mikheil Saakashvili, had no allegiance with the police, and over a two-week period in early 2004, he took what might have been considered a drastic measure. The McClatchy news service reports on his decision:

> "So we fired them," President Mikhail Saakashvili said. "We fired the Georgian police."
> He didn't mean just a few corrupt officers. He meant the entire national force. (McDonald, 2007)

The political leaders eventually wanted new police, but recruiting and training replacements would take months, and by August 2005 the 4.5-million-inhabitant nation contained only 2,500 police.[1] After they fired 30,000 police, did chaos ensue? One Georgian told me, "I did not notice any difference in crime, except I actually felt safer because I did not have to worry about being robbed by the police" (personal interview, Bakuriani, Georgia, August 8, 2012). The president stated, "People thought that we would have disaster. . . . Nothing like of this sort has happened because what it proved was that this police

---

1. The dismissals came in stages but in a fairly short period. They started with what were referred to as the traffic police (the type of police you would expect to see on the street), and in two swoops they basically fired all traffic police and gradually replaced them with what were referred to as patrol police. Replacing them took months, and their final numbers were much less. The new government then went on to dissolve the Ministry of State Security, and the end result was to have 66 percent less police (all types of police). For more specifics see Kupatadze (2012).

was not producing order, it was producing disorder" (Saakashvili, 2005). Although standard neoclassical theory teaches that "all prescriptions of behavior for individuals require enforcement" (Stigler, 1970, p. 526), in Georgia people refrained from killing each other, not because of government but for private reasons.

The most personal form of private governance is individual self-governance or internal moral constraints. Ignored by strict neoclassical economists, the importance of individual self-governance or internal moral constraints has been discussed by writers from Adam Smith to Immanuel Kant and Leo Tolstoy. Internal moral constraints are rules that people choose to follow even if other people do not impose them; these constraints are chosen from within. Manners, politeness, honesty, and trustworthiness are common examples of internal constraints that people commonly adopt independent of external rules.

Because many economists ignore morality, they attribute all cooperation to external sources of governance. The fact that Georgian police were so obviously bad indicates that the relative safety of the country should not be attributed to the police. Might individual self-governance be an important, or even the most important, form of governance? This is an empirical question that cannot be ruled out a priori. Answering this question is difficult, but many studies indicate that internal moral constraints are important. Not everyone behaves morally, but many people do, and their moral choices sometimes can be influenced. Take, for example, the experiments (described in more detail in section 9.2) with Massachusetts Institute of Technology students who do not act honestly in the baseline experiment but act honestly after being asked to list the Ten Commandments (Ariely, 2008). The first lesson (which everyone already knows) is to start with a distrust of anyone from Cambridge. But the second and more interesting lesson is that thinking about morality matters.

Consideration of the importance of individual self-governance helps explain why corporations and clubs spend so much time doing background checks and asking for character references when screening employees or members. When corporations or clubs organize among members with similar internal moral constraints (and disassociate with people who have different sets of internal moral constraints), they internalize many of the benefits of individual self-governance and lower the cost of enforcement. In college I was pleasantly surprised that the selection process had weeded out the ruffian types who attended my public high school.[2] Similarly, most large financial firms do extensive credit and background checks to decrease the likelihood that an employee will be a

---

2. For the record my high school in Brookline, Massachusetts, was not at all dangerous, but my college was far nicer, and much had to do with the character of the selected students. The dean of Students at College of the Holy Cross states that the students "are known for their character" (Peterson, 2011).

dishonest person. Of course, many less than perfect people slip through the cracks, but morality-screening mechanisms are used for a reason. A venue with more honest or reliable people will need to spend fewer resources on external governance than one where everyone is out for each other's throat.[3]

It also might be possible to enhance morality over the long run. In an ideal world, everyone would act like angels, and no external governance would be needed. But even if most people remain far from perfect, improving morality at the margin may be possible. One of the definitions of civilization is "intellectual, cultural, and moral refinement," and anything that refines morals is likely to decrease the need for external governance. Although most theorists focus on altering external governance to alter behavior, a more effective way to alter outcomes may be to utilize and influence individual self-governance. Smith (1786, p. 209) writes, "Without this sacred regard to the general rules of morality, there is no man whose conduct can be much depended upon. It is this which constitutes the most essential difference between a man of principle and honour and a worthless fellow. The one adheres, on all occasions, steadily and resolutely to his maxims, and preserves through the whole of his life one even tenour of conduct. The other, acts variously and accidentally, as humour, inclination, or interest chance to be uppermost."

9.2. HOW INDIVIDUAL SELF-GOVERNANCE MATTERS AND MAKES EXPENDITURES ON EXTERNAL GOVERNANCE LESS NECESSARY

Would you murder an innocent person if you could get away with it? I sincerely hope that most readers answered no. If you answered yes, please unfriend me on Facebook. As Thomas Babington Macaulay writes, "The measure of a man's real character is what he would do if he knew he never would be found out" (Templeton, 1997, p. 415). Many, or perhaps most, people simply will not perform certain actions that violate their most basic morals. However, reliance on individuals governing themselves is a no-no for many theorists, because it runs contrary to the basic assumption of Homo economicus. For example, Sowell (2002, pp. 29, 31) describes human beings as "tragically limited creatures whose selfish and dangerous impulses can be contained only by social contrivances" and writes that "man's nature inherently could not coincide with the social good but must be deliberately subordinated to it." This approach assumes that people are knaves (Brennan and Buchanan, 1985)

---

3. In such circumstances, unreliable or dishonest people have the option to interact with each other in less reputable venues or those that spend more on external governance. A neoclassical economist might say that such an arrangement prevents unreliable people from imposing their externalities on reliable people.

and then seeks to design political and legal institutions to elicit cooperation among amoral egoists. As Oliver Wendell Holmes (1897, p. 459) writes, "A man who cares nothing for an ethical rule which is believed and practised by his neighbors is likely nevertheless to care a good deal to avoid being made to pay money and will want to keep out of jail if he can." Buchanan (2003, p. 183) argues there must be "an agency that will, in some fashion, offer incentives, positive and negative, that will lead participants to respect behavioral constraints."[4]

But in *Theory of Moral Sentiments*, Smith describes reasons why individuals adopt constraints and govern themselves. Smith ([1759] 1853, p. 235) believes that if we do something that our moral faculties judge as wrong, "Those vicegerents of God within us, never fail to punish the violation of them, by the torments of inward shame, and self-condemnation; and on the contrary, always reward obedience with tranquility of mind, with contentment, and self-satisfaction." Smith considers these constraints as internal; the only punishments are shame or self-condemnation. The person with a conscience does not want to have to think about the questions "How can you live with yourself?" and "How can you sleep at night?"

Obviously many people, such as psychopaths, police, and politicians, do not care about morality. But just because some people lack internal moral constraints does not mean that everyone does. A notable economist who highlighted the importance of morality is my sometimes non-Hobbesian professor James Buchanan. His earlier writings focused on governmental constraints, but some of his work from the 1990s and later indicates that he moved a bit away from the legal centralist worldview (Buchanan, 2004). Buchanan writes:

> Much of human activity takes place in a setting described as "ordered anarchy," by which I refer to the simultaneous presence of apparent order and absence of formal laws governing behavior. How is such ordered anarchy possible? . . . The answer suggested by my argument here is that interacting parties choose to constrain their separate choices in such fashion as to create non-intersecting and therefore nonconflictual outcomes. (1994, p. 132)

---

4. Notable exceptions are those economists who accept the Homo economicus assumptions but then ask whether self-interested man would choose to have a conscience (Frank, 1987). However, in this perspective morality does not guide or constrain self-interested man; he chooses morality for self-interested rather than deontological or virtuous reasons.

In contrast, economists such as McCloskey (2006) argue against attempts to reduce all forms of other-regarding behavior to some form of self-interested behavior. Röpke (1960), Buchanan (1994), Rabin (1995), White (2004), and Wight (2005) offer theoretical discussions about the importance of voluntary self-restraint or internal moral constraints. For overviews of economists' treatment of ethics in a market economy, see Den Uyl (2009), Wight (2003), and Zak (2008).

In this view, internal constraints are potentially more important than external constraints. Such a view contrasts with some work by the early public choice economists, who often explicitly assumed that external constraints are the only ones possible on human behavior (Buchanan, 1972, 1975; Hogarty, 1972; Tullock, 1972, 1974). Hogarty (1972), for example, argues that in the absence of legal constraints, the world would look like the boys' society in *Lord of the Flies*, a prison camp during the Civil War, or an experiment in which brown rats bit each other.[5] But an interesting feature of *Lord of the Flies* or experiments with biting rats is that the subjects lack not only external constraints but also internal constraints, which is likely the more important factor.

For any given moral choice (such as whether or not to murder for the sole benefit of material gain) people can act in the following ways: (1) the individual does not consider trade-offs between morality and material gains (the person Adam Smith calls "the man of principle");[6] (2) the individual adopts moral constraints sometimes, or even almost always, but abandons them at a certain price (what Zamir and Medina [2008] call "threshold deontology"); (3) the individual considers morality valuable but always makes trade-offs between morality and material gains (the person Adam Smith calls "a worthless fellow");[7] or (4) the individual considers only material gains and never morality (traditional Homo economicus).[8] Do people typically act like those in categories 1, 2, 3, or 4? Advocates of the Homo economicus assumption would answer that the best description of their behavior is number 4 (that individuals will not govern themselves), but evidence suggests otherwise.

Because individual self-governance lies within, it is less easily observable than other economic factors, but just because something is difficult to observe does not mean that it does not exist. Research in economics, psychology, and anthropology indicates that individual self-governance is important.

Many historical and modern case studies show that societies can function even when external constraints are largely absent. The examples are not proof

---

5. For a critical evaluation of Hogarty's analysis, see Storr (2005).

6. These categories are not meant to be exhaustive, but I think they cover most options. White (2006) describes what can be considered an amended category 1 in which people do not consider the material gains of violating morality, but because of their human imperfection they always have a probability of violating their self-imposed rules. White (2010) contrasts this imperfection, which involves a probabilistic weakness of will, with what he calls the corrupted or impure position that intentionally considers the material benefits of violating morality (see categories 2, 3, and 4).

7. Cooter (2006, p. 1281) models all people as constantly comparing the cost of obeying versus disobeying the law (doing what's right in Cooter's model) but defines a good citizen as simply having a positive willingness to obey the law.

8. Broadly neoclassical economists who want to model morality debate whether internal constraints should be modeled as a type of constraint or as a type of preference (including multiple preferences). See Rabin (1995), White (2004), and Zamir and Madina (2008).

but are consistent with the hypothesis that internal moral constraints are important. For example, the rural California cattlemen and ranchers interviewed by Ellickson (1991) resolve disputes without any knowledge of or regard for formal law; they instead rely on norms such as the desire to be a good neighbor.[9] The diamond merchants described by Bernstein (1992) interact with others in the same tight-knit religious community. Examples such as these could indicate the potential importance of internal moral constraints, but judging to what extent cooperation is motivated by pure self-interest versus moral concerns is difficult in case studies. If only we could read minds.

An attempt to peer into people's brains to see why they cooperate comes through neuroeconomics, which uses magnetic resonance imaging (MRI) to record brain activity as subjects make choices. In a study by McCabe and co-authors (2001), subjects play trust and reciprocity games in which they can either keep a sum of money or pass some of it on (at which point the amount of money passed on is multiplied) to an anonymous counterpart, either human or computer depending on the experiment, who in turn can keep the money or pass it back. McCabe and coauthors (2001, p. 11832) find that the majority of subjects "consistently attempted cooperation with their human counterpart." The MRIs showed that certain parts of the brain light up when subjects cooperate with people but not when they interact with computers. This is consistent with the idea that people do not always make egoistic calculations; sometimes they may think about the moral way to interact with others. The same parts of the brain do not light up among people who do not cooperate. Such findings suggest that people have built-in tendencies (whether learned or genetically programmed) to want to cooperate.

Research in experimental economics shows people regularly cooperating without external constraints. Smith (2008, p. 250) provides a comprehensive summary of the findings in experimental economics and describes how cooperation is common even "in games without a punishment option." Smith (1998, p. 11) writes that even with anonymous interaction, "the data strongly reject the game theoretic hypotheses that in a single interactive play of the game subjects will overwhelmingly play noncooperatively." McCloskey (2006, p. 498) writes, "The life of man is solitary and poor unless the Max U's cooperate—as in fact experimental subjects do cooperate, because they have been children and have loved someone and are not monsters."

Many factors appear to trigger morality. Houser and coauthors (2011) describe how simply allowing subjects to communicate and to be transparent about their choices encourages large amounts of cooperation. Subjects also act honestly when asked to think about moral guidelines, such as in the Ten Commandments experiment by Ariely (2008, p. 195). In that experiment student

---

9. Posner (1996) discusses the importance of norms in depth, and Gneezy and Rustichini (2000) provide evidence that introduction of fines can undermine norms.

subjects are paid for the number of math questions they answer correctly. After administering the test several times, one can see the number of correct answers that subjects can reasonably get. The researcher then lets subsequent subjects grade their tests, shred their answers, and report their scores, and it turns out that their number of "correct" answers magically increases to an unreasonable level. Subjects in a treatment group also graded their own exams, but before the experiment began Ariely asked the subjects to list as many of the Ten Commandments as possible. Suddenly the subjects do not cheat. Students asked to think about the university's honor system also do not cheat. No changes in external constraints occurred, so what made the students behave more honestly? Were they concerned with Adam Smith's impartial spectator? Bateson, Nettle, and Roberts (2006, p. 412) conducted another experiment in which they placed a picture of a pair of eyes above an "honesty box used to collect money for drinks in a university coffee room." They found that this results in people giving three times as much on average. Such findings are clearly inconsistent with the assumptions of Homo economicus and consistent with the hypothesis that people often have regard for moral constraints. How elastic are these responses, and what are the triggers of internal constraints? Much research could be done on this subject.

The anthropologist Henrich and more than a dozen collaborators conducted behavioral experiments in fifteen small-scale societies around the world, and they found that people's likelihood of acting cooperatively (or prosocially, in the authors' terminology) instead of like Homo economicus varies across societies. Henrich and coauthors (2005, p. 795) write, "We found, first, that the canonical model—based on pure self-interest—fails in all of the societies studied." Regardless of where they were from, people were much less likely to behave opportunistically than orthodox neoclassical theory predicts. But, as one would expect, some people cooperated more than others. One of the researchers' most interesting findings is that "the higher the degree of market integration" in a society, "the greater the level of prosociality expressed in experimental games" (2005, p. 795).[10] This is consistent with McCloskey's (2006) view that markets make people more moral or perhaps that fence sitters find it easier to act morally in a market economy. The causality may go the other way, but markets and morality seem to go hand in hand (Storr, 2009; Langrill and Storr, 2012).

The experimental economics literature on this topic is vast and growing, as it should be. These academic studies confirm an important point that most people (except a few economists and paranoiacs) already know: not everyone is out to get everyone else. Of course, exceptions exist, and certain people

---

10. A few explanations are possible for such findings, but they are consistent with McCloskey's (2006) hypothesis that markets "improve our ethics" as well as with the hypothesis that markets require ethics.

are more likely to lack or to be tempted to violate internal moral rules. But this fact actually helps prove the point about the relative importance of internal and external constraints. Consider a place with lots of external constraints but also lots of conflict—prisons. Although prisons are much more policed than the outside world (a ratio of one prison guard to three prisoners is common [Mears, 2004], whereas overall in the United States the police officer to civilian ratio is 1 to 350 [Dantzker, 2005, p. 12]), the rate of crimes such as sexual assaults is upward of one hundred times higher inside prisons than outside them (Sabol and West, 2008, p. 1; Beck and Harrison, 2007, p. 5; Rand and Catalano, 2007, p. 3). Obviously, the many external constraints are not enough. A good social scientist would respond that the populations are not similar, but that is precisely the point. Whether they explicitly think about it or not, most people already consider the importance of individual self-governance. Would you rather encounter members of a prison gang with lots of police around or members of the Society of Friends (the Quakers) with no police around? I would feel much more comfortable around the Quakers.

9.3. INTERNALIZING THE BENEFITS OF INDIVIDUAL SELF-GOVERNANCE WITHIN CLUBS

Recognition of morality provides people with more options and requires spending fewer resources on external governance. Buchanan describes how being part of a community in which people have strong internal constraints is quite beneficial. Buchanan (1994, p. 133) writes, "A community that contains a larger number of members who exhibit a sense of fair play, mutual respect, and reciprocal understanding has less need of formal laws, and can avoid many of the social costs of enforcement by comparison with a community with a larger share of 'natural criminals.'" Not only does this have implications for an economy as a whole (the more individuals who govern themselves, the better), but individuals often can benefit personally if they can form individual relationships or opt into communities that utilize internal constraints. If people know they are dealing with others who have similar internal moral constraints, more trusting and less legalistic relationships become possible.

How many people would not care if they found evidence that someone with whom they were interacting lacked morals? People typically do not want to take the chance of dealing with an untrustworthy person.[11] Game theorists who portray the world as fraught with prisoners' dilemmas implicitly or

---

11. Others might deal with a known cheat, but only after taking precautions or charging a risk premium. But ceteris paribus, I cannot imagine how dealing with a deceitful person who lacks morals is a good thing.

explicitly assume that people interact with others not of their choosing, and many problems can stem from this. But as Tullock (1985, 1999) points out, we usually choose with whom we interact. One gets to select one's friends, business partners, and trading venues, and this enables individuals to trade with people they think are reliable.[12]

Many bankers refer to the "four Cs of credit" when deciding to extend a loan: collateral, capital, capacity, and character. Historically character loans, described by Merriam-Webster as "an unsecured loan made by a bank or loan company because of the known integrity of the borrower," were a common type of loan. Although people do not come with labels about their character, many proxies exist. For example, when a banker reviews a loan, he could, but need not, ask, "Are you a moral person? Do you believe in fulfilling promises that you make?" Instead, the banker can simply look at a person's credit score. Of course, reliable but amoral borrowers (people who have no qualms about defaulting but pay their loans to maintain good credit scores) may exist, but many repay their loans because they consider it a moral responsibility. A credit score is likely an indicator or a proxy of how strongly an individual governs himself.

Clubs also use mechanisms of governance that rely on internal moral constraints. For example, the brokers who formed the London Stock Exchange excluded the unreliable, and other clubs, such as private colleges, country clubs, and firms, rely on selection criteria and background checks to try to ensure that their members are upstanding.[13] People do not want to worry constantly about others stealing their wallets, so many people opt into exclusive clubs in which others have similar sets of internal moral constraints.

Membership requirements and mechanisms to fine or expel rule breakers are examples of private external governance, but stronger individual self-governance can supplement these mechanisms. Once one is inside the college, country club, or stock exchange, as a practical matter almost all interaction takes place without reliance on formally enforced rules even though such rules exist. Club members need not determine how to create and enforce contracts for the countless numbers of deals that people make within the club (consider how many trades a stockbroker can make in a given day and how costly it

---

12. Heiner (2002) and Osborne (2005) hypothesize that people garner information about the trustworthiness of others in their early stages of interaction so that they can decide whether to deal with that person. Maybe that's why ugly people are more likely to be criminals (Mocan and Tekin, 2010).

13. One could argue that having the option of showing noncooperative people the door means that clubs rely on external constraints. In some sense they do, but by establishing a safe environment for their members, they eliminate the potential for many conflicts that in theory could have required more external constraints. Thus, one can rely on external constraints at certain margins but believe internal constraints can replace them at other margins.

would be for external parties to adjudicate them); they can simply focus on determining whether those admitted to the club have an upstanding moral character.

The fact that some people are more trustworthy than others means that the optimal amount of resources spent on external mechanisms of governance will vary depending on the people interacting. A museum that allows in any paying guest will likely need to pay more for security than an equivalent private section of the Vatican where the entrance requirements are stricter. Rather than designing one-size-fits-all laws based on the assumption that all people lack internal moral constraints, individuals could gain if they could opt into clubs that have different mechanisms of private governance, and part of that structure might be reliance on individual self-governance. Laws that undermine freedom of association undermine mechanisms that depend on and encourage individual self-governance. Public streets and private venues where government mandates open access are more likely to face a tragedy-of-the-commons problem than voluntary associations where people deal with others who share similar moral views.

9.4. CAN WE RELY MORE ON INDIVIDUAL SELF-GOVERNANCE?

Individual self-governance is important, but where does it come from, and can it be strengthened? Several hypotheses have been advanced. Adam Smith ([1759] 1853, p. 233) writes that our moral faculties can be founded upon "reason, upon original instinct, called moral sense, or upon some other principle of our nature."For authors such as Thomas Paine ([1791] 1906, p. 84) self-governance is embedded in human nature. Modern authors, such as Ridley (1997), use sociobiology to suggest that humans have evolved tendencies to want to cooperate rather than cheat. Henrich (2004) describes how cultural evolution, cultural transmission, and competition within and between groups can lead to groups becoming more cooperative. True, people might cooperate only for self-interested, calculating reasons (Axelrod, 1984), but they might also cooperate because doing otherwise would be against their evolved or ingrained psyche. If our genetic makeup or a higher power predetermines our internal constraints, then they are outside human choice.

Other authors focus more on the notion that external factors, such as exposure to ideas, education, or socialization, can influence (although not enforce) individual self-governance. For example, Röpke (1960, p. 104) writes that the main sources of "self-discipline, a sense of justice," and "firm ethical norms" are "family, church, genuine communities, and tradition." Rabin (1995, p. 27) also argues that experiences such as "Sunday School and general moral socialization" can prime moral constraints. Psychological research indicates that adult psychopaths and children who have yet to be socialized are more likely to believe in the necessity of external controls. Responsible people, in contrast, realize that they must constrain their own choices.[14]

In his analysis of Smith's *Theory of Moral Sentiments*, Otteson (2002) maintains that children gradually learn what is right and wrong by observing how people react to their actions. An infant has less ability to understand how others react to their actions, but as children grow up, they understand better. Otteson (2002, p. 108) writes that children favor positive feedback and disfavor reprimands, so they "first see the need to discipline themselves when they have contact with others." Over time children become better at anticipating how others will react, and they learn how to internalize rules of proper behavior. In addition to feedback from parents or teachers, positive feedback about adoption of internal constraints may come from social norms in greater society. Norms are informal rules or customs that usually involve disapproval or extralegal sanctions if violated, so they entail a degree of constraint external to the individual. As one constantly receives feedback for acting in a certain way, one might internalize adherence to certain norms and follow them even when one does not face any repercussions.[15]

Furthermore, religion is another potential influence on individual self-governance. Those concerned with the afterlife or cosmic justice often consider how various actions will affect how they are treated later. Adam Smith ([1759] 1853, p. 233) highlights the importance of religion when he writes, "That the terrors of religion should thus enforce the natural sense of duty, was of too much importance to the happiness of mankind, for nature to leave it dependent upon the slowness and uncertainty of philosophical researches." Smith describes how people would look to God to enforce justice ([1759] 1853, p. 235): "Hence we are naturally encouraged to hope for his extraordinary favour and reward in the one case, and to dread his vengeance and punishment in the other." If one models this with game theory, a person's subjective perceptions of the payoffs include those in the afterlife or influenced by God. People who are concerned about such matters should be less likely to commit immoral acts even if they could get away with them. To John Locke, the importance of religion was tantamount. Locke ([1689] 1824, p. 47)

---

14. Debates about eating fattening foods, drinking alcoholic beverages, and consuming drugs have many similarities to those about morality. On one hand are people who believe that government must regulate, tax, or prohibit certain choices, and on the other hand are people who believe that individuals should be taught to control themselves (Leitzal, 2007).

15. For example, most American diners tip their waiter even if they are in a new city and do not intend to return to that restaurant. The norm of tipping may be internalized into an internal moral constraint that it is wrong to accept a service without paying for it.

writes, "Promises, covenants, and oaths, which are the bonds of human society, can have no hold upon an atheist." Kosmin and Keysar (2006, p. xvi) report that 91 percent of Americans profess a belief in God, so religious beliefs likely affect the choices of many people. People may also adopt morality for many other reasons (Rosser and Rosser, 1999), including a belief in tradition, a humanist philosophy, in karma, or some New Age sense of justice.

Individual self-governance is important in the short run even if its level is fixed, but it is potentially even more important if it can be enhanced. To the extent that moral socialization or economic, ethical, or religious teaching can strengthen individual self-governance, helping people do just this could be one of the most effective ways to enhance a civil society. How much influence is possible is an open question, but most parents and educators already implicitly recognize that they need to shape children's internal constraints. Psychologists have documented in depth how self-regulation and self-control are important traits that can be developed (Baumeister and Vohs, 2004), and internal moral constraints are likely quite similar. Few people assume that one can successfully raise children in a box or skip teaching them how to make responsible choices or respect others.[16] If one must be taught how to be a responsible human being, then education and socialization are of utmost importance.

For thousands of years, many religious adherents have spread commandments such as "Thou shalt not steal," "Thou shalt not lie," and "Do unto others as you would have them do unto you." Imagine if most people did not accept these principles.[17] Moral ideas that encourage individual self-governance, such as the golden rule, seem crucial for any civil society. But how much have people focused on teaching the slightly more advanced ethical norms conducive to a complex market economy? Although billions of people profess belief in the Ten Commandments, it is less obvious to them whether the implications of these commandments include "Thou shalt respect other people's private property" and "Thou shalt follow through with one's word in contracts." Although religious figures do not focus on those ideas, perhaps economists should.

My argument does not imply that betterment of society requires a complete transformation of humans; instead it implies that as individuals more

---

16. Although they skip attempting to raise their child in a box, some parents do engage in micromanagement or "helicopter parenting," in which they attempt to make or constrain their children's choices rather than to teach them to make successful decisions. Psychologists criticize this because eventually children will be in positions in which they cannot rely on their parents (Fine and Kotkin, 2003, p. 262). The parallels with legal centralism are many, except the helicopter parent is replaced by the helicopter state.

17. In a lecture Deidre McCloskey stated we know how society without morals would look, and that is a society of chimps.

effectively govern themselves, civil society can be improved at the margin.[18] Where the improvement stops, nobody knows. Economic theory is relatively new to the world; should economists spend time studying and teaching the internal moral constraints that help advance markets? Economists such as McCloskey (2006) and Storr (2009) argue that markets help make people more moral. If they are right, it might make sense to teach children and young adults economics along with ethics. Of course, Stigler (1982) would balk at anything that sounds like "economist as preacher." One can partially agree with Stigler insofar as plain vanilla positive economics always has a positive role to play, and still agree with Hayek (1967, p. 281), who states, "It is most important that a free society be based on strong moral convictions and . . . if we want to preserve freedom and morals, we should do all in our power to spread the appropriate moral convictions." Adam Smith was not just a simple economist but also a moral philosopher who taught about the beneficence of markets. Maybe we should be teaching people about the importance of respecting other people's property rights and the importance of following through on one's contracts. Increasing respect for property rights and abiding by one's contracts may not eliminate the need for other forms of governance, but they may reduce how much need we have for them.

9.5. SUMMARY AND THOUGHTS

Individual self-governance is one of the most important sources of governance. Yet out of all areas of governance, individual self-governance is the least studied and recognized. Those who pay attention to this important source of governance, rather than ignoring it as unscientific from a positive perspective or unrealistic from a normative perspective, have a better understanding of why cooperation occurs and ways in which it might be improved. In the short run, clubs can internalize the benefits of individual self-governance by organizing members with similar interests in governing themselves. And in the long run, the entire market economy may be strengthened the more that individual self-governance can be enhanced. Some forms of external governance will always be necessary, but people will need to devote fewer resources on external governance, the more people police themselves.

18. Knack and Keefer (1997, p. 1256) analyze World Values Survey data that ask people questions such as "Generally speaking, would you say that most people can be trusted, or that you can't be too careful in dealing with people?" and find that the percentage of people answering yes in a nation is correlated with many positive economic outcomes. Knack and Keefer (1997, p. 1252) write, "Individuals in higher-trust societies spend less to protect themselves from being exploited in economic transactions. Written contracts are less likely to be needed, and they do not have to specify every possible contingency. Litigation may be less frequent. Individuals in high-trust societies are also likely to divert fewer resources to protecting themselves."

CHAPTER 10

☙

When Third-Party Review Is "Necessary"

Adjudication by Contract

10.1. INTRODUCTION

It's the year 1880, and you are the captain of merchant vessel on the high seas. The hull was damaged in a storm and the vessel is taking on water. You are sure that ship and cargo will be lost, but as luck would have it, another ship appears that has the capability to help salvage your cargo and save your crew. Salvage operations are costly and quite risky for the salver, but in moments of duress, spending a long time negotiating all the terms of a contract is not practical. Your counterparty is a particularly philosophical sailor and begins: "How much should I be compensated, and how much should my firm be responsible if we damage your vessel or cargo in the process? On one hand, if we get nothing in return or are wholly responsible for any damage to a sinking ship, we have no incentive to help. On the other hand, I understand that we might not be entitled to be the full owner of boat, and if we are, it will not give you any incentive to assist us with the salvage. What legal procedures and what rules of evidence should we use? Who will determine the potential differences between us? We are in international waters, so what court will have jurisdiction, and who will select the judges? There is so much for us to talk about. Where shall we begin?" Before he has finished speaking, your boat has sunk, and both of you have nothing. Lawyers and jurists could debate the possibilities forever, but luckily common practice was for both parties to agree to a "Lloyd's salvage agreement" (also known as a "Lloyd's open form"). The agreement meant that salvage could commence quickly and the details could be sorted out later by . . . drumroll please . . . private arbitrators at Lloyd's of London (Mitcalfe, 1896).

Lloyd's of London, formerly known as Lloyd's Coffeehouse, was located just blocks from the stock market at Jonathan's Coffeehouse. Lloyd's became

THE SUBSCRIPTION-ROOM AT "LLOYD'S." *From an Old Print.*

Figure 10.1
Subscription Room at Lloyd's
Source: Thornbury (1878, p. 511).

a membership society where people could meet to buy and sell insurance and reinsurance, and it formed the Committee on Lloyd's to deal with potential differences, everything from how much a party should pay in any given case to how the proceeds from a salvage should be split.

Private third-party adjudication of disputes has a long history. As the 1795 *Ship Owner's Manual, Or, Sea-faring Man's Assistant* (1795, p. 103) explained, "It is an ordinary and laudable practice among merchants, that they do not, upon every small difference that happens, go to the law, but refer the matter in question of the decision of two men; or, in case these two cannot agree, they sometimes chuse a third, called an *Umpire*." Rather than assuming that an unbiased and knowledgeable third party must come from government, merchants selected private individuals: "All arbitrators, in difference, or disputes in assurance matters, ought always to be chosen from men of known abilities, and integrity; who dare act upon the line of equity, and fair dealing; without prejudice, or respect of persons" (Ship Owner's Manual, 1795, p. 105). Rather than relying on a bureaucrat to sort out their differences, parties in the insurance and other markets agreed to have industry experts adjudicate their potential disputes.

Third-party adjudication is not the "necessity" that legal centralists assume (scores of markets without external enforcement would not exist otherwise), but it can help minimize the problem of potential conflict or provide extra assurances. And as with the other examples of private governance, the greater the potential need, the more likely private parties are to arrange for it. Far from being libertarian fantasy, competing courts in England are analyzed by

Adam Smith, who comments that competition led to "superior dispatch and impartiality." Although government had a de jure monopoly, in many areas of law, parties had a choice among courts including local, hundred, manorial, county, ecclesiastical, law merchant, chancery, and common-law courts.[1] Adam Smith explains how various courts had to compete for business by being fast and fair:

> The fees of court seem originally to have been the principal support of the different courts of justice in England. Each court endeavoured to draw to itself as much business as it could, and was, upon that account, willing to take cognizance of many suits which were not originally intended to fall under its jurisdiction. . . . it came, in many cases, to depend altogether upon the parties before what court they would chuse to have their cause tried; and each court endeavoured, by superior dispatch and impartiality, to draw to itself as many causes as it could. (Smith [1776] 1976, p. 241)

Smith ([1776] 1976, p. 280) also writes, "Another thing which tended to support the liberty of the people and render the proceedings in the courts very exact, was the rivalship which arose betwixt them."

A system of "market chosen law" (Stringham, 1999) allows parties to evaluate and agree to a set of rules and procedures that they consider best. From various competing courts in early modern England to informal and formal alternative dispute resolution today, private adjudication is thriving.[2] Among the large corporations surveyed by Kessler (2012), 77 percent have arbitration clauses in consumer contracts and 93 percent in employment contracts. You have likely signed an arbitration agreement with your stockbroker, credit card company, and cell phone carrier. Private adjudication is common for small disputes for which going to court is not worth the time and cost, and private adjudication is common for large, complex disputes with which government courts are not equipped to deal in a knowledgeable and reasonably fast manner.

The market for private adjudication faces various regulations from government, leading survey respondents to complain about the "encroaching judicialisation" (Gerbay and Mistelis, 2013, p. 22),[3] but private adjudication is still more flexible than the government legal system. This chapter discusses some

---

1. Even though government spelled out jurisdictions for most areas, courts used various "legal fictions" to enable them to adjudicate disputes outside their official jurisdiction if parties wanted it. For example, ecclesiastical courts were officially for matters of church or morality, but parties could have a contract adjudicated by ecclesiastical courts if at contract time they swore an oath to God (Stringham and Zywicki, 2011b).

2. For overviews of the market for arbitration, see Shavell (1995), Benson (2000), Caplan and Stringham (2008), and Drahozal and Ware (2010).

3. Benson (1995) discusses how government arbitration statutes have made arbitration much more legalistic and bureaucratic than it once was or needs to be.

mechanisms that providers of adjudication adopt to cater to their clients, such as making the proceedings more likely to be fast and fair. Although certain arrangements may allow or encourage bias or waste, such problems are more prevalent when choice is absent, and lack of choice is often exacerbated by regulations. In contrast, when both parties have a free choice of rules and procedures, providers have an incentive to provide those that are ex ante beneficial to all parties. The agreement to abide by arbitration is referred to as the *compromissum* (i.e., the co-promise to arbitrate), and with this promise, both parties can gain. Ex ante selection of rules and procedures turns the rules and procedures into economic goods whose costs and benefits can be evaluated and internalized into the terms of exchange.

10.2. WHY PARTIES OPT FOR PRIVATE DISPUTE RESOLUTION

I had been so eagerly awaiting the Brooks Brothers ties I won on eBay that I was aghast to see that one of them was Oscar de la Renta, and the seller was not responding to my pleas for help. I knew that establishing jurisdiction in my local court or filing suit in the seller's state of residence would be very difficult. Fortunately, eBay offered adjudication between me and the seller, and did so for free. (The cost of adjudication had been priced into the listing fees for all transactions.) Many potentially interesting legal questions could arise. What rules of evidence would be used, how long would the proceedings be, would we have lawyers, and how many resources would we spend on the case? How would they decide who was right, and how would they make the party in the wrong pay? My "case" was likely reviewed by a single eBay employee who simply determined that the seller had not responded to my requests to exchange the item. Within a week, eBay refunded my money and let me keep the tie (please don't laugh the next time you see me in a paisley Oscar de la Renta tie). Rather than putting these decisions in the hands of legislators or courts of law, eBay transforms what could have been legal questions into business questions in which the objective is to serve buyers and sellers who use the service. Although certain actions may be right or wrong from a deontological point of view, the best way to resolve eBay disputes is not given from on high. Instead, the choice is in the hands of consumers; any burdensome or biased trials would increase the cost of transactions and negatively affect the demand for eBay.

My paisley problems were measly but still representative of a much deeper phenomenon. Private adjudication makes sense not only when the stakes are small but also when they are large. Should the procedure be more legalistic or less legalistic, more adversarial or more collaborative, drawn out or expedited? With the exception of the litigious parties whose goal is to use the legal system to extract resources from others (Haymond, 2001), trading partners typically do not want to have large sums of money tied up in legal proceedings or have lots of resources wasted in protracted disputes. Sussman and Wilkinson (2012, pp. 2–3) report that the "median length of time from filing through trial of civil cases in the U.S. District Court for the Southern District of New York was 33.2 months," and the median length of time "from filing a civil case in a lower court to disposition of appeal by the Second Superior Court of Appeals was 40.8 months." In contrast, the median period of American Arbitration Association arbitration is less than eight months from start to finish, and more informal forms of alternative dispute resolution take much less time. What sounds better to you? Speed is just one reason why the American Arbitration Association has attracted nearly 2 million cases in its history, and international arbitration is also growing in popularity (figure 10.2).

When talking about the ideal characteristics of adjudication, we should recognize that numerous variables exist, often with trade-offs between them (for example, speed versus accuracy). Consider the following potential benefits of arbitration:

1. Flexibility
2. Low cost or cost efficiencies
3. A speedy outcome and avoidance of undue delay
4. "Fairness" and "justice"
5. Legal due process
6. Results comporting with commercial, technical, or professional standards
7. Predictability and consistency in result
8. A final and binding resolution
9. Privacy and confidentiality
10. The preservation of a relationship and continuing performance (Stipawowich, 2010, p. 53)

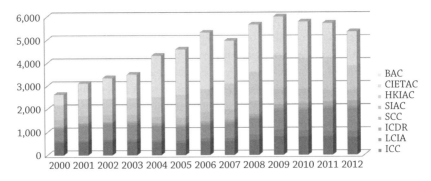

Figure 10.2
International Arbitration Cases at Eight Leading International Arbitral Institutions
Source: Data are from the International Chamber of Commerce (ICC), the London Court of International Arbitration (LCIA), the International Center for Dispute Resolution, a division of the American Arbitration Association (ICDR), the Arbitration Institute of the Stockholm Chamber of Commerce (SCC), the Singapore International Arbitration Centre (SIAC), the China International Economic and Trade Arbitration Commission (CIETAC), and the Hong Kong International Arbitration Center (HKIAC).

Given that trade-offs exist, which ones are most important, and what is the optimal combination? The person who "knows" the optimal solution for all people, is a legal centralist.

The neatness of the legal centralist solution notwithstanding, law and economics scholars should recognize that different people have different preferences and that the optimal solution will vary depending the wishes of the parties involved. In contrast to a government one-size-fits-all solution (Hasnas, 1995), private adjudication lets the parties select the priorities, which will vary based on the needs and wants of each party.

Consider, for example, the choice to have a more formal adversarial trial that can be long and drawn out or to have a more informal conciliatory process. Actually, the choice is more complicated than that. JAMS Alternative Dispute Resolution (formerly Judicial Arbitration and Mediation Services, Inc.) oversees ten thousand cases per year and offers the following choices from what it calls the alternative dispute resolution spectrum:

Direct negotiation
    Mediative processes
    Facilitative mediation
    Evaluative mediation
    Neutral evaluation
    Minitrial
    Nonbinding arbitration
    Neutral expert fact-finding
    Court-appointed special masters / discovery masters

Adjudicative processes
    Arbitration
    Bracketed arbitration
    Final-offer arbitration
    Private judging
    Med-Arb

Each choice has different advantages, and disputants have differing amounts of control through the process. With government, courts decide the procedures, but with alternative dispute resolution, they are chosen by the disputants themselves. Private adjudication (to the extent it is not restricted by government)[4] enables choice of law, choice of forum, and choice of arbitrator.

Rather than using governmentally appointed government judges or juries, users of alternative dispute resolution get to select their adjudicators based on

---

4. The contributors in Buckley (1999) provide an overview of ways in which freedom of contract for choice of law is currently restricted.

their needs. Certain disputes are so complex that parties willingly pay significant premiums for arbitrators who are subject matter experts rather than rely on some random judge (Sussman and Wilkinson, 2012, p. 3). Among corporate users, surveys indicate care about the expertise and neutrality, and companies are willing to pay more for those (figures 10.3 and 10.4).

An Ernst and Young (2011) survey of corporate users of arbitration in India found that a minority placed emphasis on hiring ex-government judges (presumably they have expertise in the law), but 68 percent believe that subject matter experts should be appointed as arbitrators. Ernst and Young (2011, p. 14) report that appointing ex-government judges as arbitrators "often leads to difficulty in understanding the technical matters" (and keep in mind they are referring to selected ex-government judges, as opposed to assigned government judges). The American Arbitration Association, for example, has

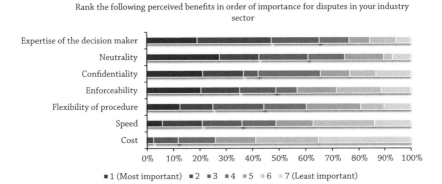

Figure 10.3
What Do Corporate Users of Arbitration Consider Most Important about Arbitration?
Source: Data are from Gerbay and Mistelis (2013).

Figure 10.4
Factors for Choosing Arbitrators
Source: Data are from Gerbay and Mistelis (2013).

different staff, arbitrators, and frameworks available for simple versus large complex commercial disputes.[5] Where North (1990, p. 35) asserts that more complex exchanges require government enforcement, as deals become more and more complex, how likely are judges and jurors in government courts to be able reasonably understand them? Some studies show that a majority of jurors do not understand basic legal directions (Thomas, 2010, p. 38), and often "judges might not understand business practice or the nuances of business law" (Aikman, 2007, p. 39).

In addition to allowing parties to choose their arbitrators, arbitration lets parties choose the set of rules and procedures that they consider best. Arbitration can allow "law by contract" (Buys, 2005) and puts the decisions in the hands of those choosing the arbitration. What set of rules and procedures should be employed? Let the people in a dispute decide. Should pretrial discovery occur? Let the people in a dispute decide. Should there be multiple levels of review? You can see where I am going with this.

Viewed from this perspective, many of the criticisms of private adjudication can be interpreted as observers simply not liking what the people in a dispute want. Consider an issue such as pretrial discovery, which is common in government courts but not with arbitration. Although pretrial discovery has the potential to make proceedings more predictable, the process is extremely costly (Sussman and Wilkinson, 2012, p. 3). For good or bad, the Bible did not instruct how much time and money we should spend on this procedure, and without market feedback, how do we know how much is optimal? Rather than putting this choice in the hands of lawmakers or judges, arbitration puts the decision in the hands of people in a dispute. The fact that few people opt for it is telling. Similarly, where the noneconomist assumes other features of arbitration, such as "no public record," are bad, they ignore the fact that parties cite privacy as one of the most desirable aspects of arbitration (PricewaterhouseCoopers, 2006, p. 6).[6]

---

5. The American Arbitration Association (2007, pp. 11–12) explains, "The large, complex case framework offered by the AAA is designed primarily for business disputes involving claims of at least $500,000, although parties are free to provide for use of the LCC [large, complex, commercial] Rules in other disputes The key elements of the program are (1) selection of arbitrators who satisfy rigorous criteria to insure that the panel is an extremely select one; (2) training, orientation, and coordination of those arbitrators in a manner designed to facilitate the program; (3) establishment of procedures for administration of those cases that elect to be included in the program; (4) flexibility of those procedures so that parties can more speedily and efficiently resolve their disputes; and (5) administration of large, complex cases by specially trained, experienced AAA staff."

6. One of the most famous partial criticisms of private adjudication comes from Landes and Posner (1979), who say it will underproduce the public good of good legal rules. Caplan (1993) provides a critique of this theory, and it turns out that many of the good rules and procedures that we see in the common law were developed privately (Stringham and Zywicki, 2011b). The same is true of the rules and procedures found at Lloyd's.

Or consider the issue of appeals, another commonly criticized aspect of arbitration. Although some types of arbitration, such as Lloyd's Open Form, allow for appeal, most arbitral decisions are meant to be final and binding. Although some consider this a bad thing, it eliminates the need to have cases adjudicated more than once, which can be extremely costly. Parties have the option of signing arbitration clauses that allow multiple levels of appeal, but in a survey by PricewaterhouseCoopers (2006, p. 15) 91 percent of respondents indicated that they did not favor an appeal mechanism. In addition, 69 percent indicated that one of the key benefits of arbitration is that it helps "minimise escalation of disputes" (PricewaterhouseCoopers, 2006, p. 2), indicating that parties prefer resolving a matter to drawing it out. Caplan and I (Caplan and Stringham, 2008) have made the analogy that being able to commit to having an issue reviewed only once is like being able to commit to not engaging in an arms race. Protracted lawsuits, like arms races, require both sides to spend resources to their ultimate detriment, and anything that can eliminate such suits can benefit both sides.

10.3. MECHANISMS FOR MAKING PRIVATE ADJUDICATION SERVE THE MUTUAL INTERESTS OF THE ADJUDICANTS

We know that alternative dispute resolution is popular, but certain authors say the process is necessarily biased. Everyone's favorite senator and American Indian Harvard Law professor, Elizabeth Warren, criticizes arbitration, stating that individuals have little choice and that arbitration is biased in favor of big business: "It is Darth Vader's Death Star—the Empire always wins" (Dougherty, 2012). Similarly, the Public Citizen Foundation states that arbitration is prone to the following problems: high costs, bias, limited discovery, prohibition of class actions, inconvenient venue, one-way requirements, no public record, limited judicial review, and limited remedies (Public Citizen, 2010). Might it be the case that arbitrators only serve one side, especially the side with more economic influence?

One should not assume that private adjudicators are perfect any more than we should assume that government judges are perfect. Imagine being roped into a tribunal without any choice in the matter (ignore for the moment that that's how government courts work). It's not difficult to think of arrangements in which tribunals compete to serve one side but not the other (Landes and Posner, 1979). That humans can have biases should be the starting point of all analysis, and the objective is how to best minimize them.

The commonly invoked option is the legal centralist route that relies on a myriad of laws and legal procedures, but a second option is to minimize problems through economic arrangements. Landes and Posner (1979, p. 247) write that private dispute resolution works best in the following two types of circumstances: "(1) those where a preexisting contract between the parties requires submission to arbitration according to specified rules for selecting an arbitrator, and (2) those where the disputants belong to an association which provides both arbitration machinery for its members and a set of effective private sanctions for refusal to submit to arbitration in good faith or to abide by its results."

Having a predispute arbitration agreement allows people to actually step behind Buchanan's veil of uncertainty (Brennan and Buchanan, 1985) and select the rules and procedures should a dispute arise. When parties agree to have a dispute adjudicated in a particular way, they will only do so if the rules are ex ante mutually beneficial.[7] Because buyers and sellers are forward looking, they weigh not just the expected costs and benefits of the good in a transaction but also the rules and procedures associated with the contract and price all of them into a transaction.

Even if one party is larger and offers the terms of adjudication on a take-it-or-leave-it basis, the requirement for a *compromissum* creates incentives to maximize joint benefit and minimize potential problems such as bias or waste. Suppose, for example, that buyers on eBay accurately predict a 10 percent chance of the seller not delivering and that eBay adjudication always found in favor of these delinquent sellers (and suppose for the moment this 90 to 10 percent ratio is stable). Here a $100 tie would be sold only for $90 (or less if we add risk aversion), meaning the cost of any *proseller bias* would be *borne by the seller*. Whether the sellers are big corporations and the buyers are little guys is irrelevant. Rules that harm buyers negatively affect their willingness to pay for a transaction.

Alternatively, suppose that sellers ship goods first, there is a 10 percent chance buyers do not end up paying, and eBay is always biased in favor of these delinquent buyers. Here forward-looking sellers would now require $110, or more if we add risk aversion, meaning the cost of any *probuyer bias* would be *borne by the buyer*. Addition of dynamic interaction effects about the choices of defaulters worsening over time does not change these basic results: adjudication biased against buyers reduces buyers' willingness to pay, and conversely, adjudication biased against sellers increases how much they need to be paid. When risk aversion drives prices away from the $100 in amounts greater $10, even Homo economicus does not gain from having a system biased in his favor. Thus, even though individuals might like bias in their favor after the fact, with ex ante market evaluation and negotiation, *eliminating proseller* bias means *buyers are willing to pay more*. (In the first example, if the buyer knows the situation will be rectified in the 10 percent of cases in which the seller does

---

7. In this chapter I focus on the many areas in which people agree, and I leave for future discussion the important question of how to deal with disputes between people who do not agree. For a good discussion of this question see Chartier (2013).

not deliver, his willingness to pay will approach $100 rather than just $90.) Conversely, *eliminating probuyer bias* means *sellers are willing to sell for less.* (In the second example, if the seller knows the situation will be rectified in the 10 percent of cases in which buyer funds do not materialize, he will be willing to sell for $100 rather than $110.) The ultimate benefit of effective rules on eBay is that delinquent buyers or sellers know they will be charged, which further eliminates the incentive to be delinquent.

Whether we are talking about potential disputes between stockbrokers and clients, banks and customers, cell phone carriers and users, or landlords and tenants, attempting to stack the deck against one side does not pay when that party can adjust his willingness to enter an agreement. The cost of biased rules or procedures is borne by the party that the rules were intended to bias.

In addition to dealing with bias, the requirement for a *compromissum* also helps minimize problems associated with wasteful disputes. Although I believe certain things are objectively right or wrong, I don't want to spend $1 million in adjudication fees to get back $100 owed to me. In contrast to government courts in which judges and lawyers do not bear the burden of protracted lawsuits, a private system internalizes the costs and benefits of adjudication and prices them into transactions. For example, if each $100 transaction wastes an average of $10 for the buyer and $10 for the seller, these procedures drive a $20 wedge between what the buyer pays and what the seller receives. In certain areas a $20 average dispute resolution cost might be the best course available, but if an alternative arrangement can eliminate unnecessary costs associated with adjudicating disputes, both parties can gain. The seller receives more, and the buyer pays less.

When rules and procedures are selected by the parties themselves rather than imposed externally, they can optimize based on what they consider most desirable. Rules and procedures can be viewed as economic goods that can be evaluated and selected, but a market for adjudication does not require potential disputants to evaluate a million rules any more than a market for automobiles requires drivers to evaluate the 10,000 parts in their car. In the automobile market consumers evaluate cars as a package deal (a package of Lancasterian goods), and producers put together the packages that consumers are likely to value most. A PricewaterhouseCoopers survey of corporate users of arbitration found that about half used a standard clause and another half used a tailored clause in their contracts (PricewaterhouseCoopers, 2006, p. 11). The market for adjudication allows consumers to evaluate the rules and procedures and select from the package, whether from Lloyd's, eBay, or the American Arbitration Association, that they consider best. Here we have a case in which Buchanan's normative ideal about agreement to rules (Brennan and Buchanan, 1985) is actually met.

If a set of rules and procedures has "high costs, bias, limited discovery, prohibition of class actions, inconvenient venue, one-way requirements, no public record, limited judicial review, and limited remedies" (Public Citizen Foundation, 2010), those negatives become priced into a transaction, and if a superior alternative exists, both sides will have an incentive to select it.[8]

Most of the literature discussing the benefits of alternative dispute resolution is not written by free-market economists, but it could be. Contributors to this literature talk about helping to discover mutually agreeable outcomes and eliminate needless disputes that harm both sides. For example, Sordin (2004) tells the story of two sisters bickering over an orange. Their legalistic mother comes in, cuts the orange in half, and tells each to go on her way. The first takes her rind to make zest for a cake while discarding the inside, and the second eats the inside of her half while discarding the rind. Each sister could have had more had the adjudicator simply assessed their wants. Such a problem is clearly evident in government courts where judges and lawyers have little incentive to look into what the people want, and many thrive on protracted and costly disputes.[9] Private adjudicators, in contrast, do not have unwilling customers and therefore must consider the well-being of their customers.

10.4. TO WHAT EXTENT DOES PRIVATE DISPUTE RESOLUTION DEPEND ON GOVERNMENT?

The more parties can rely on private adjudication, the less they "need" government courts. Many people, however, say that private adjudication ultimately depends on the state. Williamson is a pioneer in the literature on private order, but he says that at the end of the day, private order is made possible by threat of government enforcement:

> To be sure, a private ordering approach to contract requires support. For one thing, good intentions or mere agreements are prone to breakdown. This invites precisely the type of analysis of credible commitments with which transaction cost economics is concerned. Also . . . private ordering benefits from having the law available for purposes of ultimate appeal. (Williamson, 1996, p. 42)

Williamson's sentiment indicates that one can support having a massively increased role for private adjudication even if one believes that government is ultimately beneficent and necessary.

---

8. In the current world, government mandates and heavily regulates many procedures of self-regulatory organizations such as the Financial Industry Regulatory Authority, so choices are quite limited. This does not mean, however, that arbitration should be outlawed, as certain authors and lawmakers propose, when an alternative solution is to free up these markets.

9. Former West Virginia Supreme Court of Appeals judge Neely (1982) provides describes various ways that courts have little incentive to not waste resources because the decision-makers do not bear the costs.

But could arbitration agreements exist if government did not enforce them? Whereas most people assume the answer is no, a researcher of private governance should not assume either way. Whenever government exists alongside private provision of a good, there is a tendency to attribute its success to government. The government-centric mindset expressed in a vice president's statement "During my service in the United States Congress, I took the initiative in creating the Internet" (Gore, 1999) should be questioned because the Internet took off once it got in the hands of the private sector. But because Al Gore did exist when the Internet was created, simple observation cannot rule out the possibility that Al Gore created the Internet.

In many cases arbitration agreements are indeed enforceable by government, so it is theoretically possible that these agreements could not exist without government. Nevertheless, private adjudication is often completely or practically unenforceable, so examining these cases can be enlightening. In the seventeenth and eighteenth centuries, the sophisticated insurance markets of Lloyd's were a new innovation in history and, like secondary markets in company shares, they were not an innovation of government. In many cases Lloyd's rules were in direct conflict with government laws (Holman, 1896, p. 171), so in these cases we know that rules were not made possible because of government.[10] In other cases Lloyd's rules were not in direct conflict with government laws and so theoretically could be augmented by government, but that does not mean that government was helpful. Frederick Martin (1876, p. 270) describes the market in the late eighteenth and early nineteenth centuries: "Many other attempts to prevent insurance frauds simply by penal enactments followed those of Lord Ellenborough, but they were more or less inefficacious." The insurers came to a solution. Martin writes, "It was thus, gradually and slowly, the conviction came to underwriters, that the less they depended upon the legal punishing of frauds, and the more on their own vigilance to prevent them, the better it would be." Even though government courts existed, Lloyd's could not rely on them, so instead it had to rely on its own private enforcement of rules.

In modern times arbitrators face very similar dilemmas. It is theoretically possible for government courts to enforce arbitral awards in most countries (Leeson, 2008), but in practice, matters are not that simple. For example, even though China is a signatory to the Convention on the Recognition and Enforcement of Foreign Arbitral Awards (also known as the 1958 New York Convention), the convention's actual applicability in China is quite limited. The main problem is that courts in China will invalidate or simply refuse to enforce any arbitral award that was not decided by Chinese "arbitrators" (Chen

---

10. The additional fact that insurers at Lloyd's offered insurance against government arrest and seizure (*Ship Owner's Manual*, 1795, pp. 48–49) might lead us to question whether the success of Lloyd's should be attributed to government.

and Howes, 2009), who are heavily under the control of the Chinese government.[11] Hong Kong–based attorneys Blount and Rogers (2012) identify the following problems with arbitration in China:

- The enforcement regime in China is less robust for local awards.
- Arbitrations in mainland China must be administered by a mainland Chinese arbitration commission.
- The Chinese courts enjoy wide supervisory power over arbitrations seated in China.
- There is a lack of interim measures for arbitration seated in China.
- It is difficult to secure a tribunal of sufficient experience and international outlook.
- Simplified procedures are not suitable for complex disputes.

I spoke with one international commodities broker who said, "Unless one knows important people in China, arbitration in China is hopeless. I went to a lawyer about initiating a lawsuit or arbitration, and he said don't even bother" (personal interview, New York, April 7, 2013). Arbitration in China and other countries is heavily influenced or restricted by government, and not in a good way. In other countries, official restrictions on arbitration may not be great, but that does not mean that local courts have the ability or interest in actually enforcing arbitral awards. According to a PricewaterhouseCoopers (2008, p. 3) survey, "Many corporate counsel cited countries in Africa and Central America, as well as China, India and Russia, as states that they perceive as hostile to enforcement of foreign arbitral awards."

Despite the "imperfections" of these courts, trade between firms in America and these countries is thriving. The volume of trade between the United States and China is approaching a half trillion dollars per year, and arbitration between American and Chinese firms still takes place outside of China. Attorneys such as Blount and Rogers (2012) recommend that parties "arbitrate outside mainland China if possible," and if the theory that arbitration requires government enforcement were correct, we would not expect any of this arbitration to take place. How can it work? A PricewaterhouseCoopers (2008, p. 2) survey of international corporate users of arbitration found that "voluntary compliance with an award or settlement is the most common outcome from arbitration procedures" and close to full voluntary compliance happens

---

11. Zhang-Whitaker (2012) also explains that there is no guarantee courts will even decide on the legitimacy of an arbitral decision: "Chinese law gives the Chinese Intermediate Courts two months to make a decision on an enforcement petition, and if the Intermediate Court decides not to recognize and enforce the award, the case must be referred to the Chinese Supreme Court for review. Unfortunately, there are no time frames requiring the Chinese Supreme Court to act in the context of an enforcement petition, so if an arbitration award is taken up by the Supreme Court for review, it may languish in the Supreme Court indefinitely."

in 84 percent of cases. Should we attribute this voluntary compliance to the threat of enforcement from the many dysfunctional court systems around the world?[12]

Even in countries like the United States, relying on government to enforce arbitral awards is at a minimum costly, so private parties will avoid it whenever possible. Consider some of the options they have discovered. When eBay's arbitrator issued the $50 award for my paisley tie, he did not say, "Here is the judgment; now all you need to do is get the decision enforced in government court." Instead, eBay tied the arbitration procedure to our existing eBay accounts and simply transferred the funds from the delinquent seller to me. All users of eBay including my not-so-great counterpart agree to such a system. Similarly, credit cards are able to charge the party found in the wrong and issue funds to the party in the right. Here the credit card company acts not only as arbitrator but also as guarantor of payment. The credit card company assumes the debt and takes the collection into its own hands, something such companies have down to a science. And lest one think that the collection of credit card debts crucially relies on government, unsecured debt such as credit card debt is notoriously difficult to collect in government courts. In Chapter 13 bankruptcies credit card debt comes after secured debt, and in Chapter 7 bankruptcies credit card debt explicitly gets nothing, so banks must write off this bad debt. One collection agency that works with seven of the ten largest credit card companies states, "You can't squeeze blood out of a turnip. . . . The big settlements just aren't there anymore" (quoted in Dash, 2009, p. B1). Although running up credit card debt and declaring bankruptcy is relatively easy from a legal point of view (Zywicki, 2005), most credit card users prefer paying over facing other, privately generated, consequences for defaulting, such as a bad credit rating. The enforcement of this adjudication thus relies on a combination of mechanisms of private governance.

When two parties do not have accounts with a single financial institution, they have other options. The American Arbitration Association explains how parties can specify if they want to use escrow, physical deposits, or letters of credit in their arbitration agreements (2007, pp. 28–29). Certain private entities, such as the Stockholm Chamber of Commerce, provide both arbitration services and escrow services. Escrow entails parties depositing money or property with a third party; the escrow agent is authorized to release the property after everything is sorted out. Letters of credit entail a third-party financial institution pledging to pay for a buyer, thereby ensuring that a seller will be paid even if the buyer feels like backing out. Letters of credit have a

---

12. We also know that international trade and various forms of cross-border dispute resolution existed before the 1958 Convention on the Recognition and Enforcement of Foreign Arbitral Awards, so should we attribute its success to government enforcement?

long history (*Ship Owner's Manual*, 1795, p. 107) and are used because even the best government legal system cannot mandate large payments from a party without resources to pay. The arrangement puts the required diligence in the hands of the financial institution, which offers a letter of credit only if it knows the buyer can likely pay, rather than in the hands of the seller, who may know little about the buyer, or in the hands of a legal system. When a financial institution has guaranteed payment on a person's behalf, the ineffectiveness of government courts becomes irrelevant.[13]

10.5. SUMMARY AND THOUGHTS

Third-party adjudication is not always necessary, but in cases in which it is beneficial, private parties have incentives to arrange for it. Rather than assuming that the rules and procedures of adjudication must be externally imposed, we often observe the terms (rules and procedures) of adjudication bundled with a contract. In such cases, the costs and benefits of adjudication become internalized into the prices associated with a contract or series of contracts. This turns the rules and procedures of adjudication into economic goods that parties can evaluate and optimize. Instead of requiring a one-size-fits-all solution, private adjudication lets parties pick rules and procedures that they consider best. Whereas government courts do not bear the costs of, and often thrive because of, biased or drawn-out procedures, private adjudicators must consider the desires of the people in a dispute.

Should adjudication be more informal or formal, adversarial or collaborative, private or public, expedited or thorough? Predispute arbitration clauses are one way for parties to spell out their wishes regarding how their disputes will be resolved. Predispute arbitration clauses are easy standard business contracts, and with them much or all of what is subsumed by commercial law can be stipulated in arbitration agreements and adjudicated privately. The same can be true for much of what is subsumed by modern labor law in employment arbitration clauses. What people can agree to in arbitration clauses has certain restrictions, but it need not be. Similarly, many people are opting for arbitration clauses in their prenuptial agreements, and much of what is subsumed by divorce law and family law can be adjudicated privately (in cases in which it is allowed).[14] Similarly, consumer arbitration clauses cover much of what is subsumed by product liability law, and we can think about arbitration handling many other areas of law (Folmer, Heijman, and Leen, 2002). The

---

13. For the use of bonding more generally, see Friedman (2000, p. 146).
14. Authors such as Shacher (2008) claim that arbitration in family law should be restricted, and she describes how many laws do exactly that.

more people can opt out of the government legal system, the less "necessary" that legal system is.

Galanter (2004) and Stipanowich (2010) refer to "the vanishing trail" and data that show that between 1962 and 2002 the percentage of federal civil cases resolved by trial decreased by 84 percent. Cases in state courts have similar trends. The old "You'll have your day in court" mantra is becoming an increasingly mythical view of government.

To be sure, government courts are still popular in much the same way that other government agencies such as the U.S. Postal Service are still popular. Each year the Postal Service delivers 5 billion first-class letters between households (Mazzone and Pickett, 2011, p. 9), but it also delivers 83.5 billion pieces of "advertising mail" (Mazzone and Pickett, 2011, p. 10) (often classified as junk mail). Just as the Postal Service spends the majority of its time providing goods that consumers do not want, government courts also provide many "services" that people do not necessarily want. Lande's (1998) survey of executives found that 94 percent complained about the "litigation explosion," and McInturff, Weigel, and Schoen's (2010, p. 20) survey of small businesses found similar results. One litigator at a large New York City law firm told me, "At least 99 percent of the cases I see are what can be called 'stickup' cases" (personal interview, New York, March 6, 2013), and the California Chamber of Commerce states that "frivolous lawsuits hold legitimate businesses hostage and force them to pay millions to avoid paralyzing court battles" (Watson and Hassett, 2003, p. 177). Although market failure theorists justify government courts to deal with externalities, the legal system may be one of the biggest sources of externalities in a Kaldor-Hicks efficiency framework, and of rights violations in a deontological framework. Government may be providing a public good that is underprovided on the market, or it may be overproviding a "public bad" the market would not provide.[15]

One potentially important explanation of why private parties want government to recognize their arbitration agreements is so they will *not* have their arbitral agreement overturned and *not* be dragged through government courts. This perspective presents government courts as a negative to be avoided rather than a positive that help make markets work. Private adjudication is not the solution to all the world's problems, and in many or most cases, parties do not even need it. But whenever both parties agree to it, at the margin it should be viewed as unambiguously positive. When parties recognize that they need a third party to adjudicate a dispute, they can easily hire a third party to do so. Alternative dispute resolution lets parties opt out of highly imperfect government courts and opt into courts of their choosing.

---

15. Hummel (1990) and Coyne, Duncan, and Leeson (2014) make this argument in the context of national defense.

CHAPTER 11

ᴄᐯᴐ

Does Private Governance Work
in the Most Complex Markets?

Successful Risk Management on Wall Street Even
in the Wake of the 2008 Economic Downturn

11.1. INTRODUCTION

In theory, if you lend money and the borrower defaults, you simply go to government courts and get your money back.[1] In practice, however, even the best courts (whether public or private) cannot get money out of a penniless borrower, and even when the borrower uses his home as collateral, foreclosing on that collateral is often difficult. In modern America, a foreclosure process can drag on for months while the delinquent borrower makes no payments and does not maintain, or even guts, the home, and the best the lender can hope for is ending up with a home it did not want in the first place. (For homes sold in foreclosure, a 50 percent loss for investors is common [Ahmed, 2012].) Despite the inability of courts to enforce relatively straightforward contracts, the commercial and mortgage lending industries have been thriving through new forms of property rights made possible because of private governance.

In the past, loans went to people whom lenders knew personally and knew were likely to be trustworthy. Yet character loans were typically of small amounts, and they also precluded people with weaker contacts from borrowing. In recent years, however, the scope of lending has expanded dramatically thanks to a new class of financial arrangements created with the recognition that courts are not a reliable way of getting back money from delinquent borrowers. Mortgage-backed securities, collateralized debt obligations, credit

---

1. To many economists, credit transactions would be impossible otherwise (Tullock, 1972, p. 69; Landa, 1994, p. 60).

default swaps, and many other private arrangements (these are described in sections 11.2, 11.3, and 11.4) create new and tremendously complex forms of property rights and have done so largely outside the oversight of government regulators. They help price the risk of default into initial transactions and let some pay others to assume those risks.

These financial arrangements are, no doubt, some of the most complex in history, but many believe that these markets are responsible for economic ruin.[2] In 2003, Warren Buffet (2003, p. 15) stated, "Governments have so far found no effective way to control, or even monitor, the risks posed by these contracts. In my view, derivatives are financial weapons of mass destruction." By 2008 a large financial bubble was bursting, and some of the biggest losses were indeed associated with these new instruments. When all was said and done, the former masters of the universe at Lehman Brothers were bankrupt, Merrill Lynch and Bear Stearns were absorbed by commercial banks, and the government decided to nationalize American International Group (AIG), Fannie Mae, and Freddie Mac. Longtime follower of Ayn Rand Alan Greenspan said he had found a flaw in his own ideology: "I made a mistake in presuming that the self-interest of organizations, specifically banks and others, was such that they were best capable of protecting their own shareholders" (quoted in Beattie and Politi, 2008), and the forty-third president of the United States declared, "I've abandoned free market principles to save the free market system" (Cable News Network, 2008). The government-sponsored Financial Crisis Inquiry Commission (2011, p. xviii) report concluded:

> The sentries were not at their posts, in no small part due to the widely accepted faith in the self-correcting nature of markets and the ability of financial institutions to police themselves. More than 30 years of deregulation and reliance on self-regulation by financial institutions, championed by former Federal Reserve chairman Alan Greenspan and others, supported by successive administrations and Congresses, and actively pushed by the powerful financial industry at every turn, had stripped away key safeguards, which could have helped avoid catastrophe.

Although the majority of Americans still agree that "Wall Street is absolutely essential because it provides the money businesses must have for investment," 82 percent believe that "recent events have shown that Wall Street should be subject to tougher regulations" (Harris Interactive, 2012; Bowman and Rugg, 2013, pp. 24–26).

2. Mah-Hui Lim (2008, p. 4) presents the common sentiment: "The dissociation of ownership of assets from risks encouraged poor credit assessment and was fundamental in reducing the margin of safety and increasing the margin of risks . . . CDOs [collateralized debt obligations] resemble a house built on a deck of cards; when the cards slip, the house falls apart."

It is true that private governance was responsible for overseeing markets for collateralized debt obligations and credit default swaps, and it is true that many entities participating in those markets lost or went bankrupt—and add on the examples of fraud such as the Madoff scandal in the largely unregulated hedge fund industry. Many observers reached the same conclusion as *Fortune* columnist Bing (2013, p. 164): "Now we know that Wall Street needs to be overseen by regulations that make such things impossible." Is private governance something that worked in more simple times but is ill equipped for more sophisticated markets today?

These "lack of regulation caused catastrophe" and "regulation will prevent it next time" narratives are widely held, but they are actually centuries old. Since time immemorial the relative prices of assets have fluctuated, sometimes dramatically, but after major price declines one almost always sees a call for bans on certain advanced contracts. This was evident in Holland after the first major price decline in shares of the Dutch East India Company 1609, in England after the South Sea Bubble in 1720, and in America after the stock market crash in 1929. But nobody who "designed" financial markets ever designed them to avoid rising or falling relative prices, and any attempt to do is a fool's errand. Private governance helps people deal with certain types of risk (notably counterparty default risk), but it was never designed to eliminate all risk.

In the 2008 economic downturn many bad things manifested in financial markets, and many people lost a lot. But most of the problems arose from changes in underlying variables (including changes associated with monetary and regulatory policy)[3] rather than from problems of private governance. Yes, certain investment vehicles failed completely, and yes, some turned out to be fraudulently represented. But even in the midst of major problems, the market of private governance on Wall Street was working almost exactly as designed. The advanced arrangements that people blame for causing the financial crisis actually helped prevent matters from getting worse. Those who opted for aggressive investment vehicles and chose not to pay for more private governance were exposed to more risk, and those who opted for more conservative investment vehicles and chose to pay for more layers of protection limited their downside. Many criticisms of Wall Street are more sophisticated, but most stem from a fundamental misunderstanding of what financial products and private regulation were designed to do.

In this chapter I address three common misconceptions about the role of private regulation in "causing" the economic downturn and make the case that the widely misunderstood collateralized debt obligations, credit default swaps, and other advanced markets were actually great innovations. Many

---

3. For excellent book-length discussions of potential causes of the financial crisis, see Allison (2013), Friedman (2010), Friedman and Kraus (2011), and Woods (2009).

problems arose, but we must always differentiate problems that occurred *on* Wall Street from problems *with* Wall Street.

The first point, which should be obvious to everyone but for some reason isn't, is that when privately regulated financial instruments fall in value, including to zero, this does not indicate a failure of private governance. Private governance deals with certain types of risk, but it was not designed to guarantee success, and one should not be surprised if certain investment vehicles, such as intentionally riskier collateralized debt obligations, do not succeed. Many investors thought housing investments would be better than they turned out to be, but their overly bullish views were their problem and not a problem with Wall Street itself. Markets were never designed to guarantee success or stable relative prices. The net worth of Americans decreased by 38.8 percent between 2007 and 2010 (Kearns, 2012), and it has since recovered (figure 11.1). Investments in most mortgage-backed securities funds have also turned out well. This indicates that many of the problems were due simply to a large-scale fluctuation rather than to investments permanently vanishing owing to fraud. Some fraud did, and unfortunately always will, exist, but the largest losses were in the riskiest investment vehicles that investors had demanded. I feel bad for investors (including myself) whose portfolios declined in value, but not that bad.

Second, when the values of firms' portfolios are contractually intertwined and the perilous situation of one firm affects the financial well-being of another firm, this does not indicate a failure of private governance. Credit default swaps contracts enable firms to hedge against default, and when the economy soured, firms that had been paid to assume risks had to assume them. A few, most notably AIG, were having difficulty meeting new collateral requirements before government got involved with a series of bailouts. But the existence of credit default swap markets still reduced potential problems at the margin. When credit events occurred, credit default swaps backed by collateral all paid, and almost all lightly collateralized credit default swaps paid. The most prudent firms also purchased a secondary protection in case the first seller of protection (e.g., AIG) would also be unable to pay. Government bailouts did change payouts, but more defaults would not have debilitated these markets because they exist because firms know that any counterparty might default.

Third, when firms or investors choose not to purchase private governance and subsequently encounter problems, this is not a failure of private governance. Private governance allows multiple layers of protection, and although many investors demand and pay for more private governance, some refuse to do so. Those who do not conduct proper due diligence or fail to demand private third-party oversight risk being exposed to certain dangers. In notable cases such as the Madoff scandal, those dangers got the best of them. Investors who had paid for third-party administrator and custodian services were not exposed to such dangers. A private solution already existed and was working.

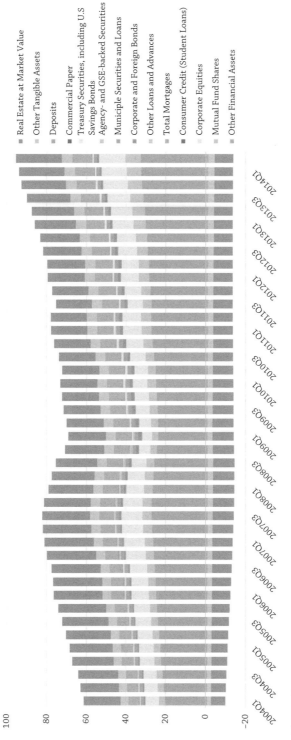

Figure 11.1
American Household Net Worth (2004–2014 in $U.S. trillions)
Source: Data are from Federal Reserve Board statistical releases.

Private governance is similar to a lock or the security system on your home. Such devices were never meant to (1) guarantee the value of your possessions, (2) eliminate the potential need for insurance or insurance payouts in the event of problems, or (3) protect your possessions if you use them. Their objective is to make burglary more difficult, and even if an adept thief thwarts a particular lock, this does not show that type of lock to be a failure. (I am guessing that you do not have bank vault doors on your home, because you consider such security measures excessive.) Furthermore, even if a particular *firm* in the lock or security industry is not living up to its promises, this does not indicate that the lock or security *industry* is a failure. Competition does not guarantee that every firm serves its customers in the best possible way, but competition overall creates pressures to weed out bad firms and to provide better customer service over the long run. The fact that some entities will fail is not a necessarily bad thing and is a reason for having competition in the first place. Government, in contrast, implements rules and regulations with little feedback about the cost or efficacy of those rules. This does not stop government from offering false promises, justifying more regulations, and then blaming the free market the next time problems occur.

During the 2008 economic downturn the advanced contracts that many people point to as causing the financial crisis were simply reacting, as they should, to changes in economic variables. Symptoms are not causal factors. Although they are usually maligned, collateralized debt obligations, credit default swaps, and other advanced financial arrangements help parties manage risk. Even in a world in which the legal system offers limited protection to lenders, these advanced markets help expand the amount of capital available to borrowers. They should be considered among the greatest innovations in history. These markets are highly complex, not the design of government, and are made possible because of private governance.

11.2. THE GREAT INNOVATION AND SUCCESS OF MORTGAGE-BACKED SECURITIES AND COLLATERALIZED DEBT OBLIGATIONS

An asset-backed security is created when an originator pools a set of assets, such as mortgages, corporate debt, auto loans, or credit card loans, to create a new financial instrument. Investors of these securities do not have personal connections with borrowers, but they become de facto lenders who own a fraction of many loans and receive income over time. In the same way a mutual fund does not go bankrupt if some stocks in its portfolio go bankrupt, an asset-backed security does not default if some loans in it default. Mortgage-backed securities are a type of asset-backed security, and investors value them based on the types of loans, borrowers' credit, loan-to-value ratio, loan-to-income ratio, type of property, income stream, or anything else that the investor deems important. Nobody can predict the future with perfect accuracy, but the better that parties estimate the probability that borrowers will repay, the more accurately the default rates are priced into the interest rate. Asset-backed securities comprised of more reliable loans (such as thirty-year fixed interest rate mortgages from borrowers with high income and high credit) are less risky but will have a lower interest rate than riskier ones comprised of subprime loans.

Once asset-backed securities exist, one can slice and arrange those pools in various ways to create new derivatives called collateralized debt obligations. Any number of collateralized debt obligations can be created to prioritize income streams or deal with various risks, such as default or prepayment, in the asset-backed security. Imagine slicing an asset-based security in two and giving one slice (tranche) senior status and the other junior status, with the latter agreeing to absorb any nonperforming loans first. If up to 50 percent of loans do not pay, the junior tranche absorbs those losses, while the senior tranche receives full income, and if more than 50 percent of the loans do not pay, the senior tranche starts absorbing losses too. Another analogy is a waterfall where the senior tranche gets first priority and the junior tranche gets its income after the senior tranche is fully paid. The senior tranche is less risky, but through different interest rates, its investors in effect pay the junior investors to bear losses first.

Creators of collateralized debt obligations usually slice asset-backed securities into many tranches, from the safest AAA tranches to the riskiest tranches, often labeled senior, mezzanine, and equity or first-loss tranches (see figure 11.2). More advanced collateralized debt obligations can be created by pooling and slicing any combination of collateralized debt obligations or other derivatives (i.e., collateralized debt obligations squared and synthetic collateralized debt obligations). These products became attractive because they enabled investing in mortgages without requiring investors to assume risks not of their liking or hold onto loans for thirty years. It also gave those willing to assume more risk the potential for, but not the guarantee of, higher returns.

These financial instruments were highly complex and not an invention of government.[4] While the average politician and government official were worrying about imposing price controls on automatic teller bank machines, firms on Wall Street were creating the most sophisticated financial instruments the world had ever seen. The market was expanding, and in 2006, $2 trillion in

---

4. Some theorists believe that these markets would not be possible without Fannie and Freddie, but the fact is that there exist mortgage-backed securities not securitized by Fannie and Freddie and for many other types of loans, including manufactured housing, credit card, automobile, and student loans (Financial Crisis Inquiry Commission, 2011, p. 45).

Collateralized Debt Obligations

Collateralized debt obligations (CDOs) are structured financial instruments that purchase and pool financial assets such as the riskier tranches of various mortgage-backed securities.

3. CDO tranches

Similar to mortgage-backed securities, the CDO issues securities in tranches that vary based on their place in the cash flow waterfall.

1. Purchase

The CDO manager and securities firm select and purchase assets, such as some of the lower-rated tranches of mortgage-backed securities.

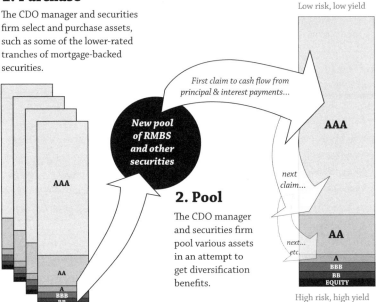

First claim to cash flow from principal & interest payments...

New pool of RMBS and other securities

AAA

Low risk, low yield

next claim...

AA

next...
etc

A
BBB
BB
EQUITY

High risk, high yield

AAA

AA

A
BBB
BB

2. Pool

The CDO manager and securities firm pool various assets in an attempt to get diversification benefits.

Figure 11.2
The Structure of Collateralized Debt Obligations
Source: Financial Crisis Inquiry Commission (2011, p. 128**)**.

mortgage-backed securities, $1.25 trillion in other asset-backed securities, and $950 billion in CDOs were issued (Hordahl and McGuire, 2007, p. 11).

These products allow parties to assume different types of risk, but they were never meant to eliminate all risk. If the profitability of the underlying assets changes, the value of the derivatives associated with those underlying assets will change. Between 2006 and 2008 the housing and mortgage markets worsened, and, as per the design of the securities, the investors that had been paid to assume more risks ended up actually assuming them. Unfortunately for them, many of the riskiest tranches saw their income stream and value of their tranche fall to zero.

One can question whether the government created or fueled a housing boom, especially by attempting to increase homeownership among low-income borrowers or by engaging in procyclical monetary policy (Allison, 2013).[5] But even assuming such elements would have existed in a pure free market, the fact remains that if future events do not go according the wishes of companies and bullish investors, this is *not* a failure of Wall Street or private governance. The fact that certain home prices, mortgage-backed securities, or collateralized debt obligations fell in value is nothing to cheer about and many were negatively affected. But such relative price declines are not that different from when a particular stock or a class of stocks fall in value, especially when investors in riskier securities agreed to assume the first losses in the event of problems. Although everyone would love an investment vehicle with all of the upside potential and none of the downside potential of stocks, that is not an option. The market requires firms and investors to test different investment strategies, just as it requires firms to experiment and test different ideas about consumer wants. Companies that develop products that best serve consumers get positive feedback through profits, whereas others get negative feedback through losses, and the same is true of investors who channel resources to more or less valuable investment opportunities.

In hindsight, we know that many investors and firms, such as Lehman Brothers and Bear Stearns, made investments that contributed to their demise. Some choices might have been good bets ex ante but turned out bad ex post. Other choices might have been fine investments for the long term because they were still generating income, but nevertheless quite illiquid in the short term and of little assistance to help firms weather the 2008 financial storm. Many investors' and firms' bullish choices, however, were simply unwise and based on models that assumed past housing appreciation would continue in the future.

Although many loans underlying the mortgage-backed securities and collateralized debt obligations did not end up performing as well many hoped, the mortgage-backed securities and collateralized debt obligations functioned pretty much as designed. Even if Standard and Poor's and Moody's estimates of the safety of mortgage-backed securities were not as accurate as they could have been, they were not wildly off and that was reflected the performance of mortgages. At any given quarter banks started foreclosures on only 1 percent of loans for prime fixed-rate mortgages (figure 11.3). When interest rates rose, foreclosure starts on prime adjustable-rate mortgages increased, but only to 3 percent of loans. The comparable figure for subprime fixed-rate mortgages

---

5. To increase homeownership rates the U.S. Department of Housing and Urban Development (2001, p. 3) had a mandate that "at least 50 percent of the dwelling units financed by each GSE's [government sponsored agency's] mortgage purchases should be for families with incomes no greater than area median income" and "at least 20 percent of the dwelling units financed by each GSE's mortgage purchase should be for very low-income families." Other policies required banks to give loans to borrowers that banks did not want to take a risk on (Block, Snow, and Stringham, 2008).

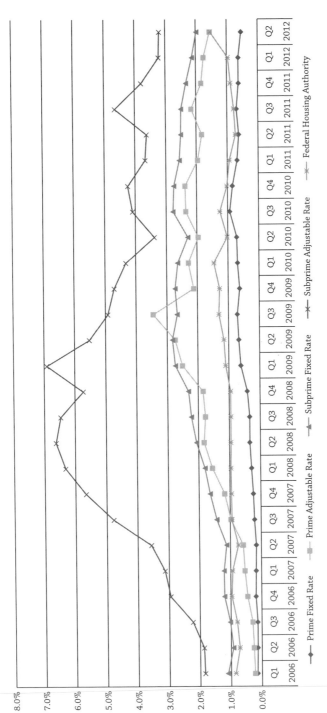

Figure 11.3
Foreclosures Started by Loan Type (2006–2012)
Source: Data are from Mortgage Bankers Association (2012, p. 3).

was slightly higher, and in a statistic that should surprise nobody, subprime adjustable-rate mortgages had the highest rate of foreclosure starts. The riskiest types of loans were to people with bad credit, low down payments, and no income documentation, and just like junk bonds, these higher risks were reflected in higher interest rates.

The value of mortgage-backed securities fell during the economic downturn, but because most underlying mortgages continue to pay, they have actually performed quite well in the long run. Figure 11.4 shows the growth from 2004 to 2014 of $10,000 invested in mortgage-backed securities funds from BlackRock, JP Morgan, Legg Mason Western Asset, PIMCO, Prudential, and Vanguard (BGPAX, OMBAX, SGSYX, PTRIX, TGMBX, and VMBIX). While a $10,000 investment in high-yield municipal bonds would have increased to $14,334 during this time, a $10,000 investment in mortgage-backed securities would have increased to between $15,964 and $16,540 depending on the fund chosen.

Of course, not all mortgage-backed securities or collateralized debt obligations can perform above average. Those based on subprime adjustable-rate mortgages have performed particularly poorly. But in all loan classes, the most junior tranches and collateralized debt obligations based on them absorbed losses first, just as the contract specified. These were not toxic securities designed to fail but simply riskier securities or ones that had been paid to absorb losses in the event of problems.

Figure 11.5 shows the percentage of collateralized debt obligations that were based on subprime debt or other collateralized debt obligations by underwriter, and figure 11.6 shows the percentage of collateralized debt obligations assets that defaulted by underwriter. Although one could interpret the incidence of default as prima facie evidence that fraud occurred, collateralized debt obligations based on subprime loans or other collateralized debt obligations are simply inherently riskier. The fact that in the aftermath of a major economic downturn only approximately 10 percent of Goldman Sachs–underwritten collateralized debt obligations assets ended up in default might indicate that Goldman Sachs was being overly conservative with their underwriting standards. Nobody claims market failure if 50 percent of new restaurants fail or 75 percent of Silicon Valley start-ups fail. Wall Street firms and investors that sought out riskier housing securities had the potential to gain or lose more, and everyone knew that.

What's more, like a bond, the price of a mortgage-backed security constantly varies, so when the value of the security falls below par, subsequent interest rates associated with the income stream go up. Consider, for example, the performance of one mortgage-backed security, JPALT 2006-S1 1A11, consisting of low-documentation loans. When 21 percent of its loans were late on payments, the value of it went to 70 percent of par, but that simply meant that initial investors ended up with less than they predicted and subsequent

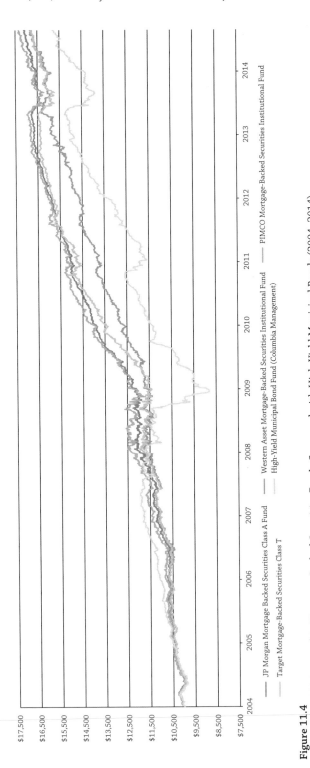

Figure 11.4
Value of $10,000 Invested in Mortgage-Backed Securities Funds Compared with High-Yield Municipal Bonds (2004–2014)
Source: Data are from Google Finance Historical Prices.

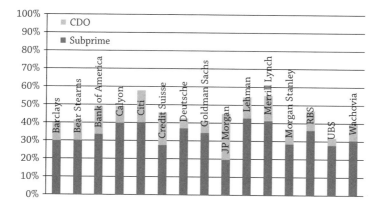

Figure 11.5
Percentage of Underwriters' Collateralized Debt Obligation Assets That Are Subprime or Collateralized Debt Obligations
Source: Reproduced by permission from Barnett Hart (2009, p. 33).

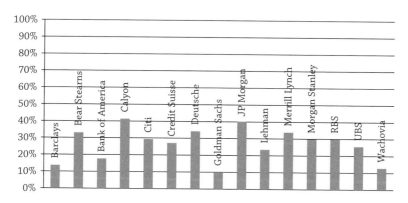

Figure 11.6
Percentage of Underwriters' Collateralized Debt Obligations Assets That Defaulted by 2008
Source: Reproduced by permission from Barnett Hart (2009, p. 33).

investors could buy a now higher-yielding security (Ahmed, 2012). If someone had created a first-loss tranche on such a security, the first-loss tranche could have easily fallen to zero. But what's the problem? Investors can choose riskier investment vehicles or more conservative ones as they wish. Some banks such as BB&T considered many of the riskier collateralized products as investments to be avoided (Allison, 2013, p. 84) and weathered the economic downturn just fine. Those that demanded riskier products ended up paying the price when economic outcomes did not go as planned. Such "failures" are not really failures; they simply exist because not everyone can predict the future. Just as big-wave surfers cannot expect to get in the ocean and see only the upside of waves, investors who choose riskier securities cannot expect only upside gains.

Rather than looking at poor performance during a downturn and conclud-ing these markets are a failure, we should take a step back and appreciate what they have done in the long run. Not only has their long-run performance been fine, mortgage-backed securities and collateralized debt obligations have done for borrowers what stock markets did for companies. These markets have dra-matically increased the amount of available capital and the ability for bor-rowers to get loans. No longer does one need to be royalty or have a close connection at the bank to access capital. These markets have also allowed eve-ryone from the most conservative to the most risk tolerant to invest in loans. Wall Street created these great products in a legal environment that offers few protections or is often hostile to lenders.

11.3. THE GREAT INNOVATION AND SUCCESS OF CREDIT DEFAULT SWAPS

In addition to pricing the estimated chance of default into interest rates, Wall Street introduced another important form of protection against de-faulters, the credit default swap. One of the chief architects of this finan-cial instrument is JP Morgan's Blythe Masters, who helped pioneer credit default swaps in 1994. Credit default swaps are contracts similar to insur-ance in which the buyer of protection pays a seller of protection to pay if a separate party that owes money (the reference entity) does not pay. Credit default swaps can be sold on mortgages, bonds for specific companies, gov-ernment debt, or anything to which a seller and buyer of protection agree.[6] The riskier the contract is, the higher the premium. Premiums for credit de-fault swaps are negotiated based on the length of the protection coverage, estimates that the reference entity will not repay, and estimates that the seller of protection will be able to pay.[7] Not only can a buyer purchase pro-tection against the first reference entity defaulting, but a buyer can purchase a second credit default swap in case the first seller of protection also cannot pay, basically insurance against their first insurance company defaulting. The future is always uncertain, but the more protection one has, the less likely one will get into trouble.

Credit default swaps have been vilified by economically illiterate comedians such as Jon Stewart and scores of politicians. In October 2008, the superintendent

---

6. Third parties who care about an entity defaulting can also buy protection as well. Such contracts can used with synthetic collateralized debt obligations whose value rises or falls based on the success or failure of underlying collateralized debt obliga-tions. For an excellent overview of credit default swaps see Stultz (2010).

7. Writers of credit default swaps with low credit ratings typically have to post more collateral (sometimes held by the buyer of protection), which influences the price of a particular credit default swap.

of insurance for New York criticized credit default swaps, stating, "It's legalized gambling. It was illegal gambling. And we made it legal gambling . . . with absolutely no regulatory controls. Zero, as far as I can tell" (CBS News, 2008). I, in contrast, believe that credit default swaps are great inventions that helped many investors, given that lenders cannot recover money in imperfect courts. They also represent a level of prudence found on Wall Street that is not found elsewhere, notably with government.

Consider, for example, credit default swaps issued in case Fannie Mae or Freddie Mac had credit events. While Federal Reserve chairman Bernanke (2008, p. 16) was saying, "The GSEs [government-sponsored agencies] are adequately capitalized. They are in no danger of failing," and 2007 Nobel laureate in economics and former chief economist for the World Bank, Joseph Stiglitz, was saying, "These results regarding the risk-based capital standard are striking: They suggest that on the basis of historical experience, the risk to the government from a potential default on GSE debt is effectively zero" (Stiglitz, Orszag, and Orszag, 2002, p. 5), firms on Wall Street had bought protection in case those entities had credit events. The existence of these markets and positive prices in these markets show that firms on Wall Street believed that Fannie and Freddie might end up in a precarious situation. The same is true of credit default swaps that pay in case government defaults. While Alan Greenspan declares, "The United States can pay any debt it has because we can always print money to do that. So there is zero probability of default" (Allen, 2011), the market for credit default swaps lets people put their money where their mouth is and establish prices associated with estimated probabilities of default. As of 2013, the implied probability that the U.S. government would default in the next year was 1.4 percent (Childs, 2013), which is not that high, but infinitely higher than Greenspan's estimate of zero. Here we see Wall Street firms being much more prudent than the "What, me worry?" attitudes of Bernanke and Stiglitz.

Credit default swap markets help indicate the market estimate of the probability of default, but markets do not guarantee that each firm or the market overall guesses the ultimate outcome correctly. Individual firms can make bad predictions, and unexpected or low-probability events can occur. By 2008 many conditions worsened, and firms that had been contracted to assume bad debts were going to have to pay.

Credit default swaps help firms mitigate certain risks, but they were never meant to eliminate all risks or the need for payouts if problems occur. Buyers of protection still retain the risk that the seller of protection will be also default, and they take many steps to mitigate this possibility. At the contract stage, buyers of protection usually negotiate collateral requirements where the seller of protection places assets in an account that is often controlled by a third party or even the buyer. Just as a bank depositor can theoretically demand that the bank hold 100 percent reserves or less depending on his preferences to pay more fees versus assume some risks, buyers of protection can require collateral up to the full amount of the reference bonds (a more expensive arrangement), or they can require less.

For example, a buyer could pay a seller of protection $50,000 to insure $1 million, and require the seller of protection to form an investment vehicle with $1 million of cash deposited with a third party that the buyer can access even if the reference loans default and have a recovery rate of zero. A reference loan suddenly jumping from being worth $1 million to $0 is possible, but unlikely, so credit default swap contracts are often more lightly collateralized. The exact amount of the collateral is negotiated based on how reliable the buyer considers the seller (International Swaps and Derivatives Association, 2009) and how much they believe the reference debt is likely to vary in the short run. One type of contract is the pay-as-you-go credit default swap, which requires the seller to pay the buyer a small amount each time the reference debt has a small write-down (and the buyer has to pay back a small amount each time there is a principal write-up) (Nolan and Dodson, 2006; Sahajwani, 2011), so big unfunded surprises in this market are less likely. Other contracts require payments to a margin account as the value of reference debt varies. With frequent payments and enough of a buffer, buyers of protection can reestablish new contracts with other sellers of protection even if the original seller goes out of business.

As a testament of how well private governance in these markets worked, consider what happened when the government nationalized Fannie and Freddie. On September 8, 2008, the private International Swaps and Derivatives Association (ISDA) determined that the government conservatorship constituted a credit event, which triggers payment in most credit default swap contracts. The notional value of credit default swaps referencing Fannie and Freddie was massive, exceeding $1.4 trillion (Biggadike and Harrington, 2008). (For perspective, the market capitalization of all firms listed on the New York Stock Exchange is approximately $10 trillion.) Right after the credit default was declared, one analyst stated, "The market is not experienced at settling a credit event for a name of this size, so it is a bit of an unknown" (quoted in Biggadike and Harrington, 2008). Yet the ISDA oversaw what turned out to be an orderly procedure.

Had parties done business through the Bloods and Crips (street gangs) Derivatives Association, the result would have been a street fight, and everyone would have gone without payment. Instead, most Wall Street firms chose to deal with other firms that were members of the ISDA, which has procedures for netting what is owed. The ISDA was founded in 1985, and its expressed goal is "to make the over-the-counter derivatives market safe and efficient." Rules and procedures are spelled out in the ISDA Master Agreement, and as with the history of other markets, the rules can evolve based on what market participants consider best.

Let us consider a few of the rules that have evolved over time. Until 2006, most credit default swap contracts required physical settlement, in which the buyer of protection delivers the obligations (usually the bonds in default) to the seller of protection, who pays the full price of the obligations. But if more credit default swap contracts exist than the number of bonds available, a rush to continue repurchasing those bonds for settlement would occur. Today most credit default swap contracts are settled with cash settlement, in which the seller of protection pays the difference between what a debt currently is worth and par (Helwege et al., 2009, p. 5; Saperia, 2008, p. 1). The ISDA helps determine the price of what is owed through an auction of the debt in default. In the case of Lehman Brothers, a bondholder with $1 of debt ended up having a bond worth $0.09 and thus was owed $0.91 from the seller of protection, and in the case of Fannie or Freddie, a bondholder with $1 of debt ended up having a bond worth approximately $0.92 or $0.94 and was owed $0.08 or $0.06 from the seller of protection. Prices of the debt and payouts were influenced by the amount of government bailouts, but the auction and settlement process functioned in each case.

What about the problems of one of the largest sellers of protection, AIG? AIG never actually defaulted on its obligations, but it was having trouble meeting new collateral requirements that were specified in contracts if AIG lost its AAA rating or certain conditions worsened. In the long run, AIG may have been able to pay for the protection had the reference entities defaulted, but in the short run, AIG likely would have had to start winding down contracts and selling certain assets, or face bankruptcy. In the fall of 2008, the government intervened and lent AIG billions (which have since been repaid) in what many portray as a backdoor bailout or guarantee for AIG's counterparties. Yet even if AIG had needed to wind down contracts or if AIG's counterparties had not received 100 percent of the protection had credit events occurred, it would not have been a failure of the credit default swap market.

Built into the price of each credit default swap is the recognition that "the protection buyer gives up the risk of default by the reference entity, and takes on the risk of simultaneous default by both the protection seller and the reference credit" (International Swaps and Derivatives Association, 2014). Credit default swaps exist because firms know that the default of any firm is possible because of unforeseen events, bad risk management, or bad business decisions, and AIG was no exception. AIG had an exceptionally risky business model with one branch of the company insuring many subprime loans and another branch of the company investing in subprime loans (Stulz, 2010, p. 83; International Swaps and Derivatives Association, 2014). Unlike other credit default swap dealers who "maintain 'matched books' that balance sold with bought protection so net exposure is low," AIG had "a 'one way' book consisting almost entirely of sold protection" (International Swaps and Derivatives Association, 2009, p. 1). Such a strategy was very profitable when payouts were uncommon, but dangerous if economic variables veered away from AIG's models. Firms that made contracts with AIG and agreed to lower collateral requirements because of AIG's high credit rating knew they were retaining certain risks.

Many of AIG's counterparties took steps to limit downside losses if AIG encountered problems. Goldman Sachs, for example, was AIG's largest banking customer and presumably trusted AIG, but Goldman Sachs intentionally bought credit default swaps from many sellers of protection, thereby limiting its exposure to AIG. Goldman Sachs also required AIG to post $7.5 billion of collateral under the control of Goldman Sachs to help prevent AIG from getting into a situation in which it could not pay the $10 billion that it could potentially owe. Furthermore, Goldman Sachs spent $100 million purchasing protection from other sellers to cover what would happen if AIG went broke. As Goldman Sachs (2013) states, "We did not take the creditworthiness of AIG for granted. On the contrary, our actions in the case of AIG are a good example of responsible risk management. . . . That is why we are able to say that whether it failed or not, AIG would have had no material direct impact on Goldman Sachs."

Even if some of AIG's counterparts did not practice as good risk management as Goldman Sachs, that does not mean the market overall was a failure. Because we live outside the Garden of Eden, we should not expect a world without problems due to unforeseen events, bad business decisions, or bad risk management. Yet today's imperfections and mistakes are signals for tomorrow's innovations. One recent innovation is that more credit default swap contracts are being traded through exchanges such as the Chicago Mercantile Exchange and the Intercontinental Exchange, which help manage counterparty default risk. As of 2014, these exchanges clear tens of trillions of dollars of credit default swap contracts, and contracts traded through an exchange will be much less likely to face AIG-like problems in the future. Those that continue to make contracts over the counter can have stricter collateral requirements than those that were potentially exposed to AIG. Credit default swaps will never eliminate default or the need for payouts when reference entities default, but they mitigate problems for risk-averse lenders and help dramatically expand the scope of trade.

11.4. THE GREAT INNOVATION AND SUCCESS OF PRIVATE CERTIFICATION, ADMINISTRATOR, AND CUSTODIAN SERVICES

In the most notable failures during the 2008 economic downturn, firms such as Bear Stearns and Lehman Brothers lost a lot of money along with their investors, so the idea that these firms intended such an outcome should be doubted. The fact that fraud accusations always jump after markets drop in value indicates the common confusion between willful malfeasance and investments simply not panning out. That said, varying amounts of fraudulent behavior, unfortunately, will always exist. Healthy ecosystems (markets) attract lots of life, but they also have the potential to attract more parasites (private and governmental fraudsters). For the purpose of this analysis, I leave aside governmental officials who cost investors billions of dollars each year (The Economist, 2012a, 2012b) and instead focus on one of the most egregious examples of private fraud that was exposed during this time, namely, the fraud perpetrated by Bernie Madoff. Although Madoff's Ponzi scheme was a big deal, it shows neither fatal flaws of private governance nor the efficacy of government. The same is true for other blatantly or borderline fraudulent actions that surfaced during the 2008 economic downturn.

Madoff was a Wall Street icon who started out as a market maker (traders that match buy and sell orders from other traders), and by 2000 Madoff Securities was the third largest market maker for NASDAQ stocks. I regularly dealt with his market makers when I worked on an over-the-counter trading desk in the late 1990s, and, as far as I could and can tell, that aspect of his business was totally legitimate. At the same time, however, Madoff also had a "hedge fund," which turned out to be a massive Ponzi scheme. Like Social Security, which does not actually have a trust fund and instead pays people who cash out with others' contributions, Madoff paid some investors—friends and family—handsome returns with other investors' money. Madoff claimed to have an investment strategy that required no management fees, involved limited volatility, and consistently returned 1 percent *per month*. The firm went from $6 billion of assets under management in 2001 to what Madoff claimed was $65 billion by 2008 (Arvedlund, 2001; Glovin, 2009). More than half of Madoff's investors took out more than they originally put in, but after all was said and done, a $13 to $17 billion shortfall existed (Delevingne and Carney, 2009).

Markets are supposed to consist of informed, nonfraudulent relationships, so does the occurrence of multi-billion-dollar fraud prove the necessity of government regulation? The first point to highlight is the fact the Securities and Exchange Commission had a $1 billion annual budget and conducted eight investigations of Madoff over the years, yet it "failed to follow incriminating evidence in plain sight" (Stout, 2009, p. B1). In late 1999 a private analyst named Harry Markopolos was asked by his firm to see if it could replicate Madoff's returns. Madoff claimed his "split strike conversion" strategy made money from owning stocks that track an index, selling out of the money call options to generate income, and buying put options to limit downside losses. Selling calls and buying puts associated with stocks is actually the common "using collars" strategy that limits both the downside and upside potential of owning stocks (Gaffen, 2008). Markopolos's firm actually had a fund that followed such a strategy, and within five minutes Markopolos concluded that Madoff's returns could not exist. Within four hours he demonstrated this mathematically (Markopolos, 2009, pp. 7–9). In 2000 Markopolos and colleagues sent a report to the Securities and Exchange Commission stating that "the entire fund is nothing more than a Ponzi Scheme" (Kotz, 2009, p. 7) and followed up with additional complaints, including Markopolos's 2005 report to the Securities Exchange and Commission titled "The World's Largest Hedge Fund Is a Fraud." Others, including *Barron's*, publicly questioned how Madoff could have annual returns averaging 15 percent, with extremely low variance, and never have a down year (Arvedlund, 2001). Another industry writer, Ocrant (2001, p. 1), also discussed Madoff's skeptics, who were "baffled by the way the firm has obtained such consistent, nonvolatile returns month after month and year after year." When the Securities and Exchange Commission asked Madoff how he could make such high returns, Madoff responded, "Some people feel the market. Some people just understand how to analyze the numbers that they're looking at" (Kotz, 2009, p. 19). After the fraud was exposed, the inspector general of the Securities and Exchange Commission concluded, "Because of the Enforcement staff's inexperience and lack of understanding of equity and options trading, they did not appreciate that Madoff was unable to provide a logical explanation for his incredibly high returns" (Kotz, 2009, p. 19). A reliable assumption is that most government officials lack an understanding of financial markets in general, and reading the full 450-page report from the inspector general of the Securities and Exchange Commission confirms it in this case. The first lesson is that government simply lacked the knowledge or incentive to notice this massive Ponzi scheme.

The more important lesson, however, is that many mechanisms of private governance that easily could have prevented such fraud were available to investors, and they *chose not to* demand them. Despite the fact that Madoff's returns were questioned by many, none demanded the private third-party administration and accounting services that other hedge funds were using. In 2001, when the newsletter writers at *MarHedge* asked Madoff many questions about how his returns were possible, they reported: "Bernie Madoff is willing to answer each of those inquiries, even if he refuses to provide details about the trading strategy. . . . The strategy and trading, he says, are done mostly by signals from a proprietary 'black box' system" (Ocrant, 2001, p. 3), and to *Barron's* Madoff said, "It's a proprietary strategy. I can't go into it in great detail" (Arvedlund, 2001). *Barron's* also reported one potential investor's account of what Madoff said:

> "What Madoff told us was, 'If you invest with me, you must never tell anyone that you're invested with me. It's no one's business what goes on here,'" says an investment manager who took over a pool of assets that included an investment

in a Madoff fund. "When he couldn't explain [to my satisfaction] how they were up or down in a particular month," he added, "I pulled the money out." (Arved-lund, 2001)

Madoff did not provide electronic access to what was in anyone's account, and his "auditing" firm had only three employees: an accountant, a secretary, and the accountant's father-in-law, who was a retired partner living Florida and Madoff's friend of fifty years (Abkowitz, 2008; Gandel, 2008). The Securities and Exchange Commission (Kotz, 2009, p. 5) reports that "numerous private entities conducted basic due diligence of Madoff's operations and . . . came to the conclusion that an investment with Madoff was unwise." In one set of al-legations that I agree with, Massachusetts regulators chided one of his biggest investors who "did not engage in any meaningful due diligence and turned a blind eye to any fact that would have burst their lucrative bubble" (quoted in Madigan, 2009). Anyone who saw Oliver Stone's *Wall Street* can recall Bud Fox telling his colleague: "Mr. Mannheim, got a sure thing"; Mannheim responds, "No such thing Bud—except death and taxes. . . . Remember there're no short-cuts, son." We should not blame the victims in this case, but Madoff's inves-tors chose to invest in something too good to be true while not requesting safeguards that others used.

One of the most straightforward solutions to prevent Madoff-like prob-lems is to use third-party or independent administrators and custodians. Madoff was not just the decision-maker guiding his "investment" strat-egy but also the trader and custodian of assets, so if one branch of the business was doing something un-kosher, nobody was around to verify. Even though the hedge fund and private equity industries lack most dis-closure requirements, investors demand them, and third-party administra-tors and custodians can provide disclosure. Third-party administrators not only provide information about activity in a fund but also create various checks to prevent parties from misusing investor assets. Third-party ad-ministrators can be independent companies such as Citco Fund Services, or they can be subsidiaries of banks such as Citigroup, Goldman Sachs, and JP Morgan. Third-party administration can handle everything from back-office functions such as daily reporting of valuations in each account to managed accounts in which the hedge fund manager becomes more like an advisor without control of the assets in the fund (HFM Week, 2010; Rose, 2009). Unlike Madoff, third-party administrators have limited in-centive or ability to walk off with investors' assets. When firms handle many accounts, a scandal with one would mean an instant scandal with many, and thus it would not be possible for such firms to create a sus-tained series of lies, as Madoff did. Hedge fund managers typically create a shadow set of books to replicate internally what the third-party adminis-trator is providing, and in some cases managers hire a second independent administrator to create a set of shadow books as well, meaning that two or three independent parties verify the value of the funds (Caplan and Ojjeh, 2011; Groenfeldt, 2013).

As Belmont (2011, p.114) explains, "Robust internal controls and procedures should be in place over each state of the trading cycle: trade authorization, execution, confirmation, settlement, reconciliation, and accounting. A breakdown in this separation of duties seems to have been a factor in almost every fraud-related fund failure." Madoff Investments used zero of these checks and internal controls. One of my friends who used to work in the industry said, "When the Madoff story broke, we were actually happy because we knew it would be a huge increase in the demand for our services" (personal interview, Arlington, Virginia, September 27, 2013). The scandal was actually a big "I told you so" moment for the third-party administrator and custodian industry. According to a survey of the hedge fund industry, 75 percent used third-party administrators in some capacity in 2006, and that number had increased to 91 percent by 2011 (BNY Mellon, 2012, p. 2; see figure 11.7).

Will third-party administrators and custodians eliminate all potential problems? Of course not. The potential for fraud will always exist, but like locks on houses, or security guards at a bank, third-party administrators make fraud more difficult. Failing to pay for locks or for various levels of protection may be a failure of good judgment, but it is not a failure of private governance. Despite what legal centralist theory might imply, paying for locks and paying for private governance are much more prudent than relying on ineffective government regulators or courts. In the wake of the Madoff scandal, third-party administrators and custodians should be celebrated as unheralded protectors of property rights and creators of transparency in the hedge fund industry.

I have focused on Madoff because his actions were a black-and-white fraud, but much of this analysis can be applied to more gray areas of fraud.

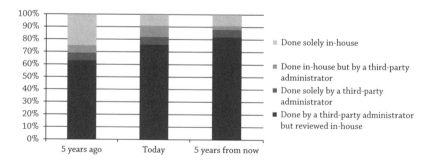

Figure 11.7
Survey of Hedge Fund Reliance on Third-Party Administrators for the Past, Current, and Future
Source: Data are from BNY Mellon (2012, p. 28).

For example, many people claim that the mortgage industry was mired in fraud, because many originators sold packages of loans from borrowers who made less than they claimed. Yet all parties involved had the option to require more documentation, and they willingly chose to give money to borrowers without any income verification (so-called liar loans). Just as "junk" bonds are not really junk when investors know they are simply high-risk and higher-interest-rate bonds, "liar" loans are not really liar loans when investors know that they involve stated income that cannot be verified. (For the record, I purchased my first condo with a no income documentation loan, and I have never missed a payment, so not all of these loans were bad.) Many investors and banks stayed far away from such products, but those who did not simply assumed additional risks, and those risks were reflected in higher interest rates. Investors who wanted more documentation could demand it, so when investors chose not to demand documentation, nobody should be surprised if some of the loans in those bundles involved less-qualified borrowers. When I buy a car or a home I willingly pay a third-party mechanic or an inspector to evaluate what I am buying, but when others choose not to, it should not be considered a failure of the inspection market. When a group of investors chooses not to pay for third-party accounting or certification services and the investors subsequently end up with less than they hoped, it should not be considered a failure of private governance.

The last point against those who say Madoff proves the necessity of regulation is that one should put the amount of the losses into perspective. Madoff's fraud was terrible for the investors who lost $13 billion, but it simply matches the $13 billion that the U.S. government recently extracted from investors in JP Morgan Chase (headlines in the *Wall Street Journal Editorial Board* (2013) and the *New York Post Editorial Board* (2013) referred to it as "The Morgan Shakedown" and "Extorting Morgan"[8] and is much less than the $22 billion that JP Morgan Chase has had to spend on regulatory compliance between 2008 and 2013 (MacDonald, 2013). Madoff's $13 billion shortfall also pales in comparison to the $20 *trillion* by which Social "Security" is underfunded (Kotlikoff, 2012). I have no respect for Madoff, but he at least had decency to trick investors into his fraudulent scheme, rather than force investors to hand over their money or force workers to

---

8. As the New York Post Editorial Board (2013) correctly points out, "If these quasi-government entities [Fannie and Freddie] were as unsophisticated about mortgage-backed securities as DOJ and the Federal Housing Finance Agency would have us believe, they ought to be put out of business altogether rather than get more taxpayer dollars to keep them afloat. Second, most of the alleged misbehavior was done by Bear Stearns and Washington Mutual before JP Morgan got them. During the 2008 financial crisis, JP Morgan bought Bear Stearns outright, as well as some of the assets and liabilities of Washington Mutual. This was done at the behest of Uncle Sam, which assured JP Morgan it would be understanding if irregularities later turned up."

"invest" 12.4 percent of all earnings in a retirement scheme. After he was exposed, he also at least had the decency to admit he was a fraud rather than continue to tell people he is investing in their future. In contrast to government, private governance lets people hire others to do due diligence, pay for various levels of production, and opt into structures of governance that they prefer. Despite examples of fraud here and there, the hedge fund market is as safe as it is not because of government but because of an advanced system of private checks.

11.5. SUMMARY AND THOUGHTS

In 2008 many problems manifested in financial markets, but just because problems with underlying variables exist does mean not a lack regulation caused those problems or that private governance failed. Those who chose to invest in the safest investment vehicles and purchase more levels of private governance were exposed to fewer problems than those who willingly assumed more risk. Most parties that bought safer tranches, credit default swaps, and third-party accounting services turned out fine. The complex financial arrangements were developed independent of government and helped markets weather a storm that could have been much worse.

If anything, providers of private governance were faced with challenges that became more difficult because of government. The housing boom and bust likely would not have been as large as it was without the Federal Reserve keeping rates at historic lows (as Krugman famously wrote in 2002, "Alan Greenspan needs to create a *housing bubble* to replace the Nasdaq bubble") and then rapidly increasing the federal funds rate by 425 percent (Allison, 2013, p. 28). The subsequent uptick in the interest of variable-rate mortgages led certain borrowers to default. Furthermore, the collapse also likely would not have been as bad had it not been for rapid and untested changes in accounting standards in which government suddenly required banks to switch to mark-to-market accounting rules when valuing assets on their books. Mark-to-market accounting (in which an asset is valued on the basis of its current market price rather than what a firm paid for it or believes the asset is worth) makes sense in many circumstances, but it makes less sense for valuing goods in illiquid markets. (You and your neighbor may each have paid a million dollars for your identical homes, and you may value them at that amount, but if your neighbor is forced to sell *his* home tonight, the "market price" of *your* home suddenly drops.) Such accounting rules wreaked havoc for banks that owned valuable but highly illiquid mortgage-backed securities. Even when mortgage-backed securities were generating income, the value of the banks' books fell dramatically, which, coupled with reserve or capital requirements, meant that banks had to dramatically reduce loans outstanding (Allison,

2013, pp. 103–18).[9] Add to all of this regime uncertainty, government picking winners and losers, and the promise of a massive increase in government regulations, and these bad policies became priced into financial markets in 2008. Regime uncertainty created by government (Higgs, 2012, p. 185) must be the free market's fault, right?

Based on the reaction to the 2008 and all past crises, we can be certain about two things moving forward: (1) No matter how many regulations are in place or how much the government did to cause the crisis, government will blame the next economic downturn on the free market and a lack of regulation, and (2) government will implement a set of new regulations that will be more onerous and do nothing to prevent the next economic downturn, leading back to point 1.

I have spoken with countless people on Wall Street, and the general sentiment is that government officials who write and implement regulations typically have little understanding of how financial markets actually work. As one of my friends from a derivatives trading firm told me, "Regulators have turned our industry upside down" (personal interview, Boston, Massachusetts, November 29, 2013). Given most government officials' lack of knowledge or outright hostility to advanced derivative markets, hedge funds, or Wall Street in general, it would be an error to say that these advanced markets were made possible by government. As Warren Buffet (2003, p. 15) stated, "The derivative genie got out of the bottle, and it's a huge genie, and it will never get back into the bottle," but rather than viewing this market innovation as a bad thing, we should be celebrating it. Even though government courts are highly imperfect, collateralized debt obligations, credit default swaps, and other advanced financial arrangements have opened up debt markets well beyond those that depend on close-knit ties. These markets are among the most complex the world has ever seen, and private governance makes them possible.

9. As Gorton (2008, p. 62) writes, "With no liquidity and no market prices, the accounting practice of 'marking-to-market' became highly problematic and resulted in massive write-downs based on fire-sale prices and estimates," and Epstein and Henderson (2009, p. 1) write, "Mark-to-market accounting helps create asset bubbles and exacerbate their negative collateral consequences when they burst."

PART THREE

Lessons of Private Governance

CHAPTER 12

ᴄᴧᴏ

The Relationship between Public and Private Governance

Does the State Help or Crowd Out Good Governance?

12.1. INTRODUCTION

The scene: Sotheby's auction house in Upper East Side, Manhattan. The crowd is filled with well-to-dos from Wall Street and their love interests who adore spending money. Some paintings are going for millions of dollars. Most of these bidders are not professional art historians, so how do they know that what they are buying is authentic? In many markets, one should not take the seller's word for it. With billions of dollars of art sold each year, the fine art market attracts many fine things, but also many counterfeits. In 2007 the value of transacted Andy Warhol art alone was $420 million (ArtPrice, 2010, p. 22), and keeping track of all prints is particularly difficult. Although the legal centralist asserts that with laws against fraud, "the state creates and preserves the environment in which the market economy can operate" (Mises, [1949] 1998, p. 258), the state has a very difficult time differentiating between authentic and fraudulent works of art. What do people do about the fact that, according to the antifraud group Art Watchdog, "the art market is the last unregulated frontier of commerce"? (Ostrovky, 2013).

The solution is private governance, or in the words of the *New York Times*, "The police and buyers mostly rely on the art market to police itself" (Cohen, 2012a, p. C1). The parts of the market with the most private governance are the large auction houses such as Christie's and Sotheby's, which hire teams of antifraud experts to investigate the legitimacy of a good before listing. Although no market can be 100 percent free of fraud (and such a state of affairs would undesirable for buyers and sellers, who would have to foot the bill for so much due diligence), the established auction houses provide many assurances, including five-year money-back guarantees for certain auctions (Sotheby's, 2013). Such due diligence and guarantees are costly and priced into listing fees, but they increase the attractiveness of these markets.

Buyers who prefer not to pay for such private regulations can trade in other markets, but they do so at their own risk. For example, some people claim that the Chinese state-owned Poly Auction house has fraud at 80 percent of auctions (Esman, 2012) (legal centralists take note: yes, governmentally regulated markets may have orders of magnitude more fraud than privately governed ones). Galleries and third-party authentication also can provide assurances against fraud. The third party may be an individual art historian with expertise in an area or a group, such as the Andy Warhol Foundation or the Roy Lichtenstein Foundation, that specializes in and lists the works of a particular artist. This private governance reduces the number of lemons (Akerlof 1970) (i.e., counterfeit or wrongly attributed paintings) in the market.

Enter government. Having a reputable third party certify that a piece is legitimate is good for a seller. A seller's finding out that his wares are bogus is not. Unfortunately in the art market, a new norm for people who receive a negative assessment is to sue in government courts. The cases often have little merit and have been described by the Supreme Court of Montana as "legal thuggery" (see *Seltzer v. Morton, Bison, Dunn, & Crutcher, LLP*, 2007) but they are costly to defend. According to one art lawyer, "This is a very serious problem. Specialists are often academics earning $100,000 [or less] a year and they can't afford litigation. [Specialists] are fearful of being a defendant in a lawsuit, even if they should win" (quoted in Adam and Pryor, 2011). Some choose to settle and pay damages rather than being dragged through court. The *New York Times* reports, "Several high-profile legal cases have pushed scholars to censor themselves for fear of becoming entangled in lawsuits" (Cohen, 2012b, p. A1). By 2005 the Lichtenstein Foundation was paying $5 million *per year* in liability insurance to deal with lawsuits. In 2011 the Warhol Foundation had to spend $7 million defending itself in a single lawsuit after it decided a particular painting did not warrant being listed in the catalogue raisonné that lists Warhol's works. The result of this government "help" in the market is that now the Lichtenstein Foundation, Warhol Foundation, and many others have completely ceased authenticating art for fear of being sued. Without understanding the economics behind the problem, many people now blame this missing market on the market (in the words of one lawyer: "Art scholarship is fighting a losing battle against commerce" [quoted in Cohen, 2012b, p. A1]) rather than attributing this problem to government.

Many theorists argue that private governance functions only because of "the shadow of the state" or "the shadow of hierarchy." For theorists Héritier and Eckert (2008, p. 113), "The willingness to engage in self-regulation is prompted by the threat of governmental legislation," and for Frye (2000, p. 2), "The prospects for self-governance may be quite favorable" but only because "Politics underpins social order." In markets such as art certification, however, the good governance preceded government and is now being undermined by government. Government intervention can undermine markets for private governance in many ways: government can put roadblocks in front of, crowd out, monopolize, or co-opt private governance.

North, Wallis, and Weingast (2009, p. 121) criticize what they call "the neo-classical economic fiction" that "holds markets exist and then politics intervenes," but I think the idea that markets precede government is precisely right. From art to financial markets, government often gets in the way of private governance. From the stocks markets in Amsterdam, London, and New York to arbitrators, colleges, and financial intermediaries today, almost all of the providers of private governance in this book still exist in some form. But almost all of them have faced various challenges from government and are often much less effective than they would be without government. In financial sector, many regulations have crowded out private regulation and interfered with private regulatory competition. In other areas such as policing in San Francisco, government has taken perfectly functioning markets of private governance and monopolized them for the sake of expanding government. Government found it could make money by requiring the public to pay for its "services" rather than letting people opt for private governance. Other times, for example with colleges or financial intermediaries, government allows providers of private governance to persist but makes them put the government's interests over that of consumers. The providers of private governance may not like it, but they often have little choice and become victims of cronyism. Although government may be a benign force that augments markets, it seems more accurate to view regulators as interfering with markets. Private governance always functions to varying degrees, but it functions much less effectively the more it is hobbled by government.

12.2. WHEN GOVERNMENT CROWDS OUT PRIVATE GOVERNANCE

Providers of private governance such as the London Stock Exchange, the New York Stock Exchange, or eBay have incentives to weigh the marginal costs and benefits of potential rules and regulations and pick ones that augment markets. Because customers of private governance can spend their money anywhere (or put it under their mattress), enticing them into particular markets requires making those markets attractive and relatively free of fraud. Although rules and regulations on a stock exchange can have benefits, they also have costs, and those costs will be borne by brokers, listing companies, and ultimately investors. Let us consider the choice of how many rules a provider of private governance will want to pick and how the market will be affected when government enters the picture.

Figure 12.1 represents the marginal, gross, and net benefits and costs of rules (or, more broadly, governance mechanisms) for a particular market, such as the London Stock Exchange, New York Stock Exchange, or eBay, in a way that will be familiar to economists and providers of private governance but foreign to legal centralists and government officials. Taking the basic set of property rights in society as given, one can analyze how adopting additional rules will make a market more or less attractive, and in this simple representation I present curves with decreasing marginal benefits and increasing marginal costs. One can analyze multiple dimensions of rules or unique rules (rather than homogenous ones with smooth curves) with discreet benefits and costs, but the basic implications are the same. If they want to attract customers, providers of private governance must adopt rules that enhance a market and reject rules that drag down the market. For example, additional disclosure requirements provide additional information to investors, but they also increase investors' cost of doing business in that venue. Just because having one rule or regulation on a topic makes sense does not mean that having a million will. In a desire to attract business, each provider of private governance must compare the marginal benefits and marginal costs of new rules and then adopt only those whose marginal benefits exceed marginal costs (q^* in figure 12.1).

A market will never be in its final state of rest, but just as markets for normal goods have built-in incentives to bring supply and demand together, the market for private governance has built-in incentives for providers of private governance to provide the "optimal" quantity of rules for each market. The optimum (q^*) in for the London Stock Exchange in 1800 will differ from the New York Stock Exchange in 1900 or the Alternative Investment Market in London in 2000 based on costs for participants and desires of investors. Those wishing to do business on more established exchanges will have different desires than those willing to assume more risks, and the optimal amount of rules in each market will vary. Some exchanges such as the Consolidated Stock Exchange of New York may be outcompeted (it opened in 1885 and closed in 1926 [Brown, Mulherin, and Weidenmier [2008]), but each provider of private governance will try to make its market as attractive as possible. Any deviation away from q^* in each market means that the market will be at a disadvantage to its competitors and the process of competition will create incentives for each provider of private governance to get to its own q^*.

This analysis can be used to explain why the London Stock Exchange and New York Stock Exchange adopted rules for its broker members and subsequently rules for listed firms. Market forces created incentives for these exchanges to adopt rules, but not just any rules, only value-enhancing ones. If the marginal benefits of a rule such as disclosure requirements exceed the

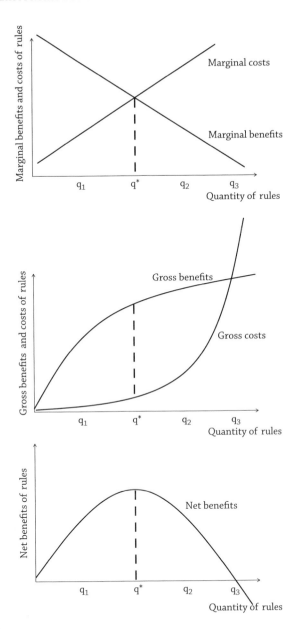

Figure 12.1
Costs and Benefits of Rules or Regulations in a Particular Market

marginal costs to market participants, then an exchange will have an incentive to adopt it.

When government enters the picture, a few things can occur. The first possibility is that government imposes rules that a market was already providing. Assuming that duplication has costs, the new government rules simply take the place of the private rules. In figure 12.1, for example, if government provides q_1 rules, the provider of private governance will now simply provide $q^* - q_1$ so that the total number of rules still equals q^*. If government happens to impose the exact rules that the market was providing (q^*), the provider of private governance will cut back and be completely crowded out of the market. Again, the optimal number of rules and the net benefits of the rules in a particular market will remain the same.

Once government starts imposing more rules than q^*, the market begins to have more rules than optimal. At q_2 the net benefit of the rules is higher than that of having no rules at all but less than what it would have been without government. Beyond q_3, the net benefit of the rules becomes negative, and the market would be better off with no rules at all.

Such an expansion of government regulation of securities markets has occurred over the past hundred years. In the United States, before the Securities Act of 1933 and Securities Exchange Act of 1934, the market for private governance in financial markets was largely competitive, and one could opt into different markets with different amounts of private regulation. After the creation of the Securities and Exchange Commission, the government started imposing rules on all parties and all exchanges. In many cases the government simply chose to impose relatively strict rules that the New York Stock Exchange had already adopted but competing exchanges had not. If a company was already listed on the New York Stock Exchange, many new rules were not additionally binding. Firms doing business on the New York Stock Exchange were now required to follow rules they had been following. Matters were different in smaller markets where q^* differed and the new rules were binding (and beyond q^*).

The results could have been predicted by economists and were subsequently shown. Stigler (1964) investigates (1) the number of new stock issues and (2) their returns relative to other stocks before and after the creation of the Securities and Exchange Commission. Stigler finds that after the creation of the Securities and Exchange Commission, the increased cost of going public meant that the number of new issues decreased. The fact that making something more expensive pushes certain firms, especially smaller firms with less ability to bear the costs, out of the market should surprise no economist. Perhaps more important is Stigler's next finding: after the creation of the Securities and Exchange Commission and all of its new regulations for new issues, the relative returns of the new issues did *not* increase. Regulations that were implemented to help investors simply precluded many firms from listing shares and also failed to enhance the performance of those that got to market. Stigler's findings are consistent with the idea that, at best, government can replicate q^* in some markets (such as the New York Stock Exchange) and go beyond q^* in others.

Since the creation of the Securities and Exchange Commission, the United States has been adding more and more rules and regulations, and they seem to be well beyond the optimum (q^*) and at the point where the regulations do more harm than good (q_3). Many questions that could easily be decided by stock exchanges are now mandated by government, reducing the decision-making power and importance of exchanges. An overprovision of rules is also making listing on an exchange in the United States much less attractive. According to the *Economist* (2012a), "The home of laissez-faire is being suffocated by excessive and badly written regulation," and these regulatory burdens are showing up in many different markets. Patricof (2011) explains that in the United States "the mounting pile of regulations forced the IPO market to shrink" and that since 2001, the number of IPOs in England exceeded the number of IPOs in the United States for the first time in decades. (In the first decade of the twenty-first century, the number of IPOs [but not their market value] on the Alternative Investment Market in London has equaled or exceeded the number of IPOs on the American Stock Exchange, NASDAQ, and the New York Stock Exchange combined [London Stock Exchange, 2012c].)[1] A record numbers of firms have gone private, and fewer firms are crosslisting in the United States because of the costs of dealing with regulations like the Sarbanes-Oxley Act (Piotroski and Srinivasan, 2008).

In modern America, the overprovision of rules and regulations is hurting more than just the stock market. In a recent survey of one thousand small businesses, 69 percent viewed policies and regulations from Washington as harmful, and 93 percent viewed increased lawsuits as a somewhat or very serious problem (McInturff, Weigel, and Schoen, 2010). Readers who have not had to deal with financial or business regulations are invited to read the Code of Federal Regulations. At 150,000 pages, it's wildly interesting reading and not too hard to keep up with: just read one hundred pages each day, and you can get through the existing set of regulations in five years, and hope that they haven't added too many others by the time you are done. Many of my friends work as compliance officers on Wall Street, and they say that although the regulations all but guarantee them employment, they would not wish the regulations on their worst enemy.

Whereas the market for private governance has built-in incentives to encourage providers of private governance to search for optimal rules, centrally imposed regulations from government do not. The best the government can do is crowd out rules that providers of private governance would have

---

1. Why are firms opting out of markets with more government regulations and into ones with few regulations such as the Alternative Investment Market in London? Vismara, Paleari, and Ritter (2012, p. 377) report that "firms transferring to the AIM often cite lower costs (31.7%), flexibility (20.3%), and minor regulation (16.3%)."

provided; or worse, government can impose rules well beyond the optimum and thereby drag down markets. The New York Stock Exchange is still great, but its effectiveness is diminished by countless government regulations.

12.3. WHEN GOVERNMENT UNDERMINES OR MONOPOLIZES WHAT WAS PROVIDED BY PRIVATE GOVERNANCE

The London Stock Exchange had done many amazing things (and still does many amazing things), but in the twentieth century it was severely undermined by government. The most harmful interferences came with World War I, when the exchange was closed and later regulated with government "measures to force Britishers to sell foreign securities and to buy only British securities, chiefly government bonds." The results of putting political interests above the interests of investors was not good, as Atwood (1917, p. 150) explains: "The restrictions placed upon the London Stock Exchange quickly forced its New York cousin in the world's first place." The predictions in Hayek's *Road to Serfdom* were coming true in England, and they led firms to do business in more free areas. As Arthur and Booth (2010, pp. 40–41) explain, "From the end of World War I onwards, we have an elegant private regulatory institution gradually becoming part of a set of cartels and corporatist institutions." Government worsened matters for the London Stock Exchange over time. In 1979 the Restrictive Practices Court challenged the entire existence of their rulebook (Glasgow Herald, 1979, p. 16) as being monopolistic and exclusionary. But as the London Stock Exchange chairman responded, "You cannot have a security market which is regulated in the interests of protecting the public, which does not have voluntary agreement—and what are voluntary agreements but restrictive practices?" (Glasgow Herald, 1980, p. 11). (In 1986 the London Stock Exchange was saved by many deregulations, but the market is still recovering.)

The fate of the London Stock Exchange is not unique, as governments have a long history of interfering with private governance. A thousand years ago the legal system in England was decentralized and largely private (Benson, 1994a; Curott and Stringham, 2010), but subsequently monopolized as a way of enhancing revenue for the government. Before the Norman invasion of 1066, free men banded together into groups of ten families called "tythings," which met regularly to talk over mutual interests and provide for their common security against crime. A man, called a tythingman, led each group. As this form of organization developed, groups of one hundred tythingmen formed a larger group called a hundred that held a court and elected a leader called a reeve. When disputes occurred, they had the equivalent of a trial within a tything or between tythings, and the wrongdoer would be asked to compensate the victim. Different tythings would pledge to honor the judgments for their members, and individuals who ignored a judgment were declared outlaws and lost privileges of the system. After the Norman invasion governments realized they could get a piece of the restitution pie by saying that a transgressor violated the king's peace and must compensate the king as well. Eventually governments mandated that all restitution go to the king, the private system broke down, and the precursor to modern criminal law emerged. In this example, government intervened with private governance not to correct a market failure but to raise revenue for itself.

One can observe similar tensions between private governance and government over time. Much of what we find in modern common law actually developed in private courts in medieval and early modern England. There were local courts, manorial courts, merchant courts, and ecclesiastical courts, which were independent from the royal courts and the King's Bench (Benson, 1990; Stringham and Zywicki, 2011a). Even when government courts had official jurisdiction, people could opt into other courts through various legal fictions. For example, even though ecclesiastical courts were supposed to deal only with matters involving religion, one could have a contract adjudicated by them if at contract time one swore an oath to God. This was an early modern equivalent of an arbitration clause. Adam Smith ([1776] 1976, p. 241) praises the competition as good for liberty, but an important disadvantage to government was that it had less control, and so gradually it began restricting these private courts. In the fourteenth century, government established admiralty courts to compete against local mercantile courts and force foreign trade to pass through them as a means of customs control (Plucknett, 1956, p. 660). In the late fifteenth century government enacted a statute restricting the law merchant's jurisdiction to the limits of fairs (Holdsworth, [1903] 1956, p. 539). In the area of church courts, "The abolition of the episcopacy in the 1640s had brought an end to the effective jurisdiction of the ecclesiastical courts" (Helmholz, 2004, p. 309). Over the following couple of centuries the government asserted more control over the commercial law of England. In all of these cases, the restrictions on private governance were not due to market failure.

Similar tensions exist in the alternative dispute resolution industry today, as some government officials want to channel disputes through government courts or have disputes adjudicated in particular ways. Benson (1995) documents how statutes that legalize binding arbitration have the downside of requiring arbitrators to follow many of the bureaucratic procedures of government courts. In flowery yet fairly Orwellian language, restrictions on arbitration are made in the name of harmonization. Who could be against harmony, after all? Such one-size-fits-all mandates mean that providers of private governance have much less ability to adjudicate disputes in ways that parties in a dispute want, and market choices are therefore reduced.

In other areas government simply forces people to use governmental "services" even though private alternatives exist. For example, the San Francisco

Police Department puts various restrictions on the Patrol Special Police to "encourage" people to hire off-duty government police. Officers working in the 10(b) overtime program get to use their government-provided equipment and earn an additional $87 per hour. Expansion of government in these areas appears to have nothing to do with correcting a market failure, but instead is a means of restricting competition and extracting resources from the public.

12.4. WHEN GOVERNMENT STRONG-ARMS OR CO-OPTS PRIVATE GOVERNANCE

The bassist for the Jerry Garcia Band, Jimmy Tebeau, is a hippie with long hair who likely does not use much shampoo. But the people around him were also hippies (thus the externalities were internalized), and he became a successful entrepreneur. He bought a 330-acre property (itself surrounded by thousands of acres of forest) in rural Missouri and organized three-day music festivals with outdoor activities that employed two hundred staff per event and grossed more than $1.7 million per year (Crone, 2013; Hamilton, 2013). Jimmy served on two chambers of commerce and in 2005 was recognized by the Missouri legislature because, among other things, his "entrepreneurship and creativity help to broaden and deepen the economic foundations of local communities and neighborhood," and because he had:

> . . . added such improvements to the property as roads, electric meters, stages, phone lines, a general store, a concession stand, an ATM, a pay phone, high speed internet satellite, and living quarters; renamed the place "Zoe Campitheater.". . . Now, therefore, be it resolved that we, the members of the Missouri House of Representatives, Ninety-third General Assembly, join unanimously to applaud the entrepreneurial spirit and creative skills embodied in the life and work of Jimmy Tebeau and to convey to him this legislative body's most heartfelt best wishes for continued personal and professional success for many more years to come. (Missouri House of Representatives, 2005)

Jimmy also lives in a country where 100 percent of the country's presidents of the past twenty years have used illicit drugs, and many of his thousands of guests did as well. In November 2010 government officials raided his festival and seized his property and bank accounts because of drug use by customers. Threatened to be sent to jail for years, this long-haired entrepreneur and father of two young children did not want to risk a trial and accepted a plea bargain in which he would be jailed for three years and have his property seized. Jimmy probably will never get back in festival business, and if he does, he likely abandon his live-and-let-live rules of the past and instead be much more diligent against drug use. Intervention such as this means that government now has a new set of (unwilling) employees to enforce its rules.

The government also forces private entities from colleges to corporations to act on its behalf. Even though the First Amendment to the U.S. Constitution states, "Congress shall make no law respecting an establishment of religion, or prohibiting the free exercise thereof; or abridging the freedom of speech," various branches of government pass laws that force private entities to restrict freedom of speech (Volokh, 1997; Barry, 2007).[2] Recently the U.S. Department of Justice and the Department of Education released a blueprint for colleges that outlines how speech codes for students (Lukianoff, 2013) should cover topics including "telling sexual or dirty jokes; spreading sexual rumors or rating other students as to sexual activity or performance; or circulating or showing e-mails or Web sites of a sexual nature" (U.S. Department of Education, 2008). Colleges and their students might want to make a commitment to free speech, but government mandates preclude them from doing so. The owners of the company that you work for may have little desire to enforce feminist speech codes, but they will be exposed to legal liabilities if they do not. These providers of private governance are forced to act against the wishes of their customers just as your bank and your email provider is being forced to spy on you. They have little choice.

The public interest theory of regulation believes that government intervenes to help the public, whereas the economic theory of regulation discusses how regulations can be imposed to benefit special interests, private or governmental (Stigler, 1971). Some regulations are used to restrict competition and benefit industry insiders and the government officials who share the proceeds (Posner, 1974). Other regulations are simply used to extract resources from successful enterprises (McChesney, 1987). In this stickup form of regulation, the threatened party hands over resources or becomes a servant of the state.

In some areas, government partners with certain industry insiders to restrict choice or to advance other governmental objectives. Just as government grants monopolist privileges in taxi cabs or cable television and gets paid for granting the monopoly privileges, government often grants monopoly privileges to "self-regulatory organizations" such as the Financial Industry Regulatory Authority (the successor to the National Association of Securities Dealers), a private but not a voluntary association. The Financial Industry Regulatory Authority sets fees with government, and any individual or firm wishing to stay in the industry cannot opt out (Carreno, 2012). Likewise, the private Financial Accounting Standards Board has become more involved with various governmental rules, and its standards are less and less voluntary.

---

2. The fact that government indirectly restricts freedom of speech is recognized by both critics (Volokh, 1997) and advocates of speech codes such as Balkin (1999), who recognizes that sexual harassment laws create "collateral censorship."

Government relies on the Financial Accounting Standards Board to help craft and impose many of its rules. Similarly, physicians' groups such as the American Medical Association (AMA) do not have forced membership, but they work closely with government to restrict the supply of doctors (in the AMA's own words, "Market forces cannot be relied upon by themselves" [quoted in Frudenheim, 1986]) or advocate certain policies. These private organizations likely do many good things, but they often oppose a free market for private governance in the same way that certain corporations oppose allowing market competition against them. If a private entity seeks to use laws to protect itself from competition, we should be unsurprised when it does not put the interests of the consumer among its primary objectives. In such industries, cronyism enables government to pick winners and losers, to give privileges to those who advance government's objectives, and to put out of business those who do not.

12.5. SUMMARY AND THOUGHTS

In a free market the customer is king, but government changes that dynamic. A casual observer could see Jimmy Tebeau, a college, or a corporation becoming stricter and subsequently blame the market for private governance for imposing rules that consumers do not want. A more accurate interpretation requires the observer to look at the impositions that interfere with the market for private governance. Rather than augmenting private governance, government is often the primary obstacle. Government often crowds out, restricts, or co-opts providers of private governance and forces them to pursue government's objectives. In some markets the government imposes rules and regulations that providers of private governance would have adopted on their own. Commonly, however, government imposes rules and regulations with little regard for whether they actually benefit market participants. Like price controls that interfere with supply and demand equilibration, government rules and regulations interfere with the searches for beneficial rules and regulations by providers of private governance.

Where providers of private governance weigh the marginal benefits and marginal costs of additional rules, government officials receive limited market feedback and almost no discipline if they impose harmful rules. Government regulations are one-size-fits-all, mute much of the potential market feedback, and receive pretty much no market discipline. It was not that difficult to predict that the extremely onerous Sarbanes-Oxley regulations imposed in 2002 would make being a publicly traded company in the United States less attractive and do nothing to prevent problems during the next economic downturn. Even though those rules led to a record number of firms going private, decreased IPOs such that the IPO market in England surpassed that in the United States for the first time in many decades, and continue to cost firms and investors tens of billions of dollars per year (Ahmed et al., 2010), the former politicians Sarbanes and Oxley will not have to repay a cent of the billions of dollars of the compliance costs that they have imposed on capital markets. The same will be true for former politicians Dodd and Frank, whose regulations cost Americans billions of dollars in explicit compliance costs (The Economist, 2012a, 2012b), not to mention the much greater but unseen costs of precluding many individuals and firms from the capital market.

Such regulations have even more costs if one considers how they reduce capital formation and the growth of businesses in the long run. Dawson and Seater (2013) argue that regulations decrease economic growth year after year, and that if one looks at how this problem compounds, in the past sixty years alone regulations have made Americans an estimated 75 percent poorer than we would be without regulations (in figure 12.1, we are well beyond q^* or in the realm past q_3). In his book *The Stealth of Nations: The Global Rise of the Informal Economy*, Neuwirth (2011) estimates that half (yes, 50 percent) of all workers worldwide work in the informal economy, and this is another indicator that governments are not creating beneficial rules and regulations and are more of a hindrance on markets than a help. These informal markets could almost certainly work more effectively if they did not have to avoid or deal with governments, but the fact that half of all workers worldwide do business outside the control of government is a strong indicator that markets are not a creation of government. The same is true of private governance. Just as markets exist in all societies to varying degrees (and their performance depends on how free they are [Gwartney, Lawson, and Block, 1996]), private governance exists in all societies to varying degrees. How well private governance solves problems depends on how free it is from government interference. Given that government often outlaws or undermines private governance and seldom supports it, we should be skeptical of the claim that government makes private governance possible. If anything, overprovision of rules and creeping legalism make the smooth functioning of private governance more and more difficult.

CHAPTER 13

☙☙

Applying Hayek's Insights about Discovery and Spontaneous Order to Governance

13.1. INTRODUCTION

SpongeBob SquarePants was a fictional sponge planning a party at his home in the sea. SpongeBob wanted a particularly good party, so he created a detailed plan of what everyone would do:

> I've taken the liberty of devising a schedule! [SpongeBob takes out list.] 8:00–8:05: Guests arrive. 8:05–8:15: Opening remarks and general discussion. 8:15–8:27: Craft corner, followed by name tag distribution. [List rolls across the table.] At 8:27, we begin the qualifying rounds for our cracker-eating slash tongue-twister contest. 9:07: Running charades. [List rolls along the wall.] 9:38: Charity apple-bob. [List is still rolling around.] 9:57: Electric jitterbug dance marathon, ladies' choice. [The list stops on SpongeBob's head.] At 10:09, things start cooking as I dig into my world-famous knock-knock joke vault! . . . And as long as we stick to this schedule, our party is a guaranteed success! (CBS Interactive, 2013)

SpongeBob had created the Sarbanes-Oxley and Dodd-Frank acts of party rules,[1] but his bash did not go as planned. Partygoers started doing their own thing and enjoying themselves, and at one point SpongeBob accidentally got locked out of his home. Viewing his unsupervised guests through the window,

---

1. In contrast to SpongeBob, the store Nordstrom's has the following one-sentence rulebook for all employees: "Rule #1: Use best judgment in all situations. There will be no additional rules."

SpongeBob lamented, "They're not using the topic cards! They're ad-libbing! . . . Look at those poor souls, they're so bored, they've gone mad! Oh, no. The party's falling into chaos without my hosting talents to guide it!" Yet the guests were having fun, and cheered as SpongeBob's starfish friend, Patrick, downed deviled egg after deviled egg. SpongeBob did not realize that the party would be fine without central control and the outcomes could emerge spontaneously.

Friedrich Hayek is well known for his theory of spontaneous order where individuals pursuing their own interests help bring about a complex outcome, not necessarily designed or intended by anyone. For example, the people who invented the first computers had little idea how computers would be used today, but interaction of countless individuals in Silicon Valley and the world leads to technological innovations that were hardly imaginable a few decades ago. The same is true of the people who created the first rules in stock markets and who helped make financial capitalism widespread.

How far we extend the scope of private governance, and how much does it need to be controlled by a monopoly government? When writing about economics Hayek refers to the competitive process of the market as a "discovery process" and argues that without markets we have no way of knowing what set of goods should be produced. Hayek also uses similar terminology about discovery in the area of law. To Hayek the role of the judge under the common law was "discovering" the law in the expectations and conventions of people in a given society. This consistent usage seems more than a mere semantic coincidence, and the concepts are remarkably similar in Hayek's thought. This chapter, based on an article I wrote with Todd Zywicki (Stringham and Zywicki, 2011a), argues that if one recognizes this conceptual similarity, one should draw the following conclusion: just as economic discovery requires the competitive process of the market to provide information and feedback to correct errors, competition in the provision of governance is essential to discovery of optimal rules. Hayek certainly did not agree with the position presented here (in fact, he expressly argued that markets need to be overseen by a monopolistic government),[2] but the same reasons that made Hayek a champion of market competition over central planning of the economy *should* have led him to support a free market for governance. Knowledge problems and accountability problems prevent a centralized government from providing rules and regulations in a manner that holds up to Hayek's ideals. Just as Hayek ([1976] 1990) abandoned his earlier belief that government needs to provide money and instead called for a system of competing currencies, he could have

---

2. In a 1978 interview Hayek said, "Our spontaneous order of society is made up of a great many organizations, in a technical sense, and within an organization design is needed. And that some degree of design is even needed in the framework within which this spontaneous order operates, I would always concede; I have no doubt about this. Of course, here it gets into a certain conflict with some of the modern anarchists."

abandoned his idea that government needs to oversee markets. About government control over money ([1976] 1990, p. 28) Hayek wrote, "It has the defects of all monopolies: one must use their product even if it is unsatisfactory, and, above all, it prevents the discovery of better methods of satisfying a need for which a monopolist has no incentive."[3] Similarly he could have taken the next step and applied the logic about "the defects of all monopolies" to the area of governance. Accepting that governance is as complex as other market phenomena should lead one to question whether governance should be monopolized or controlled by government. Instead governance can and should be produced by the market itself.

13.2. THE USE OF KNOWLEDGE IN MARKETS AND LAW
13.2.1. Hayek's Theory of Markets

Hayek's theory of market competition as a discovery process has been discussed in depth by many authors, but let us briefly review it to frame an understanding of his theory of law. Hayek believed that decentralized markets and the price system help transmit important knowledge throughout the economy.[4] The world is constantly changing, but market prices provide continually updated information and incentives to help people to coordinate over time.[5] Prices help producers see how much consumers value the cost of inputs and how they value the end products. Profits and losses provide constant feedback to help producers see if they are providing goods that consumers value. Prices also act as signals to other producers to encourage people to get into or out of a particular market. This coordination process works over a very large scale and in very complex societies, as anonymous producers produce products that meet the needs of anonymous consumers on the other side of the globe.

Of particular interest here is that Hayek considered competition to be a "discovery process" (Hayek [1968] 2002). By this he meant that competition is important because we often do not know what should be produced until a

---

3. Note Hayek's observation that a cost of monopoly is not its static inefficiency but its inability to *discover* better methods of doing things.

4. Hayek (1948, p. 54) described what he considered "the central question of all social sciences: How can the combination of fragments of knowledge existing in different minds bring about results which, if they were to be brought about deliberately, would require a knowledge on the part of the directing mind which no single person can possess?" For a discussion of the idea that many other important, perhaps much more important, questions in social science exist, see Salerno (1993).

5. In Hayek's (1948, p. 83) words, "The continuous flow of goods and services is maintained by constant deliberate adjustments, by new dispositions made every day in the light of circumstances not known the day before, by B stepping in at once when A fails to deliver."

market test occurs. More generally, Hayek observes that where competition is justified:

> it is on the ground that we do *not* know in advance the facts that determine the actions of competitors. In sports or in examinations, no less than in the award of government contracts or for prizes for poetry, it would clearly be pointless to arrange for competition if we were certain beforehand who would do best. (Hayek, 1967, p. 179)

As applied to market competition, the value of competition as a discovery process is that at any given time producers do not know what consumers want; the trial-and-error experimental process of market competition, error, and feedback provides producers with information and feedback as to what consumers want or do not want. Through this iterative process of positive and negative experimentation, the market sends signals not about "what people *have* done, but only with what they *ought* to do." Hayek noted that

> competition operates as a discovery procedure not only by giving anyone who has the opportunity to exploit special circumstances the possibility to do so profitably, but also by conveying to the other parties the information that there is some such opportunity. It is by this conveying of information in coded form that the competitive efforts of the market game secure the utilization of widely dispersed knowledge. (Hayek 1976, pp. 116–17)

Competition, Hayek ([1968] 2002, p. 10) noted, is "a procedure for discovering facts which, if the procedure did not exist, would remain unknown or at least would not be used."

Indeed, sometimes consumers themselves may not know what they want or that a product is even available, and the value of competition is to propose entrepreneurial innovations that consumers may not realize even existed previously. The desires of consumers are often inchoate until confronted with a tangible choice or opportunity. Competition simultaneously reveals consumer preferences and provides signals to transfer productive resources toward the production of some products rather than others.

Thus, although the entrepreneur forecasts that his supply will fulfill consumer wants, he cannot be sure until the competitive process has been played out. A system that lacks competition lacks this feedback mechanism. Because no one organization could gather the necessary information to coordinate behavior among millions of individuals, a system of central planning is without a rudder. Markets, on the other hand, help people determine what among the multiple possible uses of a given resource will meet human wants. Through the informal and impersonal workings of the price system, knowledge possessed by one person can be transferred to the rest of society.

Hayek thus treats the competitive process as an iterative process of constantly discovering "facts" about the economic world—extant but unarticulated consumer needs and preferences that must be translated into productive output. Indeed, Hayek expressly analogizes the process of market discovery of facts to the process of scientific discovery, as many different scientists simultaneously working independently but building on one another's findings seek an increasingly accurate understanding of the natural world. Scientific discovery, then, is also a discovery process, as scientists proffer hypotheses and then test those hypotheses through Popperian experimentation, and the web of interlocking scientists simultaneously seeking truth through experimentation combines to a spontaneous order.

13.2.2. Hayek's Theory of Law

Hayek portrayed the economy as a spontaneous order that emerges without central design. Hayek also came to apply his thinking about spontaneous order to other institutions, including law. For much of his life Hayek viewed the ideal of law through the lens of the continental *Rechsstaat* tradition, a model largely derived from the civil law system that prevailed on the continent beginning with Napoleon. This is the model of law that is implicit in Hayek's analysis of the rule of law in *The Road to Serfdom* (1944) and *The Constitution of Liberty* ([1960] 1978). The *Rechsstaat* is largely statute-based law, and Hayek's enthusiasm for this model of law seems derived from his notion that the ideal of the rule of law is predicated on formal legal rules clearly expressed, prospectively promulgated, and equally applied.

But in his three-volume work *Law, Legislation, and Liberty* (Hayek, 1973, 1976, 1979), Hayek's understanding of law shifted radically. Instead of the *Rechsstaat* tradition that dominated his early work, Hayek shifted his focus to the common law of England rather than the civil law system of Europe. Although Hayek explained his shift as being a transition from an earlier focus on "public" law to a new focus on "private" law, a careful reading of *Law, Legislation, and Liberty* makes clear that he had made a more general jurisprudential shift toward a new understanding of law itself and the ideal of law. In particular, Hayek came to believe that the bottom-up lawmaking process of the common law was more conducive to liberty, coordination of individual expectations, and efficient use of dispersed knowledge than the top-down legislature-focused approach of those earlier works. In large part this preference arose from Hayek's understanding of the common law as being analogous to a market process. Hayek argued that judges deciding concrete disputes based on their detailed, albeit often intuitive tacit and local knowledge yielded a better institutional foundation than legislators trying to anticipate all future circumstances prospectively according to detailed rules. But Hayek also argued that although each case was a judicial resolution of particular disputes in concrete factual contexts, the common law itself was abstract in nature, as coherent, abstract principles emerged from the aggregation of many decentralized judicial decisions. But these abstract articulated principles are emergent from many particular judicial decisions, not their genesis. Hayek (1973, p. 86) believed that "the chief concern of a common law judge must be the expectations which parties in a transaction would have reasonably formed on the basis of the general practices that the on-going order rests on." He thought that "in an ever changing society" judges must seek to find rules that will "aim at securing certain abstract characteristics of the overall order of our society that we would like it to possess to a higher degree" (Hayek, 1973, p. 105). Hayek claimed that the law must gradually evolve de-pending on what will help keep people's expectations relatively stable.

Underlying this approach was Hayek's (1973, p. 162) conviction, following Hume (1740, Book III, p. 541), that the essence of law is not created by the state, but rather preexists in the conventions and understandings of the indi-viduals that compose a given community. Although this underlying consensus is largely conventional, in that it emerges spontaneously from the decentralized interactions of many people living together in a society, it is far from arbitrary.[6] In fact, again following Hume, Hayek notes that every peaceful and function-ing society must have at its core a system of rules dealing with the ownership, transference, and protection of property from others—what is conventionally referred to as property, contract, and tort law. That such a system of rules is implied follows because societies that lacked such a system would be unable to prevent conflict over resources and reward investment, resulting in the group's elimination in a Darwinian-style competition among different groups defined by different systems of rules (Zywicki, 2000). Hayek wrote:

> The basic source of social order . . . is not a deliberate decision to adopt certain common rules, but the existence among the people of certain opinions of what is right and wrong. . . . Except where the political unit is created by conquest, people submit to authority not to enable it to do what it likes, but because they trust somebody to act in conformity with certain common conceptions of what is just. There is not first a society which then gives itself rules, but it is common rules which weld dispersed bands into a society. (1979, p. 33)[7]

6. Hayek (1976, p. 42) wrote, "In such an effort towards the development of a body of rules, most of which are accepted by the members of society, there will therefore also exist an 'objective' (in the sense of being inter-personally valid, but not of universal—because it will be valid only for those other members of the society who accept most of its other rules) test of what is unjust."

7. Given this preexisting consensus as to the basic principles of a community, Hayek (1973, p. 95) noted, "It is only as a result of individuals observing certain common rules that a group of men can live together in those orderly relations which we call a society. It would therefore probably be nearer the truth if we inverted the plausible and widely held idea that law derives from authority and rather thought of all authority as deriving from law—not in the sense that the law appoints authority, but in the sense that authority commands obedience because (and so long as) it enforces a law pre-sumed to exist independently of it and residing on a diffused opinion of what is right."

The role of the judge, Hayek argued, is not to "make" the law, such as by articulating the "best" rule according to some external standard of value, but to "discover" the law in this imminent consensus of norms and expectations that underlie a given community (Zywicki and Sanders, 2008). To Hayek (1973, p. 118), this judge-made law is part of the spontaneous order.[8]

Hayek (1973, p. 72) argued that law "has never been 'invented' nor can it be 'promulgated' or 'announced' before hand" (1973, p. 118). He went onto the write that rules that emerge from the judicial process:

> . . . are *discovered* either in the sense that they merely articulate already observed practices or in the sense that they are found to be required complements to the already established rules if the order which rests on them is to operate smoothly and efficiently. They would never have been discovered if the existence of a spontaneous order of actions had not set the judges their particular task, and they are therefore rightly considered as something existing independently of a particular human will; while the rules of organization aiming at particular results will be free inventions of the designing mind of the organizer. (Hayek, 1973, p. 123)

Thus, the role of the judge is to *discover* the law and apply it to a particular concrete dispute, not to create or impose the law. Hayek describes a judge articulating or discovering preexisting rules in society in much the same way that he describes market participants discovering knowledge about the economy. Hayek conceives of a judge as being in a position similar to, for example, an owner of a gasoline station who when posting prices does not concoct the price of gasoline, but merely discovers what the market will bear based on the interactions of billions of people, including himself, and then articulates what he has found (Zywicki and Sanders, 2008). Consider the analogy further. If his acts are viewed in isolation, it may appear that when the gas station owner posts the price for a gallon of gas, he is "making" or "creating" the price of gas. But in reality, of course, neither the gas station owner nor any other person creates the price of gas. Instead, the price of gas at a particular gas station at a given time reflects the decentralized interactions of billions of people around the world. The price posted at a particular gas station is therefore properly understood as merely an articulation or announcement of the outcome of all of these interactions by the gas station owner, not a "creation" or "making" of the price of gasoline, even though to the noneconomist it may appear that the gas station is doing exactly that.

---

8. Hayek (1973, p. 123) wrote, "The difference between the rules of just conduct which emerge from the judicial process, the nomos or law of liberty—and the rules laid down by authority . . . lies in the fact that the former are derived from the conditions of a spontaneous order which man has not made, while the latter serve the deliberate building of an organization serving specific purposes."

Hayek suggests that the role of a particular judge in the common-law system is analogous to that of the gas station owner in the market system. Although it appears that a judge "makes" the law, Hayek argued that in reality the common-law judge is simply doing what the gas station owner does: articulating or announcing the outcomes of an underlying spontaneous order process, not actually "making" the law. This is the notion in which Hayek argued that judges "discover" the law rather than making it.[9] Hayek wrote:

> While the process of articulation of pre-existing rules will thus often lead to alterations in the body of such rules, this will have little effect on the belief that those formulating the rules do no more, and have no power to do more, than to find and express already existing rules, a task in which fallible humans will often go wrong, but in the performance of which they have no free choice. The task will be regarded as one of discovering something which exists, not as one of creating something new, even though the result of such efforts may be the creation of something that has not existed before. (1973, p. 78)

Note that Hayek here asserts two key propositions about the role of the judge: first that he can "do no more," and second that he has "no power to do more" than to find and express already existing rule. Finally, Hayek acknowledges that judges "often will go wrong" in their efforts to discover and articulate the law. As we will see in section 13.3 below, each of these elements in Hayek's argument has important implications for the arrangement of legal institutions.

Hayek's use of the term "discover" to describe the task of the judge in the common-law system is almost certainly deliberate in the sense that it is meant to invoke Hayek's notion of competition as a discovery process articulated in his economic theory. Still further, Hayek's description of the iterative process of legal discovery by judges, of trial-and-error efforts to better articulate the underlying norms and expectations of justice of those in a given society, strongly resembles the market discovery process that he has previously described. Furthermore, this sense of the law is oftentimes tacit (Zywicki, 1998); it exists in customs and conventions that evolve over time, in Hayek's framework an intuitive knowledge of what the rules are even if it is difficult to state or define the rules precisely. Equally illuminating is Hayek's (1973, p. 120) suggestion that the judicial task of articulation of law is comparable to the hypothesis-testing of the scientific process, which Hayek described as a discovery process as well.

---

9. I take no position here on whether this characterization of the common law as a process of "discovering" law rather than "making" law is actually accurate. Here I am simply describing his view without assessing its descriptive validity.

Discovery of legal rules takes place on several different levels. We do not know what principles a society should adopt to realize the end of overcoming the knowledge problem. From this perspective, the principles that guide a society will not be known ahead of time. Rather, Hayek claims that they spontaneously emerge from the ongoing interactions of individuals. Some general truths or laws may exist, but those that best encourage cooperation must be mixed with local elements such as culture, religious beliefs, climate, or land as well (Rosser and Rosser, 2008). No one can be certain beforehand of the exact institutions that will allow each specific society and each individual within the society to make the best use of his knowledge of his local situation. As Hayek stated:

> The rules under which the citizens act constitute an adaptation of the whole of society to its environment and to the general characteristics of its members. . . . The rules may have come to exist merely because, in a certain type of situation, friction is likely to arise among individuals about what each is entitled to do, which can be prevented only if there is a rule to tell each what his rights are. (Hayek, [1960] 1978, p. 157)

Because this law is a convention created to meet the needs of the individuals in a society, it will never be completely static. Rather, it will change as human needs change, and the application of the general principles to specific cases will also change over time. In general, however, the overall principles will remain relatively constant. These general laws that develop are basically unarticulated beliefs that will differ in minor ways from society to society, depending on the local circumstances in which a society finds itself. The law of a society is given its content by the individuals that comprise this society. These rules, however, are not arbitrary; they are general ideas that emerge to resolve conflict and promote coordination. As society becomes larger, more complex, and more heterogeneous, it becomes necessary to verbalize and articulate these intuitively understood rules. But, as Hayek stresses, the verbal formulations are not "the law"; it is the underlying tacit consensus on principles and expectations that is properly the law.

13.2.3. Why Hayek Believed in Governance and Law Provided by the State

In light of Hayek's theory of the nature of law, what type of legal institutional framework did Hayek believe was best suited to effectuate the discovery of law? One thing is clear: Hayek supported governance and a legal system monopolize by the state. To Hayek, the discovery of local knowledge about law would take place among a system of somewhat decentralized *government* judges.[10] In a 1978 interview Hayek explained why he believed society needs governance from the state rather than from the market:

> I believe there is one convincing argument why you can't leave even the law to voluntary evolution: the great society depends on your being able to expect that any stranger you encounter in a given territory will obey the same system of rules of law. Otherwise you would be confined to people whom you know. And the conception of some of our modern anarchists that you can have one club which agrees on one law, another club [agrees on another law], would make it just impossible to deal with any stranger. So in a sense you have, at least for a given territory, a uniform law, and that can only exist if it's enforced by government.

Hayek argued that there must be a common framework of rules for the great society to exist, from which he infers that there must be a state to provide those rules. Hayek's ideal is a limited government that will allow for the flourishing of spontaneous order in all realms of life: economic, social, legal, and otherwise. In *Law, Legislation, and Liberty* Hayek outlines his ideal legal order that allows for the discovery, articulation, and use of the conventions that individuals recognize as justice. He argued the law should be predictable yet flexible and open to change and improvement.

For Hayek, the main basis of the legal system is common law or what he calls judge-made law. The common law is a concept most closely identified with the Anglo-American tradition of law, featuring an adversarial procedure of real cases between two conflicting parties in which legal rule-making usually derives in the first place from judges, subject to overruling by legislatures (Stringham and Zywicki, 2012).[11] Rather than deciding every case independently, however, the judges in a common-law system use a body of precedents built up over the ages to draw analogies to the particular case at hand. Hayek emphasized, however, that it is not the precedents themselves that are law, but the principles that underlie them. The written precedents are merely verbal formulations, and holdings are examples that provided evidence of the underlying principles that are the true source of law; the case decisions

---

10. And, ultimately, these government judges work within a greater legislative framework.

11. Note that the adversary process itself is a system of competitive evidence provision, in contrast to the inquisitorial system in which the judge essentially is a central planner for purposes of evidence gathering. The adversary system, it turns out, is justified primarily where competition is necessary to discover hidden or private knowledge that would be unlikely to be discovered but for that competition (Zywicki 2008). The analogy to the value of competition in market discovery is obvious.

themselves are not the law and do not make the law (Zywicki, 2003, pp. 1566–69). In that description of the nature of law, Hayek profoundly breaks with the ideology of legal positivism in favor of the historical school of jurisprudence associated with Savigny, C. K. Allen, and others. In contrast to more civil-law-based systems, Hayek believed that the common law is much better suited to discovering the law; indeed, he implies that legislative-based systems in practice generally are not "law finding" systems at all, but rather lawmaking institutions engaged in deliberate, constructivist creation of law for designated social ends (although in theory they could operate at least to some extent like the common law). He also believes that the common law helps utilize knowledge because in deciding the implications for a certain ruling, judges can use the body of precedent that has been built up. The common law thus allows judges to draw on the wisdom of their predecessors.

To Hayek the common law is a crucial element of spontaneous order in society. He also praises the common law because it provides a high degree of predictability, one of the major goals of the rule of law. Indeed, although legislation superficially appears more predictable and certain than common law because of the greater verbal precision of legislative pronouncements, Hayek argues that in reality the common law provides greater predictability because its decisions derive from widely shared notions of what is just, making it easier for most people to conform their behavior to the expectations of the law rather than having to seek technical legal advice to know whether a proposed action is permissible. By looking at how previous similar cases were decided and the principles that they illustrate, the litigants in a given controversy can to a high degree predict how a given case would be decided, and can therefore factor this decision into their individual planning.[12]

But Hayek did not believe that the law should remain fixed. He believed that changes in law over time are often beneficial, although Hayek's approach to progress may be seen as evolutionary rather than revolutionary.[13] Progress occurs through a process of a selective evolution of traditions, much like biological evolution. Hayek sees this as a gradual process of selecting a particular set of rules or laws, at particular times, and for particular reasons. Although changes send ripples into potentially all facets of life, these changes should be ripples that people can gradually adapt to, not tidal waves. Hayek

12. By emphasizing reliance on precedent, Hayek also hopes to control potentially mischievous judges by preventing them from reading their own ideological interpretations into decisions.

13. Hayek (1979, p. 167) wrote, "We can endeavour to improve the system of rules by seeking to reconcile its internal conflicts or its conflicts with our emotions. But instinct or intuition do not entitle us to reject a particular demand of the prevailing moral code, and only a responsible effort to judge it as part of the system of other requirements may make it morally legitimate to infringe a particular rule."

describes how new rules should emerge as the result of a piecemeal process of evolution:

> To become legitimized, the new rules have to obtain the approval of society at large—not by a formal vote, but by gradually spreading acceptance. And though we must constantly re-examine our rules and be prepared to question every single one of them, we can always do so only in terms of their consistency or compatibility with the rest of the system from the angle of their effectiveness in contributing to the formation of the same kind of overall order of actions which all the other rules serve. There is thus certainly room for improvement, but we cannot redesign but only further evolve what we do not fully comprehend. (Hayek, 1979, p. 167)

Thus, just as laws originally emerge from the seemingly uncoordinated interactions of numerous individuals, change and improvement should also take place through the same process. If left on their own, individuals can make the adjustments necessary to reconcile new conflicts with the old body of laws that developed spontaneously.[14]

Hayek views governmental judge-made law as a proper scope of government and a crucial element of spontaneous order—whereas the content of the law can arise spontaneously, the institutional infrastructure of courts cannot be left to competition and spontaneous order processes. But Hayek also grants to the government another important power: he grants the legislature the ability to alter the law when common law reaches a "dead end" through adherence to precedent. Hayek delegates this responsibility to legislatures because in his scheme the role of the judge is to uphold expectations and engage in an imminent criticism of the law by making new rules and situations cohere within the existing infrastructure of rules. Thus, where a well-established rule is thought to be obsolete and reform is needed, it is inappropriate for judges to adopt a new rule that would disrupt settled expectations. Legislatures, however, can legislate prospectively and thereby essentially create new expectations, rather than making decisions based on settled expectations. Hayek emphasizes, however, that when legislatures engage in this sort of rule-making they should act in a fashion consistent with the abstract purpose-independent nature of common-law rules (*cosmos*) rather than

---

14. Hayek believed that no one individual can comprehend the origin of the social world around him. Describing our moral rules, Hayek (1979, pp. 166–67) wrote, "We do not really understand how it maintains the order of actions on which the co-ordination of the activities of many millions depends. And since we owe the order of our society to a tradition of rules which we only imperfectly understand, all progress must be based on tradition. We must build on tradition and can only tinker with its products. It is only by recognizing the conflict between a given rule and the rest of our moral beliefs that we can justify our rejection of an established rule."

the command-oriented nature of many legislative rules (*taxis*). He also supports legislation when the law develops in ways that are inconsistent with the market economy. Ultimately, Hayek believed in a system of law that builds on precedent and emerges and changes slowly over time, but when it reaches a dead end, he says, the legislature is justified in intervening to remove the bad precedent and prospectively set the legal system onto a new and better track. To Hayek it is the best of all worlds: reliance on individuals who use accumulated knowledge and operate within a greater framework to ensure that the market persists. Individual judges could rely on precedent in law in much the same way that individual producers in markets rely on prices.

13.3. WHY HAYEK SHOULD HAVE EMBRACED A MARKET OF PRIVATE GOVERNANCE

Hayek thus describes the nature of the law and the relationship of judges to the legal process as one of "discovery," drawing an analogy to the similar process in markets. With respect to economics and science, Hayek argues that their nature as discovery processes implies the necessity of competition in institutional arrangements.

Yet Hayek shies away from reaching the obvious logical implication of his modeling of law as a discovery process: the need for competition in legal provision. In particular, as suggested above, Hayek treats as normative concepts what are fundamentally questions of positive analysis and institutional design: his admonition that judges "do no more" and "have no power to do more" than discover the law. But his institutional structure is inadequate to ensure that judges in fact do no more and that they lack the power to do more than discover the law. Each of these two statements of the problem suggests a different challenge for Hayek: the first raises the knowledge problem as to the institutional circumstances under which judges can actually discover the law accurately, and the second raises an accountability problem regarding the agency-cost relationship between judges and society as to whether judges can be constrained to discover the law rather than pursue their own interests.

13.3.1. The Knowledge Problem with Centrally Provided Rules and Regulations

Although Hayek attempted to draw parallels between the market order and his ideal monopolized legal order, the crucial differences are that markets have competition and feedback through price, profits, and losses, whereas his or any other monopolized legal system does not. To understand why the judges in Hayek's ideal legal will be unable to discover the law, one should differentiate between two different types of competition: first, the one-on-one competition identified with the adversary system, and, second, a broader type of competition between multiple providers of a service. Even though the adversaries are in one sense competing under a centrally provided system, there are no market feedback mechanisms to indicate whether the judges or the overall system is doing a good job. The usual market feedback mechanisms of competition are absent, yet Hayek does not identify how a monopolist legal system would overcome what can be considered knowledge problems.[15] At the outset even well-intentioned judges will have little idea if they are discovering the type of laws people support in society, just as a well-intentioned economic planning board will lack the knowledge to discover the appropriate prices of goods and services in the economy without competition and market feedback. Although judicial decisions will be subject to critique and analysis by other judges and scholars, that intellectual critique is only tangentially related to the real measure of judicial success—whether the judicial decision dovetails with existing societal expectations and whether the decision promotes social and economic coordination. The real test of the usefulness of a legal rule is found in the *unseen* effects of the rule in terms of the number of accidents avoided or conflicts averted, not the *seen* effects of the cases that come before the judge. On this question the judge will have almost no relevant knowledge or, crucially, a way of possibly acquiring the relevant knowledge to make that assessment (Zywicki and Stringham, 2012). Without any measurement of market demand, judges will be unable to determine whether their decisions are really right or wrong as measured by whether they actually do reflect parties' expectations and social consensus. Judges will also be vulnerable to mistakes in articulating the unarticulated law. Hayek recognizes that this process of articulation may oftentimes be inaccurate and supports minimizing it. But with a monopoly and no feedback mechanism, how will the judges know initially or as consumer demands change whether a particular decision or verbal articulation is consistent with underlying expectations? Hayek's nomos or law of liberty is ever-changing, so even if a monopolistic legal system could discern the content of the law, the specifics would be useful for only a short period of time.

If such a system is combined with a strict adherence to precedent, stare decisis, then errors can create path-dependency effects that build upon each other and spread to other areas of the legal framework (Zywicki and Stringham, 2012). Although knowledge of the past, as embodied in the process of precedent, may be superior to no body of knowledge at all, it seems inferior

---

15. Rowley (1989, p.372) wrote that Hayek has not "presented a convincing explanation as to why, or through what mechanism, the judiciary should be supportive of the law of liberty or the law of efficiency in a largely monopolistic court bureaucracy such as that which characterizes twentieth century Britain and the U.S."

to knowledge of the past as well as the present. If, on the other hand, the common law allows judges to overrule precedent, it does not indicate when or what the new decision should be. Whatever the court decides will be enforced, so how the "right" or "wrong" decision could even be compared is not clear. Lacking a feedback mechanism, the judge is on his own. Furthermore, the stakes are extremely high, because if the judge chooses incorrectly, he could set off a chain reaction of unintended consequences. One has to ask, at what point does one determine that a precedent is wrong? Should a judge with a different opinion overrule the initial precedent as incorrect? Or the second interpretation of it? Or the third, or the tenth? A view of law wedded to precedent must start with the assumption that all previous precedents are correct. After this, without a feedback mechanism, judges are effectively without guidance in trying to decide which precedents are no longer relevant or which to overrule. But giving judges such discretion would defeat the purpose of Hayek's legal order: to discover and implement what society recognizes as law.

These problems are not solved by pushing the decision into the hands of the legislature. The same knowledge problems that pose difficulties in judges' attempts to discover the law are also present when the legislature attempts to intervene. Because legislators are confounded by the knowledge problem just as everyone else is, they will have difficulty determining how the rest of the human expectations, conventions, and other interlocking institutions will respond to changes in the legal structure. Pushing the problem back to the voting public will not solve the problem either. With little way to evaluate the goodness of any given rule or the performance of any individual judge, the public will be left wondering if the judge's opinion or the legislature's laws are simply personal opinions shrouded in false cloak of justice. Without profits and losses providing a feedback mechanism, judges and legislatures have little way of determining Hayek's nomos or law of liberty.

13.3.2. Accountability Problems with Centrally Provided Rules and Regulations

In addition to knowledge problems, centralized law enforcement suffers from accountability problems. Hayek's formulation creates an agency-cost relationship with judges: he says how judges *should* act—articulate parties' expectations—but institutional arrangements determine whether they *will* act in that manner. The knowledge problem deals with the well-intentioned judge; the accountability problem deals with the judge who doesn't want to be constrained.

Judges can attempt to discover Hayek's preferred law of liberty, or they can pursue other agendas. As Judge Posner and others correctly point out, government judges maximize their utility just like everyone else, which can include increasing fame, leisure, money, specific political outcomes, or state power

(Rowley, 1987; Posner 1994; Stephenson, 2009). No matter how strictly a set of laws are drafted, or adherence to judicial precedent may be commanded, any rule of law will still have to be implemented, interpreted, and executed by human beings (Hasnas, 1995). Absent competition, there are no obvious constraints on judicial agency costs for judges to pursue their personal preferences rather than seeking to "discover" the law as Hayek says that they should. Absent competition, there are no incentives for judges to even *seek* to supply Hayek's law of liberty as opposed to pursuing their ideological predilections or simply shirking and consuming leisure. Difficulties are magnified when power-seeking individuals are attracted to government, as Hayek (1944) suggests in his theory of why the worst get on top. No matter how stringent the selection process of these individuals is, a large amount of room exists for them to err and exploit their power.

Why is monitoring government judges or other lawmakers difficult? Hayek argued that no one party can understand the wisdom of the law, which implies that evaluating whether a judge is acting prudently or venally is inherently difficult. Citizens or watchdog groups may know their own position on a specific law, but they cannot know the exact feelings of others. They are therefore in the same position as judges who lack a measure about how a particular case "should" be decided. Judges or lawmakers wanting to use the law to advance a particular agenda can very easily come up with justifications of their actions that sound interested in public betterment (hence the existence of law reviews). These problems are not solved by the fact that adversaries compete and make their case about what is right in any given dispute. Although this system does provide a type of competition, the judges are the ones who ultimately call the shots, which leaves them room to pursue their own agenda. With a system of judicial review, the problem is simply pushed to a higher level, which gives even more power to the appellate or supreme courts.

Hayek's proposed solution of granting to the legislature the power to control judges and improve the law merely shifts the problem one level higher. The problem now becomes one of controlling the actions of the legislature instead of the judges.[16] But in making this logical move, Hayek betrays his own insights about the nature of law as a spontaneous order: in a world of legislative supremacy, law at root rests on top-down positivism rather than bottom-up polycentrism. Hayek's theory rests on a radical decentralization and polycentrism of law in which courts are engaged in an ongoing, dynamic discovery process of experimentation, trial and error, and feedback. In fact, Hayek's vision of law seemingly pushes toward the less-hierarchical polycentric institutional structure of his friend Bruno Leoni ([1961] 1972, pp. 23–24), who argued that a "Supreme Court" with authority to issue top-down binding

16. In fact, Hayek saw the gradual usurpation of power by the legislature from the courts as the most troublesome development of the era in which he wrote.

pronouncements on lower courts was actually an anomaly in a true common-law system. Leoni also argued that it would be possible to rely on entirely judge-made law rooted in custom and dispense with legislation completely—an argument that Hayek (1973, p. 68, n. 35) rejects with minimal explanation. If the legislature has the trump card and can intervene whenever it does not like a judicial decision, the incentives for the politicization of law are quite clear. In Hayek's system the express purpose of the legislature is to overturn precedents and start in new uncharted directions, which seems to go against his other goals of having stability and the rule of law rather than men. For Hayek's system to work, the rest of the problems of politics that Hayek and other public choice scholars identify would have to not exist.

13.3.3. Competition among Providers of Governance as the Solution

Hayek thus argued that the goal of the judge should be to "discover" the law. But the institutional structure that he has devised is inadequate to actually ensuring that result. What is the solution? By applying Hayek's insights about the knowledge problem in the economy to the workings of the legal system, one is led to a logical, albeit seemingly radical, institutional conclusion: governance, like other goods and services, should be provided in a competitive marketplace. We must have competition among providers of governance, and consumers must be allowed to choose among those suppliers.

Moving beyond the "central provision or no provision" mindset enables one to realize that governance can be provided in a plethora of ways. A centralized system of law is one size fits all (Hasnas, 1995; Stringham, 1999), and everyone receives rules and procedures whether they like them or not. But in a system in of private governance, consumers can have the set of rules and enforcement procedures that they actually value.

Hayek did worry that in a society without a monopoly governance, people would encounter others who do not follow the exact same rules. In an important sense he is correct that if rules were left to voluntary evolution, different clubs would have different rules. But what he does not realize is that this already happens all over the world today. Not only do people cross international boundaries that have differences in laws, laws differ between states and between towns. For example, rules about everything from carrying firearms to drinking alcohol on public property vary across the United States, but ask most Europeans, and they will be surprised that carrying firearms is legal anywhere or that drinking on public property is illegal anywhere. Yet Europeans travel to the United States all of the time without major problems. The whole basis of international trade, which has been taking place for hundreds if not thousands of years, is that it can take place between people of very different backgrounds (Leeson, 2006). Obviously Hayek is wrong to state that having different rules in different regions "would make it just impossible to deal with any stranger." If we move beyond the political sphere, in any given territory rules of conduct also vary greatly within different private establishments. English tearooms have very different rules than motorcycle bars, and golf clubs have very different rules than boxing rings. What is allowed in a boxing ring is prohibited outside it, and most people think twice before entering a motorcycle bar or a boxing ring. But even though house rules at bars can differ, most establishments choose to have fairly similar rules. This is not a problem with voluntarily evolved rules, but an advantage.

Private governance allows rules to vary or change over time depending on the preferences of club members.[17] For example, the private rules in rugby differ from those in football, and the same is true between a strict or less strict college. As preferences evolve, people might decide they now like football over rugby or a less strict college to a strict one, and private providers of rules can adapt accordingly. By contrast, under a monopoly system, the decisions of a court will be enforced regardless of what people want. Private providers of rules that respond to the type of law demanded by society will profit, and those that do not will incur losses. The profit-and-loss system will thus signal that a certain kind of law is demanded at any given point in time.

To illustrate the benefits of competition in the law, let us take a parallel from regular market competition that Hayek would certainly praise, the question of how many and what types of shirts should be produced (including what size, fabric, color, and style). A system based on legislation, even

---

17. The system described here overlaps with the ideals of Rothbard (1973), Friedman (1973), or Hasnas (1995), with some minor differences. In Rothbard, adherence to the nonaggression principle (or, to use Leonard Read's phrase, anything that's peaceful) is key, and I agree, but emphasize that once people opt into a particular club, the particulars have a lot of room to vary and evolve based on custom. A lot of the specifics of the legal rules, such as rules of evidence or punishments for crimes, which Rothbard (1973, p. 227) thought had to be laid down with "precise guidelines for private courts," could, as a practical matter, be decided differently by different clubs.

Friedman talks about rules varying across legal providers, including on issues such as whether or not drugs should be allowed. In Hasnas, any rule or procedure is okay as long as it is the product of market evolution. Hummel (1973), however, points out that despite what Friedman may imply, Friedman's system necessarily cannot be an anything-goes system, as it requires a bright-line rule that competing law enforcement agencies are not allowed to collect taxes; otherwise, the system differs little from government. From there it's a question of where one draws the bright line of what is acceptable and what is not (what constitutes a violation of the nonaggression principle and what does not). In the same vein, to support market evolution (as opposed to coercive government changes in law), Hasnas has to have a bright-line definition of what constitutes market evolution and what constitutes violations of it. Doing this ultimately requires having some definition of what counts as a market (voluntary) and what counts as a violation of it (aggression), similar to that of Rothbard. To use phraseology similar to Den Uyl and Rasmussen (2005), once one agrees on the metarule or metanorm of respecting basic rights, the particular norm or rule systems that people opt into can vary quite a bit.

democratically based, would basically need to guess on all counts. A legislator could guess whether his constituents wanted more shirts or fewer than provided the last time he or his predecessor was elected, but he would have little idea about how his guesses are related to the real ranking of what each citizen prefers. A shirt provision system based on Hayek's view of the common law might come closer to fulfilling individual wants, as it would use historical precedent to decide the types of shirts that will be manufactured now. But it's unclear how government would innovate or respond to changing consumer wants. As the shirt example illustrates, there is no optimal number of uniform shirts or even an optimal combination of different types of shirts. What is best varies from place to place and over time depending on what people want.

Similarly, with laws and legal procedures, what people want will vary from place to place and over time. In fact, of particular interest here is that the legal system that Hayek holds up as the model for his ideal of law was the English common-law system. But that system itself was characterized by multiple providers of legal services competing side-by-side for centuries, including multiple common-law courts, church courts, the law merchant, and other private courts such as the Courts of the Staple (Helmholz, 2004; Stringham and Zywicki, 2012). This competition among rival providers of legal services ensured that judges, who were paid in part according to the number of cases they heard, would seek to discover the law in the expectations of the private parties to the dispute rather than pursing their own self-interests and that the judges would provide speedy and fair justice.[18] Parties who were able to vote with their feet could simply refuse to patronize those judges and legal systems that sought to use law to promote their own goals rather than to further the needs of the parties. As Adam Smith ([1776] 1976, p. 423) wrote, "During the improvement of the law of England there arose rivalships among the several courts," and Smith praised the competition, saying that "each court endeavoured, by superior dispatch and impartiality, to draw to itself as many causes as it could" (Smith [1776] 1976, p. 241). Thus not only is competition in the provision of legal services an implication of Hayek's theory of law, Hayek's theory of law itself arose in exactly that institutional context.

If Hayek is correct that lawmaking is a discovery process similar to the discovery process of economics, it follows that the optimal system for provision of legal services should be predicated on a competition-based, rather than a monopoly-based, system. The need for judges to receive both positive and negative feedback in the provision of dispute resolution services is as relevant in the provision of legal services as it is in anything else.

---

18. For a discussion of the conditions under which this competition can yield a beneficent spontaneous order see Stringham and Zywicki (2011b) and DiIanni (2010).

13.4. SUMMARY AND THOUGHTS

Just as competition enables discovery and innovation in markets, competition enables discovery and innovation in governance. If one takes Hayek's discussion of the importance of discovery through competition seriously, one should question the idea that the state must centrally provide governance. Centralized governance faces knowledge and accountability problems similar to those of central economic planners. Hayek's proposed institutional system was simply not radical enough to capture the benefits of a decentralized competitive order. Rosser (2010) makes the case that although Hayek's economics was oriented toward a complexity approach, in many ways he did not go far enough. One can reach a parallel conclusion about Hayek's legal theory. Even though Hayek thought that government judge-made law could help encourage spontaneous order, such judges lack feedback mechanisms, so whether they are doing a good or a bad job will always be unclear. Hayek praises relying on precedent as a way of basing decisions on accumulated wisdom, although he supports allowing the law to change. Yet centrally provided systems have no way to measure the unseen or indirect consequences of relying on precedent versus changing the law. Monitoring judges becomes difficult, and the door opens wide for self-seeking individuals to attain their own ends in the name of improving the law, the common good, or any of the other of the myriad of euphemisms justifying state action.

Instead of relying on centrally provided governance, markets can provide rules and regulations that can vary from place to place and over time. Given Hayek's internal logic about the need for experimentation and openness, he should have been favored a system of private governance. At the very least, if Hayek is correct, there should be room for greater experimentation and competition among providers of governance. There is no reason to categorically rule out a whole host of ways society can be organized. Through competition, individuals and groups can discover what types of governance fit their needs best.

CHAPTER 14

ⲟⲗⲟ

The Unseen Beauty
that Underpins Markets

14.1. INTRODUCTION

"Stringham. Ed Stringham." I am on a rooftop bar in eastern Europe surrounded by some of the most beautiful blondes in the world. None are spies. I give a stranger a rectangular piece of plastic. In return he gives me a martini. I see a bunch of uniformed men staring at me. None are out to get me. James Bond never had it so good. My Slovenian friend's brother asks me, "Do you ever get pessimistic? Government is so pervasive, and we are so far from a world that relies on private rules and regulations?" I respond: "Quite the opposite!" How much of this venue was made possible because of government? How did the bartender know he would get money from me, because of government or because of American Express? Is the safety in this bar attributable to the police station a few miles away or to the niceness of the people and (in case something goes wrong) the uniformed security guards throughout? Things are as good as they are, not because of ex-Communist officials who are commonly outright hostile to markets, but in spite of them. Rothbard ([1974] 2000, p. 86) describes "history as a race" between state power and peaceful cooperation. At many times such as under communism and under war, state power prevailed. At this moment in Slovenia, peaceful cooperation is winning.

Even where governments are pervasive, so too is private governance, and the important source of order might not be a mythical market augmenting government but private governance. Each person involved in a market has numerous relationships, each of which is governed by multiple layers of private governance. Order can be attributable to a combination of trust, reciprocity, reputation, due diligence, bonding, risk management, and various business relationships for profit. As Thomas Paine ([1791] 1906, p. 84) states:

> The landholder, the farmer, the manufacturer, the merchant, the tradesman, and every occupation, prospers by the aid which each receives from the other, and from the whole. Common interest regulates their concerns, and forms their law; and the laws which common usage ordains, have a greater influence than the laws of government. In fine, society performs for itself almost everything which is ascribed to government.

Paine is right. Private parties have mutual interests to create rules to regulate their concerns, and such order comes about independent of government.

Although potential problems such as fraud are ubiquitous and unfortunately can never be eliminated, private governance does an extraordinarily good job of dealing with them. When solving a problem is a profit opportunity, market participants are extraordinarily good at finding mechanisms for dealing with problems of noncooperation and predation. Anyone who holds up peaceful cooperation as a normative ideal should be extremely impressed with all of these nonviolent mechanisms for eliciting good behavior. Just as entrepreneurs in product markets continually work to satisfy unmet needs of consumers, providers of private governance continually work to solve problems on behalf of consumers.

Private governance has been tremendously important for centuries, but its mechanisms are often not easily seen. When you do not have to worry about paying for fraudulent transactions on your credit card or about counterparty default risk in a stock purchase, the time you spend thinking about the problem is minimal. Behind the scenes, however, your credit card company spends hours designing, perfecting, and monitoring its fraud mitigation system, and your stock exchange spends hours making sure people who are permitted to trade in a market can actually deliver what they promise. Most people are not even aware that a potential problem even existed, whereas others simply misattribute the solution to government. Because private governance is neither hierarchical nor imposed on all, historians and economists often miss it. Research on private governance, however, helps shed light on the private parties that create the order in markets. Throughout history people have experimented with ways to deal with potential problems. In their search for profits, providers of private governance discover new ways of facilitating exchange, protecting property rights, and creating the framework that underpins markets.

Whereas Milton Friedman argues that successful examples of private enforcement are historical anomalies, and Douglass North argues that they work only in limited circumstances (Doherty and Friedman, 1995; North, 1990), they are pervasive and work under a wide range of conditions. Private governance works in simple markets with small numbers of homogeneous traders who have low discount rates, but it also works in large groups (chapters 5, 6, 7), among heterogeneous traders (chapters 4, 7, 8), with nonrepeat interaction (chapters 6, 7, 10), and for tremendously complex deals that take place through time (chapters 4, 6, 11). Private governance is responsible for the development of stock markets, derivatives markets, electronic commerce, and all of the advanced transactions associated with them.

The rules and regulations *of the* markets came *endogenously from* the markets. One cannot look at the first stock markets and say, "These markets emerged only after government started enforcing contracts in these markets," and one cannot look at the history of electronic commerce and say, "Trade emerged only because of technologically competent police and courts." Government is not the chicken that lays the egg of markets. Instead I would liken it to salmonella, a pathogen associated with but not responsible for chicken and eggs, or to a very large parasite (Hummel, 2001). Like money (Menger, [1871] 2007; White, 1999; Selgin, 2011), the rules of private governance have coevolved with markets rather than being created by the state.

When one sees tremendously complex financial instruments, one should not attribute their existence to politicians and bureaucrats who rarely know the meaning, let alone the purpose, of derivatives. When one sees thriving cross-border exchange, one should not attribute its existence to government officials who have little appreciation for free-market or international trade. Without private governance, markets probably would be as advanced as the U.S. Postal Service or the Department of Motor Vehicles. The London Stock Exchange and the New York Stock Exchange have done far more to underpin advanced financial markets than any bureaucrat from the Securities and Exchange Commission. American Express, MasterCard, and Visa have done far more to facilitate exchange around the world than any lawmaker, regulator, or cop. Private governance is responsible for much more, but even if it were only responsible for the examples in this book, its accomplishments should still be considered among the greatest achieved by humanity.

14.2. RESEARCH IMPLICATIONS OF PRIVATE GOVERNANCE

Everything built upon the work of the London Stock Exchange, the New York Stock Exchange, or modern financial intermediaries is only made possible because of private governance. Without it markets as we know them would not be here today. Although some authors criticize libertarians for cherry-picking the few examples in which private solutions work, the examples in this book just scratch the surface of what exists, and their influence on the world is enormous. This book has focused on specific case studies because they (1) are relatively clean examples in which one can more easily differentiate the contribution of private governance versus government and (2) let us examine private governance in complex settings. Countless other examples, some less complicated or clean, exist, and good social science can help us understand them (Benson, 1998; Williamson, 2005; Boettke and Aligica, 2009). The field of private governance is wide open and ripe for research.

A researcher of private governance can ask some of the following questions: What are the potential problems in a given market, and what are some of the potential solutions? Has government solved the problem, and if not, why? Does a private solution exist, and, if so, why does it exist and how does it work? Most of these are empirical questions that must be investigated rather than assumed.[1] Whereas legal centralism does not consider such questions, research in private governance can give a much better understanding of how markets work. Although normative discussions are necessary and useful, simply stating, "Defaulting on futures contracts with unlimited downside risk ought to be illegal" or "Defaulters on futures contracts who owe billions of dollars should be locked in a debtors' prison until they pay back their billions" is not as helpful as describing how a futures exchange actually prevents those problems to begin with.

In many cases, solutions do not exist, or have yet to be invented. For example, cavemen, and for that matter the vast majority of people in human history, did not have the luxury of the New York Cotton Exchange or Chicago Mercantile Exchange acting as a rule-enforcing clearinghouse. Such is the world. But innovations are always popping up, and a researcher can help document them rather than assuming the markets are made possible by declarations of law.

Because private governance is not a one-size-fits-all solution, research in private governance can analyze the various ways that parties deal with problems. Consider the simple but much-worried-about prisoners' dilemma problem, which authors such as Buchanan (1975) use to justify government. Rather than assuming a prisoners' dilemma must be dealt with by threats, research in private governance can document how people eliminate the problems by dealing with friends, creating long-lasting relationships, relying on reputation mechanisms, dealing with intermediaries, using escrow, posting performance bonds, hiring a third party to manage and assume risk, or many other methods. By transforming what could have been legal issues into issues of risk management, the effectiveness or ineffectiveness of a government legal system becomes irrelevant. This market creates incentives for providers of private governance to constantly optimize, experiment, and discover better ways of solving problems.

---

1. Although economic theory teaches that certain economic laws are forever true, good praxeologists do not assert that everything in the world can be known a priori. For example, whether how people act in a potential prisoners' dilemma situation cannot be known a priori depends on many variables, such as whether people know each other, can communicate, or expect to see each other again.

A better understanding of private governance leads to a better understanding of how markets work. Just as looking at the Charles River Bridge in Boston and mistakenly assuming it was built by government (rather than the Charles River Bridge Company) is easy, it is easy to look at markets and assume that order was created by a "policeman who protects men from the use of force" and from "law courts to settle disputes among men" (Rand, 1964). Instead of assuming that markets are underpinned and supported by bureaucrats in blue costumes and black robes, one should recognize the potential shortcomings of government and observe the steps that private parties take to facilitate exchange and protect their property.

Ignoring private order and misattributing that order to threats are common mistakes. Even many radical libertarians have strong legal centralist tendencies and believe that exchange crucially depends on police and courts, albeit private ones. Some compose science fiction-length speculations about how defaulters must be jailed until they pay off their debts, and critics are right to worry about such proposals. By retaining many of the bad aspects of legal centralism, these theorists miss the fact that some of the most sophisticated contracts in the world today are already enforced privately without the use of force. The London Stock Exchange need not threaten incarceration when it has rules limiting who is let in and the threat of excluding rule breakers from the club. American Express need not threaten incarceration when it can encourage merchants and cardholders to follow their rules or else get kicked out of the network and be given a bad credit report. A condominium complex need not threaten incarceration to subcontractors who accidentally damage a building when they have a security deposit from the unit owners or a surety bond from an insurer. From a positive perspective, voluntary associations already enforce most rules without the threat of force. All of this will give us a better understanding of markets, how they work, and what underpins them.

14.3. IMPORTANCE OF PRIVATE GOVERNANCE FOR SHORT-RUN POLICY DEBATES

A better understanding of private governance has many implications for the short run. Klein (2004, pp. 15–16) uses a football analogy and criticizes advocates of markets who focus on "the endzone" and refuse to "converse between the 30 yard lines." Holcombe (2004) also criticizes advocates of markets for discussing topics that Holcombe believes are unlikely to be implemented. Holcombe (2004, p. 338) states, "Whether private arrangements are superior to government activity . . . is largely irrelevant." I, however, hope that Klein and Holcombe agree that private governance is always present to varying degrees, and the question is how much. Just as some societies have more economic freedom, some societies have more private governance or pockets thereof, and discussions of either can be relevant to policy today.[2] For those interested in short-run policy, private governance can help inform the following debates:

- Listing and disclosure requirements. Should the state or stock exchanges decide the conditions and firms that can be invested in? Should the state mandate what firms disclose and in what formats, or should investors be able to choose what information they want? If regular investors can invest in foreign companies that do not follow the Sarbanes-Oxley regulations and small-scale and qualified investors can invest in American companies that do not follow the Sarbanes-Oxley regulations, should some or all Americans be able to invest in companies that do not follow Sarbanes-Oxley regulations?
- Accounting rules. Should the state mandate accounting rules for everyone or allow private groups such as the Financial Accounting Standards Board (FASB) to offer suggestions for people to evaluate and choose? If government-mandated accounting rules are so beneficial, why require them instead of letting firms opt into them?
- Terms of arbitration. Should the state prohibit arbitration agreements for specific industries such as securities, cell phones, or credit cards or allow people to select mutually agreed-upon terms?
- Marriage. Should the state determine the terms of marriage and who can or cannot be married, or should matters of family be determined and overseen privately by churches or other voluntary associations?
- Drug use among athletes and hippies. Should the state or sports leagues set the rules of what performance-enhancing drugs are allowed or disallowed for a particular sport? Should the state impose a blanket prohibition on recreational drugs (ones that the president of the United States chose to ignore), or should individual communities decide how to best deal with drugs? Should organizers of music festivals such as James Tebeau be jailed if attendees of their festivals use drugs?
- Police at festivals. Should organizers of festivals or street fairs be forced to hire government police, or should they be allowed to hire private security or private police who are paid to cater to the well-being of guests?
- Underage drinking. Should the state mandate a minimum drinking age and jail violators and their parents, or should individual families and colleges be allowed to teach responsible drinking in a safe and monitored atmosphere?
- Speech codes. Should the state restrict what speech is allowed on college campuses and in workplaces, or should individual colleges or workplaces be able to set their own rules based on the preferences of consumers and employees?

2. Building on the Economic Freedom of the World index (Gwartney, Lawson, and Block, 1996) many researchers have found that freedom matters at the margin and is correlated with many good things (for example, economic freedom is correlated with lower rates of homicide [Stringham and Levendis, 2010]). Future research could attempt to quantify and test the hypothesis that private governance matters at the margin.

- Zoning. Should government mandate the rules of neighborhoods or put more decisions in the hands of private cities, proprietary communities, or homeowners' associations?
- Immigration. Should the state determine whether an individual can be allowed in a continent or large land mass with political borders, or should the rules of who enters a property be determined by individual property owners?

Without awareness of private governance, it would be easy to assume that government needs to set the rules in each case. The person who answers "There ought to be a law" for each question and knows the "optimal rules for society" is a strong legal centralist and likely a "man of system," whom Adam Smith ([1759] 1853, pp. 233–34) describes as one who hopes to "arrange the different members of a great society with as much ease as the hand arranges the different pieces upon a chess-board." Yet even supporters of government law enforcement can support varying degrees of private governance, meaning that private governance need not be an all-or-nothing position. Whether or not one supports private governance in some or all of the above cases, they can help influence policy debates. None of this discussion involves pie-in-the-sky questions that can only be considered after government is cut back in other areas; instead, the questions have policy relevance today.[3]

14.4. IMPORTANCE OF PRIVATE GOVERNANCE IN THE LONG RUN

Private governance is also important for creating a better world in the long run. Mises and Bastiat argue that economic policy, for good or bad, is ultimately determined by public opinion (Caplan and Stringham, 2005), and although a widespread misunderstanding of how markets work likely translates into bad policies (Caplan, 2007), public opinion can, and often does, change. Until a half-century ago, arguments such as "We need more housing. Therefore government should provide housing" or "We need more affordable housing. Therefore government should put price controls on housing" were common, whereas today no serious person would make such as argument. When even

---

3. Further note that none of this discussion requires a radical transformation of man and instead takes humans' mix of goodness and badness as given and recognizes that markets can arise to deal with certain problems. Instead of assuming that topics involving rules must be the domain of the state, those who advocate private governance can highlight areas in which the private sector can solve problems quickly and cheaply in ways that government cannot. They can highlight ways in which providers of private governance internalize many of the costs and benefits of their rules and regulations and enhance markets as a result. The more that people can opt into voluntary associations, the less they will need to deal with a monolithic and coercive bureaucracy.

the median voter in Massachusetts can understand the problems with and vote to eliminate rent control (Powell and Stringham, 2005), there is hope about the spread of economic ideas.

Still, arguments such as "We need to reduce fraud. Therefore government needs more regulations" or "Risk is a problem. Therefore government should assume and manage risk" are much more accepted than they should be. When a U.S. president can state that a new set of regulations for Wall Street, such as the 2010 Dodd-Frank Act, "provides certainty to everybody" (Forty-Fourth President of the United States, 2010), and more than one person actually believes him, we are in trouble. We are in more trouble when people believe him that, with this 2,400-page bill, "unless your business model depends on cutting corners or bilking your customers, you've got nothing to fear" (Forty-Fourth President of the United States, 2010). This legal centralism run amok helps explain why the Federal Register now has 80,000 pages (Crews, 2013), and it explains the creeping criminalization of all types of activities and the government's record incarceration rates.

Although faith in government is still widespread, it may be passing its apex and declining. Surveys find that in the late 1960s about 75 percent of Americans said they trusted "the government in Washington all or most of the time," whereas now the number is only 20 percent. Gallup (2013) reports that a "record high in U.S. say big government greatest threat" to the country, and Pew (2013) reports that "majority views government as a threat to personal rights." People are also abandoning faith in politicians, and today only 9 percent have a favorable view of Congress. (Congress does rank as more popular than gonorrhea but less popular than cockroaches [Public Policy Polling, 2013, so the results are mixed.)

Many people do not make a connection between the unreliability of politicians and the inefficacy of the laws they impose, but if they can recognize the untrustworthiness of the former, they might be able to recognize the harmfulness of the latter. As more people recognize that order in markets is as attributable to government as much as good literature is attributable to the Government Printing Office, they will not so willingly support rules and regulations, and that can aid in replacing government rules and regulations with private ones.

One of the most important contributions of economics has been to elucidate invisible hand mechanisms and to describe how supply and demand come together to satisfy consumer wants. Buying and abstention from buying are all that is needed to coordinate the actions of buyers and sellers (Mises, [1949] 1998), and just as markets have built-in incentives to deal with unmet needs such as housing, the market for private governance has incentives to deal with unmet needs for problems such as fraud. Just as markets for housing worked long before economists understood of them, the same is true for private governance.

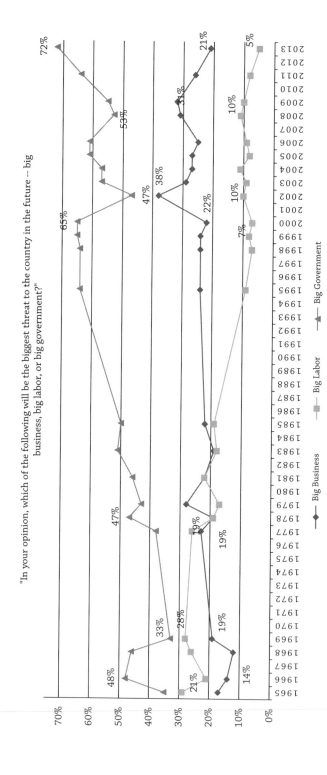

Figure 14.1
Views of Biggest Threat to United States in Future
Source: Data are from Gallup (2013).

Although conservatives worry about potential disorder in free markets, I suggest that private governance will be much more orderly than rules from a monolithic bureaucracy. And although progressives worry about corporate power, I suggest private governance will allow more choice and be markedly more liberal than government impositions on all people. Allowing people to voluntarily opt into, or out of, different systems lets people find the rules that benefit them. As Hayek writes:

> There is an advantage in obedience to such rules not being coerced, not only because coercion as such is bad, but because it is, in fact, often desirable that rules should be observed only in most instances. . . . It is this flexibility of voluntary rules which in the field of morals makes gradual evolution and spontaneous growth possible, which allows further experience to lead to modifications and improvements. Such an evolution is only possible with rules which are neither coercive or deliberately imposed. . . . Unlike any deliberately imposed coercive rules, which can be changed only discontinuously and for all at the same time, rules of this kind allow for gradual and experimental change. The existence of individuals and groups simultaneously observing partially different rules provides the opportunity for selection of the more effective ones. ([1960] 1978, pp. 62–63)

Choice is beneficial in markets for regular products and in markets for private governance. Sometimes people want the same thing, and markets can provide that. Widely desirable structures of private governance will become profitable and encourage others to mimic them without any need for coercive "harmonization." In other cases, variety of rule is a good thing. Just as it does not make sense for the corner store to comply with the listing requirements of the New York Stock Exchange or recreational sailors to comply with the rules of America's Cup, a market for private governance allows people to select from different structures that make sense for them. The market allows people to opt into different rule-enforcing clubs in different areas of their lives in various ways they like.

In "I, Pencil," Read (1958) describes how countless individuals cooperate to make even the simplest writing utensil. The typical consumer does not think about the markets for wood, graphite, paint, metal, and rubber and all of the submarkets required to produce those ingredients; the consumer is concerned only with the final product. The same is true for private governance. The consumer does not think about whether the pencil manufacturer is vertically integrated or how it contracts for graphite from Sri Lanka, a country that scores low on contract enforcement. The consumer does not think about the relationships between managers and the investors in the bauxite mining company in Guinea, a country that scores low on protecting investors (World Bank, 2013). The consumer does not think about whether aluminum was purchased over-the-counter using letters of credit or through the London Metal Exchange, a market where "80 percent of global non-ferrous business is conducted." The consumer can be completely unaware of all of the intricacies and multiple sources of oversight, whether formal or informal, individualistic, or club based. He can be completely unaware of the private governance that is ultimately provided on his behalf and simply priced into the final product. The fact that so many contracts along the way are unenforceable is irrelevant to the consumer, who just cares about getting the pencil. Simply walk into a store anywhere around the globe, give the clerk a credit card, and you can have anything within your credit limit. Private governance solves problems seamlessly with few people noticing, but it underpins economic exchange.

Private governance, in all of its forms—driven principally by the reliable engine of self-interest—brings people together to cooperate and to expand the scope of mutually beneficial exchange. With so much at stake and so much to gain, providers of private governance constantly experiment and collaborate to discover ways of eliminating problems. The mechanisms of private governance are potentially limitless. They facilitate cooperation in close-knit groups and among relative strangers. They facilitate cooperation between billions of people across political boundaries and anywhere where the government legal system is not capable of or uninterested in facilitating exchange. Private governance is responsible for cooperation in simple informal markets as well as the most advanced markets: stock markets, insurance markets, futures markets, and electronic commerce. Private governance makes markets work. Private governance replaces threats of coercion with numerous noncoercive mechanisms that expand the scope of trade, and it should be seen as one of the most successful peace projects in the history of the world.

ACKNOWLEDGMENTS

My interest in banking and finance spans longer than I can remember, and maybe has something to do with my grandfather, Richard Ver Valen Stringham, who worked in financial services and gave me bonds for Christmas. Those were best gifts a future economist could have asked for, so thanks Grandfather! I also thank my mother for encouraging me to study economics. The idea to write this book came during my two months as the Hayek Endowed Visiting Professor at Klagenfurt University in Austria, so I thank Barbara Kolm of the Hayek Institute and Professor Reinhard Neck for the opportunity. Thinking about economics in Austria, overlooking the Alps, and consuming sausage and beer for breakfast were great. *Besten Dank!* This book builds on my research of the past decade and half and I am most appreciative for ideas, inspiration, and feedback from professors including Walter Block, Peter Boettke, James Buchanan, Bryan Caplan, Tyler Cowen, Leonard Liggio, Nicolas Sanchez, Gordon Tullock, Walter Williams, and Todd Zywicki, and colleagues including Mark Brady, William Butos, Gerald Gunderson, Jeffrey Rogers Hummel, Adam Martin, and Benjamin Powell. I have also received helpful comments from members of the Financial Policy Council in Manhattan, former colleagues and current friends on Wall Street, members of the Colloquium on Market Institutions and Economic Processes at New York University: William Butos, Young Back Choi, Sanford Ikeda, David Harper, Luc Marest, Mario Rizzo, and Joseph Salerno; and seminar participants at George Mason University: Peter Boettke, Rosolino Candela, Christopher Coyne, Peter Leeson, Phil Magness, Alex Salter, Paola Suarez, Solomon Stein, and Lawrence White.

For written comments on chapters I thank Abha Banerjee, Bryan Caplan, Amy Fontinelle, Doug French, Walter Grinder, Gil Guillory, Linley Hall, Andreas Hoffmann, Aisha Jaleel, Michael Malice, Barkley Rosser, Nicholas Snow, Daniel Sutter, Virgil Storr, Alex Tabarrok, Jeffrey Tucker, Carl Watner, Claudia Williamson, Tom Woods, and J. Robert Subrick his most helpful James Madison University team: Mary Arczynski, Wes Boswell, Markus Brun Bjoerkheim, Devin Cates, Sarah Hollenbeck, Kevin Huber, Mohammed Idrees, Anton Konjevoda, Nolan Morris, Benjamin Orzolek, and Isabela Fleurine Reeves. Taylor Smith provided helpful research assistance. Parts of chapters 2, 3, 4, 5, 6, 7, 8, 9, 10, 11, and 13 build on or draw from Stringham (2013, 2014a, 2003, 2002),

Stringham and Chen (2012), Stringham (2005b, 2009, 2011), Caplan and Stringham (2008), Stringham (2014b), and Stringham and Zywicki (2011) respectively, so I acknowledge coauthors, editors, and publishers that have made this research possible. I thank Scott Parris and Terry Vaughn at Oxford University Press for their work on this manuscript, and the Earhart Foundation for its generous support.

As I finish this book I am overlooking the Hudson River and glorious skyscrapers surrounding Wall Street. I think Ayn Rand is right to say: "Come to New York, stand on the shore of the Hudson, look and kneel." I want to acknowledge the providers of private governance for making all of this possible. Without private governance the Dutch East India Company would not have financed Henry Hudson's voyage to this harbor in 1609, and the Dutch West India Company would not have founded New Amsterdam as a city based on profit. The City would not have attracted my ancestors, Jacob Van Wyck in 1640 or Peter Stringham in 1678, or the millions of other immigrants since. Without private governance the New York Stock Exchange would not have financed American capitalism, and markets would nothing close to what they are today. To the providers of private governance that have made the modern world possible, thank you.

Edward Peter Strigham
Davis Chair in Economic Organizations and Innovation, Trinity College

REFERENCES

Abel, Herbert D. 1954. "Euripides' Deus Ex Machina: Fault or Excellence." *Classical Association of the Middle West and South* 50 (3): 127–30.

Abkowitz, Alyssa. 2008. "Madoff's Auditor . . . Doesn't Audit?" *CNN Money*, December 19.

Adam, Georgina and Riah Pryor. 2011. "The Law vs Scholarship: Taking Academics to Court Over Authentication Issues Is Eroding Independent Expertise." *The Art Newspaper*, December.

Ahmed, Anwer S., Mary Lea McAnally, Stephanie Rasmussen, and Connie D. Weaver. 2010. "How Costly Is the Sarbanes Oxley Act? Evidence on the Effects of the Act on Corporate Profitability." *Journal of Corporate Finance* 16 (3): 352–69.

Ahmed, Azam. 2012. "Bonds Backed by Mortgages Regain Allure." *New York Times*, February 18.

Aidman, Alexander B. *The Art and Practice of Court Administration*. Boca Raton, FL: Taylor and Francis.

Akerlof, George A. 1970. "The Market for 'Lemons': Quality Uncertainty and the Market Mechanism." *Quarterly Journal of Economics* 84 (3): 488–500.

Albert, Miriam R. 2002. "E-Buyer Beware: Why Online Auction Fraud Should Be Regulated." *American Business Law Journal* 39 (4): 575–644.

Allen, Patrick. 2011. "No Chance of Default, U.S. Can Print Money: Greenspan." *CNBC*, August 7.

Allison, John A. 2013. *The Financial Crisis and the Free Market Cure: How Destructive Banking Reform in Killing the Economy*. New York: McGraw Hill.

American Arbitration Association. 2007. *Drafting Dispute Resolution Clauses—a Practical Guide*. New York: American Arbitration Association.

Amzalak, Moses. 1944. "Joseph Da Vega and Stock Exchange Operation in the Seventeenth Century." In *Essays in Honour of the Very Rev. Dr. J. H. Hertz*, ed. E. Levine, 33–49. London: E. Goldston.

Anderson, Terry L., and Peter J. Hill. 2004. *The Not So Wild, Wild West: Property Rights on the Frontier*. Palo Alto, CA: Stanford University Press.

Anti-Lounger. 1772. "Letter to the Printer of Town and Country Magazine." *Town and Country Magazine*, October 23, 524–25.

Ariely, Dan. 2008. *Predictably Irrational: The Hidden Forces That Shape Our Decisions*. New York: HarperCollins.

Arthur, Terry, and Philip Booth. 2010. *Does Britain Need a Financial Regulator? Statutory Regulation, Private Regulation and Financial Markets*. London: Institute of Economic Affairs.

ArtPrice. 2010. *Art Market Trends 2010*. Paris: ArtPrice.

Arvedlund, Erin E. 2001. "Don't Ask, Don't Tell: Bernie Madoff Is So Secretive, He Even Asks His Investors to Keep Mum." *Barron's*, May 7.

Atwood, Albert William. 1917. *The Exchanges and Speculation*. New York: Hamilton Institute.

Axelrod, Robert. 1984. *The Evolution of Cooperation*. New York: Basic Books.

Azfar, Omar, Charles Caldwell, eds. 2003. *Market Augmenting Government: The Institutional Foundations for Prosperity*. Ann Arbor: University of Michigan Press.

Balkin, J. M. 1999. "Free Speech and Hostile Environments." *Columbia Law Review* 99: 2295–305.

Balko, Radley. 2006. *Overkill: The Rise of Paramilitary Police Raids in America*. Washington, DC: Cato Institute.

Balko, Radley. 2013. *Rise of the Warrior Cop: The Militarization of America's Police Forces*. New York: Public Affairs.

Bancroft, Hubert Howe. 1887. *History of the Pacific States of North America: Popular Tribunals*. San Francisco: History Company.

Banner, Stuart. 1998. *Anglo-American Securities Regulation: Cultural and Political Roots, 1680–1860*. Cambridge: Cambridge University Press.

Barber, John W., and Henry Howe. 1865. *The Loyal West in the Times of the Rebellion*. Cincinnati, OH: F.A. Howe.

Barbour, Violet. [1950] 1976. *Capitalism in Amsterdam in the Seventeenth Century*. Ann Arbor: University of Michigan Press.

Barnett, Randy. 1985. "Pursuing Justice in a Free Society. Part 1: Power versus Liberty." *Criminal Justice Ethics* 4: 50–72.

Barnett, Randy. 1986. "Pursuing Justice in a Free Society. Part 2: Crime Prevention and the Legal Order." *Criminal Justice Ethics* 5: 30–53.

Barnett, Randy. 1998. *The Structure of Liberty*. New York: Oxford University Press.

Barnett-Hart, Anna Katherine. 2009. "The Story of the CDO Market Meltdown: An Empirical Analysis." Honors thesis, Harvard College.

Barry, Bruce. 2007. *Speechless: The Erosion of Free Expression in the American Workplace*. San Francisco: Berrett-Koehler.

Bartlett, John Russell. [1859] 1877. *Dictionary of Americanisms: A Glossary of Words and Phrases Usually Regarded as Peculiar to the United States*. Boston: Little, Brown.

Barzel, Yoram. 2002. *A Theory of the State*. New York: Cambridge University Press.

Bastiat, Frédéric. [1848] 1995. *Selected Essays on Political Economy*. Trans. Seymour Cain. Irvington, NY: Foundation for Economic Education.

Bastiat, Frédéric. [1850] 1996. *Economic Harmonies*. Irvington, NY: Foundation for Economic Education.

Bates, Victoria. 2010. "Astaire Securities Sold Off to Canada's Northland Capital Partners for £2.45m." *City A.M.*, October 18.

Bateson, Melissa, Daniel Nettle, and Gilbert Roberts. 2006. "Cues of Being Watched Enhance Cooperation in a Real-World Setting." *Biology Letters* 2: 412–14.

Baumeister, Roy F., and Kathleen D. Vohs. 2004. *Handbook of Self-Regulation*. New York: Guilford Press.

Bayles, W. Harrison. 1915. *Old Taverns of New York*. New York: Frank Allaben Genealogical Company.

BBC. 2005. "How the Rose Revolution Happened." *BBC News*, May 10.

BBC. 2012. "Britain's Private War." *BBC Scotland Investigates*, October 4.

Beattie, Alan and James Politi. 2008. "'I Made a Mistake,' Admits Greenspan." *Financial Times*, October 23.

Beaulier, Scott. 2005. "Polycentrism and Power: A Reply to Warren Samuels." In *Anarchy, State and Public Choice*, ed. Edward Peter Stringham, 178–90. Cheltenham, UK: Edward Elgar.

Beck, Allen, and Paige Harrison. 2007. "Sexual Victimization in State and Federal Prisons Reported by Inmates, 2007." Bureau of Justice Statistics Special Report NCJ 219414, December.

Beito, David, Peter Gordon, and Alexander Tabarrok. 2002. *The Voluntary City: Choice, Community, and Civil Society*. Ann Arbor: University of Michigan Press.

Bell, Maya. 1997. "Mickey's Identity Crisis: Courts Deciding If Disney World Is a Government, Business or Both." *Orlando Sentinel*, May 4.

Belmont, David P. 2011. *Managing Hedge Fund Risk and Financing: Adapting to a New Era*. Singapore: John Wiley and Sons.

Benjamin, Rich. 2009. *Searching for Whitopia: An Improbable Journey to the Heart of White America*. New York: Hyperion.

Benson, Bruce L. 1988. "Legal Evolution in Primitive Societies." *Journal of Institutional and Theoretical Economics* 144: 772–88.

Benson, Bruce L. 1989. "The Spontaneous Evolution of Commercial Law." *Southern Economic Journal* 55: 644–61.

Benson, Bruce L. 1990. *The Enterprise of Law: Justice without the State*. San Francisco: Pacific Research Institute for Public Policy.

Benson, Bruce L. 1994a. "Are Public Goods Really Common Pools? Considerations of the Evolution of Policing and Highways in England." *Economic Inquiry* 32 (April): 294–71.

Benson, Bruce L. 1994b. "Third Thoughts on Contracting Out." *Journal of Libertarian Studies* 11: 44–78.

Benson, Bruce L. 1995. "An Exploration of the Impact of Modern Arbitration Statutes on the Development of Arbitration in the United States." *Journal of Law, Economics, and Organization* 11 (2): 479–501.

Benson, Bruce L. 1998. *To Serve and Protect: Privatization and Community in Criminal Justice*. New York: New York University Press.

Benson, Bruce L. 2000. "Arbitration." In *Encyclopedia of Law and Economics*, Vol. 5, ed. B. Bouckaert and G. De Geest, 159-193. Chelthenham, UK: Edward Elgar.

Bernanke, Benjamin. 2008. *Monetary Policy and the State of the Economy: Hearing before the Committee on Financial Services, U.S. House of Representatives, One Hundred Tenth Congress, Second Session, July 16, 2008*. Vol. 4. Washington, DC: Government Printing Office.

Bernstein, Lisa. 1992. "Opting Out of the Legal System: Extralegal Contractual Relations in the Diamond Industry." *Journal of Legal Studies* 21: 115–57.

Bernstein, Lisa. 1996. "Merchant Law in a Merchant Court: Rethinking the Code's Search for Immanent Business Norms." *University of Pennsylvania Law Review* 144 (5): 1765–821.

Biggadike, Oliver, and Shannon D. Harrington. 2008. "Fannie, Freddie Credit-Default Swaps May Be Settled." *Bloomberg*, September 8.

Bing, Stanley. 2013. "Lessons from the Fall." *Fortune*, August 29, 164.

Black, Jane. 2002. "Max Levchin: Online Fraud-Buster." *Bloomberg-Businessweek*, September 30.

Blackstone, Erwin, and Simon Hakim. 2010. "Privatizing the Police." *Milken Institute Review: Journal of Economic Policy* 12 (3): 54–61.

Blackstone, Erwin, and Simon Hakim. 2013. "Competition versus Monopoly in the Provision of Police." *Security Journal* 26: 157–79.

Blakely, E., and M. Snyder. 1998. "Separate Places: Crime and Security in Gated Communities." In *Reducing Crime through Real Estate Development and Management*, ed. M. Felson and B. Peiser, 53–70. Washington, DC: Urban Land Institute.

Block, Walter. [1976] 1991. *Defending the Undefendable*. San Francisco: Fox & Wilkes.

Block, Walter, and William Barnett II. 2009. "Coase and Bertrand on Lighthouses." *Public Choice* 140 (1–2): 1–13.

Block, Walter, and Thomas DiLorenzo. 2001. "Constitutional Economics and the Calculus of Consent." *Journal of Libertarian Studies* 15: 37–56.

Block, Walter, Nicholas A. Snow, and Edward Peter Stringham. 2008. "Banks, Insurance Companies, and Discrimination." *Business and Society Review* 113 (3): 403–19.

Bloom, Herbert Ivan. 1937. *The Economic Activities of the Jews of Amsterdam in the Seventeenth and Eighteenth Centuries.* Williamsport, PA: Bayard Press.

Blount, Jeffrey, and James Rogers. 2012. "China-Related Arbitration Agreement: A Guide to Best Practice for International Parties Engaged in China-Related Transactions." *International Arbitration Report* 1 (April): 2–4.

BNY Mellon. 2012. "Risk Roadmap: Hedge Funds and Investors' Evolving Approach to Risk." New York: BNY Mellon.

Boer, Harm den, and Jonathan Israel. 1991. "William III and the Glorious Revolution in the Eyes of Amsterdam Sephardi Writers: The Reactions of Miguel De Barrios, Joseph Penso de La Vega, and Manuel De Leão." In *The Anglo-Dutch Moment: Essays on the Glorious Revolution and Its World Impact*, ed. J. Israel, 439–61. New York: Cambridge University Press.

Boettke, Peter J. 1993. *Why Perestroika Failed: The Politics and Economics of Socialist Transformation.* New York: Routledge.

Boettke, Peter J. 2005. "Anarchism as a Progressive Research Program in Political Economy." In *Anarchy, State and Public Choice*, ed. Edward Peter Stringham, 206–19. Cheltenham, UK: Edward Elgar.

Boettke, Peter J. 2012. "Anarchism and Austrian Economics." *New Perspectives on Political Economy* 7 (1): 125–40.

Boettke, Peter J., and Paul Dragos Aligica. 2009. *Challenging Institutional Analysis and Development: The Bloomington School.* New York: Routledge.

Boettke, Peter J. and Christopher Coyne. 2008. "The Political Economy of the Philanthropic Enterprise." In *Non-market Entrepreneurship: Interdisciplinary Approaches*, ed. G. Shockley, P. Frank, and R. Stough, 71–88. Cheltenham, UK: Edward Elgar.

Boettke, Peter J., and Christopher Coyne. 2009. "Context Matters: Institutions and Entrepreneurship." *Foundations and Trends in Entrepreneurship* 5 (3): 135–209.

Boettke, Peter J., and Anne Rathbone. 2002. "Civil Society, Social Entrepreneurship and Economic Calculation: Toward a Political Economy of the Philanthropic Enterprise." Working paper, Department of Economics, George Mason University.

Boot, Arnoud, Stuart Greenbaum, and Anjan Thakor. 1993. "Reputation and Discretion in Financial Contracting." *American Economic Review* 83: 1165–83.

Bowman, Karlyn, and Andrew Rugg. 2013. *Five Years after the Crash: What Americans Think about Wall Street, Banks, Business, and Free Enterprise.* Washington, DC: American Enterprise Institute.

Brennan, Geoffrey, and James M. Buchanan. 1985. *The Reason of Rules.* New York: Cambridge University Press.

Brewer, John. 1983. *An Ungovernable People: The English and Their Law in the 17th and 18th Centuries.* New Brunswick, NJ: Rutgers University Press.

Brown, William O., J. Harold Mulherin, and Marc D. Weidenmier. 2008. "Competing with the New York Stock Exchange " *Quarterly Journal of Economics* 123 (4): 1679–719.

Buchanan, James M. 1965. "An Economic Theory of Clubs." *Economica* 32: 1–14.

Buchanan, James M. 1972. "Before Public Choice." In *Explorations in the Theory of Anarchy*, ed. Gordon Tullock, 27–37. Blacksburg, VA: Center for the Study of Public Choice.

Buchanan, James M. 1975. *The Limits of Liberty: Between Anarchy and Leviathan*. Chicago: University of Chicago Press.

Buchanan, James M. 1994. "Choosing What to Choose." *Journal of Institutional and Theoretical Economics* 150: 123–35.

Buchanan, James M. 2003. "Politics as a Tragedy in Several Acts." *Economics and Politics* 15: 181–91.

Buchanan, James M. 2004. "Heraclitian Vespers." In *The Production and Diffusion of Public Choice Political Economy*, ed. J. Pitt, D. Salehi-Isfahami, and D. Echel, 263–71. Malden, MA: Blackwell.

Buckley, F.H. 1999. *The Fall and Rise of Freedom of Contract*. Durham, NC: Duke University Press.

Buffet, Warren. 2003. *Berkshire Hathaway Inc. 2002 Annual Report*. Omaha, NE: Berkshire Hathaway.

Buys, Cindy G. 2005. "The Arbitrators' Duty to Respect the Parties' Choice of Law in Commercial Arbitration." *St. John's Law Review*, 79(1): 59–96.

Cable News Network. 2008. "Looking at Bailout Options: CNN'S Candy Crowley Asks President Bush about Whether He Will Bail Out the Auto Industry." December 16.Caplan, Bryan. 1993. "The Economics of Non-State Legal Systems." Thesis. Princeton University.

Caplan, Bryan. 2007. *The Myth of the Rational Voter: Why Democracies Choose Bad Policies*. Princeton, NJ: Princeton University Press.

Caplan, Bryan, and Edward Peter Stringham. 2005. "Mises, Bastiat, Public Opinion, and Public Choice: What's Wrong with Democracy?" *Review of Political Economy* 17 (1): 79–105.

Caplan, Bryan, and Edward Peter Stringham. 2008. "Privatizing the Adjudication of Disputes." *Theoretical Inquiries in Law* 9 (2): 503–28.

Caplan, Keith, and Samer Ojjeh. 2011. "Hedge Fund Administrator Shadowing: Lowering the Costs of Third-Party Oversight." New York: Ernst and Young Financial Services.

Carlos, Ann, and Larry Neal. 2006. "The Micro-foundations of the Early London Capital Market: Bank of England Shareholders during and after the South Sea Bubble, 1720–1725." *Economic History Review* 59 (3): 498–538.

Carlton, Dennis. 1984. "Futures Markets: Their Purpose, Their History, Their Growth, Their Successes and Failures." *Journal of Futures Markets* 4 (3): 237–71.

Carreno, Kevin. 2012. "Letter to the Editor." *Investment News*, July 23.

Casey, Gerard. 2012. *Libertarian Anarchy: Against the State*. New York: Bloomsbury.

CBS Interactive. 2013. "Quotes from Spongebob Squarepants Season 3 Episode 10: Spongebob's House Party." CBS Interactive TV.com.

CBS News. 2008. "The Bet That Blew up Wall Street: Steve Kroft on Credit Default Swaps and Their Central Role in the Unfolding Economic Crisis." *CBS News 60 Minutes*, October 26.

Chartier, Gary. 2013. *Anarchy and Legal Order: Law and Politics for a Stateless Society*. New York: Cambridge University Press.

Chen, Brian X. 2012. "Developers Have Mixed Reactions to Blackberry 10 News." *New York Times*, May 1.

Chen, Henry (Litong), and B. Ted Howes. 2009. "The Enforcement of Foreign Arbitration Awards in China." *Bloomberg Law Reports—Asia Pacific* 2 (6).

Chertoff, Michael. 2001. "Fighting Cyber Crime: Efforts by Federal Law Enforcement: Oversight Hearing before the Subcommittee on Crime of the House of Representatives, Committee on Judiciary."

Childs, Mary. 2013. "Credit Swaps See U.S. Default Odds Less Than 2%: Reality Check." *Bloomberg News*, October 10.

Clark, J. R., Jennifer Miller, and Edward Peter Stringham. 2010. "Internalizing Externalities through Private Zoning: The Case of Walt Disney Company's Celebration, Florida." *Journal of Regional Analysis and Policy* 40 (2): 96–103.

Clay, Karen. 1997a. "Trade, Institutions, and Credit." *Explorations in Economic History* 34: 495–521.

Clay, Karen. 1997b. "Trade without Law: Private-Order Institutions in Mexican California." *Journal of Law, Economics, and Organization* 13: 202–31.

CME Group. 2011. *OTC Derivatives Market Monitor*. Chicago: CME Group.

Coase, Ronald. 1974. "The Lighthouse in Economics." *Journal of Law and Economics* 17 (October): 357–76.

Coffee, John C. 1995. "Competition Versus Consolidation: The Significance of Organizational Structure in Financial and Securities Regulation." *Business Lawyer* 50: 1–38.

Cohen, Patricia. 2012a. "Fake Art May Keep Popping Up for Sale." *New York Times*, November 5, C1.

Cohen, Patricia. 2012b. "In Art, Freedom of Expression Doesn't Extend to 'Is It Real?'" *New York Times*, June 19, A1.

Committee for General Purposes of the Stock-Exchange. 1812. *Rules and Regulations Adopted by the Committee for General Purposes of the Stock-Exchange*. London: Stephen Couchman Printers.

Coolidge, Mary Roberts. 1909. *Chinese Immigration*. New York: Henry Holt and Company.

Cooter, Robert D. 2006. "The Intrinsic Value of Obeying a Law: Economic Analysis of the Internal Viewpoint." *Fordham Law Review* 75: 1275–85.

Cormick, Alixe B. 2010. "Summary of the Listing Requirements of the NYSE, NYSE-MKT, TSX, Nasdaq, TSX Venture Exchange, CSE and U.S. OTCBB." Vancouver: Venture Law Corporation.

Cowen, Tyler. 1992. *Public Goods and Market Failures*. New Brunswick, NJ: Transaction Publishers.

Coyne, Christopher, Thomas Duncan, and Peter Leeson. 2014. "A Note on the Market Provision of National Defense." *Journal of Private Enterprise* 29 (2): 51–56.

Crews, Clyde Wayne. 2013. *Ten Thousand Commandments: An Annual Snapshot of the Federal Regulatory State*. Washington, DC: Competitive Enterprise Institute.

Crone, Thomas. 2013. "Encore: Jimmy Tebeau Is Still 'Truckin' While Waiting for the Law." *St. Louis Beacon*, March 21.

Crouzet, François. 2001. *A History of the European Economy, 1000–2000*. Charlottesville: University of Virginia Press.

Curott, Nicholas A., and Edward Peter Stringham. 2010. "The Historical Development of Public Policing, Prosecution, and Punishment." In *Handbook on the Economics of Crime*, ed. B. Benson and P. Zimmerman, 109–126. Cheltenham, UK: Edward Elgar.

Cuzan, Alfred. 1979. "Do We Ever Really Get Out of Anarchy?" *Journal of Libertarian Studies* 3: 151–58.

CyberSource Corporation. 2012a. *2012 Online Fraud Report: Online Payment Fraud Trends, Merchant Practices and Benchmarks*. San Francisco: CyberSource Corporation.

CyberSource Corporation. 2012b. *How It Started*. San Francisco: CyberSource Corporation.

Daily Alta California. 1851. "A Volunteer Night Patrol." *Daily Alta California*, May 19: 1.

Daily Alta California. 1854. "The Grand Jury." *Daily Alta California*, December 2.

D'Amico, Daniel J. 2009. "The Business Ethics of Incarceration: The Moral Implications of Treating Prisons Like Businesses." *Reason Papers* 31: 125–47.

D'Amico, Daniel J. 2012. "The Use of Knowledge in Proportionate Punishment." Working paper, Joseph A. Butt, S. J., College of Business, Loyola University, New Orleans.

Dantzker, Mark L. 2005. *Understanding Today's Police*. Monsey, NJ: Criminal Justice Press.

Dash, Eric. 2009. "Credit Card Companies Willing to Deal Over Debt." *New York Times*, January 3: B1.

Dawber, Alistair. 2010. "Small Talk: AIM Delistings Still on the Rise but Experts See Hopeful Signs." *Independent*, January 4.

Dawson, John W., and John J. Seater. 2013. "Federal Regulation and Aggregate Economic Growth." *Journal of Economic Growth* 18 (2): 137–77.

Defoe, Daniel. 1727. *The Complete English Tradesman*. Vol. 11. London: Charles Rivington.

Dehing, Pit, and Marjolein 't Hart. 1997. "Linking the Fortunes: Currency and Banking, 1550–1800." In *A Financial History of the Netherlands*, ed. M. 't Hart, J. Jonker, V. Zanden, and J. Luiten, 37–63. New York: Cambridge University Press.

de la Vega, Josef Penso. [1688] 1996. *Confusion de Confusiones*. New York: John Wiley & Sons.

Delevingne, Lawrence and John Carney. 2009."Half of Madoff's Victims Withdrew More Than They Invested" *Business Insider*, September 23.

Demsetz, Harold. 1967. "Toward a Theory of Property Rights." *American Economic Review* 57: 347–59.

Demsetz, Harold. 1969. "Information and Efficiency: Another Viewpoint." *Journal of Law and Economics* 12 (1): 1–22.

Deng, F. Frederic. 2002. "Ground Lease-Based Land Use System versus Common Interest Development." *Land Economics* 78 (2): 190–206.

Deng, F. Frederic, Peter Gordon, and Harry W. Richardson. 2007. "Private Communities, Market Institutions and Planning." In *Institutions and Planning*, ed. N. Verma, 187–206. New Brunswick, NJ: CUPR Press.

den Uyl, Douglas J. 2009. "Homo Moralis." *Review of Austrian Economics* 22: 349–85.

De Russailh, Albert Bernard. [1851] 1931. *Last Adventure: San Francisco in 1851*. San Francisco: Westgate Press.

Deutsche Börse Group. 2008. "The Global Derivatives Market an Introduction." White Paper, Frankfurt am Main.

de Vries, Jan, and Ad van der Woude. 1997. *The First Modern Economy: Success, Failure, and Perseverance of the Dutch Economy, 1500–1815*. New York: Cambridge University Press.Dey, Iain. 2006. "You Have to Go into AIM with Your Eyes Open," *The Telegraph*, June 18.

Dickson, Peter George Muir. [1967] 1993. *The Financial Revolution in England: A Study in the Development of Public Credit, 1688–1756*. Aldershot, Hampshire, England: Gregg Revivals.

DiIanni, I. 2010. "The Role of Competition in the Market for Adjudication." *Supreme Court Economic Review* 19: 203–31.

DiLorenzo, Thomas. 2005. *How Capitalism Saved America: The Untold History of Our Country, from the Pilgrims to the Present*. New York: Random House Digital.

DiLorenzo, Thomas. 2011. "A Note on the Canard of 'Asymmetric Information' as a Source of Market Failure." *Quarterly Journal of Austrian Economics* 14 (2): 249–55.

DiLorenzo, Thomas, and Walter Block. 2000. "Is Voluntary Government Possible? A Critique of Constitutional Economics." *Journal of Institutional and Theoretical Economics* 156: 567–82.

Dodd, S. C. T. 1894. "The Present Legal Status of Trusts." *Harvard Law Review* 7: 159–69.

Doherty, Brian, and Milton Friedman. 1995. "Best of Both Worlds: Milton Friedman Reminisces about His Career as an Economist and His Lifetime 'Avocation' as a Spokesman for Freedom." *Reason*, June.

Dore, Mohammed, and J. Barkley Rosser Jr. 2007. "Do Nonlinear Dynamics in Economics Amount to a Kuhnian Paradigm Shift?" *Nonlinear Dynamics, Psychology & Life Sciences* 11: 119–47.

Dougherty, Carter. 2012. "Consumers May See New Limits on Mandatory Arbitration." *Bloomberg Businessweek*, May 21.

Drahozal, Christopher R., and Stephen J. Ware. 2010. "Why Do Businesses Use (or Not Use) Arbitration Clauses?" *Ohio State Journal on Dispute Resolution* 25 (2): 433–76.

DTSM. 2007. *Downtown Santa Monica Demographics*. Santa Monica, CA: DTSM.

Duffie, Darrell, and Haoxiang Zhu. 2011. "Does a Central Clearing Counterparty Reduce Counterparty Risk?" *Review of Asset Pricing Studies* 1 (1): 74–95.

Duke University Police Department. 2010. *Security at Duke University, 2010–2011*. Durham, NC: Duke University.

Duke University Police Department. 2012. *2012–2013 Annual Clery Security Report*. Durham, NC: Duke University.

Easterbrook, Frank H., and Daniel R. Fischel. 1996. *The Economic Structure of Corporate Law*. Cambridge, MA: Harvard University Press.

The Economist. 2012a. "Over-regulated America: The Home of Laissez-Faire Is Being Suffocated by Excessive and Badly Written Regulation." *Economist*, February 18.

The Economist. 2012b. "The Dodd-Frank Act: Too Big Not to Fail: Flaws in the Confused, Bloated Law Passed in the Aftermath of America's Financial Crisis Become Ever More Apparent." *Economist*, February 16.

Ellickson, Robert C. 1991. *Order without Law: How Neighbors Settle Disputes*. Cambridge, MA: Harvard University Press.

El Nasser, Haya. 2002. "Gated Communities More Popular, and Not Just for the Rich." *USA Today*, December 15.

Epstein, Richard A. 1999. "Hayekian Socialism." *Maryland Law Review* 58: 271–99.

Epstein, Richard A., and M. Todd Henderson. 2009. "Marking to Market: Can Accounting Rules Shake the Foundations of Capitalism." University of Chicago John M. Olin Law and Economics Working Paper No. 458.

Ernst and Young. 2011. "Changing Face of Arbitration in India: A Study by Fraud Investigation and Dispute Services." Mumbai.

Esman, Abigail. 2012. "China's $13 Billion Art Fraud—And What It Means For You." *Forbes*, August 13.

Espenlaub, Susanne, Arif Khurshed, and Abdulkadir Mohamed. 2012. "IPO Survival in a Reputational Market." *Journal of Business Finance and Accounting* 39 (3–4): 427–63.

Euripides. [408 B.C.] 1893. *Orestes*. Trans. Edward P. Coleridge. London: George Bell and Sons.

European Magazine and London Review. 1811. "The Stocks." *European Magazine and London Review* 59: 34–37.

Evening Standard. 2008. "Nabarro Sold to Rival for £1m." *Evening Standard*, April 4, B35.

Federal Bureau of Investigation. 2004. *Crime in the United States, 2004*. Washington, DC: Federal Bureau of Investigation.

Federal Realty. 2011. *Santana Row Leasing Opportunities, May 2011*. Rockville, MD: Federal Realty.

Ferguson, Niall. 2001. *The Cash Nexus: Money and Power in the Modern World, 1700–2000*. New York: Basic Books.

Financial Crisis Inquiry Commission. 2011. *Final Report of the National Commission on the Causes of the Financial and Economic Crisis in the United States*. Washington, DC: Government Printing Office.

Financial Times. 2006. "A Healthy, Flourishing Market for the Future." *Financial Times*, October 6.

Fine, Aubrey, and Ronald Kotkin. 2003. *Therapists Guide to Learning and Attention Disorders*. Oxford: Academic Press.

Fisher, John Robert. 1997. *The Economic Aspects of Spanish Imperialism in America: 1492–1810*. Liverpool: Liverpool University Press.

Foldvary, Fred. 1994. *Public Goods and Private Communities: The Market Provision of Social Services*. Cheltenham, UK: Edward Elgar.

Folmer, Henk, Wim J. M. Heijman, and Auke Leen. 2002. "Product Liability: A Neo-Austrian Based Perspective." *European Journal of Law & Economics* 13: 73–84.

Forty Fourth President of the United States. 2009. "Remarks by the President at the Signing of the Helping Families Save Their Homes Act and the Fraud Enforcement and Recovery Act." Washington, DC: White House.

Forty Fourth President of the United States. 2010. "Remarks by the President on the Passage of Financial Regulatory Reform, July 2010." Washington, DC: White House.

Francis, John. 1850. *Chronicles and Characters of the Stock Exchange*. Boston: WM. Crosby and H.P. Nichols.

Frank, Robert H. 1987. "If Homo Economicus Could Choose His Own Utility Function, Would He Want One with a Conscience?" *American Economic Review* 77: 593–604.

French, Doug. 2006. "The Dutch Monetary Environment during Tulipmania." *Quarterly Journal of Austrian Economics* 9 (1): 3–14.

Frey, Bruno S. 2001. "A Utopia? Government without Territorial Monopoly." *Journal of Institutional and Theoretical Economics* 157: 162–75.

Friedman, David D. 1989. *The Machinery of Freedom, Guide to Radical Capitalism*. La Salle, IL: Open Court.

Friedman, David D. 2000. *Law's Order: An Economic Account*. Princeton, NJ: Princeton University Press.

Friedman, David D. 2008. *Future Imperfect: Technology and Freedom in an Uncertain World*. New York: Cambridge University Press.

Friedman, Devin. 2012. "The Best Night $500,000 Can Buy." *GQ*, September.

Friedman, Jeffrey, ed. 2010. *What Caused the Financial Crisis*. Philadelphia: University of Pennsylvania Press.

Friedman, Jeffrey, and Wladimir Kraus. 2011. *Engineering the Financial Crisis: Systemic Risk and the Failure of Regulation*. Philadelphia: University of Pennsylvania Press.

Friedman, Milton. 1962. *Capitalism and Freedom*. Chicago: University of Chicago Press.

Frudenheim, Milt. 1986. "A.M.A. Board Studies Ways to Curb Supply of Physicians." *New York Times*, June 14.

Frumkin, Jessica. 2010. "Operant Conditioning." In *Psychology: Seventh Edition, in Modules*, ed. David G. Myers, 318–37. New York: Macmillan.

Frye, Timothy. 2000. *Brokers and Bureaucrats: Building Market Institutions in Russia*. Ann Arbor: University of Michigan Press.

Gaffen, David. 2008. "Madoff's Not-So-Unique Options Strategy." *Wall Street Journal*, December 16.

Galanter, Marc. 1981. "Justice in Many Rooms: Courts, Private Ordering, and Indigenous Law." *Journal of Legal Pluralism* 19: 1–47.

Galanter, Marc. 2004. "The Vanishing Trial: An Examination of Trials and Related Matters in Federal and State Courts." *Journal of Empirical Legal Studies* 460–63.

Galanter, Marc, and David Lubin. 1992. "Poetic Justice: Punitive Damages and Legal Pluralism." *American University Law Review* 42 (4): 1393–463.

Gallup. 2013. "Record High in U.S. Say Big Government Greatest Threat." Survey conducted December 5–8, 2013.

Gambetta, Diego. 1993. *The Sicilian Mafia: The Business of Private Protection*. Cambridge, MA: Harvard University Press.

Gandel, Stephen. 2008. "The Madoff Fraud: How Culpable Were the Auditors?" *Time Business and Money*, December 17.

Garber, Peter. 1994. "Tulipmania." In *Speculative Bubbles, Speculative Attacks, and Policy Switching*, ed. R. Flood and P. Garber, 55–82. Cambridge, MA: MIT Press.

Garber, Peter. 2000. *Famous First Bubbles*. Cambridge, MA: MIT Press.

Gerbay, Remy, and Loukas Mistelis. 2013. "International Arbitration Survey 2013: Corporate Choices in International Arbitration." London: PricewaterhouseCoopers.

Gerstäcker, Friedrich. 1853. *Narrative of a Journey Round the World, Comprising a Winter-Passage across the Andes to Chili: With a Visit to the Gold Regions of California and Australia, the South Sea Islands, Java, & C.* New York: Harper and Brothers.

Glaeser, Edward I., Simon Johnson, and Andrei Shleifer. 2001. "Coase versus the Coasians." *Quarterly Journal of Economics* 116: 853–99.

Glaeser, Edward L., and Andrei Shleifer. 2003. "The Rise of the Regulatory State." *Journal of Economic Literature* 41 (2): 401–25.

Glasgow Herald. 1979. "Goodison Supports Investors." *Glasgow Herald*, April 5, 16.

Glasgow Herald. 1980. "Exchange Costs Mount to Over £1m." *Glasgow Herald*, September 24, 11.

Glovin, David. 2009. "Madoff Prosecutors May Hire Picard to Help Distribute Assets." *Bloomberg*, September 23.

Gneezy, Uri, and Aldo Rustichini. 2000. "A Fine Is a Price." *Journal of Legal Studies* 29: 1–18.

Goldman Sachs. 2013. *Overview of Goldman Sachs' Interaction with AIG and Goldman Sachs' Approach to Risk Management*. New York: Goldman Sachs.

Goldstein, Amy. 2007. "The Private Arm of the Law." *Washington Post*, January 2.

Gomme, Paul, and Peter Rupert. 2004. "Measuring Labor's Share of Income." Policy Discussion Papers of the Research Department of the Federal Reserve Bank of Cleveland.

Gore, Al. 1999. "Vice President Gore on CNN's 'Late Edition.'" *Late Edition with Wolf Blitzer*, CNN, March 9, 1999.

Gorton, Gary B. 2008. "The Panic of 2007." National Bureau of Economic Research Working Paper No. 14358.

Gralla, Preston. 2012. "Microsoft Subsidizes Developers up to $600,000 Per Windows Phone App." *Computer World*, April 6.

Granovetter, Mark. 1995. *Getting a Job: A Study of Contracts and Careers*. Chicago: University of Chicago Press.

Great Britain House of Commons. 1810. "Stock Market Petition." *Journals of the House of Commons* 65 (February 8): 60.

Greif, Avner. 1989. "Reputation and Coalitions in Medieval Trade: Evidence on the Maghribi Traders." *Journal of Economic History* 49: 857–82.

Greif, Avner. 1993. "Contract Enforceability and Economic Institutions in Early Trade: The Maghribi Traders' Coalition." *American Economic Review* 83: 525–48.

Greif, Avner. 2006. *Institutions and the Path to the Modern Economy: Lessons from Medieval Trade*. New York: Cambridge University Press.

Grigg, Neal S. 2010. *Economics and Finance for Engineers and Planners: Managing Infrastructure and Natural Resources*. Reston, VA: ASCE Publications.

Groenfeldt, Tom. 2013. "Major Hedge Fund Will Run Two Sets of Books." *Forbes*, January 28.

Grote, Jim, and John McGeeney. 1997. *Clever as Serpents: Business Ethics and Office Politics*. Collegeville, MN: Liturgical Press.

Grunfeld, Raphael. 2006. "AIM to Knock the Sox Off." *Legal Week*, May 25.

Gunderson, Gerald. 1989. *The Wealth Creators: An Entrepreneurial History of the United States*. New York: Dutton.

Gwartney, James, Robert Lawson, and Walter Block. 1996. *Economic Freedom of the World, 1975–1995*. Vancouver, Canada: Fraser.

Gwartney, James, Robert Lawson, and Joshua Hall. 2014. *Economic Freedom of the World: 2014 Annual Report*. Vancouver, Canada: Fraser Institute.

Hamilton, Keegan. 2013. "He's Gone: As Schwagstock Founder Jimmy Tebeau Enters Federal Prison, Should Other Music-Festival Organizers Worry about On-Site Drug Use?" *Riverfront Times*, June 13.

Hamon, Henry. 1865. *New York Stock Exchange Manual: Containing Its Different Modes of Speculation: Also, a Review of the Stocks Dealt in on 'Change*. New York: John F. Trow.

Hanson Westhouse. 2012. "Flotation Report." *AIM Listing*, April 24.

Hardin, Russell. 1997. "Economic Theories of the State." In *Perspectives on Public Choice: A Handbook*, ed. D. C. Mueller, 21–34. New York: Cambridge University Press.

Harris, Ron. 2000. *Industrializing English Law: Entrepreneurship and Business Organization, 1720–1844*. New York: Cambridge University Press.

Harris Interactive. 2012. "The Harris Poll #42." May 10.

Hart, Marjolein 't. 1997. "The Merits of a Financial Revolution: Public Finance, 1550–1700." In *A Financial History of the Netherlands*, ed. Marjolein 't Hart, Joost Jonker, and Jan Luiten van Zanden, 11–36. New York: Cambridge University Press.

Hart, Marjolein 't, Joost Jonker, and Jan Luiten van Zanden, eds. 1997. *A Financial History of the Netherlands*. New York: Cambridge University Press.

Hart, Oliver, and John M. Moore. 1999. "Foundations of Incomplete Contracts." *Review of Economic Studies* 66: 115–39.

Hasnas, John. 1995. "The Myth of the Rule of Law." *Wisconsin Law Review*: 199–233.

Hasnas, John. 2003. "Reflections on the Minimal State." *Politics, Philosophy, and Economics* 2: 115–28.

Hayek, Friedrich A. 1944. *The Road to Serfdom.* Chicago: University of Chicago Press.

Hayek, Friedrich A. 1945. "The Use of Knowledge in Society." *American Economic Review* 35 (4): 519–30.

Hayek, Friedrich A. 1948. *Individualism and Economic Order.* Chicago: University of Chicago Press.

Hayek, Friedrich A. [1960] 1978. *The Constitution of Liberty.* Chicago: University of Chicago Press.

Hayek, Friedrich A. 1967. *Studies in Philosophy, Politics and Economics.* Chicago: University of Chicago Press.

Hayek, Friedrich A. 1968 [2002]. "Competition as a Discovery Procedure." Trans. Marcellus S. Snow. *Quarterly Journal of Austrian Economics* 5: 9–23.

Hayek, Friedrich A. 1973. *Law, Legislation and Liberty.* Vol. 1: *Rules and Order.* Chicago: University of Chicago Press.

Hayek, Friedrich A. 1976. *Law, Legislation and Liberty.* Vol. 2: *The Mirage of Social Justice.* Chicago: University of Chicago Press.

Hayek, Friedrich A. 1976 [1990]. *The Denationalisation of Money.* 3rd ed. London: Institute of Economic Affairs.

Hayek, Friedrich A. 1978. "Tom Hazlett Interviews Friedrich A. Hayek November 12, 1978." UCLA Oral History Program and the Pacific Academy of Advanced Studies.

Hayek, Friedrich A. 1979. *Law, Legislation and Liberty.* Vol. 3: *The Political Order of a Free People.* Chicago: University of Chicago Press.

Haymond, Jeffrey E. 2001. "Blowing Smoke: A Case of Rent Extraction." *Journal of Public Finance and Public Choice* 19: 23-38.

Hazlitt, Henry. [1946] 1979. *Economics in One Lesson.* New York: Random House.

Heiner, Ronald A. 2002. "Robust Evolution of Contingent-Cooperation in Pure One-Shot Prisoners' Dilemmas." Working paper, George Mason University.

Helmholz, R. H. 2004. *The Canon Law and Ecclesiastical Jurisdiction from 597 to the 1640s.* New York: Oxford University Press.

Helper, Hinton Rowan. 1855. *The Land of Gold: Reality versus Fiction.* Baltimore: Henry Taylor, Sun Iron Bldg.

Helwege, Jean, Samuel Maurer, Asani Sarkar, and Yuan Wang. 2009. "Credit Default Swap Auctions." *Journal of Fixed Income* 19(2): 34-42.

Henrich, Joseph. 2004. "Cultural Group Selection, Coevolutionary Processes and Large-Scale Cooperation." *Journal of Economic Behavior and Organization* 53 (1): 3–35.

Henrich, Joseph, Robert Boyd, Samuel Bowles, Colin Camerer, Ernst Fehr, Herbert Gintis, Richard McElreath, Michael Alvard, Abigail Barr, Jean Ensminger, et al. 2005. "'Economic Man' in Cross-Cultural Perspective: Behavioral Experiments in 15 Small-Scale Societies." *Behavioral and Brain Sciences* 28: 795–855.

Héritier, Adrienne, and Sandra Eckert. 2008. "New Modes of Governance in the Shadow of Hierarchy: Self-Regulation by Industry in Europe." *Journal of Public Policy* 28 (1): 113–38.

Hertog, Johan den. 1999. "General Theories of Regulation." In *Encyclopedia of Law and Economics,* vol. 1, *The History and Methodology of Law and Economics,* ed. B. Bouckaert and G. De Geest, 223–70. Cheltenham, UK: Edward Elgar.

HFM. 2010. "Third-Party Administration." *HFMWeek:* February 25–March 3.

Higgs, Robert. 2012. *Delusions of Power: New Explorations of the State, War, and Economy.* Oakland: Independent Institute.

Hing, Julianne. 2011. "Report: Blacks and Latinos Make up 86 Percent of Pot Arrests in NYC." *Colorlines*, February 15.

Hittel, Theodore H. 1878. *A History of the City of San Francisco*. San Francisco: A.L. Bancroft.

Hittel, Theodore H. 1898a. *History of California*. Vol. 2. San Francisco: N.J. Stone.

Hittel, Theodore H. 1898b. *History of California* Vol. 4. San Francisco: N.J. Stone and Company.

Hogarty, Thomas. 1972. "Cases in Anarchy." In *Explorations in the Theory of Anarchy*, ed. Gordon Tullock, 51–64. Blacksburg, VA: Center for Study of Public Choice.

Hogg, James. 1850. "California in the Last Months of 1849." *Hogg's Weekly Instructor* 5: 343–45.

Holcombe, Randall. 2004. "Government: Unnecessary but Inevitable." *Independent Review* 8 (3): 325–42.

Holdsworth, William S. [1903] 1956. The History of English Law. London: Methuen and Company.

Holman, Herbert. 1896. *A Handy Book for Shipowners & Masters*. London: W.H. Maisey.

Holmes, Oliver Wendell. 1897. "Path of Law." *Harvard Law Review* 10 (8): 457–78.

Hoppe, Hans-Hermann. 1989. *A Theory of Socialism and Capitalism: Economics, Politics, and Ethics*. Boston: Kluwer Academic.

Hordahl, Peter, and Patrick McGuire. 2007. "Overview: Markets Rally until Late February." *BIS Quarterly Review*, March 2007: 1–15.

Houghton, John. [1692] 1727. *Husbandry and Trade Improv'd*. London: Woodman and Lyon.

Houser, Daniel, David M. Levy, Kail Padgitt, Sandra J. Peart, and Erte Xiao. 2011. "Doing and Saying: An Experimental Analysis of Transparent Leadership." Working paper, George Mason University.

Huemer, Michael. 2013. *The Problem of Political Authority: An Examination of the Right to Coerce and the Duty to Obey*. New York: Palgrave Macmillan.

Hulbert, Mark. 2005. "Membership Has Its Privileges." *MarketWatch*, December 6.

Hume, David. 1740. *A Treatise of Human Nature*. Book III. London: John Noon.

Hummel, Jeffrey Rogers. 1973. "A Comparison of Libertarian Primers." *Libertarian Alternative* 1: 3–5, 8.

Hummel, Jeffrey Rogers. 1990. "National Goods versus Public Goods: Defense, Disarmament, and Free Riders." *Review of Austrian Economics* 4: 88–122.

Hummel, Jeffrey Rogers. 2001. "The Will to Be Free: The Role of Ideology in National Defense." *Independent Review: A Journal of Political Economy* 5 (4): 523–37.

International Association of Campus Law Enforcement Administrators. 2013. *Campus Public Safety Standards*. West Hartford, CT: International Association of Campus Law Enforcement Administrators.

International Swaps and Derivatives Association. 2009. "AIG and Credit Default Swaps." New York.

International Swaps and Derivatives Association. 2014. "Key CDS Facts and FAQ." New York.

Israel, Jonathan. [1989] 1991. *Dutch Primacy in World Trade, 1585–1740*. New York: Oxford University Press.

Israel, Jonathan. 1995. *The Dutch Republic: Its Rise, Greatness, and Fall, 1477–1806*. New York: Oxford University Press.

Jackson, Eric M. 2004. *The PayPal Wars: Battles with eBay, the Media, the Mafia, and the Rest of Planet Earth*. Torrance, CA: World Ahead.

James, Scott. 2013. "King of My Castle? Yeah, Right." *New York Times*, June 7, A27.

Jasay, Anthony de. 1997. *Against Politics: On Government, Anarchy, and Order*. New York: Routledge.

Jenkins, Alan. 1973. *The Stock Exchange Story*. London: Heinemann.

Jenkins, Morris. 2006. "Gullah Island Dispute Resolution: An Example of Afrocentric Restorative Justice." *Journal of Black Studies* 37 (2): 299–319.

Johnsen, D. Bruce. 1986. "The Formation and Protection of Property Rights among the Southern Kwakiutl Indians." *Journal of Legal Studies* 15 (1): 41–67.

Johnson, Glen. 2011. "Elizabeth Warren Says She 'Created Intellectual Foundation' for Occupy Wall Street Movement." *Boston Globe*, October 25

Johnstone, Andrew. 1814. *The Caluminous Aspersions Contained in the Report of the Sub-Committee of the Stock-Exchange*. London: W. Lewis.

Katz, Michael, and Carl Shapiro. 1994. "Systems Competition and Network Effects." *Journal of Economic Perspectives* 8: 93–115.

Kearns, Jeff. 2012. "Fed Says U.S. Wealth Fell 38.8% in 2007–2010 on Housing." *Bloomberg Personal Finance*, June 12.

Kellenbenz, Hermann. [1957] 1996. "Introduction to Confusion de Confusiones." In *Confusion de Confusiones*, ed. M. Fridson, 125–46. New York: John Wiley and Sons.

Kennedy, Siobhan. 2007. "Adviser Fined for Not Making Proper Checks on AIM Listings." *Times* (London), October 20, 61.

Kessler, Amalia D. 2012. "Stuck in Arbitration." *New York Times*, March 7, A27.

Khurshed, Arif, Stefano Paleari, and Silvio Vismara. 2005. "The Operating and Share-price Performance of Initial Public Offerings: The UK Experience." Working paper, Manchester Business School.

Kindleberger, Charles P. 1984. *A Financial History of Western Europe*. London: George Allen and Unwin.

Kirzner, Israel M. 1985. "Liberalism and Limited Government." *Freeman* 35 (11): 678–80.

Kirzner, Israel M. 2000. *The Driving Force of the Market: Essays in Austrian Economics*. New York: Routledge.

Klein, Alex. 2011. "Are You Smarter Than a Wall Street Occupier?" *New York Magazine*, October 18.

Klein, Benjamin, Robert Crawford, and Armen Alchian. 1978. "Vertical Integration, Appropriable Rents, and the Competitive Contracting Process." *Journal of Law and Economics* 21 (2): 297–326.

Klein, Benjamin, and Keith Leffler. 1981. "The Role of Market Forces in Assuring Contractual Performance." *Journal of Political Economy* 89 (4): 615–41.

Klein, Daniel B. 1987. "Tie-Ins and the Market Provision of Public Goods." *Harvard Journal of Law and Public Policy* 10: 451–74.

Klein, Daniel B. 1997. *Reputation*. Ann Arbor: University of Michigan Press.

Klein, Daniel B. 2002. "The Demand for and Supply of Assurance." In *In Market Failure or Success: The New Debate*, ed. T. Cowen and E. Crampton, 172–92. Cheltenham, UK: Edward Elgar.

Klein, Daniel B. 2004. "Mere Libertarianism: Blending Hayek and Rothbard." *Reason Papers* 27: 7–43.

Knack, Stephen, and Philip Keefer. 1997. "Does Social Capital Have an Economy Payoff? A Cross-Country Investigation." *Quarterly Journal of Economics* 112 (4): 1251–88.

Knight, Frank. 1924. "Some Fallacies in the Interpretation of Social Cost." *Quarterly Journal of Economics* 38 (4): 582–606.

Kosmin, Barry, and Ariela Keysar. 2006. *Religion in a Free Market*. Ithaca, NY: Paramount Market.

Kotlikoff, Laurence. 2012. "What Neither Candidate Will Admit—Social Security Is Desperately Broke." *Forbes*, July 13.

Kotz, H. David. 2009. *Executive Summary of S.E.C. Madoff Report*. Washington, DC: Securities and Exchange Commission.

Kregel, J. A. 1995. "Neoclassical Price Theory, Institutions and the Evolution of Securities Market Organisation." *Economic Journal* 105: 459–70.

Kretkowski, Paul D. 1995. "Cops vs. Cops." *SF Weekly*, April 19.

Kubic, Thomas T. 2001. "Statement for the Record." Washington, DC: House Committee on the Judiciary, Subcommittee on Crime, June 12.

Kukathas, Chandran. 2007. *The Liberal Archipelago: A Theory of Diversity and Freedom*. New York: Oxford University Press.

Kupatadze, Alexander. 2012. "Police Reform in Georgia." Report for the Center for Social Sciences Foreign Policy and Security Programme, September.

Khurshed, Arif, Stefano Paleari, and Silvio Vismara. 2005. "The Operating and Share-Price Performance of Initial Public Offerings: The UK Experience." Manchester Business School Working Paper.

Lachmann, Ludwig. 1994. *Expectations and the Meaning of Institutions*. London: Routledge.

Lancaster, Kevin. 1966. "A New Approach to Consumer Theory." *Journal of Political Economy* 74 (2): 132–57.

Landa, Janet. 1981. "A Theory of Ethnically Homogenous Middleman Group: An Institutional Alternative to Contract Law." *Journal of Legal Studies* 10 (2): 349–62.

Landa, Janet. 1994. *Trust, Ethnicity, and Identity*. Ann Arbor: University of Michigan Press.

Lande, John. 1998. "Failing Faith in Litigation? A Survey of Business Lawyers' and Executives' Opinions." *Harvard Negotiation Law Review* 3: 1-69.

Landes, William M., and Richard A. Posner. 1979. "Adjudication as a Private Good." *Journal of Legal Studies* 8: 235–84.

Landsburg, Steven. 2010. *Price Theory & Applications*. Mason, OH: South-Western Cengage Learning.

Langrill, Ryan, and Virgil Henry Storr. 2012. "The Moral Meanings of Markets." *Journal of Markets and Morality* 15 (2): 347–62.

Leeson, Peter T. 2006. "Cooperation and Conflict: Evidence on Self-Enforcing Arrangements and Heterogeneous Groups." *American Journal of Economics and Sociology* 65: 891–907.

Leeson, Peter T. 2007a. "Anarchy, Monopoly, and Predation." *Journal of Institutional and Theoretical Economics* 163 (3): 467–82.

Leeson, Peter T. 2007b. "An-Arrgh-Chy: The Law and Economics of Pirate Organization." *Journal of Political Economy* 115: 1049–94.

Leeson, Peter T. 2007c. "Better Off Stateless: Somalia before and after Government Collapse." *Journal of Comparative Economics* 35: 689–710.

Leeson, Peter T. 2007d. "Efficient Anarchy." *Public Choice* 130 (1–2): 41–53.

Leeson, Peter T. 2008. "How Important Is State Enforcement for Trade?" *American Law and Economics Review* 10: 61–89.

Leeson, Peter T. 2009. *Invisible Hook*. Princeton, NJ: Princeton University Press.

Leeson, Peter T. 2011. "Trial by Battle." *Journal of Legal Analysis* 3 (1): 341–75.

Leeson, Peter T. 2012. "Ordeals." *Journal of Law and Economics* 55 (3): 691–714.

Leeson, Peter T. and Peter J. Boettke. 2009. "Two-Tiered Entrepreneurship and Economic Development." *International Review of Law and Economics* 29(3): 252–259.

Le Goix, Renaud. 2005. "The Impact of Gated Communities on Property Values: Evidence of Changes in Real Estate Markets—Los Angeles, 1980–2000." *Cybergeo: European Journal of Geography*, Article 375: 1-23

Leitzal, Jim. 2007. *Regulating Vice*. Cambridge: Cambridge University Press.

Leoni, Bruno. [1961] 1972. *Freedom and the Law*. Menlo Park, CA: Institute for Humane Studies.

Levchin, Max. 2008. "Interview between Max Levchin and Jessica Livingston." In *Founders at Work: Stories of Startups' Early Days*, ed. J. Livingston, 1–16. New York: Springer-Verlag.

Levy, David, Kail Padgitt, Sandra J. Peart, Daniel Houser, and Erte Xiao. 2011. "Leadership, Cheap Talk and *Really* Cheap Talk." *Journal of Economics Behavior and Organization* 77 (1): 40–52.

Lind, Hans, and Johan Nyström. 2007. "'Observable' and 'Verifiable': Can These Be the Basic Concepts in Incomplete Contract Theory?" In *Partnering: Definition, Theory and Evaluation*, ed. Johan Nyström, Stockholm: KTH Royal Institute of Technology.

Lipsey, Richard George, and K. Alec Chrystal. 2007. *Principles of Economics*. 11th ed. Oxford: Oxford University Press.

Litvintsev, Sergey G. 2009. "At What Do Venture Capitalists AIM?" Working paper, Duke Law School.

Locke, John. [1689] 1824. "A Letter Concerning Toleration." In *The Works of John Locke*, vol. 5, ed. C. a. J. Rivington, 1–58. London: Rivington.

London Stock Exchange. 2010a. "A Guide to AIM." London: London Stock Exchange.

London Stock Exchange. 2010b. "AIM Rules for Companies." London: London Stock Exchange.

London Stock Exchange. 2012a. "AIM Advisory Group." London: London Stock Exchange.

London Stock Exchange. 2012b. "Becoming a Nomad." London: London Stock Exchange.

London Stock Exchange. 2012c. "AIM Statistics." London: London Stock Exchange.

London Stock Exchange. 2015. "AIM Factsheet." London: London Stock Exchange.

London Stock Exchange Commission. 1878. *Report of the Commissioners*. London: George Edward Eyre and William Spottiswoode.

Long, Roderick, and Tibor Machan, eds. 2008. *Anarchism/Minarchism: Is a Government Part of a Free Country?* Aldershot, UK: Ashgate.

Lopez, Edward J. 2010. *The Pursuit of Justice: Law and Economics of Legal Institutions*. Basingstoke, Hampshire, UK: Palgrave Macmillan.

Lopez-de-Silanes, Florencio. 2004. "A Survey of Securities Laws and Enforcement." World Bank Policy Research Working Paper Series, No. WPS3405.

Lukianoff, Greg. 2013. "Feds to Students: You Can't Say That." *Wall Street Journal*, May 16.

Macaulay, Stewart. 1963. "Non-contractual Relations in Business: A Preliminary Study." *American Sociological Review* 28 (1): 1–23.

MacCallum, Spencer Heath. 1970. *The Art of Community*. Menlo Park, CA: Institute for Humane Studies.

MacCallum, Spencer Heath. 2002. "The Case for Land Lease versus Subdivision." In *The Voluntary City*, ed. D. Beito, P. Gordon, and A. Tabarrok, 371–400. Ann Arbor: University of Michigan Press.

Macey, Jonathan. 2013. *The Death of Corporate Reputation: How Integrity Has Been Destroyed on Wall Street*. Upper Saddle River, NJ: Pearson Education.

Macey, Jonathan, and Hideki Kanda. 1990. "The Stock Exchange as a Firm: The Emergence of Close Substitutes for the New York and Tokyo Stock Exchanges." *Cornell Law Review* 75: 1007–52.

Macey, Jonathan, and Maureen O'Hara. 1999. "Regulating Exchanges and Alternative Trading Systems: A Law and Economics Perspective." *Journal of Legal Studies* 28: 17–53.

Machan, Tibor R. 2002. "Anarchism and Minarchism: A Rapprochement." *Journal des Economistes et des Etudes Humaines* 12 (4): 569–88.

Madigan, Peter. 2009. "Massachusetts Charges Fairfield Greenwich for 'Profound' Due Diligence Failings." *Risk*, April 1.

Mah-Hui Lim, Michael. 2008. "Old Wine in New Bottles: Subprime Mortgage Crisis—Causes and Consequences." *Journal of Applied Research in Accounting and Finance* 3 (1): 3–13.

Mahoney, Paul. 1997. "The Exchange as Regulator." *Virginia Law Review* 83: 1453–500.

Malmendier, Ulrike M. 2009. "Law and Finance at the Origin." *Journal of Economic Literature* 47 (4): 1076–108.

Maltzev, Yuri. 1996. "Murray N. Rothbard as a Critic of Socialism." *Journal of Libertarian Studies* 12 (1): 99–119.

Markham, Jerry. 2002. *A Financial History of the United States*. Vol. 2. *From J.P. Morgan to the Institutional Investor*. New York: M.E. Sharpe.

Markopolos, Harry. 2009. *Testimony of Harry Markopolos*. Boston: McCarter & English.

Martin, Frederick. 1876. *The History of Lloyd's and of Marine Insurance in Great Britain: With an Appendix Containing Statistics Relating to Marine Insurance*. London: Macmillan.

Mason, Rowena. 2011. "Langbar Chief Jailed for Phantom £570m AIM Fraud." *Daily Telegraph*, June 21, B1.

Matthews, Dan. 2010. "Are Small Cap Public Markets 'Open' Again?" *Growing Business*, June 17.

Mazzone, John, and John Pickett. 2011. *The Household Diary Study: Mail Use & Attitudes in FY 2010*. Washington, DC: United States Postal Service.

McCabe, Kevin, Daniel Houser, Lee Ryan, Vernon Smith, and Theodore Trouard. 2001. "A Functional Imaging Study of Cooperation in Two-Person Reciprocal Exchange." *Proceedings of the National Academy of Sciences* 20 (98): 11832–35.

McChesney, Fred S. 1987. "Rent Extraction and Rent Creation in the Economic Theory of Regulation." *Journal of Legal Studies* 16: 101–18.

McCloskey, Deirdre N. 2006. *The Bourgeois Virtues*. Chicago: University of Chicago.

McDonald, Mark. 2007. "Firing of Traffic Police Force Stands as a Symbol of Hope in Georgia." *McClatchy News Service*, June 7.

McDonald, Elizabeth. 2013. "JPMorgan Beefs Up Controls as Fed Submission Looms." *Fox Business*, September 13.

McInturff, Bill, Lori Weigel, and Douglas Schoen. 2010. *National Survey of 1,000 Small Businesses, Including 600 Phone and 400 Internet Interviews Conducted August 19–31, 2010*. Alexandria, VA: Public Opinion Strategies.

McNally, Christopher A. 2007. "China's Capitalist Transition: The Making of a New Variety of Capitalism." *Capitalisms Compared* 24: 177–203.

Mears, Dan P. 2004. "Prisoner Abuse Is Avoidable." *The Hill*, June 16.

Meese, Edwin III. 1997. "Big Brother on the Beat: The Expanding Federalization of Crime." *Texas Review of Law and Politics* 1 (1): 1–22.

Melady, Mark. 1999. "Tougher Enforcement Sought." *Worcester Telegram and Gazette*, October 24.

Mendoza, Jose Miguel. 2008. "Securities Regulation in Low-Tier Listing Venues: The Rise of the Alternative Investment Market." *Fordham Journal of Corporate and Financial Law* 13 (2): 257–328.

Menger, Carl. [1871] 2007. *Principles of Economics*. Auburn, AL: Mises.

Merten, Robert. 1974. "On the Pricing of Corporate Debt: The Risk Structure of Interest Rates." *Journal of Finance* 29 (2): 449–70.

Michie, Ranald. 1985. "The London Stock Exchange and the British Securities Market 1850–1914." *Economic History Review Second Series* 38 (1): 61–82.

Michie, Ranald. 2001. *The London Stock Exchange: A History*. New York: Oxford University Press.

Milgrom, Paul, Douglass North, and Barry Weingast. 1990. "The Role of Institutions in the Revival of Trade: The Law Merchant, Private Judges, and the Champagne Fairs." *Economics and Politics* 2: 1–23.

Mirowski, Philip. 1981. "The Rise (and Retreat) of a Market: English Joint Stock Shares in the Eighteenth Century." *Journal of Economic History* 41 (3): 559–77.

Mises, Ludwig. [1920] 1990. *Economic Calculation in a Socialist Commonwealth*. Auburn, AL: Mises.

Mises, Ludwig. [1927] 2002. *Liberalism*. Auburn, AL: Mises.

Mises, Ludwig. [1949] 1998. *Human Action*. Auburn, AL: Mises.

Missouri House of Representatives. 2005. House Resolution No. 3899 (Adopted July 1, 2005) Honoring Jimmy Tebeau.

Mitcalfe, J. Stanley. 1896. *Suggestions to Managing Owners of Steamers and Their Captains: Containing Instructions to Captains and Officers for the Consideration and Approval of Managing Owners*. Newcastle, UK: North of England Protecting & Indemnity Association.

Mocan, H. Naci, and Erdal Tekin. 2010. "Ugly Criminals." *Review of Economics and Statistics* 92 (1): 15–30.

Morgan, E. Victor, and W. A. Thomas. [1962] 1969. *The London Stock Exchange*. New York: St. Martin's Press.

Mortgage Bankers Association. 2012. *National Delinquency Survey Results Q2 2012*. Washington, DC: Mortgage Bankers Association.

Mortimer, Thomas. 1762. *Every Man His Own Broker: Or, a Guide to Exchange-Alley*. London: S. Hooper.

Mortimer, Thomas. 1801. *Every Man His Own Broker; or, a Guide to the Stock Exchange*. *13th Ed.* London: W. J. & J. Richardson.

Mueller, Dennis C. 2003. *Public Choice III*. New York: Cambridge University Press.

Musgrave, Peggy. 2009. "Remembering Richard Musgrave, 1910–2007." In *Tax Reform in the 21st Century: A Volume in Memory of Richard Musgrave*, ed. J. Head and R. Krever, 3–16. New York: Kluwer Law International.

Musgrave, Richard. 1999. "The Nature of the Fiscal State." In *Public Finance and Public Choice: Two Contrasting Visions of the State*, ed. J.M. Buchananand R Musgrave, 29–50. Cambridge, MA: MIT Press.

Myers, David G., ed. 2004. *Psychology: Seventh Edition, in Modules*. New York: Macmillan.

Narveson, Jan. 2008. "The State: From Minarchy to Anarchy." In *Anarchism/Minarchism: Is a Government Part of a Free Country?*, ed. R. Long and T. Machan, 103–10. Aldershot, UK: Ashgate.

Neal, Larry. 1987. "The Integration and Efficiency of the London and Amsterdam Stock Markets in the Eighteenth Century." *Journal of Economic History* 47 (1): 97–115.

Neal, Larry. 1990a. "The Dutch and English East India Companies Compared." In *The Rise of Merchant Empires*, ed. J. Tracy, 195–223. New York: Cambridge University Press.

Neal, Larry. 1990b. *The Rise of Financial Capitalism: International Capital Markets in the Age of Reason*. New York: Cambridge University Press.

Neal, Larry. 1997. "On the Historical Development of Stock Markets." In *The Emergence and Evolution of Stock Markets*, ed. H. Brezinski and M. Fritsch, 59–79. Cheltenham, UK: Edward Elgar.

Neal, Larry. 2000. "How It All Began: The Monetary and Financial Architecture of Europe during the First Global Capital Markets, 1648–1815." *Financial History Review* 7: 117–40.

Neal, Larry, and Lance Davis. 2005. "The Evolution of the Rules and Regulations of the First Emerging Markets: The London, New York and Paris Stock Exchanges, 1792–1914." *Quarterly Review of Economics and Finance* 45: 296–311.

Neal, Larry, and Lance Davis. 2006. "The Evolution of the Structure and Performance of the London Stock Exchange in the First Global Financial Market, 1812–1914." *European Review of Economic History* 10 (3): 279–300.

Neal, Larry, and Stephen Quinn. 2001. "Networks of Information, Markets, and Institutions in the Rise of London as a Financial Center in the Seventeenth Century." *Financial History Review* 8: 7–26.

Neely, Richard 1982. *Why Courts Don't Work*. New York: McGraw-Hill.

Nelson, Robert H. 2005. *Private Neighborhoods and the Transformation of Local Government*. Washington, DC: Urban Institute Press.

Neuwirth, Robert. 2011. *The Stealth of Nations: The Global Rise of the Informal Economy*. New York: Pantheon Press.

New America Foundation. 2012. *The Year of the Drone: An Analysis of U.S. Drone Strikes in Pakistan, 2004–2012*. Washington, DC: New America Foundation.

New York Post Editorial Board. 2013. "Extorting JPMorgan." *New York Post*, November 20.

New York Stock Exchange. 1869. *Constitution and by-Laws of the New York Stock Exchange*. New York: Martin England.

New York Stock Exchange. 1914. *Constitution of the New York Stock Exchange and Resolutions Adopted by the Governing Committee: With Amendments to February 1914*. New York: Searing & Moore Company.

New York Stock Exchange. 1925. *The Constitution of the New York Stock Exchange (as Revised in 1925)*. New York: New York Stock Exchange.

New York Stock Exchange. 2013. "About Us/History/Timeline."

Nolan, Anthony, and Anna Dodson. 2006. "Pay as You Go and Don't Forget Your Cap: Demystifying CDS of ABS." Goodwin Procter, New York.

North, Douglass C. 1990. *Institutions, Institutional Change, and Economic Performance*. New York: Cambridge University Press.

North, Douglass C. 1995. "The Paradox of the West." In *The Origins of Modern Freedom in the West*, ed. R. W. Davis, 7–34. Stanford, CA: Stanford University Press.

North, Douglass C., John J. Wallis, and Barry R. Weingast. 2009. *Violence and Social Orders: A Conceptual Framework for Interpreting Recorded Human History*. Cambridge: Cambridge University Press.

Nozick, Robert. 1974. *Anarchy, State, and Utopia*. New York: Basic Books.

Ocrant, Michael. 2001. "Madoff Tops Charts; Skeptics Ask How." *MAR/Hedge (RIP)* 89: 1–5.

Oh, Inae. 2012. "NYC School Arrests: 96 Percent of Students Arrested by NYPD in 2011 Were Black or Latino." *Huffington Post*, August 15.

O'Hara, Maureen. 1995. *Market Microstructure Theory*. Oxford: Blackwell.

Olson, Mancur. 1965. *The Logic of Collective Action: Public Goods and the Theory of Groups*. Cambridge, MA: Harvard University Press.

Olson, Mancur. 1996. "Big Bills Left on the Sidewalk: Why Some Nations Are Rich, and Others Poor." *Journal of Economic Perspectives* 10 (2): 3–24.

Olson, Mancur. 2000. *Power and Prosperity: Outgrowing Communist and Capitalist Dictatorships*. New York: Basic Books.

Osborne, Jason. 2005. "Jungle or Just Bush." In *Anarchy, State, and Public Choice*, ed. Edward Peter Stringham, 24–35. Cheltenham, UK: Edward Elgar.

Ostrom, Elinor. 1990. *Governing the Commons: The Evolution of Institutions for Collective Action*. New York: Cambridge University Press.

Ostrom, Elinor. 2005. *Understanding Institutional Diversity*. Princeton, NJ: Princeton University Press.

Ostrom, Vincent. 2007. *The Political Theory of a Compound Republic: Designing the American Experiment*. Lanham, MD: Lexington Books.

Ostrovky, Victor. 2013. "Legal Talk." Scottsdale, AZ: Art Watch Dog.

Otteson, James R. 2002. *Adam Smith's Marketplace of Life*. New York: Cambridge University Press.

Paine, Thomas. [1791] 1906. *Rights of Man*. London: J. M. Dent.

Pastor, James F. 2003. *The Privatization of Police in America: An Analysis and Case Study*. Jefferson, NC: McFarland.

Patricof, Alan. 2011. "It's Official: The IPO Market Is Crippled—and It's Hurting Our Country." *Business Insider*, January 12.

PayPal. 2012. "Security for Merchants." San Jose, CA.

Pennington, Mark. 2011. *Robust Political Economy: Classical Liberalism and the Future of Public Policy*. Cheltenham, UK: Edward Elgar.

Penslar, Derek. 1997. "The Origins of Jewish Political Economy." *Jewish Social Studies* 3 (3): 26–60.

Peters, Bethany, and Edward Peter Stringham. 2006. "No Booze? You May Lose: Why Drinkers Earn More Money Than Nondrinkers." *Journal of Labor Research* 27 (3): 411–21.

Peterson, Jacqueline. 2011. "Message from the Dean of Students." College of the Holy Cross, Worcester, MA, September 8.

Pew Research Center for the People and the Press. 2010. *Distrust, Discontent, Anger and Partisan Rancor: The People and Their Government*. Washington, DC: Pew Research Center.

Pew Research Center for the People and the Press. 2013. *Public Trust in Government: 1958–2013*. Washington, DC: Pew Research Center.

Pigou, Arthur C. 1918. *Economics of Welfare*. New Brunswick, NJ: Macmillan.

Piotroski, Joseph D., and Srinivasan Suraj. 2008. "Regulation and Bonding: The Sarbanes-Oxley Act and the Flow of International Listings." *Journal of Accounting Research* 46 (2): 383–425.

Plucknett, Theodore F. T. 1956. *A Concise History of the Common Law*. Boston: Little, Brown.

Police Forums and Law Enforcement Forums. 2008. "Duke University Police." Officer. com, August 31.

Posner, Eric. 1996. "The Regulation of Groups: The Influence of Legal and Nonlegal Sanctions on Collective Action." *University of Chicago Law Review* 63 (1): 133–97.

Posner, Eric. 2002. *Law and Social Norms*. Cambridge, MA: Harvard University Press.

Posner, Richard A. 1974. "Theories of Economic Regulation." *Bell Journal of Economics and Management Science* 5: 335–58.

Posner, Richard A. 1994. "What Do Judges and Justices Maximize? (the Same Thing Everyone Else Does)." *Supreme Court Economic Review* 3: 1–41.

Powell, Benjamin, Ryan Ford, and Alex Nowrasteh. 2008. "Somalia after State Collapse: Chaos or Improvement?" *Journal of Economic Behavior & Organization* 67 (3–4): 657–70.

Powell, Benjamin, and Edward Peter Stringham. 2005. "The Economics of Inclusionary Zoning Reclaimed: How Effective Are Price Controls?" *Florida State University Law Review* 33 (Winter): 471–99.

Powell, Benjamin, and Edward Peter Stringham. 2009. "Public Choice and the Economic Analysis of Anarchy: A Survey." *Public Choice* 140 (3–4): 503–38.

Prashanth, Konakanchi. 2004. *Paypal.Com's Business Model*. Hyderabad, India: ICFAI Center for Management Research (ICMR).

Prentice, Robert. 2002. "Whither Securities Regulation? Some Behavioral Observations Regarding Proposals for Its Future." *Duke Law Journal* 51 (5): 1397–151.

President's Working Group on Unlawful Conduct on the Internet. 2000. "The Electronic Frontier: The Challenge of Unlawful Conduct Involving the Use of the Internet, President's Working Group on Unlawful Conduct on the Internet." U.S. Department of Justice.

PricewaterhouseCoopers. 2006. "International Arbitration: Corporate Attitudes and Practices." London.

PricewaterhouseCoopers. 2008. "International Arbitration: Corporate Attitudes and Practices." London.

Public Citizen Foundation. 2010. "Mandatory Arbitration Clauses: Undermining the Rights of Consumers, Employees, and Small Businesses." Washington, DC.

Public Policy Polling. 2013. "Congress Less Popular Than Cockroaches, Traffic Jams." Public Policy Polling, Raleigh, NC, January 8.

Punch. 1882. "A Handbook of Knowledge: The Coffee-Shop." *Punch*, August 19, 84.

Qualkenbush, Robert. 2012. *Company Police Are Part of North Carolina History*. Charlotte, NC: Allied Barton Company Police.

Quinn, Stephen. 1997. "Goldsmith-Banking: Mutual Acceptance and Interbanker Clearing in Restoration London." *Explorations in Economic History* 34 (4): 411–32.

Rabin, Matthew. 1995. "Moral Preferences, Moral Constraints, and Self-Serving Biases. Working paper, Department of Economics, University of California at Berkeley.

Rajan, Raghuram, and Luigi Zingales. 2004. *Saving Capitalism from the Capitalists: Unleashing the Power of Financial Markets to Create Wealth and Spread Opportunity*. Princeton, NJ: Princeton University Press.

Rand, Ayn 1964. "Playboy Interview: Ayn Rand." *Playboy*, March, 35–43.

Rand, Ayn. 1966. *Capitalism: The Unknown Ideal*. New York: New American Library.

Rand, Michael, and Shannon Catalano. 2007 "Criminal Victimization, 2006." Bureau of Justice Statistics Bulletin NCJ 219413.

Rasmussen, Douglas B., and Douglas J. den Uyl. 2009. "Making Room for Business Ethics: Rights as Metanorms for Market and Moral Values." *Journal of Private Enterprise* 24 (2): Spring: 1–19.

Rasmussen, Douglas B., and Douglas J. den Uyl. 2010. *Norms of Liberty: A Perfectionist Basis for Non-perfectionist Politics*. University Park: Pennsylvania State University Press.

Read, Leonard. 1958. "I, Pencil." *Freeman* 8 (December): 12.

Read, Leonard. 1964. *Anything That's Peaceful*. Irvington-on-Hudson, NY: Foundation for Economic Education.

Reed, M. C. 1975. *A History of James Capel & Co.* London: James Capel & Co.

Reno, Janet. 2000. "'Cybercrime': Statement of Janet Reno Attorney General of the United States." U.S. Senate Committee on Appropriations, Subcommittee on Commerce, Justice, and State, February 16.

Ridley, Matt. 1997. *The Origins of Virtue*. New York: Viking.

Roback, Jennifer. 1986. "The Political Economy of Segregation: The Case of Segregated Streetcars." *Journal of Economic History* 46 (4): 893–917.

Roberts, Paul Craig, and Lawrence M. Stratton. 2008. *The Tyranny of Good Intentions: How Prosecutors and Law Enforcement Are Trampling the Constitution in the Name of Justice*. New York: Three Rivers Press.

Romano, Roberta. 1998. "Empowering Investors: A Market Approach to Securities Regulation." *Yale Law Journal* 107: 2365–99.

Röpke, Wilhelm. 1960. *A Humane Economy*. Chicago: Henry Regnery.

Rose, Christopher. 2009. "Hedge Fund Managed Accounts: Panacea or Source of New Risks?" *FIN Alternatives*, August 14.

Rosser, J. Barkley, Jr. 2010. "How Complex Are the Austrians?" *Advances in Austrian Economics* 14: 165–79.

Rosser, J. Barkley, Jr., and Marina V. Rosser. 1999. "The New Traditional Economy: A New Perspective in Comparative Economics." *International Journal of Social Economics* 26 (6): 763–78.

Rosser, J. Barkley, Jr., and Marina V. Rosser. 2008. "A Critique of the New Comparative Economics." *Review of Austrian Economics* 21: 81–97.

Rothbard, Murray N. 1973. *For a New Liberty: The Libertarian Manifesto*. New York: Collier Books / Macmillan.

Rothbard, Murray N. [1974] 2000. *Egalitarianism as a Revolt against Nature*. Auburn, AL: Mises.

Rothbard, Murray N. 1977. *Power and Market: Government and the Economy*. Kansas, MO: Sheed Andrews and McMeel.

Rothbard, Murray N. 1980. "Introduction." In *Capital, Interest, and Rent: Essays in the Theory of Distribution*, F. A. Fetter, 1–24. New York: New York University Press.

Rothbard, Murray N. 1990. "Karl Marx: Communist as Religious Eschatologist." *Review of Austrian Economics* 4: 123–79.

Rothbard, Murray N. 1995. *Making Economic Sense*. Auburn, AL: Mises.

Rothbard, Murray N., and Leonard P. Liggio. 1975. *Conceived in Liberty*. Vol. 1: *A New Land, a New People, the American Colonies in the Seventeenth Century*. New Rochelle, NY: Arlington House.

Rousseau, Stephane. 2007. "London Calling? The Experience of the Alternative Investment Market and the Competitiveness of Canadian Stock Exchanges." *Banking and Finance Law Review* 23 (1): 51–105.

Rowley, Charles K. 1987. "A Public Choice Perspective on Judicial Pragmatism." In *Economic Liberties and the Judiciary*, ed. J. A. Dom and H. G. Manne, 219–24. Fairfax, VA: George Mason University Press.

Rowley, Charles K. 1989. "The Common Law in Public Choice Perspective: A Theoretical and Institutional Critique." *Hamline Law Review* 12: 372–384.

Royce, Josiah. 1886. *American Commonwealths: California, from the Conquests in 1846 to the Second Vigilance Committee in San Francisco.* Boston: Riverside Press.

Russo, Steven, and Samuel J. Reyes v. Willis Casey, et al. 1993. No. 93-15686. United States Court of Appeals, Ninth Circuit.

Ryan, John Augustine. 1907. "Right of Voluntary Association." In *The Catholic Encyclopedia,* ed. C. G. Herbermann, 1–4. New York: Robert Appleton.

Saakashvili, Mikhail. 2005. "Georgia's National Police Corruption Project: Robert Siegel Interviews Mikhail Saakashvili." *All Things Considered,* NPR, September 15.

Sabol, William J., and Heather C. West. 2008. "Prisoners in 2007." NCJ 224280. December. Bureau of Justice Statistics.

Sachs, Stephen. 2006. "From St. Ives to Cyberspace: The Modern Distortions of the Medieval Law Merchant." *American University International Law Review* 21 (5): 685–812.

Sahajwani, Manish. 2011. "Pay-as-You-Go Credit Default Swaps (PAUG CDS)." Finance Train, Bangalore.

Salerno, Joseph T. 1990. "Why a Socialist Economy Is 'Impossible.'" In *Economic Calculation in the Socialist Commonwealth,* ed. J. T. Salerno, 34–46. Auburn, AL: Mises.

Salerno, Joseph T. 1993. "Mises and Hayek Dehomogenized." *Review of Austrian Economics* 6: 113–46.

Samuels, Warren. 1974. "Anarchism and the Theory of Power." In *Further Explorations in the Theory of Anarchy,* ed. Gordon Tullock, 33–57. Blacksburg, VA: Center for Study of Public Choice.

Samuelson, Paul A., and William D. Nordhaus. 2010. *Economics.* 19th ed. New York: McGraw Hill.

Sanders, John T., and Jan Narveson. 1996. *For and against the State: New Philosophical Readings.* Lanham, MD: Rowman and Littlefield.

Saperia, Nishul. 2008. *Credit Event Auction Primer.* New York: Creditex.

Schama, Simon. 1987. *The Embarrassment of Riches: An Interpretation of Dutch Culture in the Golden Age.* New York: Alfred Knopf.

Schwartz, Evan. 2001. "Digital Cash Payoff: Online Payment Services Like PayPal Are Catching On." *Technology Review,* December.

Securities and Exchange Commission. 2012. "What We Do." Washington, DC.

Seidl, D., P. Sanderson, and J. Roberts. 2012. "Applying the 'Comply-or-Explain' Principle: Conformance with Codes of Corporate Governance in the UK and Germany." *Journal of Management and Governance* 17 (3): 791–826.

Selgin, George. 2011. *Good Money: Birmingham Button Makers, the Royal Mint, and the Beginnings of Modern Coinage, 1775–1821.* Ann Arbor: University of Michigan Press.

Sengupta, Somini. 2012. "Paypal Strength Helps eBay Exceed Forecasts." *New York Times,* April 18, B10.

Shavell, Steven 1995. "Alternative Dispute Resolution: An Economic Analysis." *Journal of Legal Studies* 24 (1): 1–28.

Shearmur, Jeremy, and Daniel Klein. 1997. "Good Conduct in a Great Society: Adam Smith and the Role of Reputation." In *Reputation: Studies in the Voluntary Elicitation of Good Conduct,* ed. D. Klein, 29–45. Ann Arbor: University of Michigan Press.

Ship Owner's Manual. 1795. *The Ship Owner's Manual, or, Sea-Faring Man's Assistant: Containing a General System of the Maritime Laws, on the Most Interesting Subjects.* Newcastle, UK: D. Akenhead and Sons, on the Sandhill.

Shorto, Russell. 2004. *Island at the Center of the World*. New York: Doubleday.

Sidman, Murray. 1989. *Coercion and Its Fallout*. Ann Arbor, MI: Authors Cooperative.

Skarbek, David. 2014. *The Social Order of the Underworld: How Prison Gangs Govern the American Penal System*. New York: Oxford University Press.

Skibell, Reid. 2003. "Cybercrimes & Misdemeanors: A Reevaluation of the Computer Fraud and Abuse Act." *Berkeley Technology Law Journal* 18 (909): 910–44.

Skoble, A. J. 2008. *Deleting the State: An Argument About Government*. Chicago: Open Court.

Smith, Adam. [1759] 1853. *The Theory of Moral Sentiments*. London: H. G. Bohn.

Smith, Adam. [1766] 1982. *Lectures on Jurisprudence*. Indianapolis: Liberty Classics.

Smith, Adam. [1776] 1976. *Wealth of Nations, Book 5*. Chicago: University of Chicago Press.

Smith, Adam. 1786. *The Philosophical Dictionary: Or, the Opinions of Modern Philosophers on Metaphysical, Moral, and Political Subjects*. Vol. 2. London: G. G. J. and J. Robinson.

Smith, C. F. 1929. "The Early History of the London Stock Exchange." *American Economic Review* 19 (2): 206–16.

Smith, Vernon L. 1998. "The Two Faces of Adam Smith." *Southern Economic Journal* 65 (1): 1–19.

Smith, Vernon L. 2008. *Rationality in Economics*. New York: Cambridge University Press.

Smollett, Tobias George. 1814. *The Critical Review, or, Annals of Literature*. London: W. Simpkin and R. Marshall.

Sordin, Tania. 2004. *Alternative Dispute Resolution and the Courts*. Sydney: Federation Press.

Sotheby's. 2013. "How to Buy and Sell." New York.

Soto, Hernando de. 1989. *The Other Path: The Economic Answer to Terrorism*. New York: Basic Books.

Soto, Hernando de. 2000. *Mystery of Capital: Why Capitalism Triumphs in the West and Fails Everywhere Else*. New York: Basic Books.

Soulé, Frank, John H. Gihon, and James Nisbet. 1854. *The Annals of San Francisco*. New York: D. Appleton.

Southwick, Lawrence, Jr. 2005. "Economies of Scale and Market Power in Policing." *Managerial and Decision Economics* 26 (8): 461–73.

Sowell, Thomas. 2002. *A Conflict of Visions*. New York: Basic Books.

Spinoza, Benedict de. 1670. *Tractatus Theologico-Politicus*. Hamburg: Henricus Kunraht.

Staten, Michael, and Robert Johnson. 1995. "The Case for Deregulating Interest Rates on Consumer Credit." Monograph 31, Credit Research Center, Krannert Graduate School of Management, Purdue University.

Stedman, Edmund C., and Alexander N. Easton. 1905. "History of the New York Stock Exchange." In *The New York Stock Exchange: Its History, Its Contribution to National Prosperity, and Its Relation to American Finance at the Outset of the Twentieth Century*, ed. E. C. Stedman, 15–410. New York: Stock Exchange Historical Company.

Stenning, Philip C. 2000. *Police Powers and Accountability in a Democratic Society: Proceedings, Reports Presented to the 12th Criminological Colloquium*. Strasbourg: Council of Europe Publishing.

Stephenson, M. C. 2009. "Legal Realism for Economists." *Journal of Economic Perspectives* 23: 191–211.

Stigler, George J. 1964. "Public Regulation of Securities Markets." *Journal of Business* 37 (2): 117–42.

Stigler, George J. 1970. "The Optimum Enforcement of Laws." *Journal of Political Economy* 78 (3): 526–36.

Stigler, George J. 1971. "The Economic Theory of Regulation." *Bell Journal of Economics and Management Science* 2: 3–21.

Stigler, George J. 1975. *The Citizen and the State: Essays on Regulation.* Chicago: University of Chicago Press.

Stigler, George J. 1982. *The Economist as Preacher.* Oxford: Blackwell.

Stiglitz, Joseph E. 2003. *Globalization and Its Discontents.* New York: Norton.

Stiglitz, Joseph E. Jonathan M. Orszag, and Peter R. Orszag. 2002. "Implications of the New Fannie Mae and Freddie Mac Risk-Based Capital Standard." *Fannie Mae Papers* 1 (2): 1–10.

Stipanowich, Thomas J. 2010. "Arbitration: The New Litigation." *University of Illinois Law Review* 1: 27–38.

Storr, Virgil Henry. 2005. "Defining Anarchy as Rock 'N' Roll: Rethinking Hogarty's Three Cases." In *Anarchy, State, and Public Choice*, ed. E.P. Stringham, 113–122. Cheltenham, UK: Edward Elgar.

Storr, Virgil Henry. 2009. "Why the Market? Markets as Social and Moral Spaces." *Journal of Markets and Morality* 12 (2): 277–96.

Stout, David. 2009."Report Details How Madoff's Web Ensnared S.E.C." *New York Times*, September 9: B1.

Stringham, Edward Peter. 1999. "Market Chosen Law." *Journal of Libertarian Studies* 14 (1): 53–77.

Stringham, Edward Peter. 2002. "The Emergence of the London Stock Exchange as a Self-Policing Club." *Journal of Private Enterprise* 17 (2): 1–19.

Stringham, Edward Peter. 2003. "The Extralegal Development of Securities Trading in Seventeenth Century Amsterdam." *Quarterly Review of Economics and Finance* 43 (2): 321–44.

Stringham, Edward Peter. 2005a. *Anarchy, State and Public Choice.* Cheltenham, UK: Edward Elgar.

Stringham, Edward Peter. 2005b. "The Capability of Government in Providing Protection against Online Fraud." *Journal of Law, Economics, and Policy* 1 (2): 371–92.

Stringham, Edward Peter. 2006. "Overlapping Jurisdictions, Proprietary Communities, and Competition in the Realm of Law." *Journal of Institutional and Theoretical Economics* 162 (3): 516–34.

Stringham, Edward Peter, ed. 2007. *Anarchy and the Law: The Political Economy of Choice.* Somerset, NJ: Transaction Publishers.

Stringham, Edward Peter. 2009. "A Report on the Patrol Special Police and Community Safety in San Francisco." Independent Institute Report, Oakland, CA.

Stringham, Edward Peter. 2011. "Embracing Morals in Economics: The Role of Internal Moral Constraints in a Market Economy." *Journal of Economic Behavior and Organization*, 78(1–2): 98–109.

Stringham, Edward Peter. 2013. "When Formal Institutions of Property Rights and Law Fail." In *Law, Rules and Economic Performance*, ed. Aleksandra Jovanovic and Ljunomir Madzar, 93-109. Belgrade: University of Belgrade Faculty of Law.

Stringham, Edward Peter. 2014a. "Extending the Analysis of Spontaneous Market Order to Governance." *Atlantic Economic Journal* 42 (2): 171–80.

Stringham, Edward Peter 2014b. "It's Not Me, It's You: The Functioning of Wall Street during the 2008 Economic Downturn." *Public Choice* 161(3–4): 269–288.

Stringham, Edward Peter, and Ivan Chen. 2012. "The Alternative of Private Regulation: The London Stock Exchange's Alternative Investment Market as a Model." *Economic Affairs* 32 (3): 37–43.

Stringham, Edward Peter, and John Levendis. 2010. "The Relationship between Economic Freedom and Homicide." In *Economic Freedom of the World: 2010 Annual Report*, ed. J. Gwartney, J. Hall, and R. Lawson, 203–17. Vancouver: Fraser Institute.

Stringham, Edward Peter, and Mark White. 2004. "Economic Analysis of Tort Law: Austrian and Kantian Perspectives." In *Law and Economics: Alternative Economic Approaches to Legal and Regulatory Issues*, ed. M. Oppenheimer and N. Mercuro, 374–92. New York: M.E. Sharpe.

Stringham, Edward Peter, and Todd J. Zywicki. 2011a. "Hayekian Anarchism." *Journal of Economic Behavior and Organization* 78 (3): 290–301.

Stringham, Edward Peter, and Todd J. Zywicki. 2011b. "Rivalry and Superior Dispatch: An Analysis of Competing Courts in Medieval and Early Modern England." *Public Choice* 147: 497–524.

Stulz, René M. 2010. "Credit Default Swaps and the Credit Crisis." *Journal of Economic Perspectives* 24 (1): 73–92.

Sunday Business. 2007. "Wrapped in Red Tape, New York Takes AIM at LSE Rules." *Sunday Business*, February 27.

Susman, Edna, and Wilkerson, John. 2012. "Benefits of Arbitration for Commercial Disputes." Working paper. Chicago: American Bar Association Section of Dispute Resolution.Swartz, Jon. 2004. "Is the Future of E-Mail under Cyberattack?" *USA Today*, June 14.

Tannehill, Morris, and Linda Tannehill. 1970. *Market for Liberty*. Lansing, MI: Linda and Morris Tannehill.

Taylor, Peter. 2009. "Astaire's Public Punishment Is a Warning to Others." *Telegraph*, June 28.

Telser, L. G. 1980. "A Theory of Self-Enforcing Agreements." *Journal of Business* 53 (1): 27–44.

Telser, L. G. 1987. *A Theory of Efficient Cooperation and Competition*. New York: Cambridge University Press.

Templeton, J. M. 1997. *Worldwide Laws of Life: 200 Eternal Spiritual Principles*. Radnor, PA: Templeton Foundation.

Thiel, Peter. 2004. "Innovation, Entrepreneurship and the Global Marketplace." Presentation, Independent Institute, San Francisco, April 21.

Thomas, Cheryl. 2010. "Are Juries Fair?" Ministry of Justice Research Series 1/10: 10–87.

Thornbury, Walter. 1887. *Old and New London: A Narrative of Its History, Its People, and Its Places*. London: Cassel and Company.

Thorsnes, Paul. 2000. "Internalizing Neighborhood Externalities: The Effect of Subdivision Size and Zoning on Residential Lot Prices." *Journal of Urban Economics* 48 (3): 397–418.

Tiebout, Charles M. 1956. "A Pure Theory of Local Expenditures." *Journal of Political Economy* 64 (5): 416–24.

Timbs, John. 1866. *Club Life of London with Anecdotes of the Clubs, Coffee-Houses and Taverns of the Metropolis During the 17th, 18th, and 19th Centuries*. London: Richard Bentley.

Tirole, Jean. 1999. "Incomplete Contracts: Where Do We Stand?" *Econometrica* 67 (4): 741–81.

Tocqueville, Alexis de. [1835] 2010. *Democracy in America*. Trans. James T. Schleifer. Indianapolis: Liberty Fund.

Tontine Coffee House. 1796. *The Constitution and Nominations of the Subscribers to the Tontine Coffee-House*. New York: Tontine Coffee House.

Treanor, Jill. 2007. "City Hits Out Over U.S. 'Casino' Jibe at A.I.M." *The Guardian*, March 10.

Tullock, Gordon, ed. 1972. *Explorations in the Theory of Anarchy*. Blacksburg, VA: Center for Study of Public Choice.

Tullock, Gordon, ed. 1974. *Further Explorations in the Theory of Anarchy*. Blacksburg, VA: Center for Study of Public Choice.

Tullock, Gordon. 1985. "Adam Smith and the Prisoners' Dilemma." *Quarterly Journal of Economics* 100: 1073–81.

Tullock, Gordon. 1999. "Non-prisoner's Dilemma." *Journal of Economic Behavior and Organization* 39 (4): 455–58.

Urbina, Ian. 2009. "Debate Follows Bills to Remove Clotheslines Bans." *New York Times*, October 10, A23.

U.S. Department of Education. 2008. "Sexual Harassment: It's Not Academic." Washington, DC.

U.S. Department of Housing and Urban Development. 2001. "HUD's Affordable Lending Goals for Fannie Mae and Freddie Mac." Office of Policy Development and Research Issue Brief No. V.

U.S. Department of Justice. 2010. "Local Police Departments, 2007." Washington, DC.

Vandenberghe, Ann-Sophie. 2000. "Labor Contracts." In *Encyclopedia of Law and Economics*, ed. B. Bouckaert and G. De Geest, 541–58. Cheltenham, UK: Edward Elgar.

Vismara, Silvio, Stefano Paleari, and Jay Ritter. 2012. "Europe's Second Markets for Small Companies." *European Financial Management* 18 (3): 352–88.

Volokh, Eugene. 1997. "What Speech Does 'Hostile Work Environment' Harassment Law Restrict?" *Georgetown Law Journal* 85: 627–48.

Voltaire. [1733] 1961. "On the Church of England." In *Philosophical Letters*, ed. E. Dilworth, 22–26. Upper Saddle River, NJ: Prentice-Hall.

Wall Street Journal Editorial Board. 2013. "The Morgan Shakedown." *Wall Street Journal*, October 20.

Ward, Theresa. 2010. *Strategies for Reducing the Risk of Ecommerce Fraud*. Atlanta: First Data Corporation.

Wary, Mr. 1691. *Plain Dealing: In a Dialogue between Mr. Johnson and Mr. Wary His Friend, a Stock-Jobber, and a Petitioner against the E—— I—— Company, About Stock-Jobbing and the Said Company*. London: S. Eddowes.

Watner, Carl, George H. Smith, and Wendy McElroy. 1983. *Neither Bullets nor Ballots: Essays on Voluntaryism*. Orange, CA: Pine Tree Press.

Watson, Douglas J., and Wendy L. Hassett, eds. 2003. *Local Government Management: Current Issues and Best Practices*. Armonk, NY: M.E. Sharpe.

Welles, C. 1975. *The Last Days of the Club*. New York: E.P. Dutton.

Werner, Walter, and Steven T. Smith. 1991. *Wall Street*. New York: Columbia University Press.

Westhouse, Hanson. 2012. "Joining AIM: Flotation." AIM Listing, West Yorkshire.

White, Lawrence. 1999. *The Theory of Monetary Institutions*. Malden, MA: Blackwell.

White, Mark D. 2004. "Can Homo Economicus Follow Kant's Categorical Imperative?" *Journal of Socio-economics* 33 (1): 89–106.

White, Mark D. 2006. "Multiple Selves and Weakness of Will: A Kantian Perspective." *Review of Social Economy* 64 (1): 1–20.

White, Mark D. 2010. "Resisting Procrastination: Kantian Autonomy and the Role of the Will." In *The Thief of Time: Philosophical Essays on Procrastination*, ed. C. Andreou and M. White, 216–32. Oxford: Oxford University Press.

Wible, Brent. 2003. "A Site Where Hackers Are Welcome: Using Hack-in Contests to Shape Preferences and Deter Computer Crime." *Yale Law Journal* 112 (6): 1577–1623.

Wight, Jonathan B. 2003. "Teaching the Ethical Foundations of Economics." *Chronicle of Higher Education* 49: B7–B9.

Wight, Jonathan B. 2005. "Adam Smith and Greed." *Journal of Private Enterprise* 21 (1): 46–58.

Williamson, Oliver E. 1983. "Credible Commitments: Using Hostages to Support Exchange." *American Economic Review* 73 (4): 519–40.

Williamson, Oliver E. 1996. *The Mechanisms of Governance*. New York: Oxford University Press.

Williamson, Oliver E. 2005. "The Economics of Governance." *American Economic Review* 95 (2): 1–18.

Wilson, Charles. 1941. *Anglo-Dutch Commerce in the Eighteenth Century*. New York: Cambridge University Press.

Wincott, Harold. 1946. *The Stock Exchange*. London: Sampson Low, Marston.

Withers LLP. 2011. "AIM—the Market for International Companies." Geneva.

Woods, Thomas E. 2004. *The Church and the Market*. Lanham, MD: Lexington Books.

Woods, Thomas E. 2009. *Meltdown: A Free-Market Look at Why the Stock Market Collapsed, the Economy Tanked, and Government Bailouts Will Make Things Worse*. Washington, DC: Regnery.

Workmen's Compensation Reporter. 1951. *California Compensation Cases: Comprising All Decisions of the Supreme and Appellate Courts in Cases Originating from the Industrial Accident Commission*. Berkeley, CA: Workmen's Compensation Reporter.

World Bank. 2013. *Doing Business 2013: Comparing Business Regulations for Domestic Firms in 185 Economies*. Washington, DC: World Bank.

Zak, Paul. 2008. *Moral Markets: The Critical Role of Values in the Economy*. Princeton, NJ: Princeton University Press.

Zamir, Eyal, and Barak Medina. 2008. "Law, Morality, and Economics: Integrating Moral Constraints with Economic Analysis of Law." *California Law Review* 96 (2): 323–91.

Zero Hedge. 2013. "U.S. Households Have Never Been More Reliant on the Stock Market for Their 'Net Worth.'" March 7.

Zhang-Whitaker, Pang. 2012. "China: Looking for a Viable Dispute Resolution Forum for China Deals." *Mondaq*, July 27.

Zywicki, Todd J. 1998. "Epstein and Polanyi on Simple Rules, Complex Systems, and Decentralization." *Constitutional Political Economy* 9: 143–50.

Zywicki, Todd J. 2000a. "The Economics of Credit Cards." *Chapman Law Review* 3 (79): 80–172.

Zywicki, Todd J. 2000b. "Was Hayek Right about Group Selection after All? Review Essay of *Unto Others: The Evolution and Psychology of Unselfish Behavior* by Elliott Sober and David Sloan Wilson." *Review of Austrian Economics* 13 (1): 81–95.

Zywicki, Todd J. 2003. "The Rise and Fall of Efficiency in the Common Law: A Supply-Side Analysis." *Northwestern Law Review* 97: 1551–634.

Zywicki, Todd J. 2005. "An Economic Analysis of the Consumer Bankruptcy Crisis." *Northwestern University Law Review* 99(4): 1463–1541.

Zywicki, Todd J. 2008. "Spontaneous Order and the Common Law: Gordon Tullock's Critique." *Public Choice* 135: 35–53.

Zywicki, Todd J. 2011. "The Dick Durbin Bank Fees." *Wall Street Journal*, September 29.

Zywicki, Todd J., and Anthony B. Sanders. 2008. "Posner, Hayek, and the Economic Analysis of Law." *Iowa Law Review* 93: 559–604.

Zywicki, Todd J., and Edward Peter Stringham. 2012. "Common Law and Economic Efficiency." In *Encyclopedia of Law and Economics*, ed. F. Parisi and R. Posner, 107–31. Cheltenham, UK: Edward Elgar.

INDEX

Note: The letter 't' following locators refers to tables; the letter 'f' refers to figures.

Adjudication. *See* Private adjudication
Akerlof, George A., 28–29
Albert, Miriam R., 34, 59
Alternative Investment Market (AIM),
    81, 89–98
  admission document for, 90,
    91t–92t
  costs of listing on, *vs.* NASDAQ,
    90–92, 93t
  flexible (private) regulation on,
    94–98, 96f, 99
  fraud on, 96–98
  functions and operations of, 89
  IPOs in, 93, 94f, 204–205
    process for, 90
    survival of, 95
  liquidity of firms on, 96
  listing process at, 89–92, 91t
  Nomads in, 89–90, 93t, 97
  number of companies and market
    values of firms on, 94, 95f
  performance of, *vs.* Dow
    Jones Industrial Average,
    96–97, 96f
  success of, 93–94, 94f, 95f
American International Group (AIG),
    166, 168, 181–182
American Medical Association
    (AMA), 203
Amsterdam, as center of world trade,
    42, 43f
Amsterdam Bourse, 46–50, 47f, 48f
  anti-speculator plates and, 48, 49f
  brokers at, 57
  eBay similarities to, 59

  self-regulation of, 48–50
  short sales in, ordinances against,
    46–47
  "wind traders" in, 48, 49f
Arbitration, 150. *See also* Private
    Adjudication
  benefits of, 152
  in China, problems with, 160–161
  escrow services in, 162
  government competition and
    regulation of, 201
  international corporate use of,
    160–162
  letters of credit in, 162–163
Arbitration agreements
  enforceability of, government, 160
  law by contract in, 155
  predispute, 157, 163–164
Arthur, Terry, 200
Art market
  Chinese state-owned Poly Auction
    house in, 194
  lack of regulation of, 193
    self-policing for, 193–194
Asset-backed securities, 170–175,
    176f
Associations, voluntary. *See* Voluntary
    associations
Assurance, demand and supply of, 34
Atwood, Albert William, 200
Augmenting markets, 12, 13

Background checks, 136–137
Bastiat, Frédéric, 13, 232
Bay, Dan, 126

Bear Sterns, 166, 173, 177f, 182
Benjamin, Rich, 131
Big Board. *See* New York Stock
    Exchange (NYSE)
Bilateral reputation mechanism, 41
Block, Walter, 23, 26, 27, 52, 173, 205,
    231
Boettke, Peter, 6, 12, 26, 34, 77, 229
Bonding, 60
Bond, irrecoverable, 58
Booth, Philip, 200
Bourse, Amsterdam. *See* Amsterdam
    Bourse
Brennan, Geoffrey, 27
Bubble Act, 26, 66
Buchanan, James, 11, 14, 17, 23, 27,
    40, 137, 138, 139, 142, 157,
    158, 229
  on community, 142
  economic theory of clubs of, 23
  on exchange and property rights,
    11–12
  on internal constraints and
    morality, 138–139
  on public choice, law and, 17
  on rules, costs and benefits of, 27
Buffet, Warren, on derivatives, 166,
    189

Caplan, Bryan, 156
Captcha, 105
Carlton, Dennis, 78
Casey, James P., 119–120
Centralism, legal. *See* Legal centralism
Character loans, 143, 165
Charles River Bridge, 230
Cheating. *See also* Fraud
  eliminating, reciprocity for, 40–41
  Reputation on, 59–60
  in trading partners', information
    on, 60
Chertoff, Michael, 104
China
  arbitration in, problems with,
    160–161
  state-owned Poly Auction house in,
    194
Choice, on rules and regulations, 235
Club good
  definition of, 22

governance as, 21–36 (*See also*
    Voluntary associations,
    governance as club good in)
Clubs, 3. *See also* Voluntary
    associations
  Buchanans' economic theory of,
    23
  definition of, 22
  exclusion ability of, 32–33
  externalities in, 25
  functions of, 36
  governance of, 24, 143
  homogeneous groups in, 31–32
  internalizing benefits of individual
    self-governance in, 142–144
  membership of, 24
    rules for, 30–32, 143–144
  rule-enforcing, stock exchange as,
    77–78
  rules in, 22–26 (*See also* Voluntary
    associations, governance as
    club good in)
  structure, management, and
    ownership of, 30
  as voluntary association, 25–26
Clubs, exclusive
  Jonathan's Coffee House as,
    69–70
  London Stock Market as (*See*
    London Stock Exchange)
  New Jonathan's (The Stock
    Exchange) as, 69–72, 71f
  rule-enforcing, stock exchange as,
    77–78
Coffee houses. *See also specific coffee
    houses*
  London Stock Exchange in, 3,
    61–63, 64, 66f, 67f, 69–72
  New York Stock Exchange in, 82,
    83f
Collateralized debt obligations (CDOs),
    171–178, 172f, 176f, 177f
Common law
  from English private courts, 150,
    155, 201
  Hayek on, 16, 201, 207, 210–211,
    213, 215–217, 224
Communities, private. *See also*
    Voluntary associations
  rules in, 131, 133f, 211

Competition
  as discovery process, 16, 207, 208–210
  one-on-one *vs.* between multiple providers, 219
Compromis is not compromise, 4
Compromissum, 151, 157–158
Computer Fraud and Abuse Act, 103
Confusion de Confusiones, 50–55, 57–58. *See also* Stock market, world's first
The Constitution of Liberty, 210
Continuous dealings, discipline of, 40–41
Contract, adjudication by. *See* Private adjudication
Cooperation
  benefits and costs of new mechanisms for, 34–35
  gains from, 28
  game theory and, 40–41
  individual self-governance and, 140–142
  in legal centralism, 22
  without external constraints, 140
Cosmopolitan (Las Vegas), private policing in, 131
Costs of disputes, minimizing, 35, 40. *See also specific entities*
Courts. *See also* Law; Rules and regulations
  cost of use of, 14–15, 40
  ecclesiastical, 150
  as governmental, 3
  solutions to problems in, 12–18
    incentive for, 12, 17–18
    knowledge for, 12, 15–16
    low-cost, 12, 13–15
Courts, English private
  common law from, 150, 155, 201
  competing, 149–150
    Adam Smith on, 150, 201, 224
Credit
  etymology of, 56
  four Cs of, 143
  letters of, for arbitration, 162–163
Credit card transaction fraud, reducing, 227
  CyberSource for, 106–107
  First Data programs for, 107–108
Credit checks, 136–137

Credit default swaps, 168, 178–182
  of AIG, 166, 168, 181–182
Cybercrime. *See also* eBay; PayPal
  government enforcement for, ineffective, 102–103, 111
  President's Working Group on, 103–104
CyberSource, 106–107

de la Vega, Josef Penso, 48–55, 57–58. *See also under* Stock market, world's first
Derivatives, 165–166
  as anything but derivative, 4
  Buffet on, 166, 189
  ducaton as, 54–55
  without external enforcement, in first stock market, 54–55
Deux ex machina
  Euripides's *Orestes* and, 9–10
  in Greek plays, 9–10
  as plot device, 10
Deux ex machina theory of law, 9–20
  legal centralism in, 10
    failings of assumptions of, 12–20 (*See also under* Legal centralism)
Direct negotiation, 153
Discipline of continuous dealings, 40–41
Discovery process, 16, 207, 208–210. *See also* Hayek, Friedrich
  for legal rules, 212–214, 222
Disputes
  minimizing costs of, 35, 40
  private resolution of, 150–163 (*See also* Private adjudication)
Ducaton shares, 54–55
Duke University, private police of, 125–126, 129, 130

East Asia Company, 39
Easterbrook, Frank H., 111
eBay
  Amsterdam Bourse similarities to, 59
  fraud rate in, 59
  PayPal purchase by, 106
  private dispute resolution by, 151
  as private governance, 3

Eckert, Sandra, 194–195
Economic theory of regulation, 203
Electronic commerce. *See also* eBay;
　　PayPal
　　fraud in, 100–101 (*See also* Fraud,
　　　cybercrime (ecommerce))
Electronic Fund Transfer Act, 105
Ellickson, Robert C., 10
Enforcement. *See also specific types*
　　local (*See also* Policing, private)
　　of laws, 25
Enforcers, private, 3. *See also* Policing,
　　private
English courts, competing, 149–150,
　　155, 201, 224
Epstein, Richard A., 11, 108
Escrow services, for arbitration, 162
Ethics. *See also* Morality
　　natural human, 137–138
Euripides, *Orestes* of, 9–10
Ex ante risk management, 100–112.
　　See also Technologically
　　advanced markets
Exchange and property rights
　　Buchanan on, 11
　　legal centralism on, 11–12
Exclusion, 30
　　from Jonathan's Coffee House, 69
　　from private clubs, 32–33 (*See also*
　　　Clubs, exclusive)
　　from voluntary associations, 32–33
Externalities
　　in clubs, 25
　　internalizing, private communities
　　　in, 129–131, 133f
　　rules for, 24–25

Failures. *See specific types*
Financial Accounting Standards Board,
　　203–204
Financial Crisis Inquiry Commission,
　　166
Financial Industry Regulatory
　　Authority, 203
Financial instruments. *See also specific
　　instruments*
　　failures of, 167, 168
Financial intermediaries. *See*
　　Intermediaries
First Board, 83, 86

FirstData, 107
Fischel, Daniel R., 111
Force, threat of, 21
Foreclosure
　　in 2008 crash, 173–175, 174f
　　process of, 165–166
Forward contracts
　　for East India Company, 46
　　in England, unenforceable, 56
Fraud
　　on Alternative Investment Market,
　　　96–98
　　in art market
　　　Chinese state-owned Poly
　　　　Auction house in, 194
　　　lawsuits on authentication in, 194
　　credit card, reducing, 227
　　　CyberSource for, 106–107
　　　FirstData programs for,
　　　　107–108
　　government and, 34
　　on investor confidence, 80
　　in London Stock Exchange, 72–73
　　North on, 101
　　private governance on, 227
　　securities, 94–95
　　tragedy-of-the commons in, 67–68,
　　　77
Fraud, cybercrime (ecommerce),
　　100–101
　　Computer Fraud and Abuse Act on,
　　　103
　　in eBay, 59
　　example of, 79–80
　　government policing of, inadequate,
　　　102–103, 111
　　merchant losses from, 108, 108f
　　in PayPal, 100, 104–105
　　President's Working Group on,
　　　103–104
　　success of programs for, 106
Fraud management market, 108–111
　　Epstein on need for, 108
　　intermediary pooling and risk
　　　sharing in, 109–111
　　pricing risks in, 109
　　probability *vs.* risks in, 109
　　quantifying losses in, 108
Friedman, Milton, 7, 223, 227
Frye, Timothy, 11, 117

Galanter, Marc, 5, 7, 14
Garraway's Coffee House, 64, 65f
Gated communities, 129–131, 133f
Gausbeck-Levchin test, 105
Georgia, post-Soviet, self-governance
    and policing in, 134–136
Goldman Sachs
    AIG credit default swaps of, 182
    collateralized debt obligations of,
        175, 177f
Governance. *See also* Private
    governance; *specific topics*
    as club good, 22–26
    economics of, as unfinished
        project, 5
    as product, 34
    state law and, 214–218
    threat of force in, 21
    varieties of, 222
Government, 3. *See also specific topics*
    in advancing markets, 40
    faith in, 233
    in private adjudication, 159–163, 164
    on private governance
        crowding out by, 195–200, 197f
        intervention by, 194–195
        as primary obstacle, 204
        strong-arming or co-opting by,
            200–202
        undermining/monopolizing by,
            200–202
Government property, ownership
    issues in, 18
Greenspan, Alan, 166, 179, 188
Grigg, Neal S., 27

Hardin, Russell, 31, 41, 56–57
Harmony of interests, 29
Hasnas, John, 223
Hayek, Friedrich, 33
    on common law, 16, 201, 207,
        210–211, 213, 215–217, 224
    The Constitution of Liberty of, 210
    on discovery and spontaneous
        order, 206–225
    discovery process in, 16, 207,
        208–210
    market of private governance in,
        218–224 (*See also* Market
        of private governance)

    state law and governance in,
        214–218
    state law *vs.* market law in,
        215
    theory of law in, 210–214
    theory of markets in, 208–210
    theory of spontaneous order in,
        207–208
    on judges and judicial process,
        212–213
    Law, Legislation, and Liberty of,
        210–212, 215
    on price system, 7
    The Road to Serfdom of, 200, 210
    on rules and regulations, individual
        choice on, 235
Henrich, Joseph, 141, 144
Héritier, Adrienne, 194–195
Hidden law of online commerce, 4
Hittel, Theodore H., 117
Hobbes, Thomas, 10–11
Holcombe, Randall, 230–231
Holmes, Oliver Wendell, 138
Household net worth, 2004-2014, 168,
    169f
Housing price fluctuations, before
    2008 downturn, 172–173
Housing price decreases, 187
Hypothecation without external
    enforcement, in first stock
    market, 53–54

Identity verification systems, real-time,
    106–107
Incentives
    of provider of private governance,
        28–29
    to solve problems, of regulators,
        police, and courts, 12, 17–18
Inclusion, benefits of, 30–31
Individual self-governance, 134–147
    in California cattlemen and
        ranchers, 140
    in clubs, internalizing benefits of,
        142–144
    cooperation in, 140–142
    credit and background checks in,
        136–137
    in diamond merchants, 140
    in Georgia, post-Soviet, 134–136

Individual self-governance (*continued*)
  morality in, 136–140, 144–145
    Buchanan on, 138–139
    choices in, 138
    enhancing, 137
    factors triggering, 140–141
    internal, 137–138
    internal moral constraints in,
      136
  neuroeconomics of, 140
  norms in, 144–145
  police in, necessity for, 134
  reliance on, 144–147
  religion in, 145–146
  self-regulation and self-control in,
    146
Informal economy, 205
Initial public offerings (IPOs). *See* IPOs
Interests. *See also specific parties and
    types*
  harmony of, 29
Intermediaries
  financial, 80, 101 (*See also* PayPal;
    Technologically advanced
    markets)
  for risk management, 101, 109–111
    in futures markets transactions,
      111
    in online transactions, 108–111
Internal constraints, 138–139
Internalizing externalities, private
    communities in, 129–131,
    133f
Internal moral constraints, 136
International Swaps and Derivatives
    Association (ISDA), 180–181
Invisible hand analogy, 8, 233
Involuntary associations, *vs.* voluntary
    associations, 30–33
"I, Pencil," 235
IPOs
  on Alternative Investment Market,
    93, 94f, 204–205
  process for, 90
  survival of, 95
  on NASDAQ, 93, 94f, 204–205
  on New York Stock Exchange, 93,
    94f, 204–205
Irrecoverable bond, 58

JAMS Alternative Dispute Resolution,
    153
Jonathan's Coffee House, 3, 64, 66f,
    67f
  exclusions from, early, 69
  lameducks in, 68f, 69
  as private club, transformation into,
    69–70
JP Morgan Chase settlements,
    187
Judges and judicial process, 212–213
Junk bonds, 36, 109, 175, 187

Kaldor-Hicks efficiency, 23
Keefer, Philip, 147
Kirzner, Israel M., 11, 34, 62
Klein, Daniel B., 34, 230
Knack, Stephen, 147
Knowledge
  with centrally provided rules and
      regulations, 207, 218–220,
      225
  in markets and law, Hayek on,
      208–218
    governance and state law in,
        214–218
    theory of law in, 210–214
    theory of markets in, 208–210
  for solving problems, 12, 15–16
Kukathas, Chandran, 30

Labor markets, implicit, unenforceable
    contracts in, 15
Laissez-fare tradition, 119
Landa, Janet, 41
Law. *See also specific topics*
  competition in, 222–224
  as discovery process, 207, 208–210
  Hayek's theory of, 210–214
  market chosen, 150
  state
    governance and, Hayek on,
        214–218
    vs. market law, 215
Law, Legislation, and Liberty, 210–212,
    215
Leeson, Peter T., 27
Legal centralism, 5
  assumptions of, 12–13

assumptions of, failings of, 12–20
  ability to solve problem in
      low-cost way in, 12, 13–15
  incentive to solve problem in,
      12, 17–18
  knowledge to solve problem in,
      12, 15–16
  unmet needs in, 12, 18–19
  cooperation in, 22
  definition of, 5, 10
  as *deux ex machina* theory of law,
      10
  Ellickson on, 10
  on exchange and property rights,
      11–12
  failings of, 5
  government as source of order in,
      7
  Hobbes on, 10–11
  on individual preferences, 153
  judges and judicial process in,
      212–213
  normative frameworks in, 6, 7, 10
  problems in, solutions for
      government, 12
      private party, 12–13
  radical libertarians and, 5–6
  strong *vs.* weak forms of, 10
  Williamson on, 10
Legal disputes, minimizing costs of, 35,
    40. *See also* Arbitration; Private
    adjudication
Legal system, government. *See also*
    Law; *specific topics*
  classical liberals on functions for,
      11
  cost of use of, 14–15, 40
  judges in, 212–213
Legitimate market systems, 6
Lehman Brothers, 166, 173, 177f, 181,
    182
Lemon problem, with used cars,
    28–29
Leoni, Bruno, 221–222
Letters of credit, for arbitration,
    162–163
Levchin, Max, 105–106
Liar loans, 176
Lighthouse, as public good, 23

Lim, Mah-Hui, 166
Listing and disclosure requirements
  of Alternative Investment Market,
      89–98 (*See also* Alternative
      Investment Market (AIM))
  of New York Stock Exchange
      1865, original, 83
      1914 and 1924, 83
      costs and benefits of, 84–85
      current, 87t–88t
  of North American stock exchanges,
      86, 87t–88t
Lloyd's Coffeehouse, 148
Lloyd's of London, 148–149, 149f
Lloyd's salvage agreement (open form),
    148
Loans
  character, 143, 165
  liar, 176
Local enforcement, of laws, 25
Locke, John, 145–146
London Stock Exchange, 61–78
  Alternative Investment Market
      of, 81, 89–98 (*See also*
      Alternative Investment
      Market (AIM))
  coffee house beginnings of, 61–63
  fraud in, harm from, 73
  government undermining of, 20th
      century, 200
  motto of, 3
  origins of, 3
  as rule-enforcing club, 77–78
  rules evolution in, government *vs.*
      endogenous, 63–73
      'Change Alley and stock-jobbers
          in, 64–68, 65f
      defaulters in, brokers' rules on,
          68–69
      Garraway's Coffee House in, 64,
          66f
      Jonathan's Coffee House in, 3,
          64, 66f, 67f, 68–70
      lame ducks in, 68f, 69
      monopoly privileges of early
          companies and, 63
      at New Jonathan's (The Stock
          Exchange), 70–72, 71f
      ownership of stocks in, 63–64

London Stock (*continued*)
  Royal Exchange in, 64
  Stock Exchange at Capel Court
    in, 72–73
  Stock Subscription Room in,
    70–72, 71f
  tragedy-of-the commons
    potential in, 68, 77
  rules in, first, 73–76, 73f
  settings for trading stocks in, late
    18th century, 77–78
  stock companies in, first major, 63
  success of, 93–94, 94f, 95f
  summary and thoughts on, 76–78

Macaulay, Thomas Babington, 137
Madoff, Bernie, 183–185, 187
Mahoney, Paul, 78
Man of system, 232
Market-augmenting government, state
    as, 16
Market chosen law, 150
Market of private governance, 218–224
  competition among providers of
    governance for, 222–224
  embracing, 33–36
Markets
  as a discovery process, 16, 207,
    208–210
  on governance, beneficence of,
    33–34
  government in advancing of, 40
  Hayek's theory of, 208–210
  legitimate systems of, 6
  rules and regulations of,
    endogenous, 228
  voluntary choice in, 26
Markets, transparency from, 79–99
  Alternative Investment Market
    in, 81, 89–98 (*See also*
    Alternative Investment
    Market (AIM))
  financial intermediation in, 80
  fraud on (*See also* Fraud)
    internet example of, 79–80
    investor confidence and, 80
  New York Stock Exchange in,
    81–88, 98–99 (*See also* New
    York Stock Exchange (NYSE))
  SEC and, 80–81

Masters, Blythe, 178
Membership rules, 30–32
Menger, Carl, 33–34
Merchant Coffee House, 82, 83f
Mises, Ludwig von, 11, 16, 33, 232
Money, Hayek on government control
    over, 208
Monopolies, defects of, 208
Morality, 137–139. *See also* Individual
    self-governance
  in civilization, 137
  enhancing, 137
  factors triggering, 140–141
  in individual self-governance,
    136–140
    Buchanan on, 138–139
    choices in, 138
    factors triggering, 140–141
    internal, 137–138
    internal moral constraints in,
      136
  markets in creation of, 147
  screening for, 136–137
  Smith on, 137, 139, 144–145, 147
  without external constraints,
    137–140
Mortgage-backed securities, 170–178,
    176f
Motivation, coercive *vs.* noncoercive,
    21
Mueller, Dennis C., 26
Multilateral reputation mechanism,
    41
Murder Incorporated, 127
Musgrave, Richard, 26
Myers, David G., 21
My word is my bond, 3, 4

NASDAQ
  costs of listing on, *vs.* AIM, 90–92,
    93t
  IPOs at, 93, 94f, 204–205
Negotiation, direct, 153
Neuroeconomics, 140
Neuwirth, Robert, 205
New York Stock Exchange (NYSE),
    81–88, 98–99
  competition of, 85–86
  First Board in, 83, 86
  importance of, 81–82, 85

IPOs at, 93, 94f, 204–205
listing and disclosure requirements
   for
   1865, original, 83
   1914 and 1924, 83
   costs and benefits of, 84–85
   current, 87t–88t
locations of
   current building (1903), 83, 86f
   Tontine Tavern and Coffee
      House, 82, 83f
   Wall Street and Broad (1882),
      83, 85f
as membership club, 82
membership in, original rules on,
   82–83, 84f
as private and voluntary
   organization, 26
Second Board of, 86
Securities and Exchange Commission
   on, 80–81, 198–199
Nomads, 89–90, 93t, 97
Normative frameworks, in legal
   centralism, 6, 7, 10
Norms, 145
North Carolina, private policing in,
   125–126
North, Douglass C.
   on cooperation breakdown with
      large numbers of traders, 41,
      56–57
   on fraud in large markets, 101
   on neoclassical economic fiction,
      195
   on politics in efficient economies,
      42
   on private governance, 227–228
   on third-party enforcement, 39
Nozick, Robert, 23, 36

Occupy Wall Street movement, 15
Olson, Mancur, 118–119
Online commerce
   fraud in (*See* Fraud, cybercrime
      (ecommerce))
   hidden law of, 4
Options without external enforcement,
   in first stock market, 52–53
Order, spontaneous. *See* Hayek,
   Friedrich

Orestes, 9–10
Ostrom, Elinor, 24
Ostrom, Vincent, 24
Otteson, James R., 145

Paine, Thomas, 7–8, 144, 227
Patrol Special Police. *See* Policing,
   private; San Francisco Patrol
   Special Police
Payment processors, fraud risk
   management for, 108–111
PayPal. *See also* Technologically
   advanced markets
   eBay purchase of, 106
   private governance in, 3
   suboptimalities in, elimination of,
      19
PayPal, fraud and fraud management
   in, 100–112
   assumption of risks in, 104–105
   Chertoff on, 104
   early days of, 100
   Electronic Fund Transfer Act and,
      105
   Gausbeck-Levchin test and Captcha
      of, 105
   internal solutions for, 105
   international, 103
   Levchin's fraud-monitoring and
      prevention system at,
      105–106
   membership for, increasing,
      110
   pre-crime detection in, 105–106
   success of programs for, 106
   Thiel's early experience with,
      101–103
   Government incompetence in,
      102–103, 111
Peters, Bethany, 61, 62
Police
   armed private, 115
   government, 3
      numbers and cost of, current,
         120, 121t, 122t
      solutions to problems for,
         12–18
      incentive for, 12, 17–18
      knowledge for, 12, 15–16
      low-cost, 12, 13–15

Policing, private
  consumers of, 126–132
    bundling on behalf of consumers
      in, 126–129
    internalizing externalities by
      private communities in,
      129–131, 132f
    at Cosmopolitan (Las Vegas), 131
    at Duke University, 125–126, 129,
      130
    in North Carolina, 125–126
    as private protection of property
      rights, 132–133
    vs. private security guards, 114–115
    at Walt Disney, 131
Policing, private, in San Francisco, 4,
    113–125
  history and background on, 113–116,
    115f, 116f
  public vs. private space interactions
    and, 115–116
  rationale for, 116–126
    de facto anarchy in, 116–117
    financing in, 118–119
    government police in, corrupt,
      118
    politicians in, corrupt, 118
    private group policing and trials
      in, early, 117–119
    work of, vs. government police,
      119–120
  San Francisco Patrol Special Police
    in, 114, 115f, 116f, 133
    beats and placards for, 122–124,
      123f, 124f
    newspaper headlines on, 130f
    present-day use of, 122–123
    San Francisco Police Department
      regulation of, 202
    services and funding of, early,
      118–119, 120–122
  tying and bundling arrangements
    in, 114–116
Policy debates, short-run, 230–232
Poly Auction house, 194
Predispute arbitration clauses, 157,
  163–164
Price system, Hayek on, 7
Prisoners' dilemma, 28
  two-person vs. n-person, 31, 41

Private, 3
  invisible hand analogy and, 8,
    233
Private adjudication, 150–163
  compromissum in, 151, 157–158
  direct negotiation vs., 153
  by eBay, 151
  government competition and
    regulation of, 201
  government role in, 159–163, 164
  growth of, 152, 152f
  law by contract in, 155
  legal centralists on, 153
  market for, 150–151
  mutual interests of adjudicants in,
    serving, 156–159
  predispute arbitration clauses in,
    157, 163–164
  reasons for, 151–156, 163
    arbitrator choice in, 154–155
    benefits in, 152
    corporate users on, 154, 154f
    finality in, 156
    speed in, 151–152
    subject-matter experts in, 154
  rules and procedures for, 158–159
Private communities, 129–131, 133f
Private dispute resolution. See Private
  adjudication
Private governance, 236. See also
  specific topics
  definition of, 3–4
  Friedman on, 7
  Frye on, 11
  government intervention in,
    194–195
  government on
    crowding out by, 195–200,
      197f
    as primary obstacle, 204
    strong-arming or co-opting by,
      200–202
    undermining/monopolizing by,
      200–202
  importance of, long run, 232–236,
    234f
  key examples of, 4
  vs. legal centralism, 5
  legal centralists on, strongest,
    11–12

marketplace of, embracing,
33–36
mechanisms of
major, 5
ubiquity and power of, 6–7
North on, 227–228
order in, 226–227
Paine on, 7–8, 227
parties benefiting from, 27–29
pervasiveness of, 226–227
as prisoners' dilemma, 28
public governance and, 193–205
(*See also* Public and private
governance)
purchase of, declining to, 168–169
research on, 7, 228–230
role of, 170
for short-run policy debates,
230–232
ubiquity of, 226–236
for unmet needs, 12, 18–19
Private order, Williamson on, 159
Private organizations, rules in, 22
Private police, armed, 115
Private policing. *See* Policing, private
Probuyer bias, 157–158
Proseller bias, 157
Public and private governance,
193–205
art auctions and, 193–194
benefits and costs of, 196–198,
197f
governments in
crowding out by, 195–200,
197f
interventions by, 194–195
as primary obstacle, 204
as shadow of the state,
194–195
strong-arming or co-opting by,
202–204
undermining/monopolizing by,
200–202
Public choice hypothesis, 17
Public good, 23
Public interest theory of regulation,
203

Rajan, Raghuram, 11
Read, Leonard, 235

Real-time identity verification systems,
106–107
Rechsstaat, 210
Regulations. *See* Rules and regulations
Regulators
as governmental, 3
costliness of, 12, 13–15
incentives of, 12, 17–18
knowledge of, 12, 15–16
Religion, 145–146
Reno, Janet, 102, 103
Reputation
bilateral *vs.* multilateral mechanisms
of, 41
bonding and, 60
building of, in specific market, 60
vs. cheating, 59–60
third-party certification agencies
on, 60
Research, on private governance, 7,
228–230
Residual claimant, 18
Rights violations, rules for, 24
Risk management
by financial intermediaries, 101 (*See
also* Technologically advanced
markets)
for online fraud, 109–110
on Wall Street, after 2008 (*See* Wall
Street risk management, after
2008)
The Road to Serfdom, 200, 210
Rosser, J. Barkley, Jr., 225
Rothbard, Murray N., 134, 223, 226
Rule makers, as private, 3
Rules and regulations
in art market, lack of, 193
self-policing for, 193–194
benefits and costs of, 196–198,
197f
centrally provided
accountability problems with,
220–222, 225
knowledge problem with, 207,
218–220, 225
costs and benefits of, 27
economic theory of, 203
for externalities, 24–25
government enforcement of,
problems with, 40

Rules and regulations (*continued*)
  individual choice on, 235
  on London Stock Exchange, first,
    73–76, 73f
  of markets, endogenous, 228
  public interest theory of, 203
  for rights violations, 24
  rule makers in, favoring of, 27
Ryan, J. A., 25–26

"Safety and protection of the property
    and interests of the members of
    the stock-exchange," rules for,
    73–76, 73f
San Francisco, 1800s
  crime in, 113–114
  de facto anarchy in, 116–117
  policing in
    lack of, 114
    private, 4, 113–133 (*See also*
      Policing, private)
San Francisco Patrol Special Police,
    114, 116f, 133
  badge of, 114, 115f
  beats and placards for, 122–124,
    123f, 124f
  in Chinatown, 119–120
  funding of, 118–119, 122–123
  newspaper headlines on, 132f
  present-day use of, 122–123
  San Francisco Police Department
    regulation of, 202
  services offered by, 120–121
Sarbanes-Oxley Act (SOX), 92, 99, 199,
    204, 205
Schama, Simon, 48
Securities and Exchange Commission
    (SEC)
  on financial markets, 198–199
  goals of, 80
  New York Stock Exchange and,
    80–81
  as private and voluntary
    organization, 26
Securities fraud, 94–95
Security guards
  vs. private police, 114–115
  unarmed, 115
Self-control, 146
Self-governance

individual (*See* Individual
    self-governance)
  Paine on, 7–8, 144
Self-regulation, 146
Shadow-of-the state theories of order,
    14, 59, 194–195
Shares, East India Company
  creation of, 42, 43t
  prices of, early, 45f
Shevardnadze, Eduard, 134–135
Short-run policy debates, 230–232
Short sales, in first stock market
  of East India Company, 46–47
  ordinances against, 46–47
  without external enforcement,
    50–51
Smith, Adam, 33, 40, 56
  on competing English courts, 150,
    201, 224
  on man of system, 232
  on morality, 137, 139, 144–145,
    147
  Theory of Moral Sentiments of, 138,
    145
Social Security actuarial deficit,
    187–188
Sordin, Tania, 159
Special Police Officers. *See* San
    Francisco Patrol Special Police
Spinoza, Benedit de, 7
Spontaneous order, 206–225. *See also*
    Hayek, Friedrich
State
  on good governance, 193–205
    (*See also* Public and private
    governance)
  as market-augmenting government,
    16
State law, Hayek on
  governance and, 214–218
  vs. market law, 215
Stigler, George J., 147, 198
Stock Exchange at Capel Court, 72–73
Stock exchanges. *See also specific
    exchanges*
  London Stock Exchange, 61–78 (*See
    also* London Stock Exchange)
  New York Stock Exchange, 81–88
    (*See also* New York Stock
    Exchange (NYSE))

North American, listing and
 disclosure requirements of,
 86, 87t–88t
as rule-enforcing club, 77–78
Stock market, world's first, 39–60
 de la Vega's description of, 48–55,
  57–58
  hypothecation without external
   enforcement in, 53–54
  options without external
   enforcement in, 52–53
  other derivatives without
   external enforcement in,
   54–55
  short sales without external
   enforcement in, 50–51
 history of, 41–50 (*See also*
  Amsterdam Bourse)
  Amsterdam as center of world
   trade in, 42, 43f
  Amsterdam Bourse in, 46–50,
   47f, 48f
  East India Company in, 42–46,
   43t (*See also* East India
   Company)
  The Netherlands at time of, 42
  vs. predictions of government-
   centric academics, 41–42
  West India Company in, 42–44,
   45f
 mechanisms of, 56–58
 multilateral reputation mechanism
  in, 41
 summary and thoughts on, 59–60
 theoretical underpinnings of,
  39–41
Stock Subscription Room, 70–72, 71f
Success of private governance, in post-
 2008 Wall Street. *See* Wall Street
 risk management, after 2008

Tebeau, Jimmy, 202–203, 204
Technologically advanced markets,
 fraud in, 100–112
 CyberSource and credit card
  transactions in, 106–107
 FirstData work in, 107–108
 management market for, 108–111
  (*See also* Fraud management
  market)

North on, 101
 in PayPal, 101–106 (*See also* PayPal)
Theory of law, Hayek's, 210–214
Theory of markets, Hayek's, 208–210
Theory of Moral Sentiments, 138, 145
*The Stealth of Nations: The Global Rise of
 the Informal Econo*my, 205
Thiel, Peter, 19, 101–102. *See also*
 PayPal
Third-party certification agencies, 60
Third-party intermediaries, risk
 management
 for futures markets transactions,
  111
 for online transactions, 108–111
Third-party review, "necessary,"
 148–164
 arbitration in, 150
 competing English courts in,
  149–150, 201, 224
 compromissum in, 151, 157–158
 by Lloyd's of London, 148–149,
  149f
 Lloyd's salvage agreement in,
  148
 market chosen law in, 150
 mutual interests of adjudicants in,
  serving, 156–159
 private dispute resolution in,
  150–163 (*See also* Private
  adjudication)
  government role in, 159–163,
   164
  market for, 150–151
  reasons for, 151–156, 163
 in shipping industry, early,
  147–148
 value and use of, 148–149
Threat of force, 21
Threshold deontology, 139
Tontine Tavern and Coffee House, 82,
 83f
Trading partners
 interests of, 27
 reliability of, information on, 60
 trustworthiness of, 56
Tragedy-of-the commons, 68, 77
Trustworthiness, 56, 144
Tullock, Gordon, 11, 17, 28, 40, 41, 56,
 139, 143, 165

Tullock (*continued*)
　on public choice, law and, 17
　on transactions, 41
Tying and bundling arrangements, in
　　private policing, 114–116
Tythings, 200–201

Unarmed security, 115
United States. *See also specific topics*
　biggest future threats to, 234f, 235
Unmet needs, private governance for,
　　12, 18–19
Used cars lemon problem with, 28–29

Voluntary associations
　definition of, 25–26
　exclusion ability of, 32–33
　in free society, 30
　functions of, 36
　governance as club good in, 21–36
　　vs. involuntary associations,
　　　30–33
　　marketplace of, embracing,
　　　33–36
　　parties benefiting from, 27–29
　　rules in, 22–26
　government denial of the right of,
　　26
　membership rules for, 30–32
　private clubs as, 25–26
Voluntary choice, market, 26

Wallis, John J., 195
Wall Street fluctuations, 2008,
　　165–167
　credit default swaps contracts in,
　　168
　derivatives in, 165–166
　Financial Crisis Inquiry Commission
　　on, 166
　financial instrument failures in,
　　168
　institutional collapses in, 166
　private governance in, not
　　purchasing, 168–169
　private regulation as "cause" of,
　　167–170, 169f
　regulating Wall Street as solution
　　for, 167

Wall Street risk management, after
　　2008, 165–189
　AIG in, 166, 168, 181–182
　Bear Sterns in, 166, 173, 177f,
　　182
　collateralized debt obligations in,
　　171–178, 172f, 176f, 177f
　credit default swaps in, 168,
　　178–182
　events leading to, 165–167
　firms' poor investments in, 173
　foreclosures in, 173–175, 174f
　Goldman Sachs in, 175, 177f, 182
　government challenges to private
　　governance in, 188–189
　Greenspan's role in, 166, 179,
　　188
　household net worth 2004-2014
　　and, 168, 169f
　housing price fluctuations in,
　　172–173
　housing price decreases in, 188
　International Swaps and Derivatives
　　Association in, 180–181
　junk bonds in, 36, 109, 175, 187
　Lehman Brothers in, 166, 173,
　　177f, 181, 182
　mortgage-backed securities in,
　　170–178, 176f
　private certification, administrator,
　　and custodian services in,
　　182–188
　　vs. Bernie Maddoff's Ponzi
　　　scheme, 183–185, 187
　　vs. JP Morgan Chase settlements,
　　　187
　　vs. Social Security actuarial
　　　deficit, 187–188
　　third-party administrators and
　　　custodians in, 185–188,
　　　187f
　private governance and, 167–170
Walt Disney, private policing by, 131
Warren, Elizabeth, 156
Weingast, Barry R., 195
West India Company, 42–45
　failure of, 43–44
　in New Amsterdam, 44–45
　share prices of, 45f

White, Mark D., 25
Williamson, Oliver E., 5, 22, 159
  on irrecoverable bond, 57
  on legal centralism, 10

Zingales, Luigi, 11
Zywicki, Todd, 207
  on common law, private
    development of, 155, 201
  on ecclesiastical courts, 150
  on Hayek, 16 (*See also* Hayek,
    Friedrich)
    discovery and spontaneous order
      of, 206–225

.